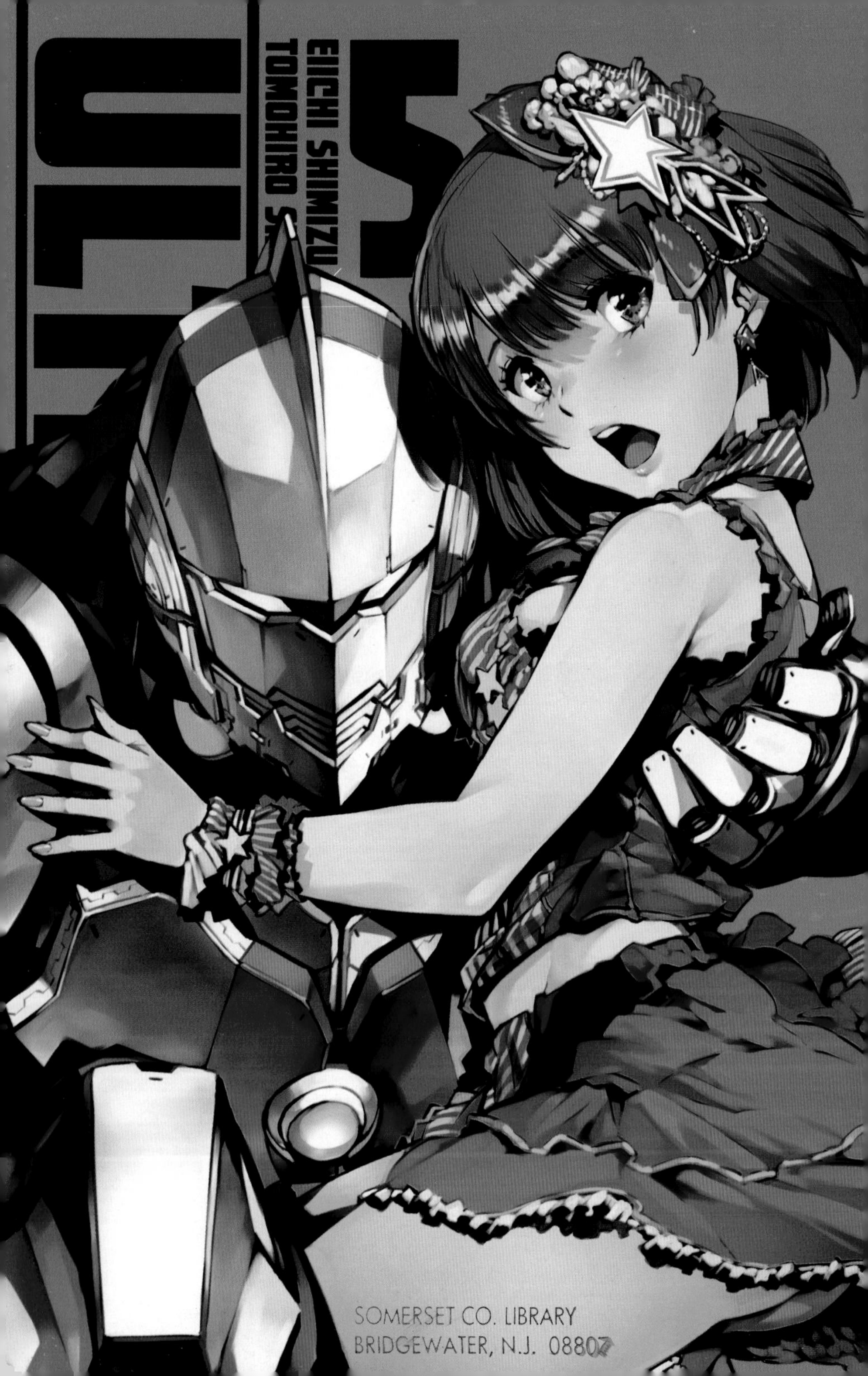
5
EIICHI SHIMIZU
TOMOHIRO

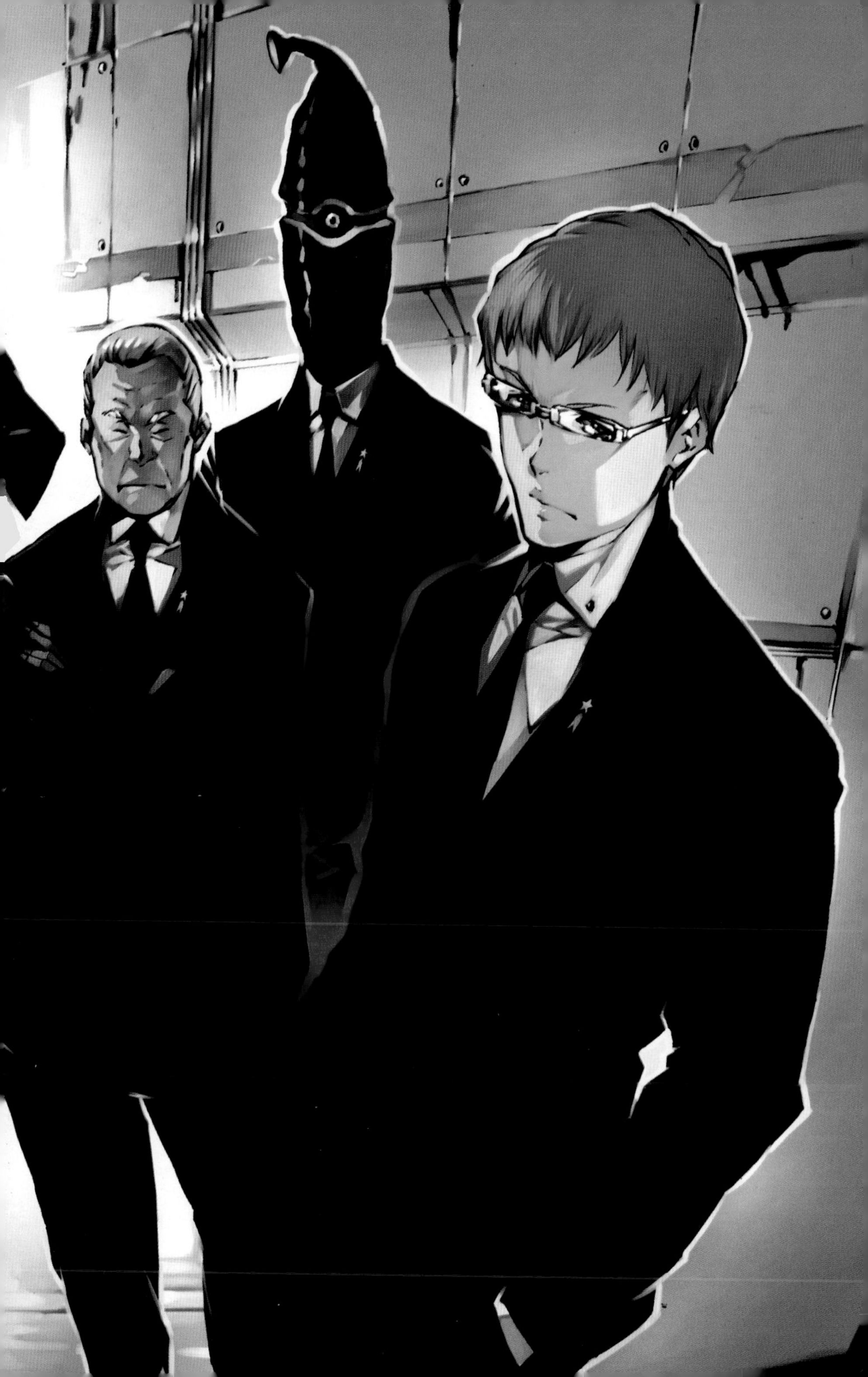

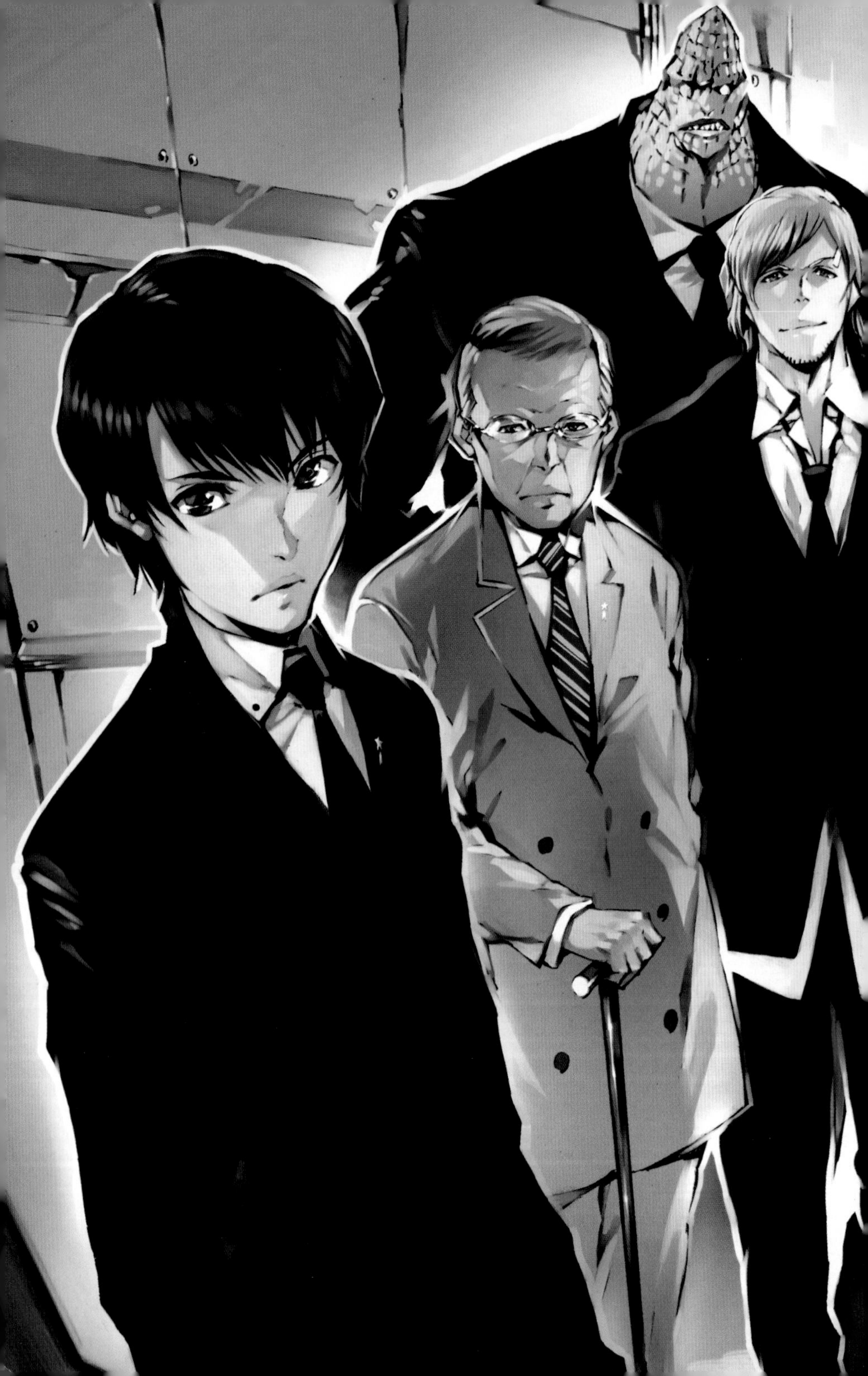

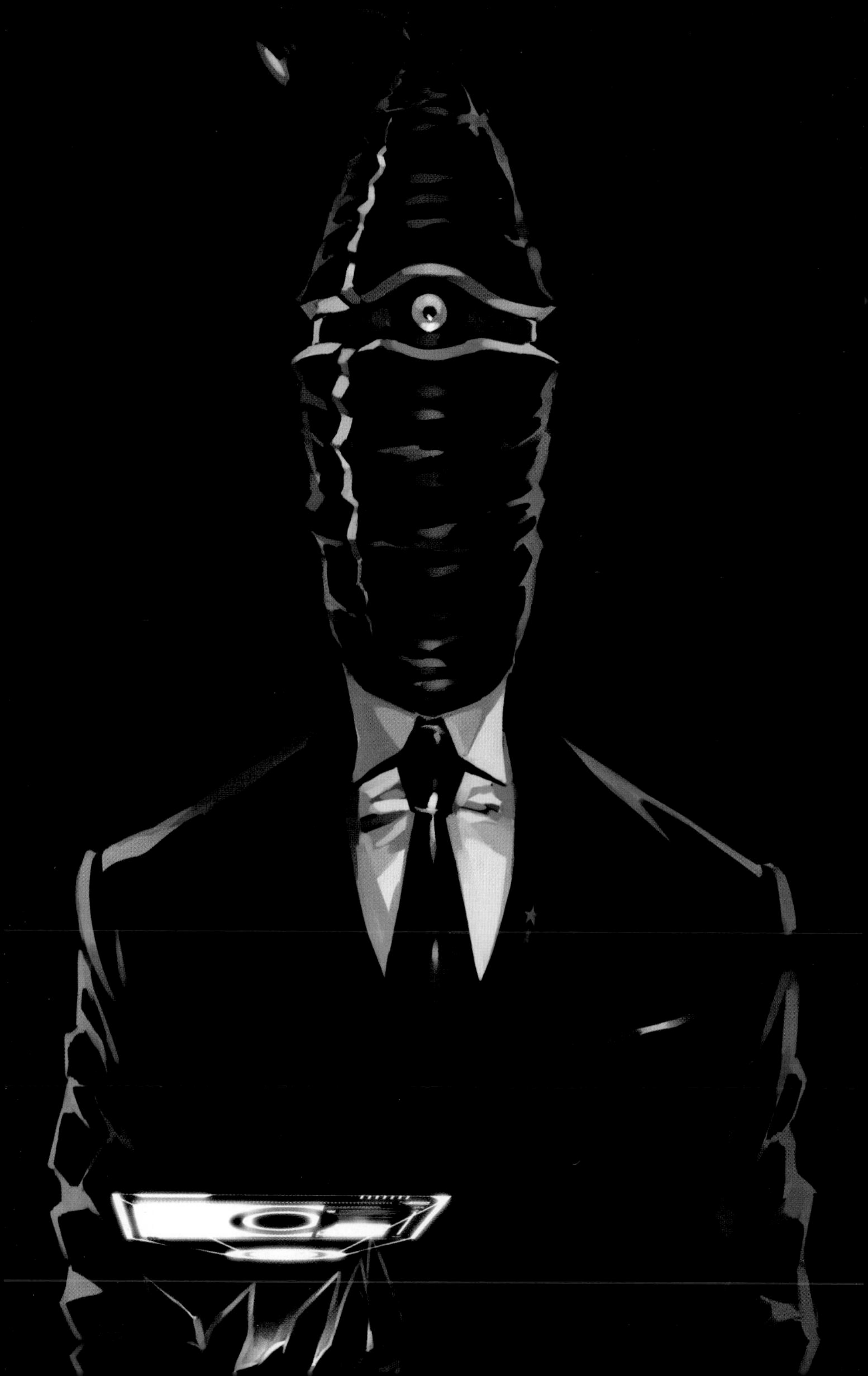

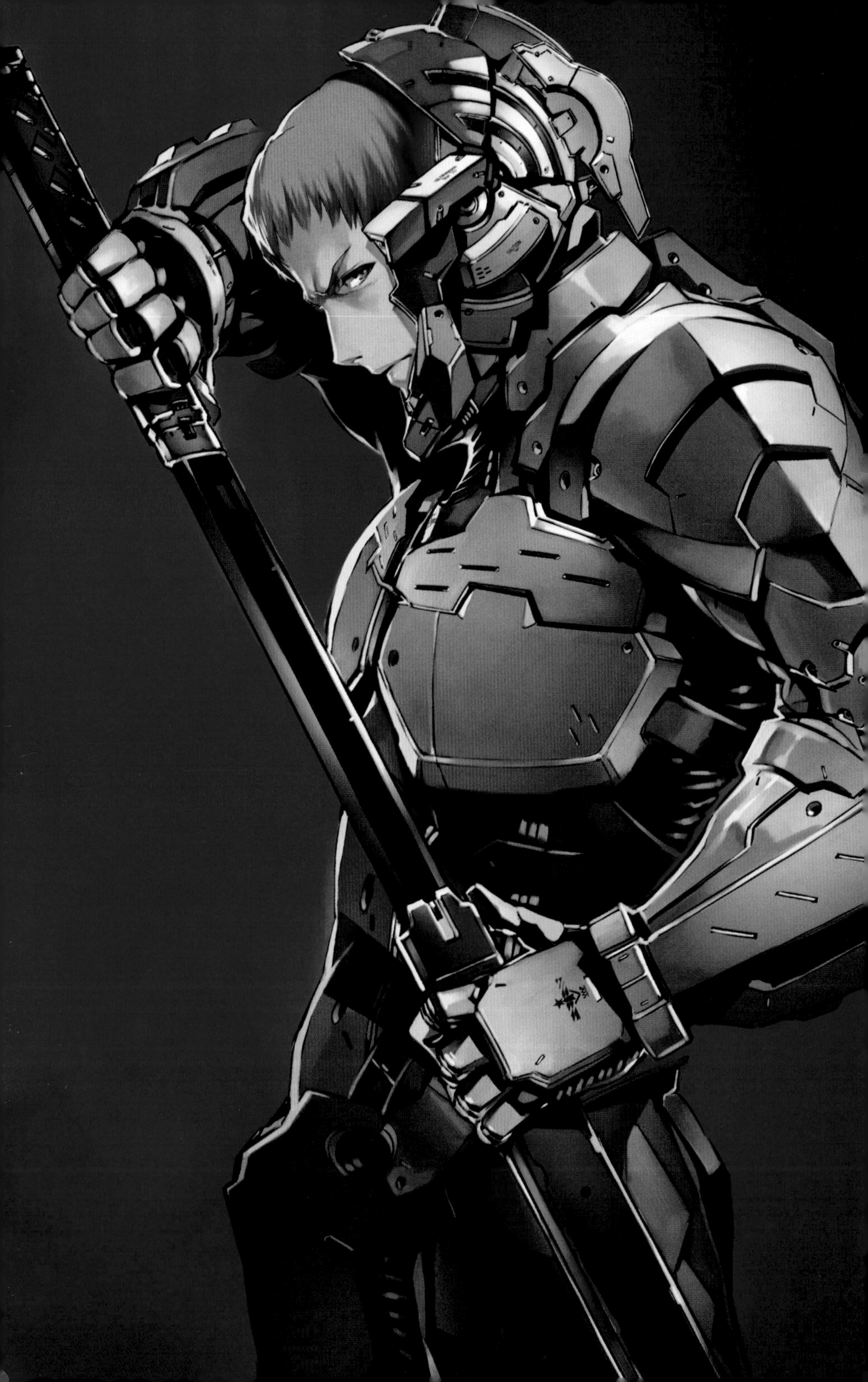

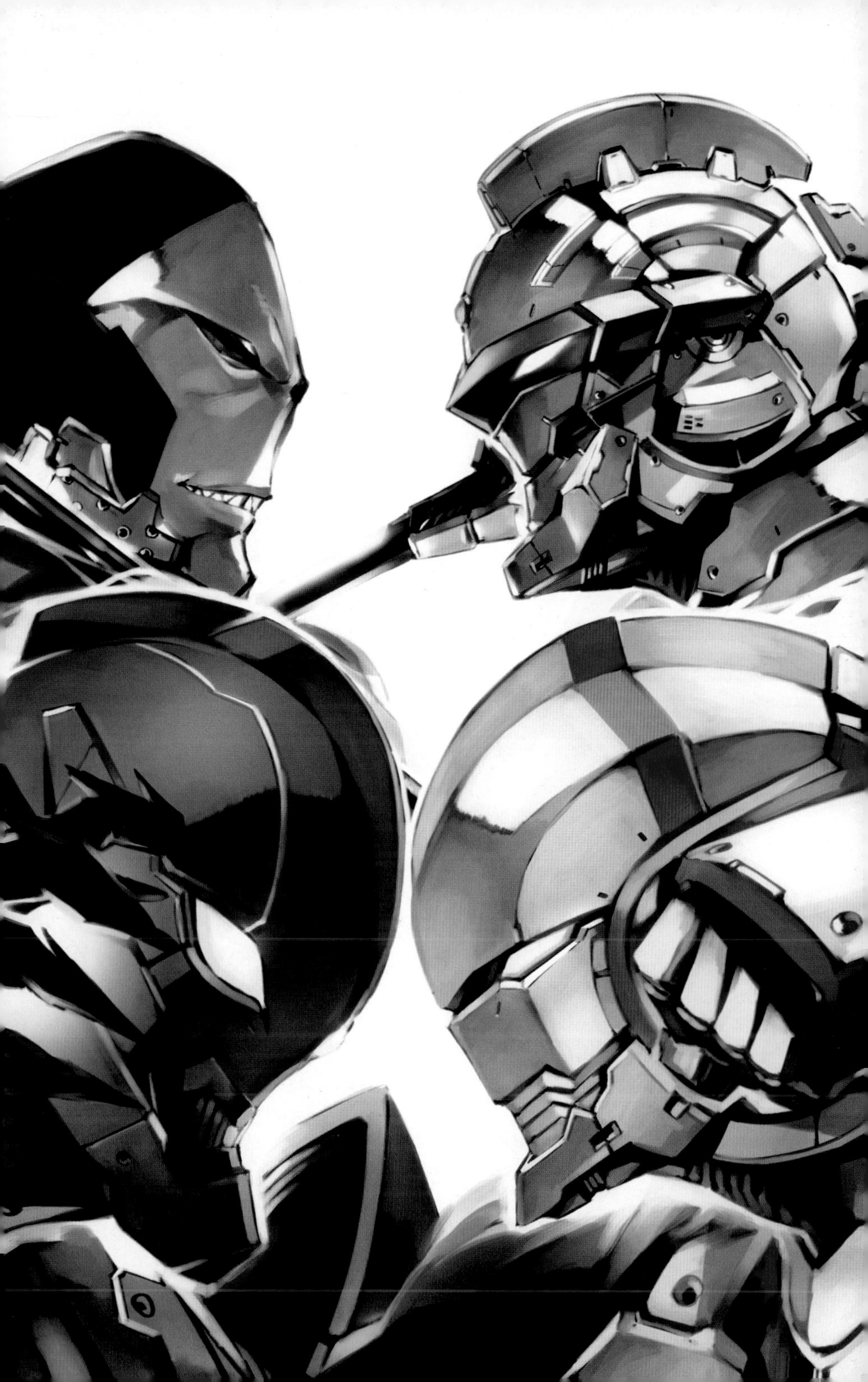

THIS IS THE BEGINNING OF A NEW AGE.

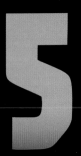

CONTENTS

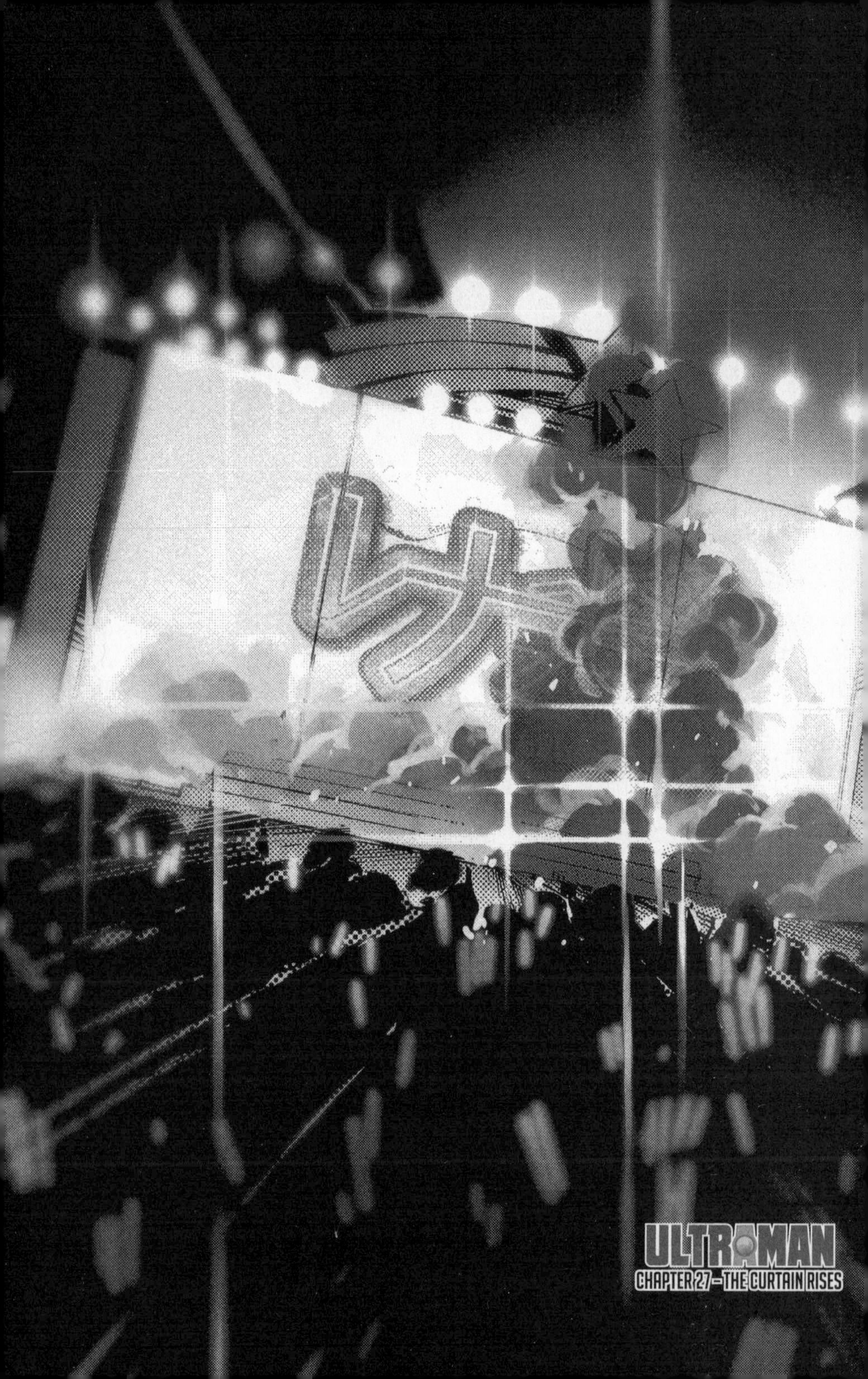
ULTRAMAN
CHAPTER 27 – THE CURTAIN RISES

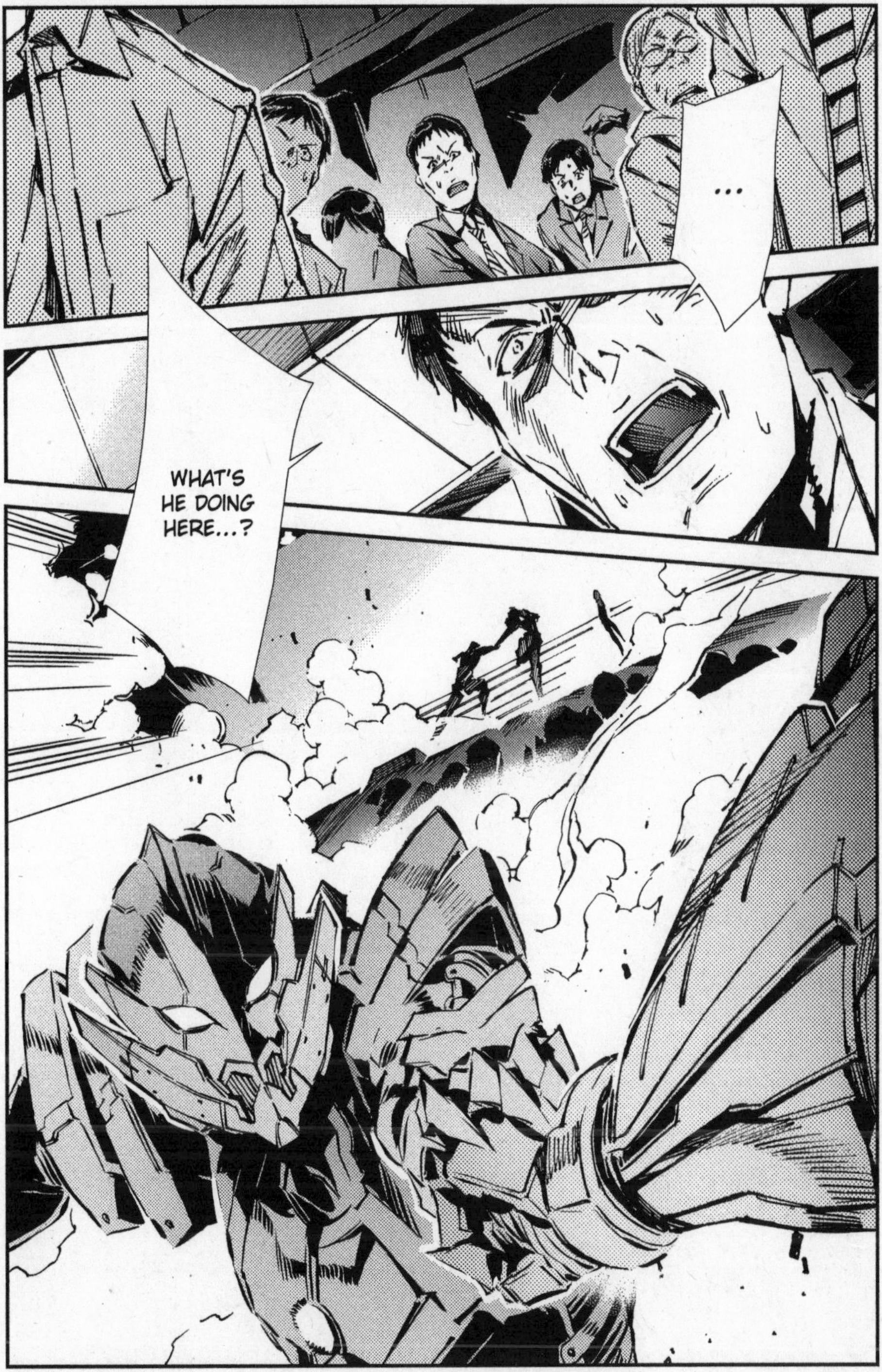
...
WHAT'S HE DOING HERE...?

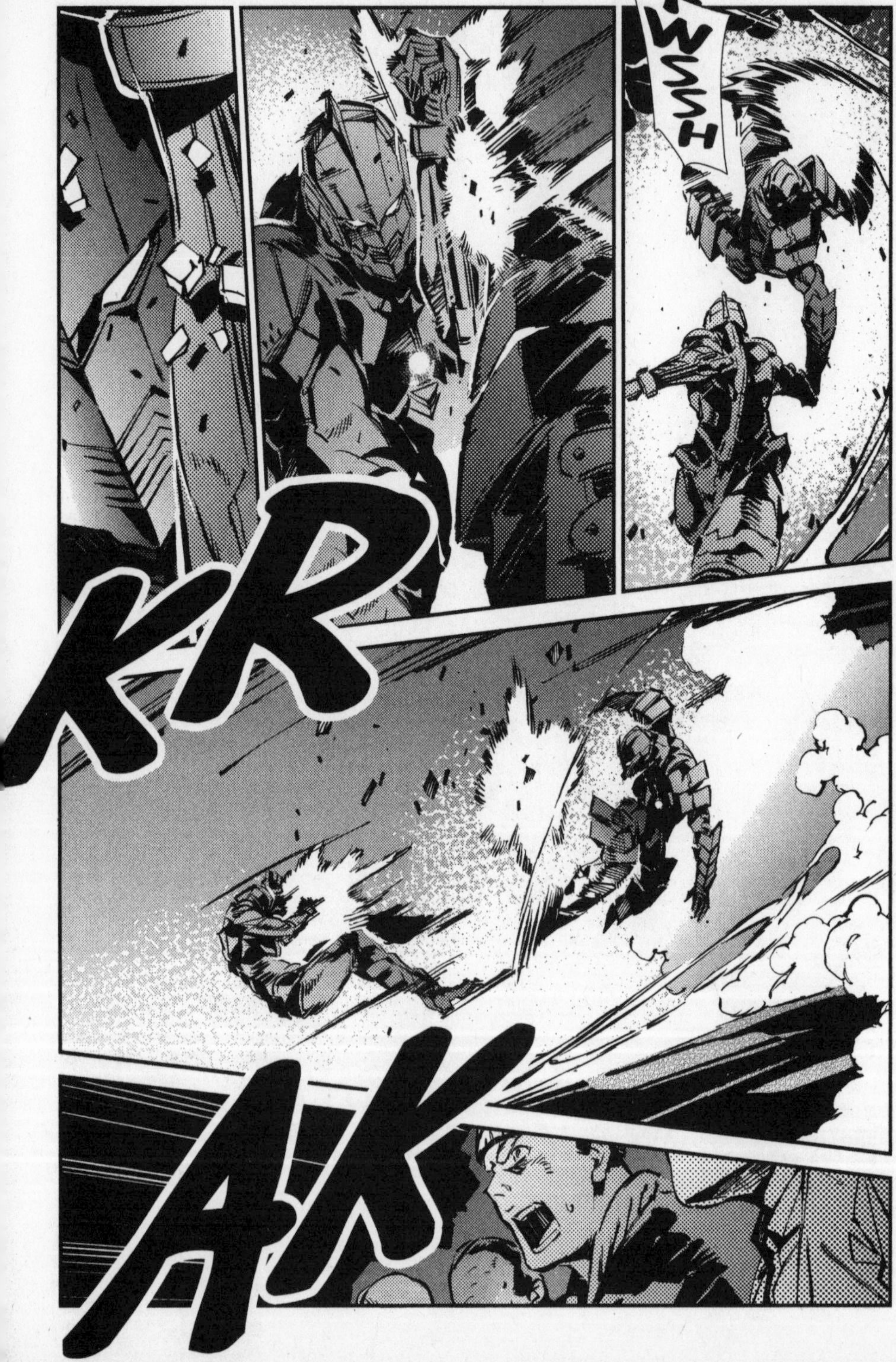
FWSSH
KR
AK

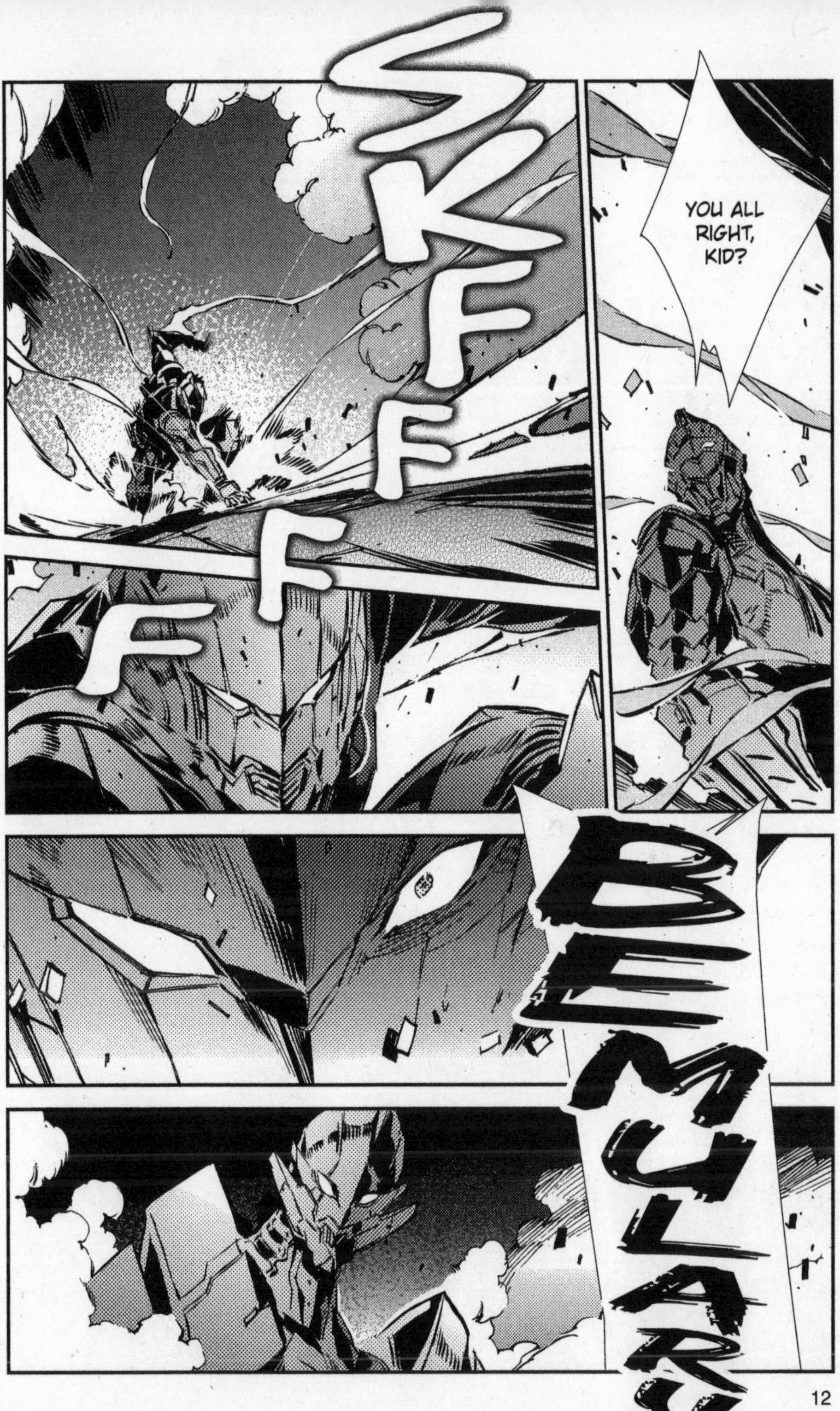
YOU ALL RIGHT, KID?
SKFFFF
BEMULAR!!

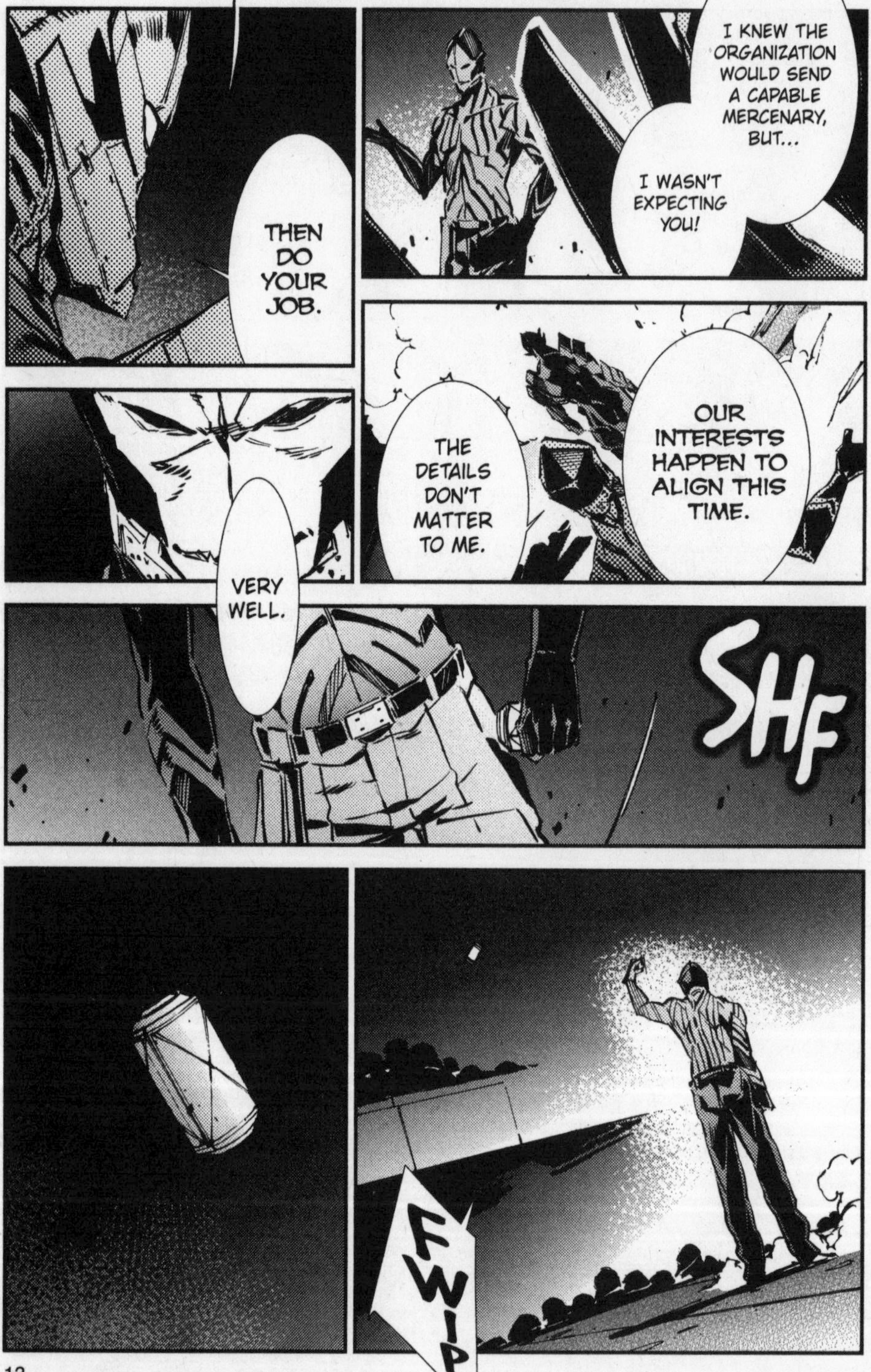
I KNEW THE ORGANIZATION WOULD SEND A CAPABLE MERCENARY, BUT...
I WASN'T EXPECTING YOU!
THEN DO YOUR JOB.
OUR INTERESTS HAPPEN TO ALIGN THIS TIME.
THE DETAILS DON'T MATTER TO ME.
VERY WELL.
SHF
FWIP

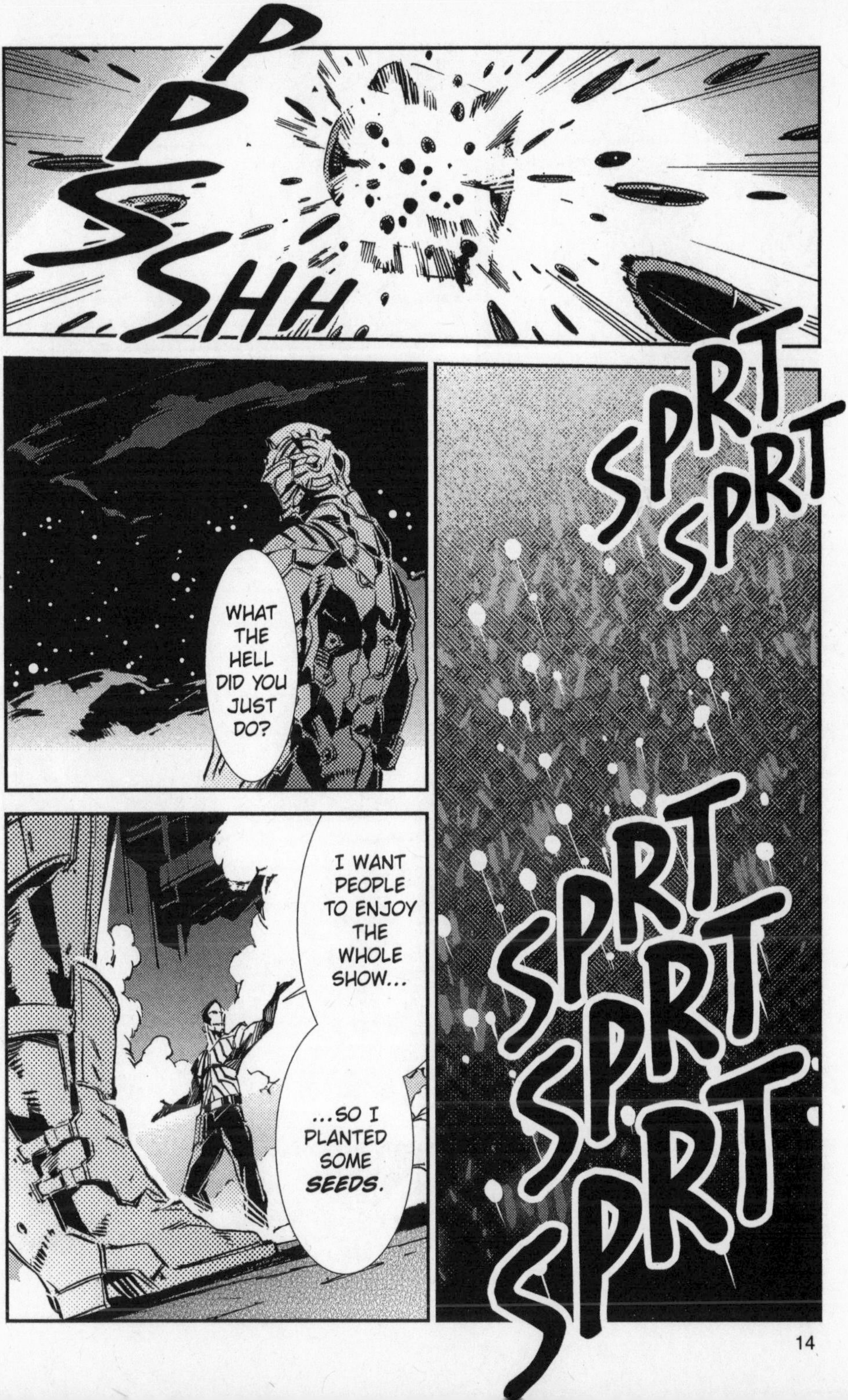
PPSSHH
SPRT SPRT
SPRT SPRT SPRT SPRT
WHAT THE HELL DID YOU JUST DO?
I WANT PEOPLE TO ENJOY THE WHOLE SHOW...
...SO I PLANTED SOME *SEEDS*.

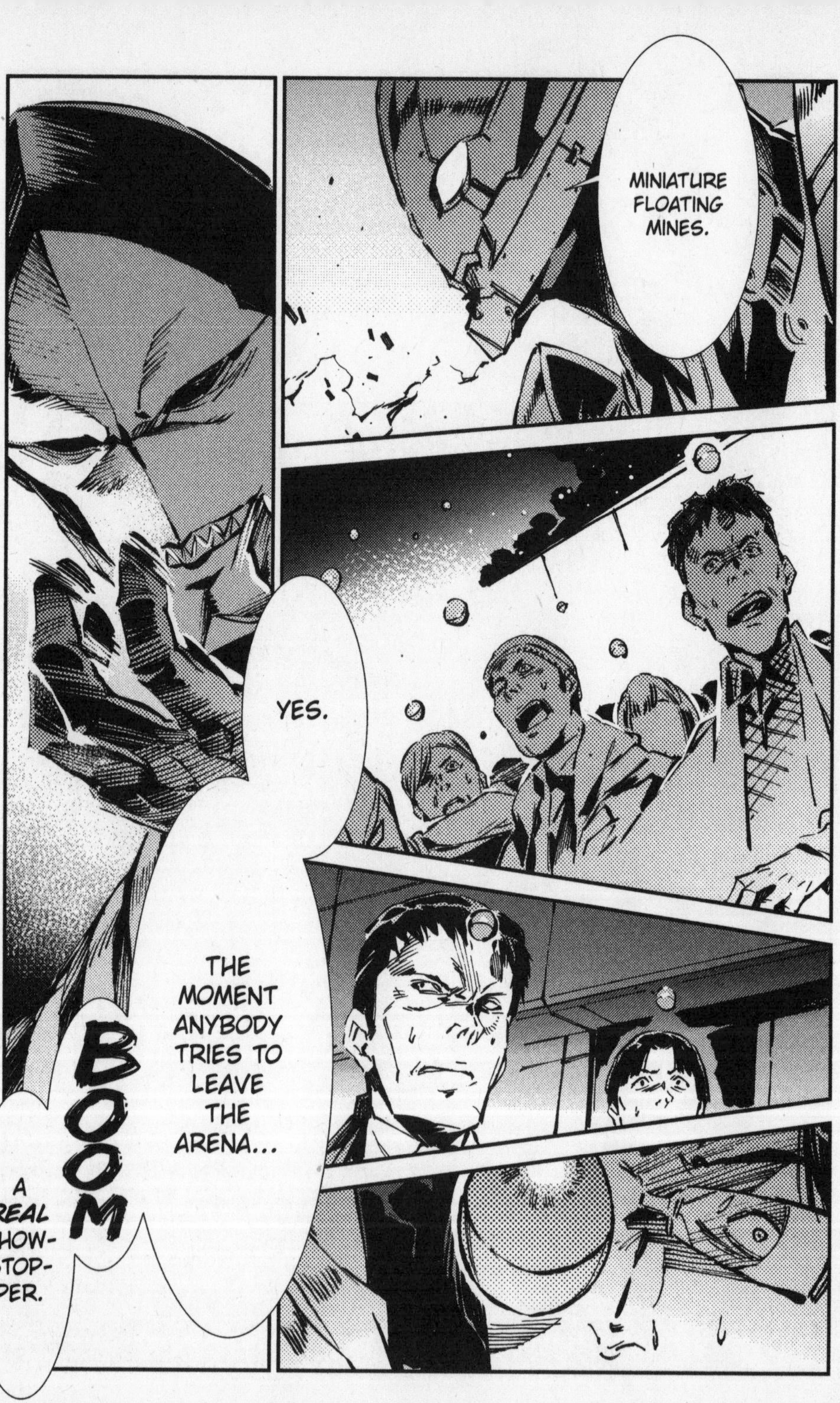
MINIATURE FLOATING MINES.
YES.
THE MOMENT ANYBODY TRIES TO LEAVE THE ARENA...
BOOM
A *REAL* SHOW-STOP-PER.

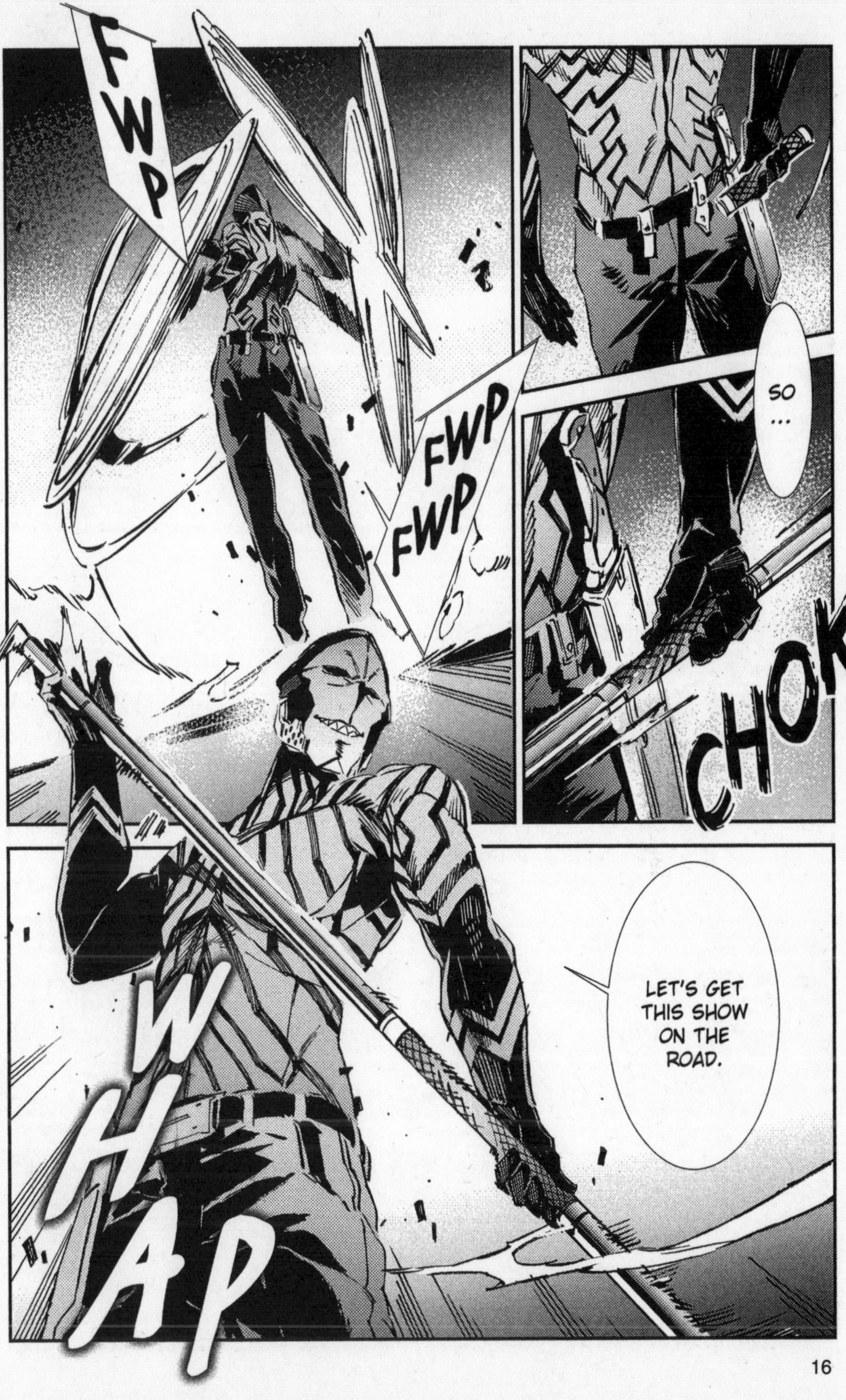

SO ...
CHOK
FWP
FWP FWP
LET'S GET THIS SHOW ON THE ROAD.
WHAP

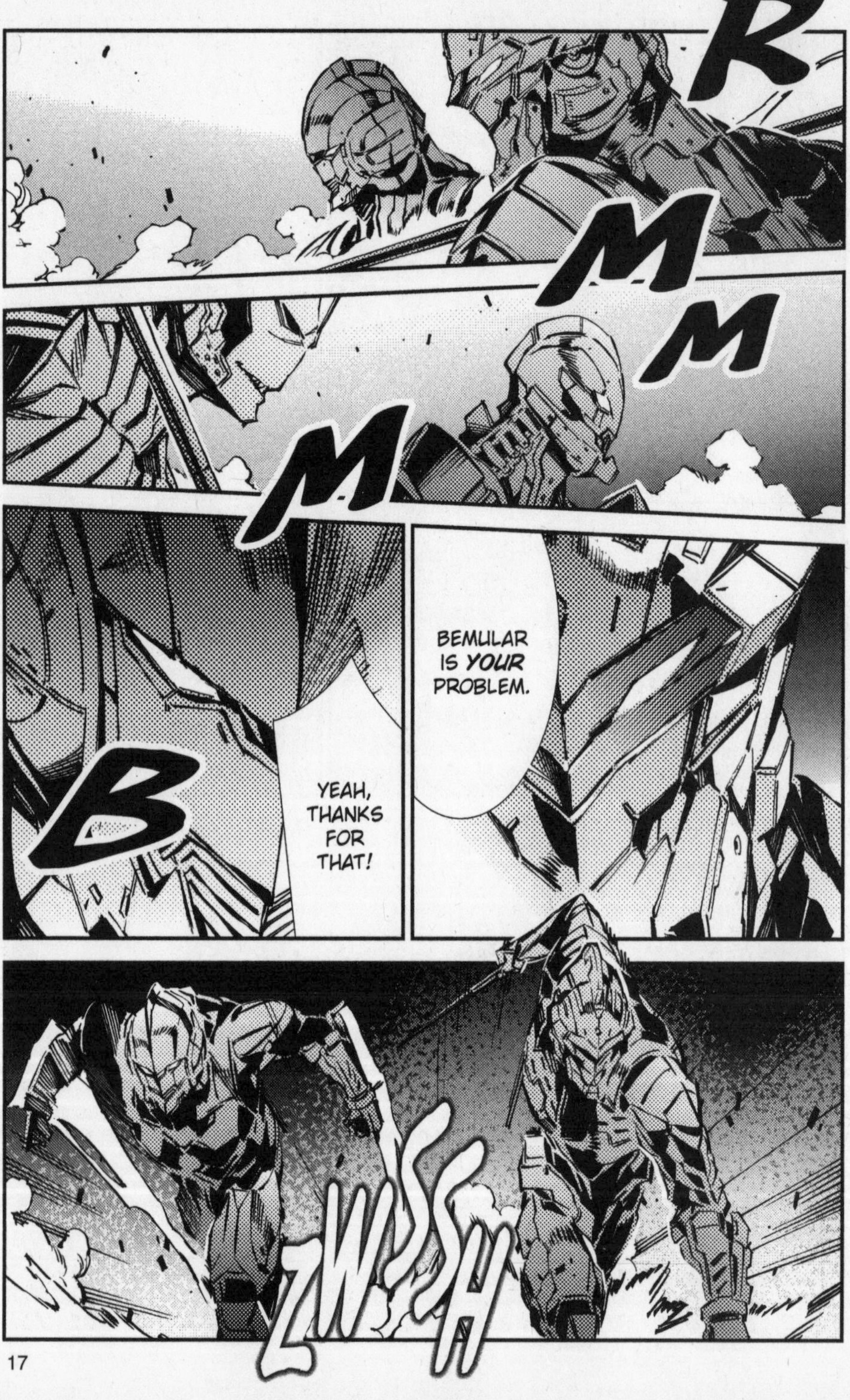
R
M
M
M
BEMULAR IS *YOUR* PROBLEM.
B
YEAH, THANKS FOR THAT!
ZWISSH

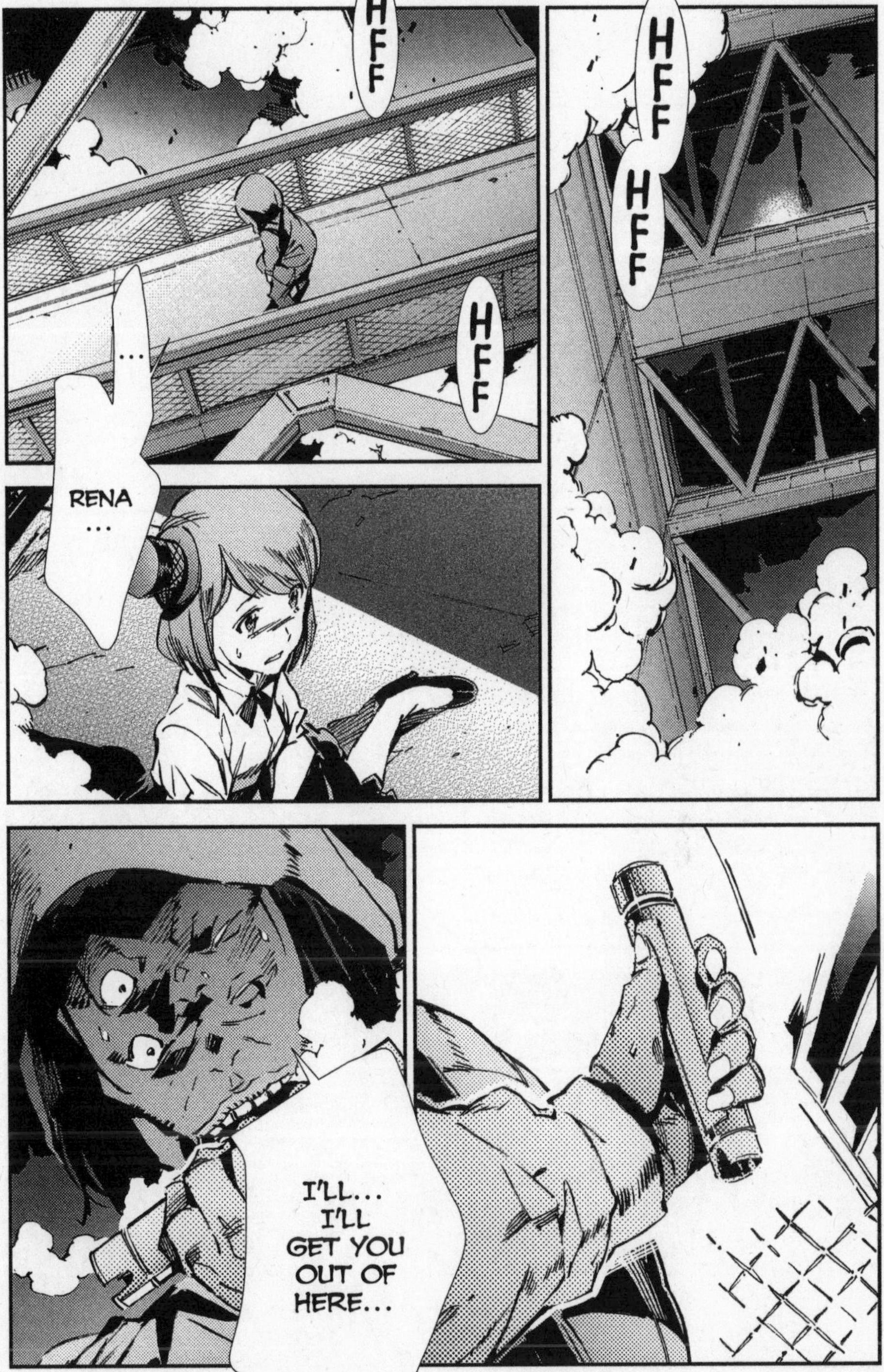
HFF HFF
HFF HFF
HFF
HFF
...
RENA ...
I'LL... I'LL GET YOU OUT OF HERE...

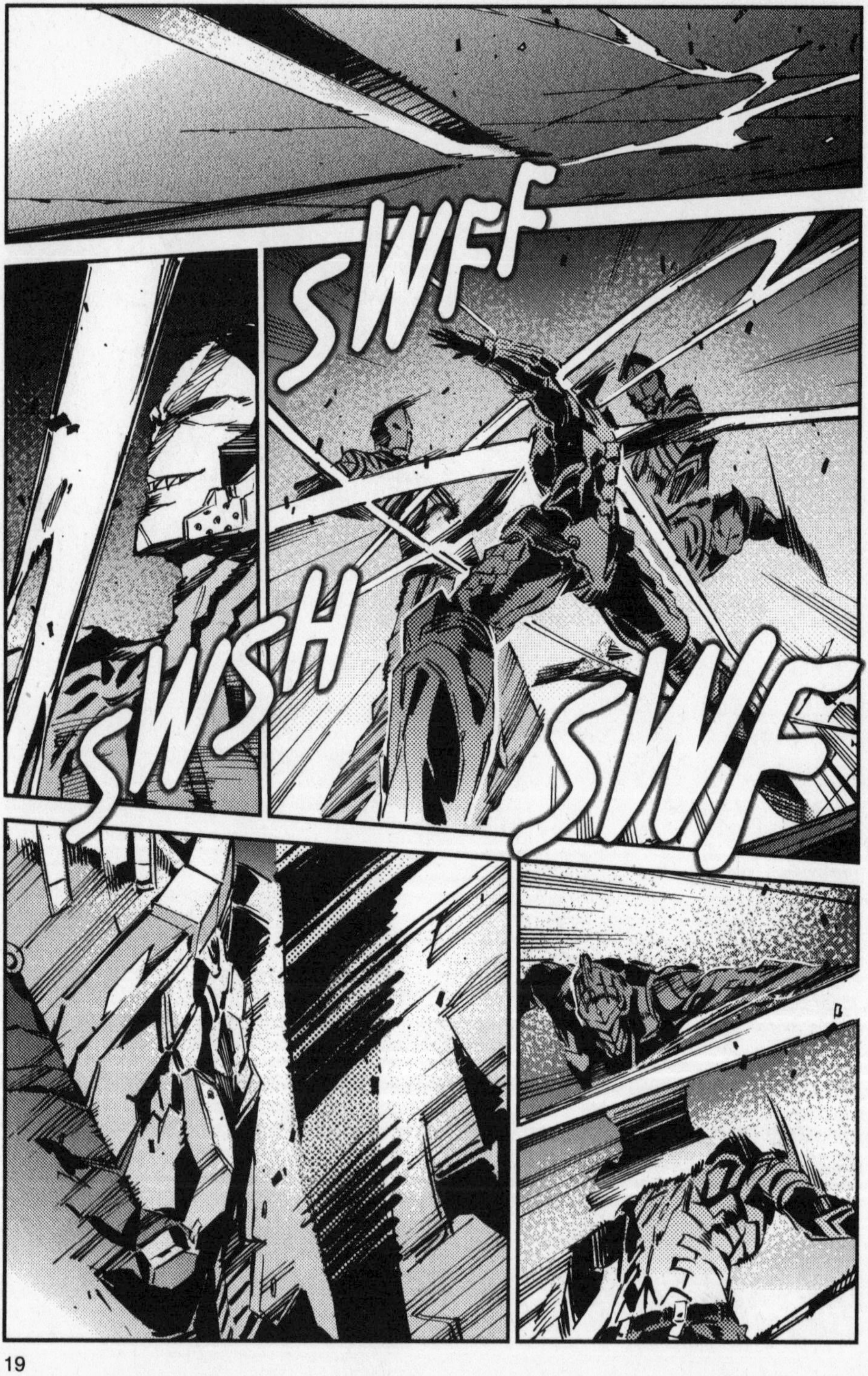
SWFF
SWF
SWSH

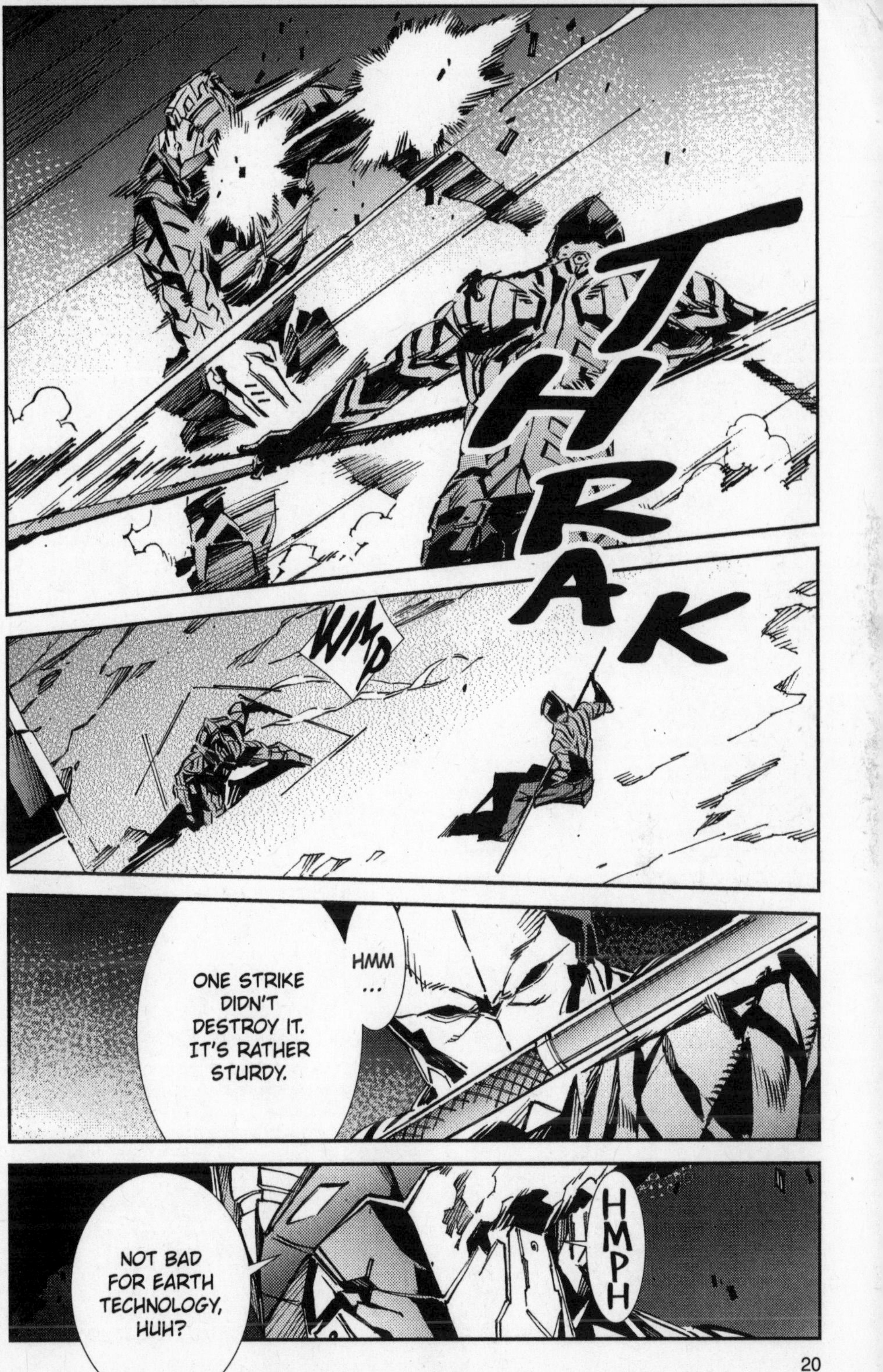
THRAK
WMP
HMM ...
ONE STRIKE DIDN'T DESTROY IT. IT'S RATHER STURDY.
HMPH
NOT BAD FOR EARTH TECHNOLOGY, HUH?

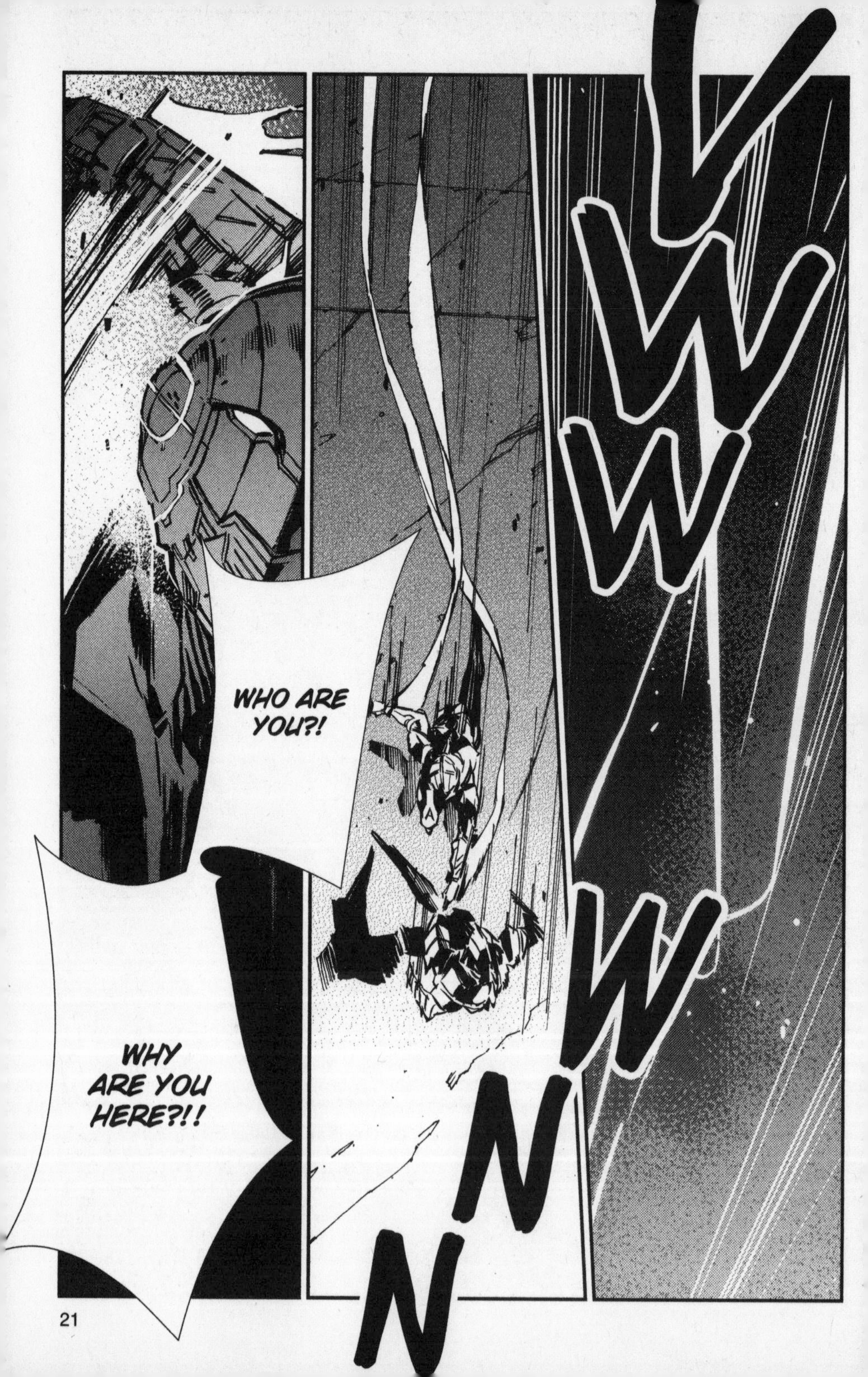
WHO ARE YOU?!
WHY ARE YOU HERE?!!

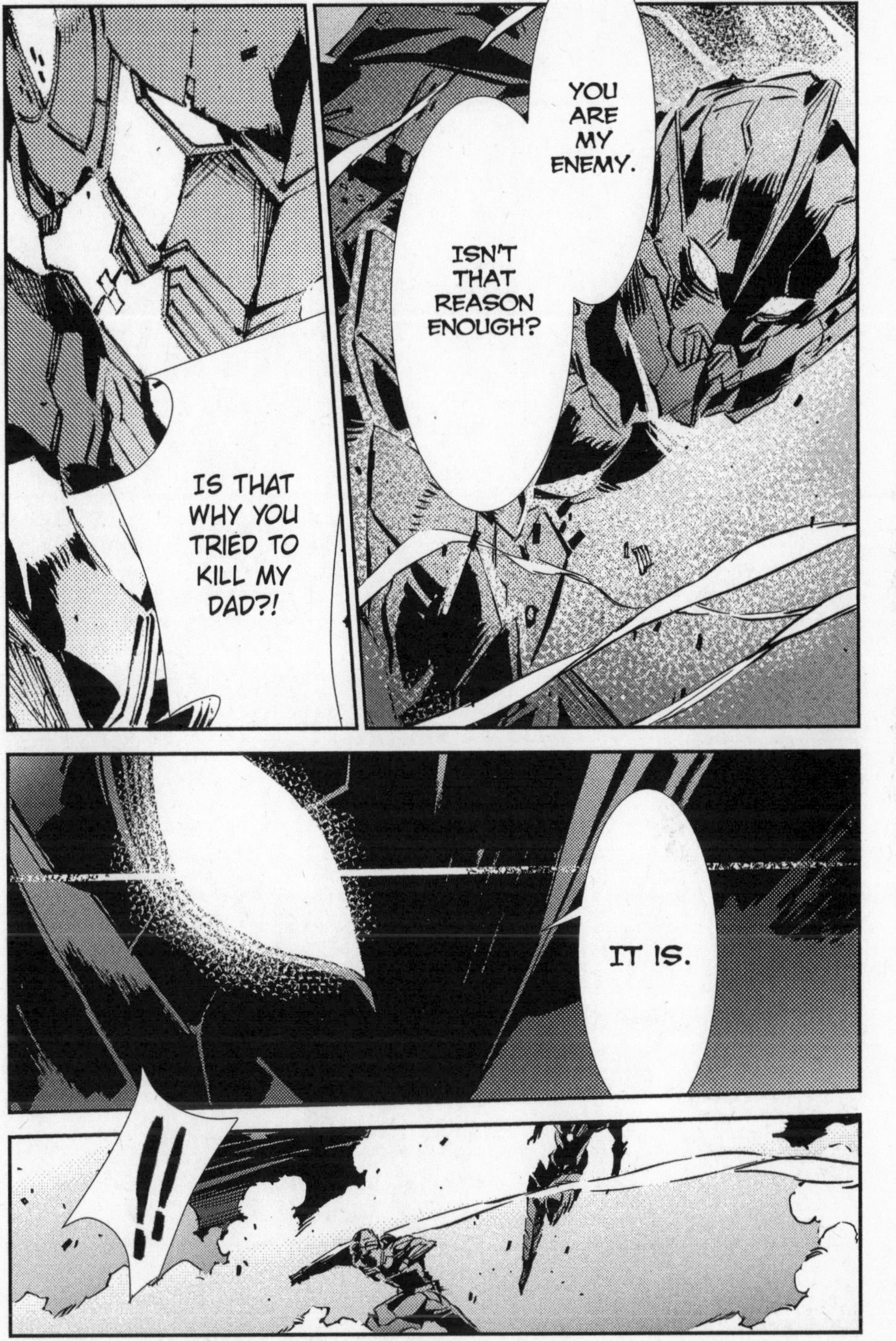
YOU ARE MY ENEMY.
ISN'T THAT REASON ENOUGH?
IS THAT WHY YOU TRIED TO KILL MY DAD?!
IT IS.
!!

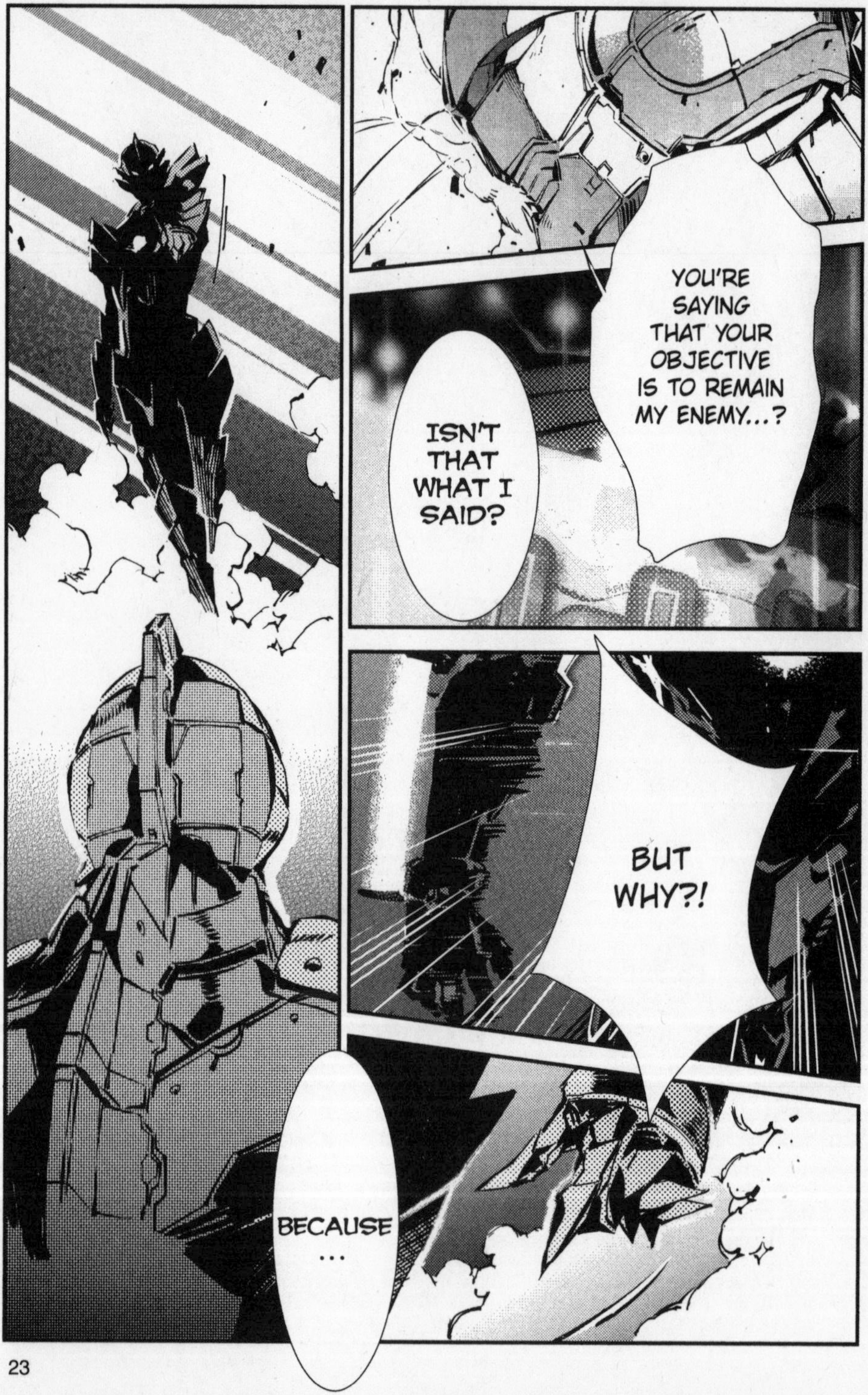
YOU'RE SAYING THAT YOUR OBJECTIVE IS TO REMAIN MY ENEMY...?
ISN'T THAT WHAT I SAID?
BUT WHY?!
BECAUSE ...

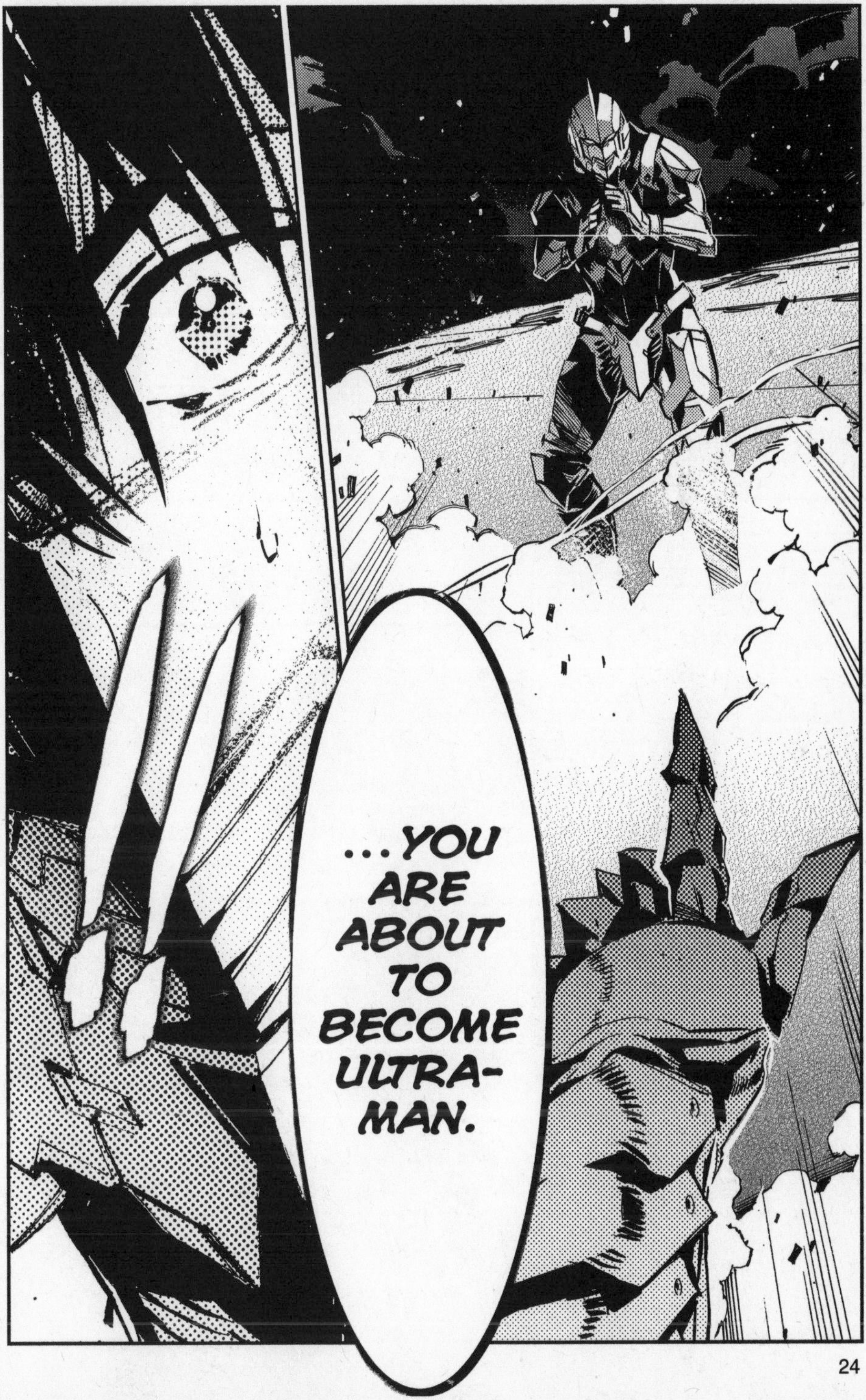
...YOU ARE ABOUT TO BECOME ULTRA-MAN.

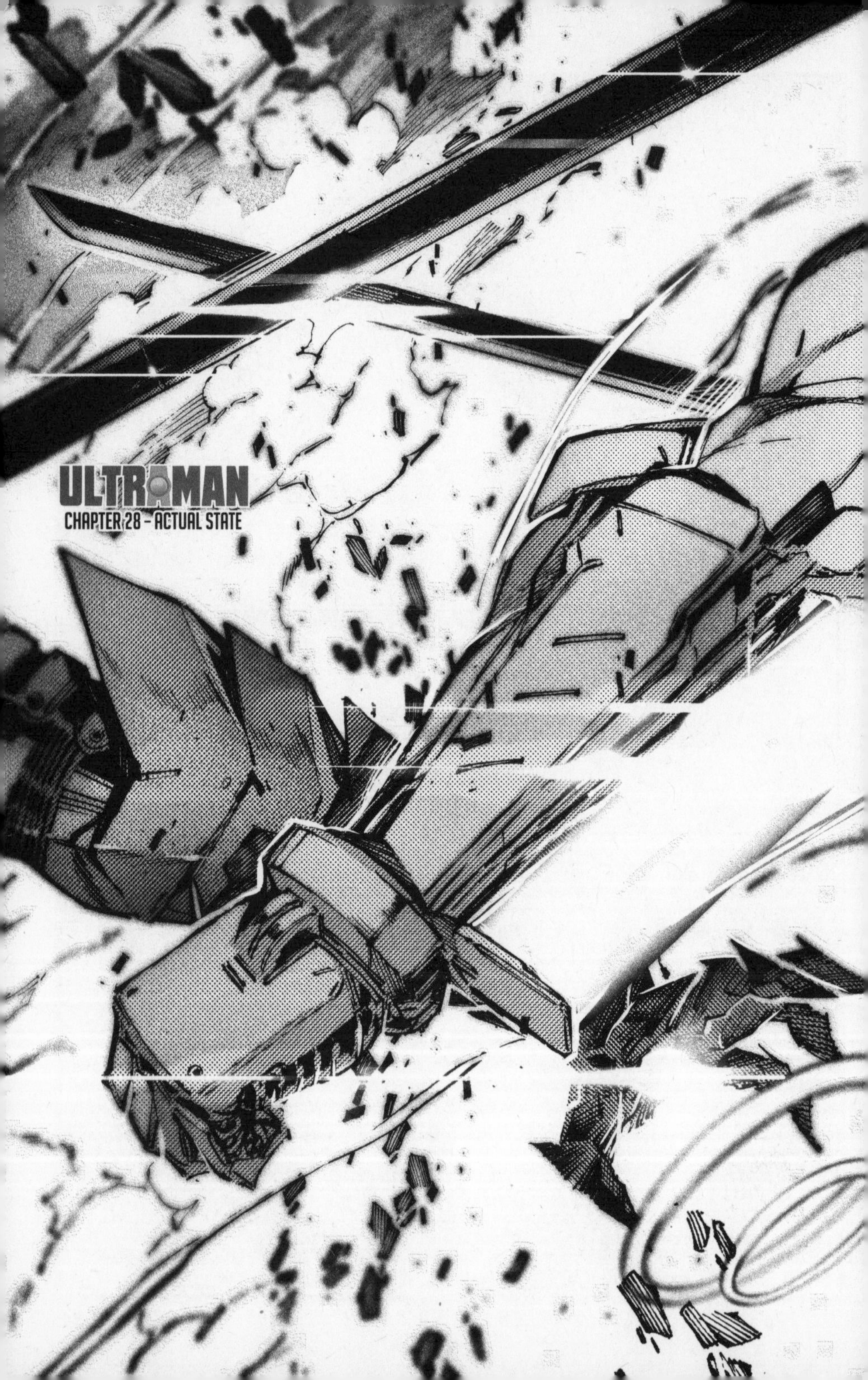
ULTRAMAN
CHAPTER 28 - ACTUAL STATE

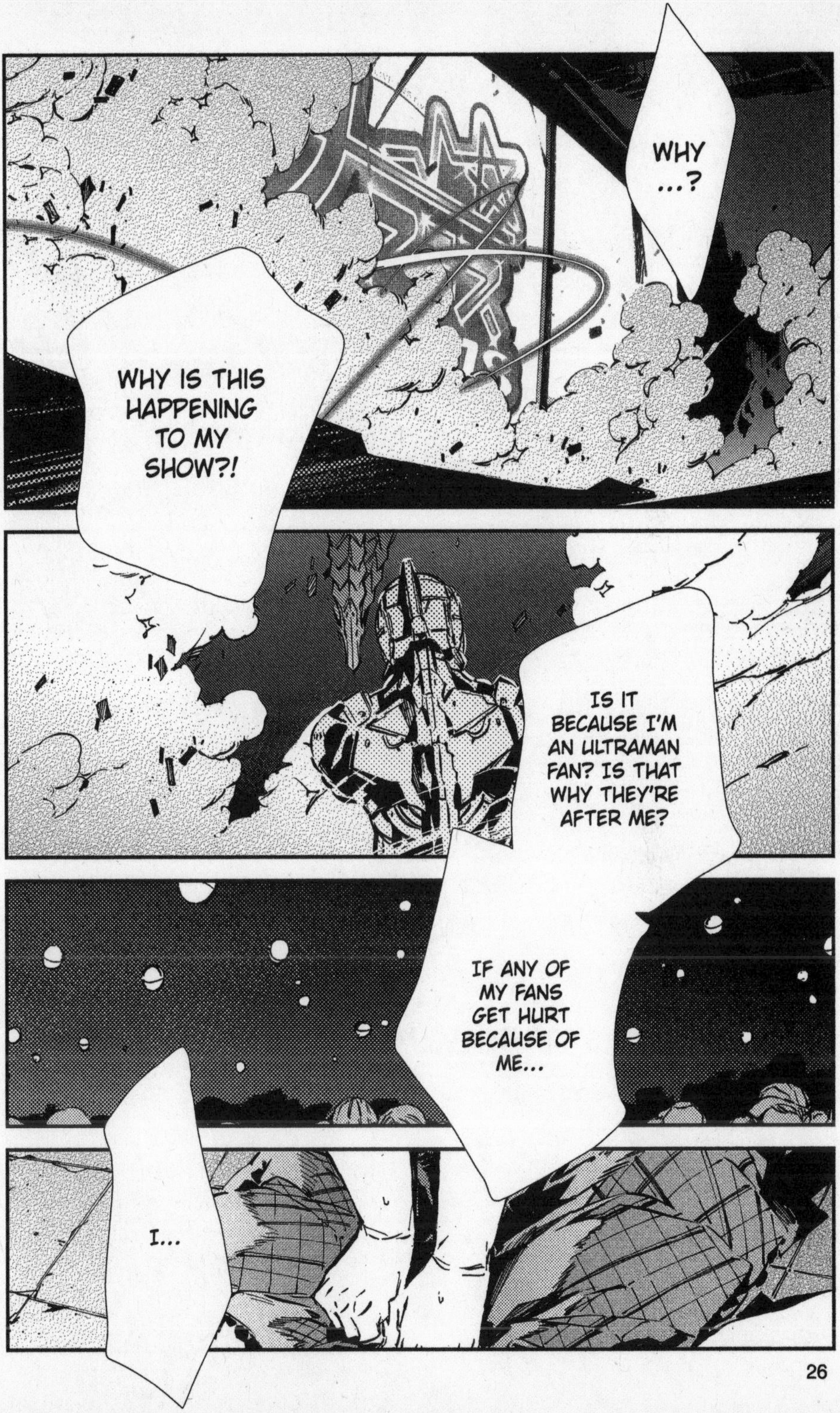
WHY ...?
WHY IS THIS HAPPENING TO MY SHOW?!
IS IT BECAUSE I'M AN ULTRAMAN FAN? IS THAT WHY THEY'RE AFTER ME?
IF ANY OF MY FANS GET HURT BECAUSE OF ME...
I...

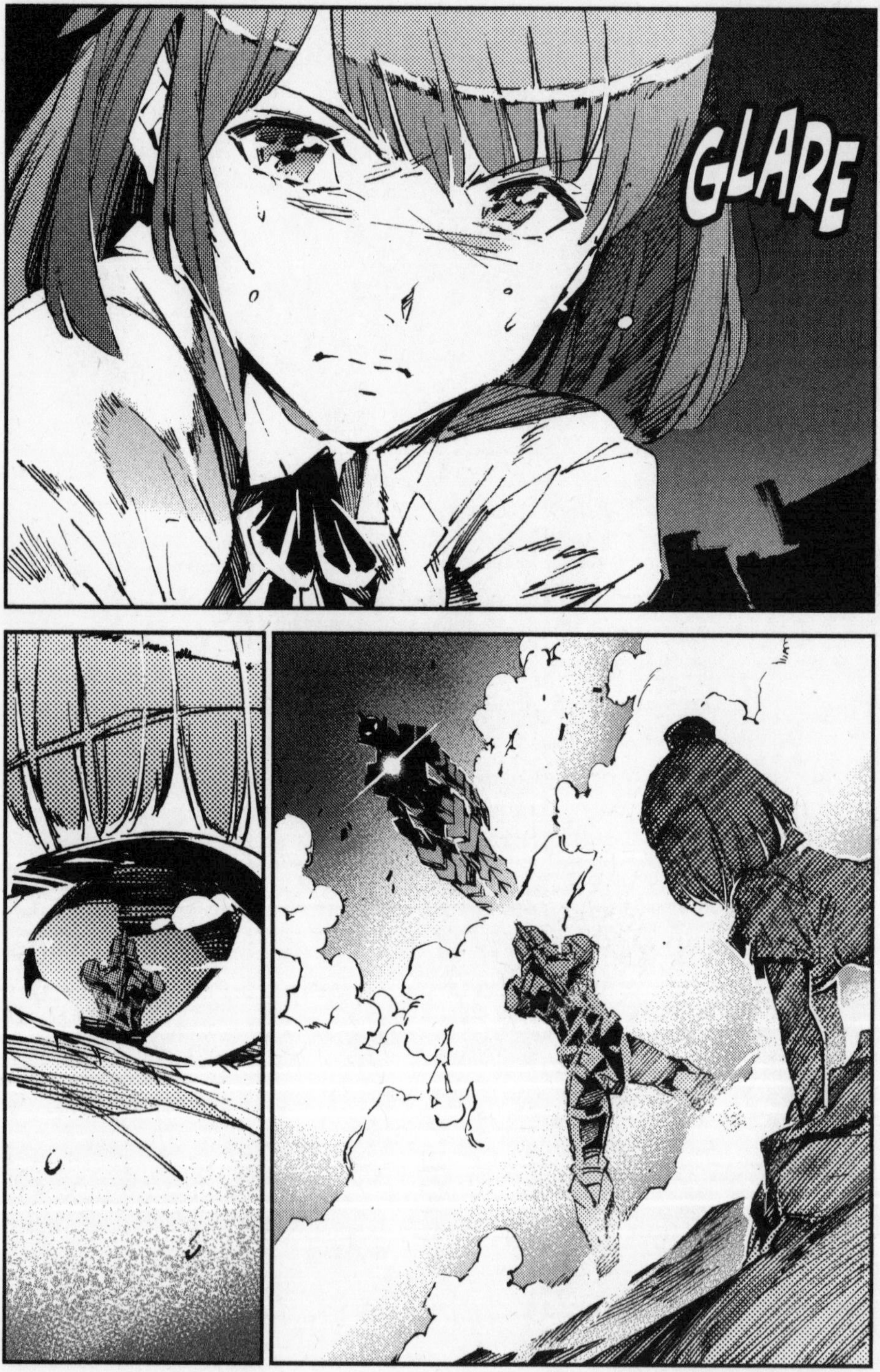
GLARE

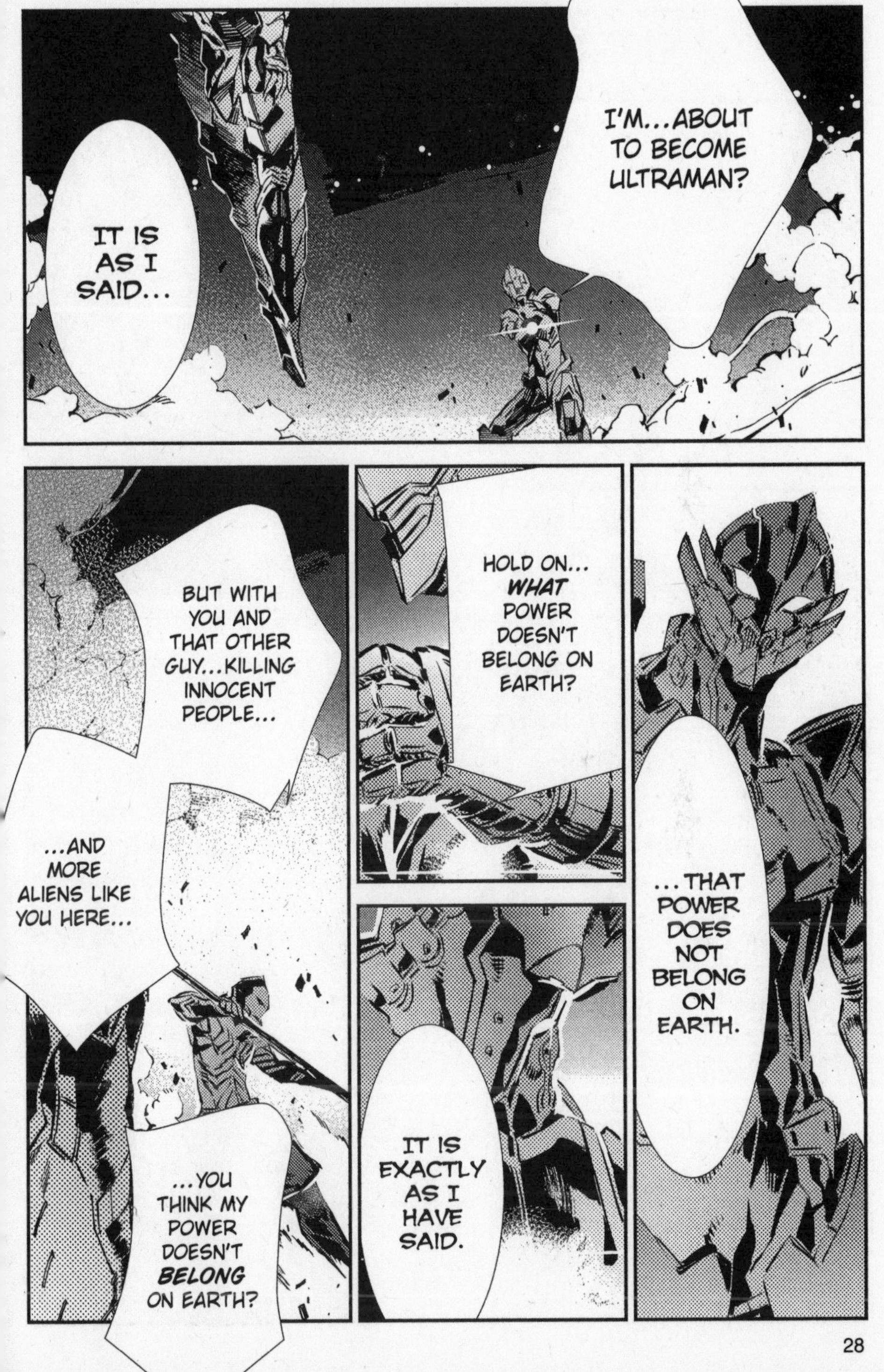
I'M...ABOUT TO BECOME ULTRAMAN?
IT IS AS I SAID...
...THAT POWER DOES NOT BELONG ON EARTH.
HOLD ON... *WHAT* POWER DOESN'T BELONG ON EARTH?
IT IS EXACTLY AS I HAVE SAID.
BUT WITH YOU AND THAT OTHER GUY...KILLING INNOCENT PEOPLE...
...AND MORE ALIENS LIKE YOU HERE...
...YOU THINK MY POWER DOESN'T *BELONG* ON EARTH?

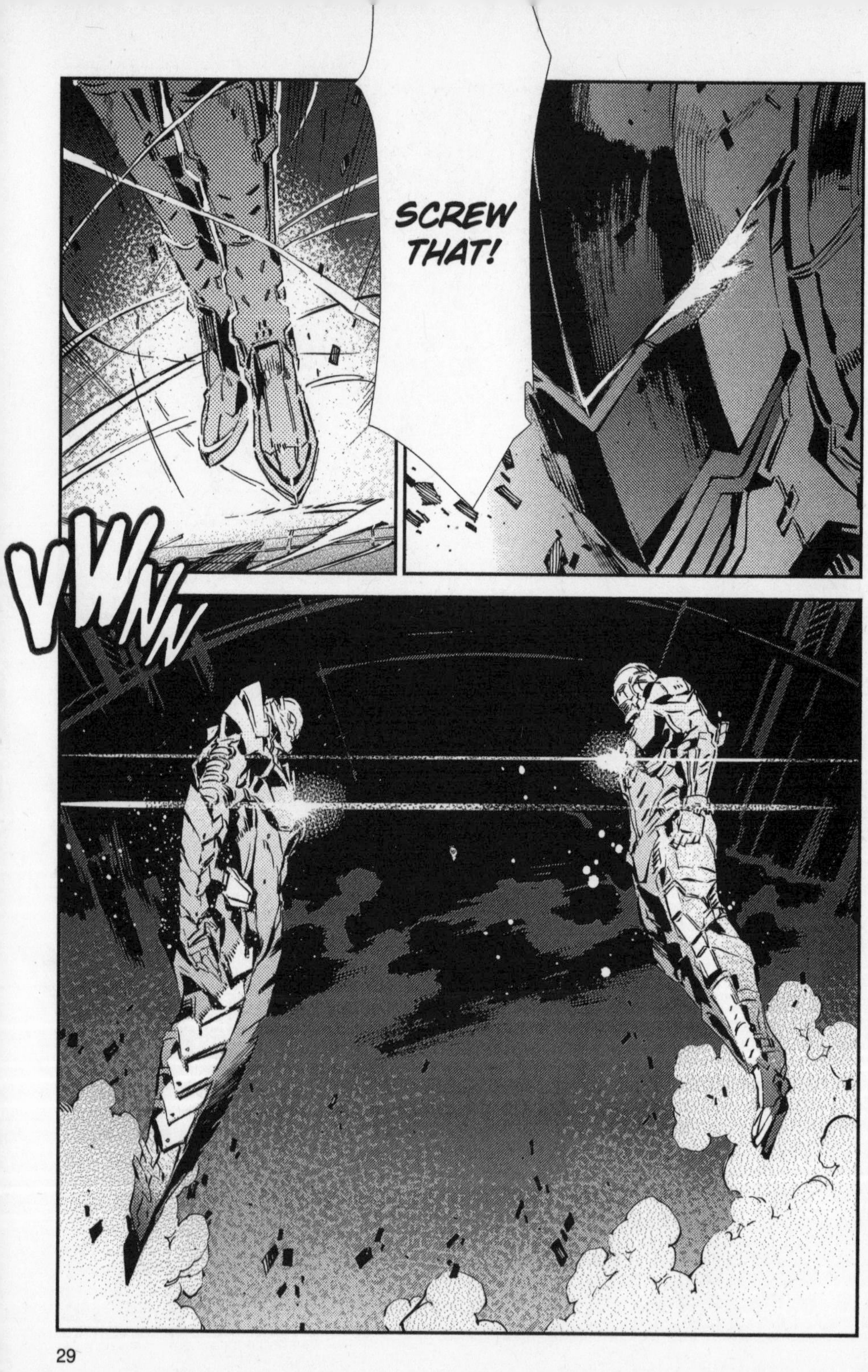
SCREW THAT!
VWNN

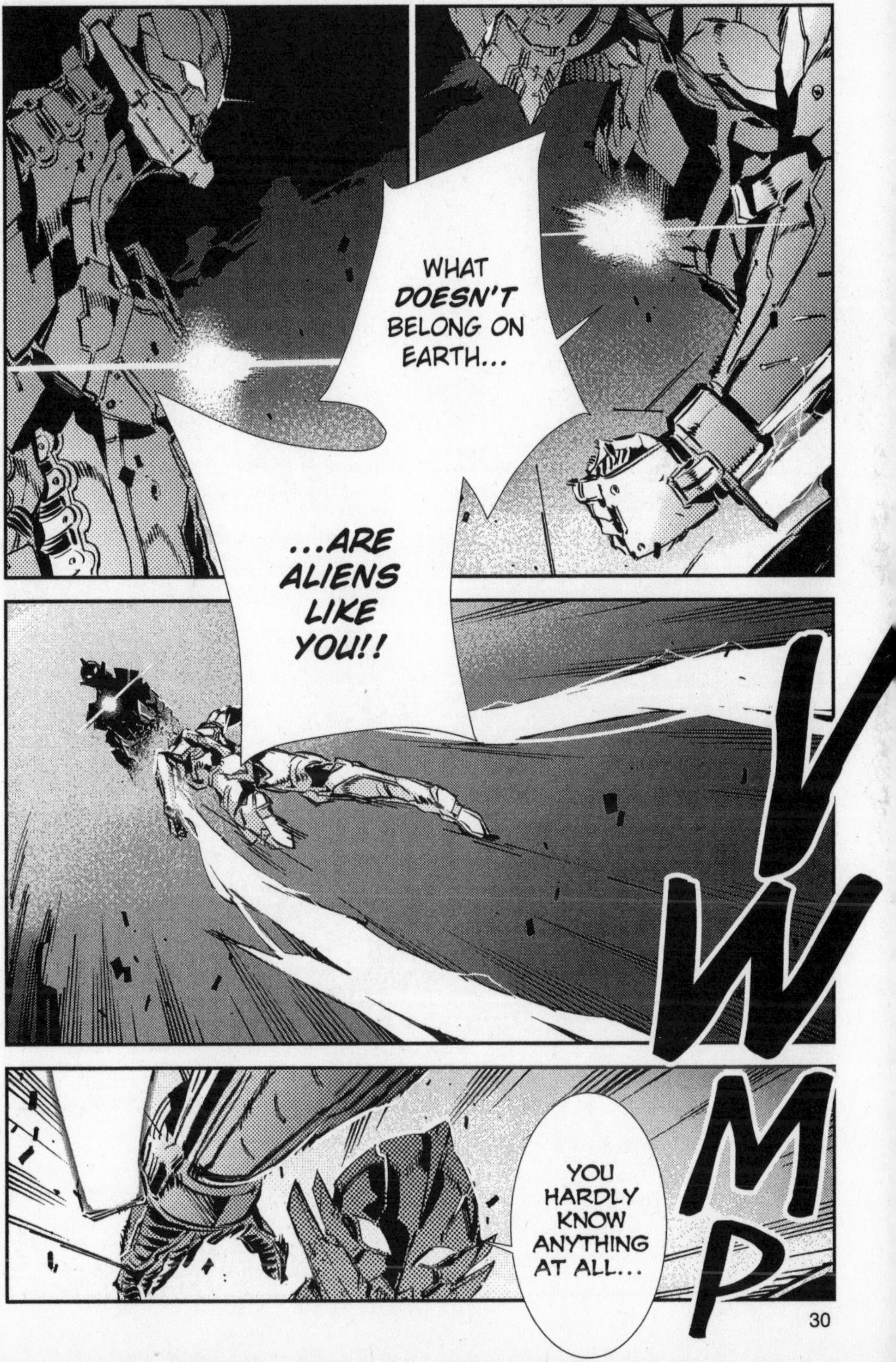
WHAT *DOESN'T* BELONG ON EARTH...
...ARE ALIENS LIKE YOU!!
VWWMP
YOU HARDLY KNOW ANYTHING AT ALL...

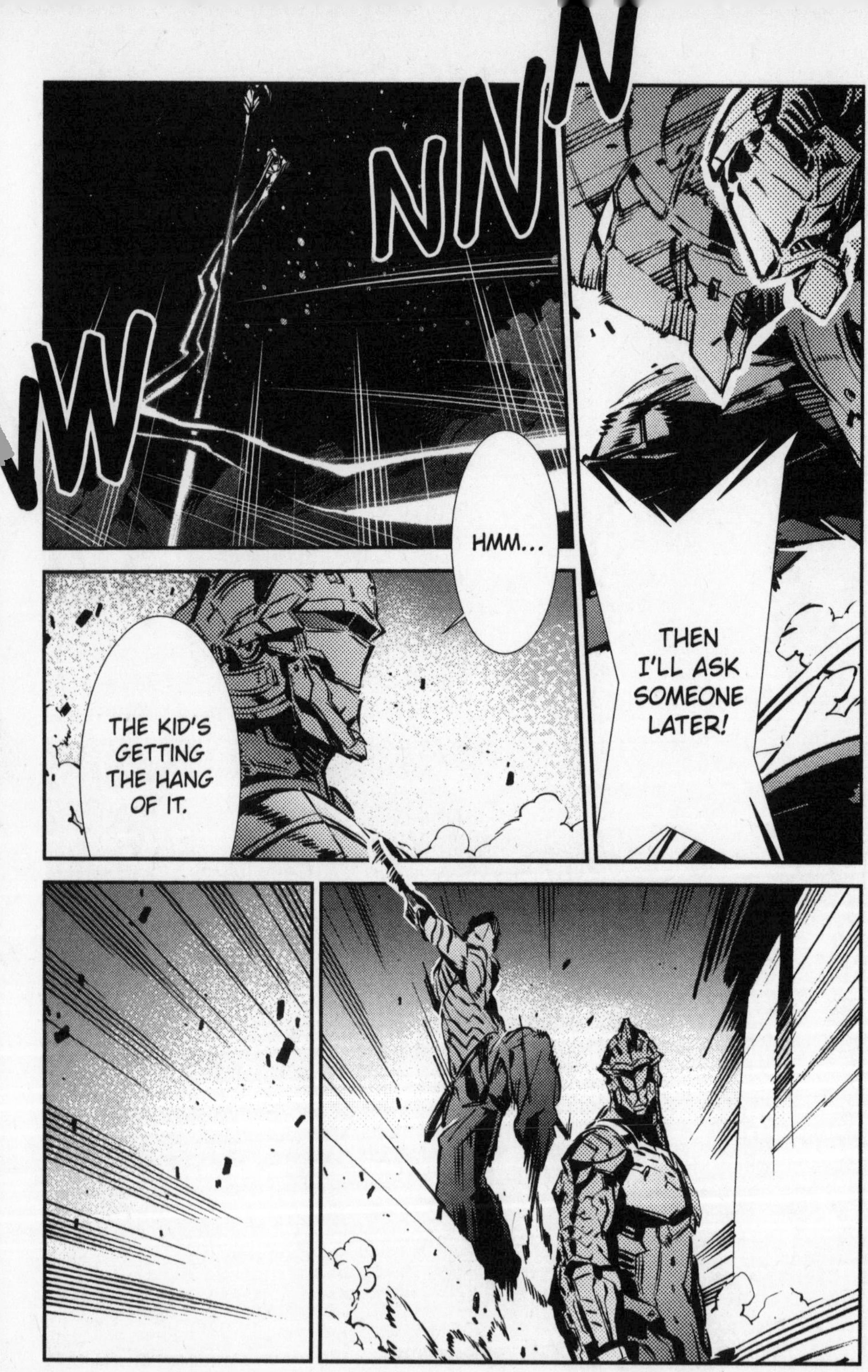
THEN I'LL ASK SOMEONE LATER!
WWNNNN
HMM...
THE KID'S GETTING THE HANG OF IT.

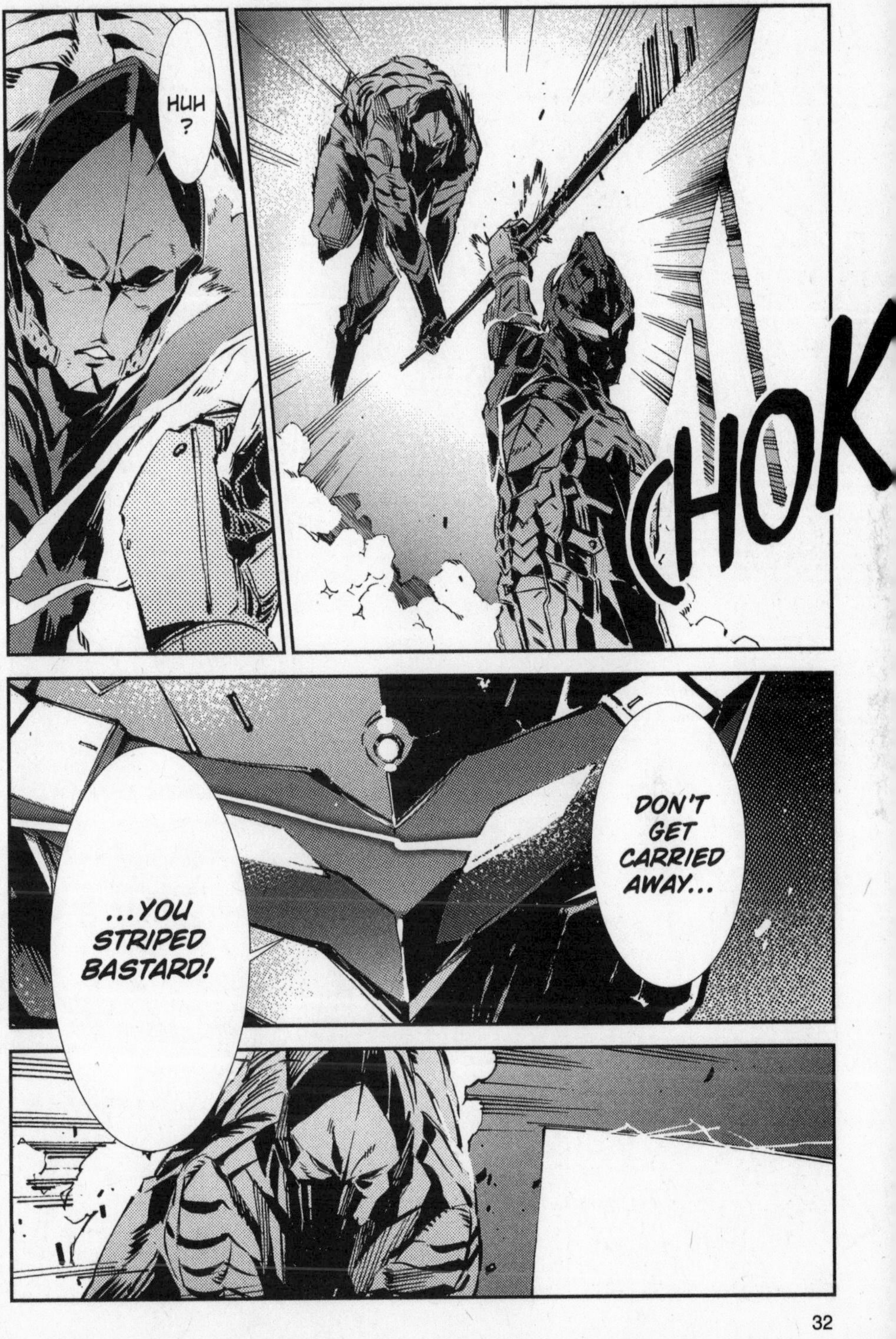
CHOK
HUH ?
DON'T GET CARRIED AWAY...
...YOU STRIPED BASTARD!

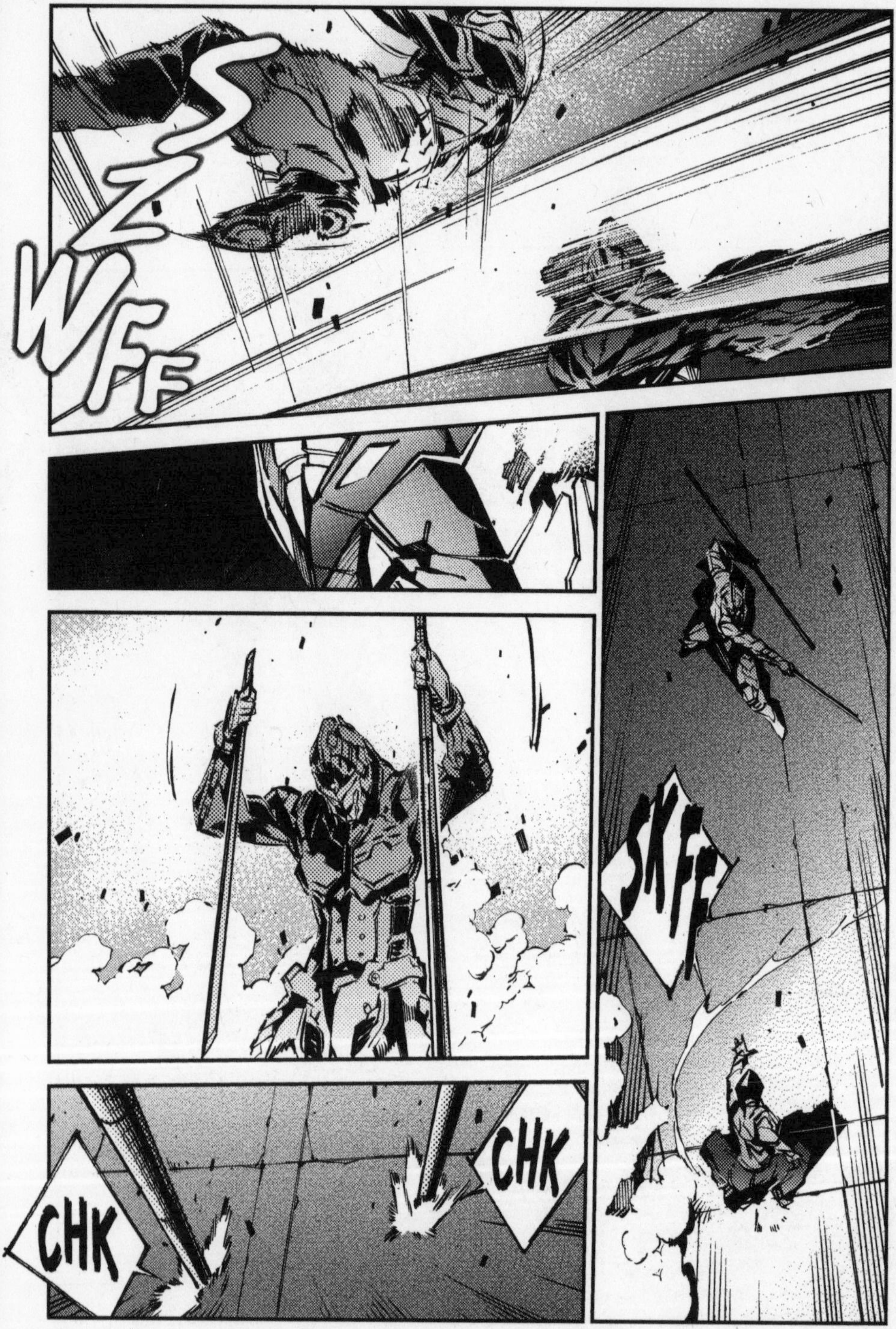
SWFF
SKFF
CHK
CHK

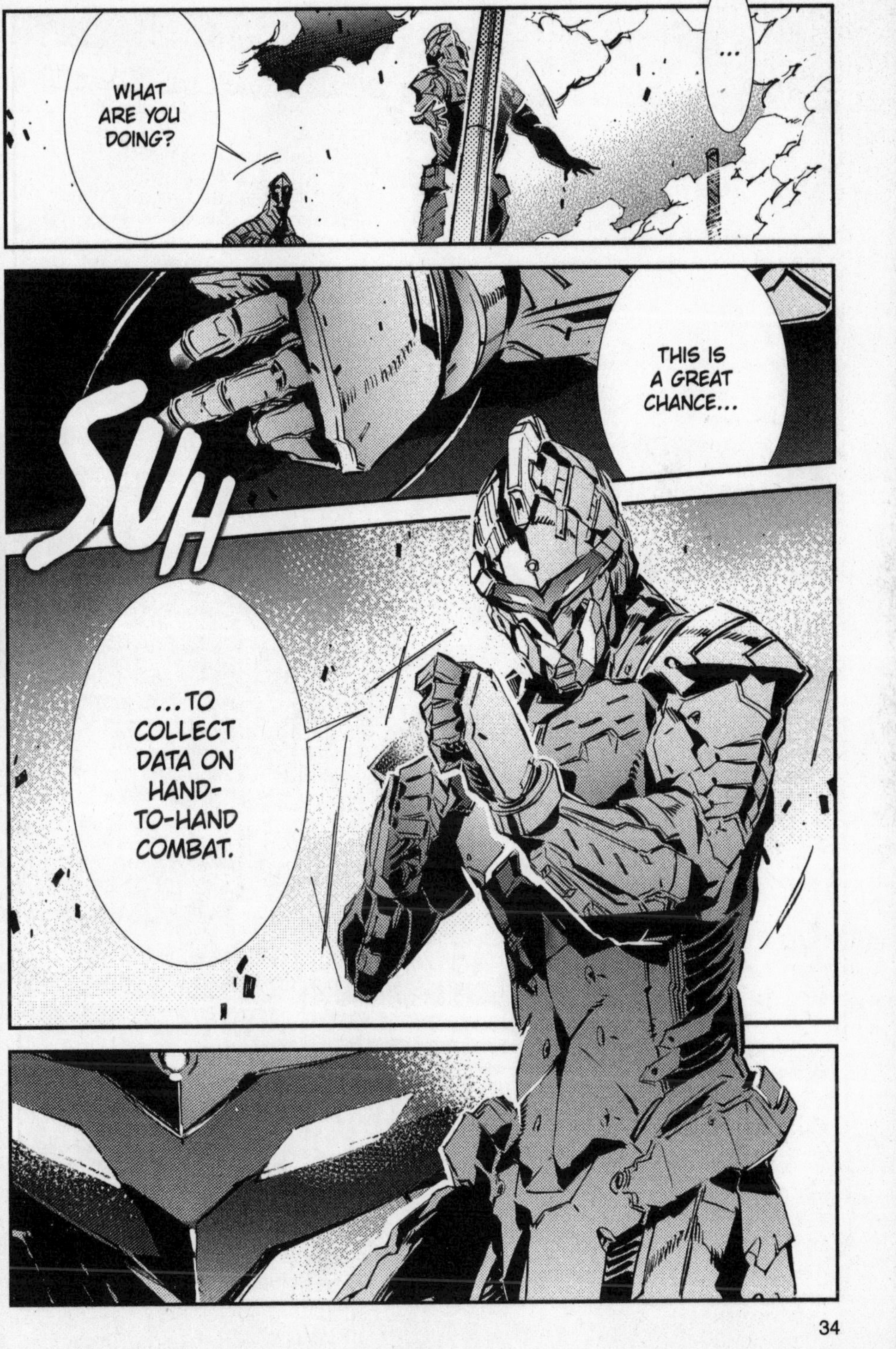
...
WHAT ARE YOU DOING?
THIS IS A GREAT CHANCE...
SUH
...TO COLLECT DATA ON HAND-TO-HAND COMBAT.

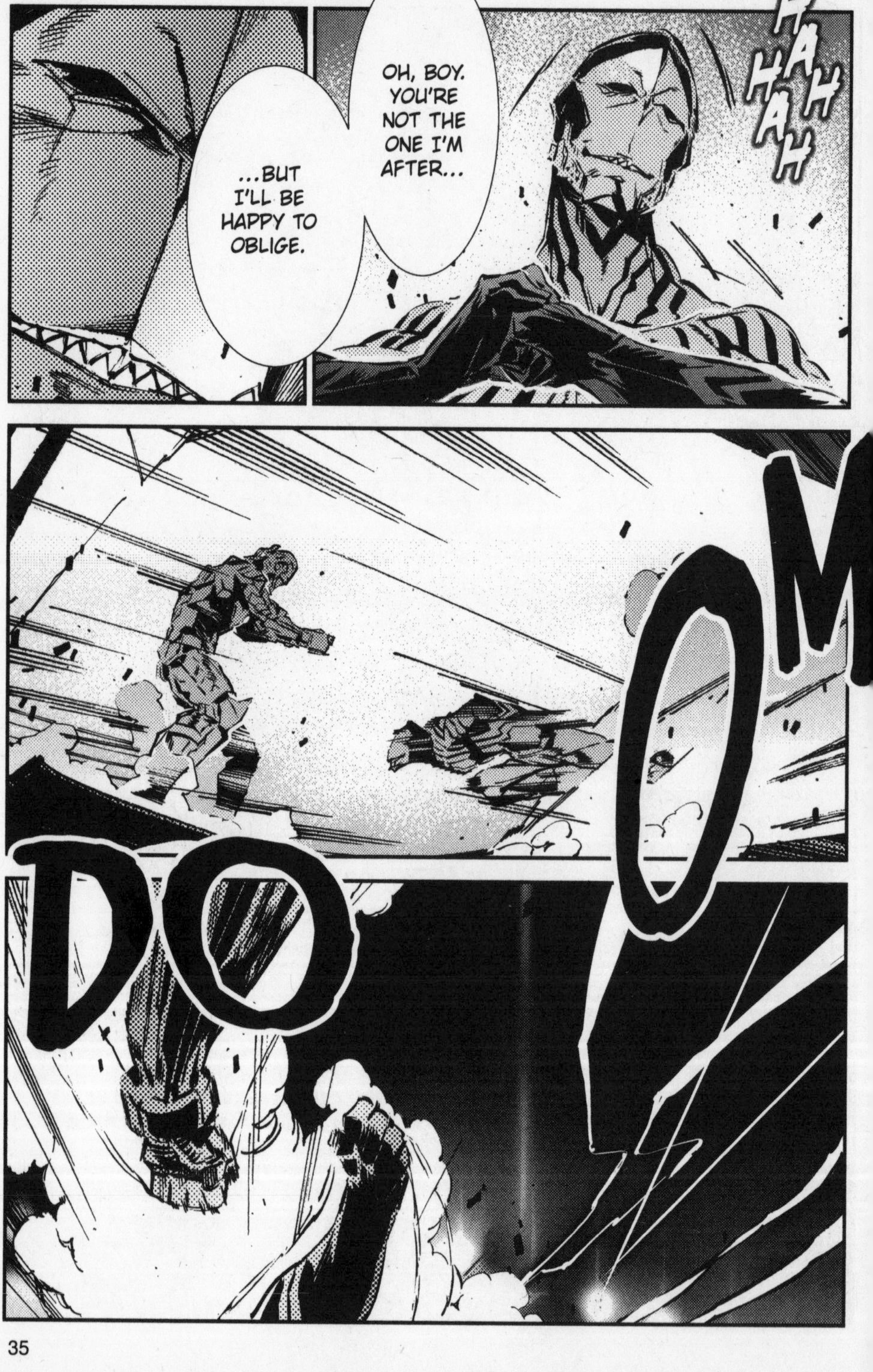
HAH HAH
OH, BOY. YOU'RE NOT THE ONE I'M AFTER...
...BUT I'LL BE HAPPY TO OBLIGE.
DOOM

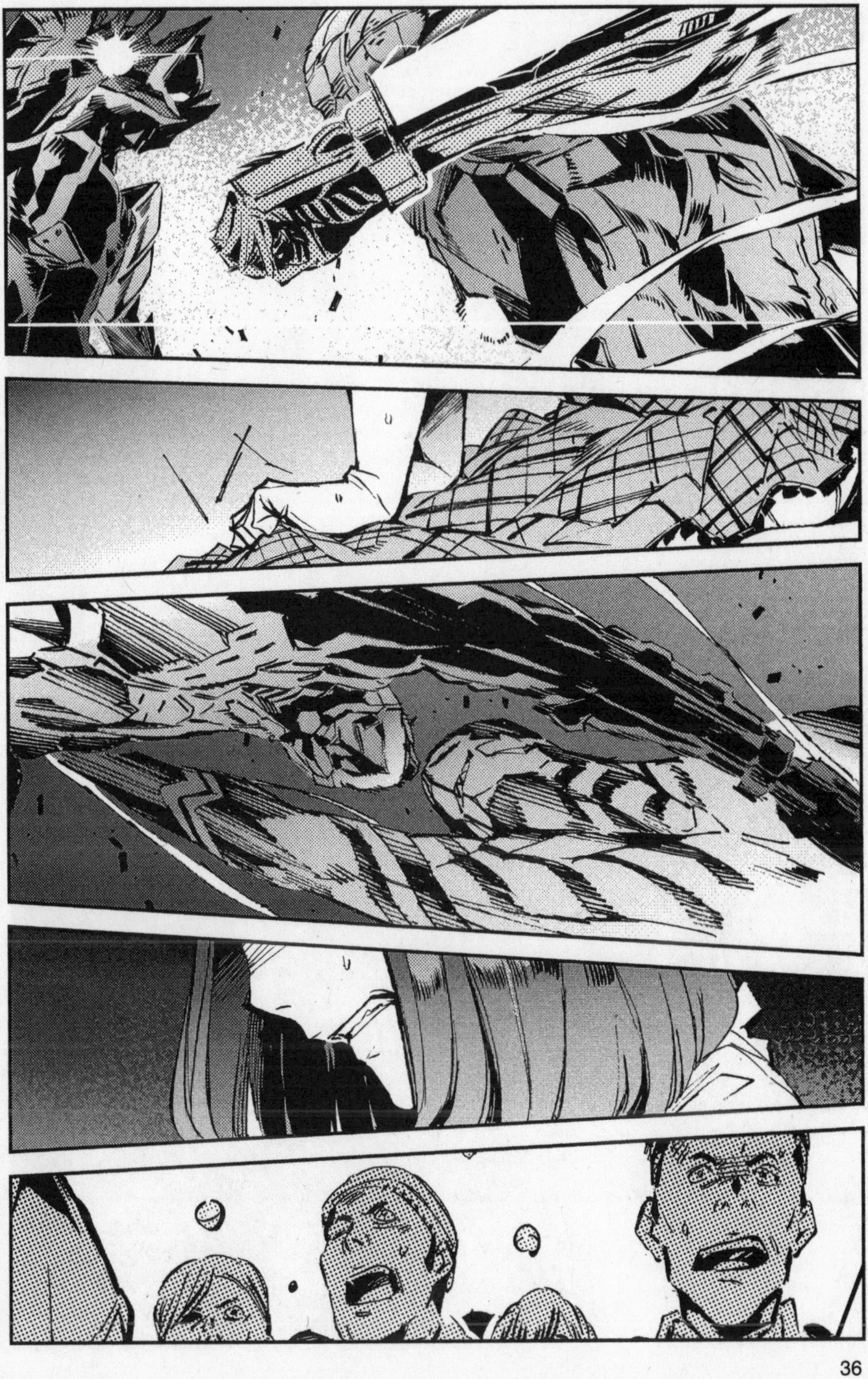

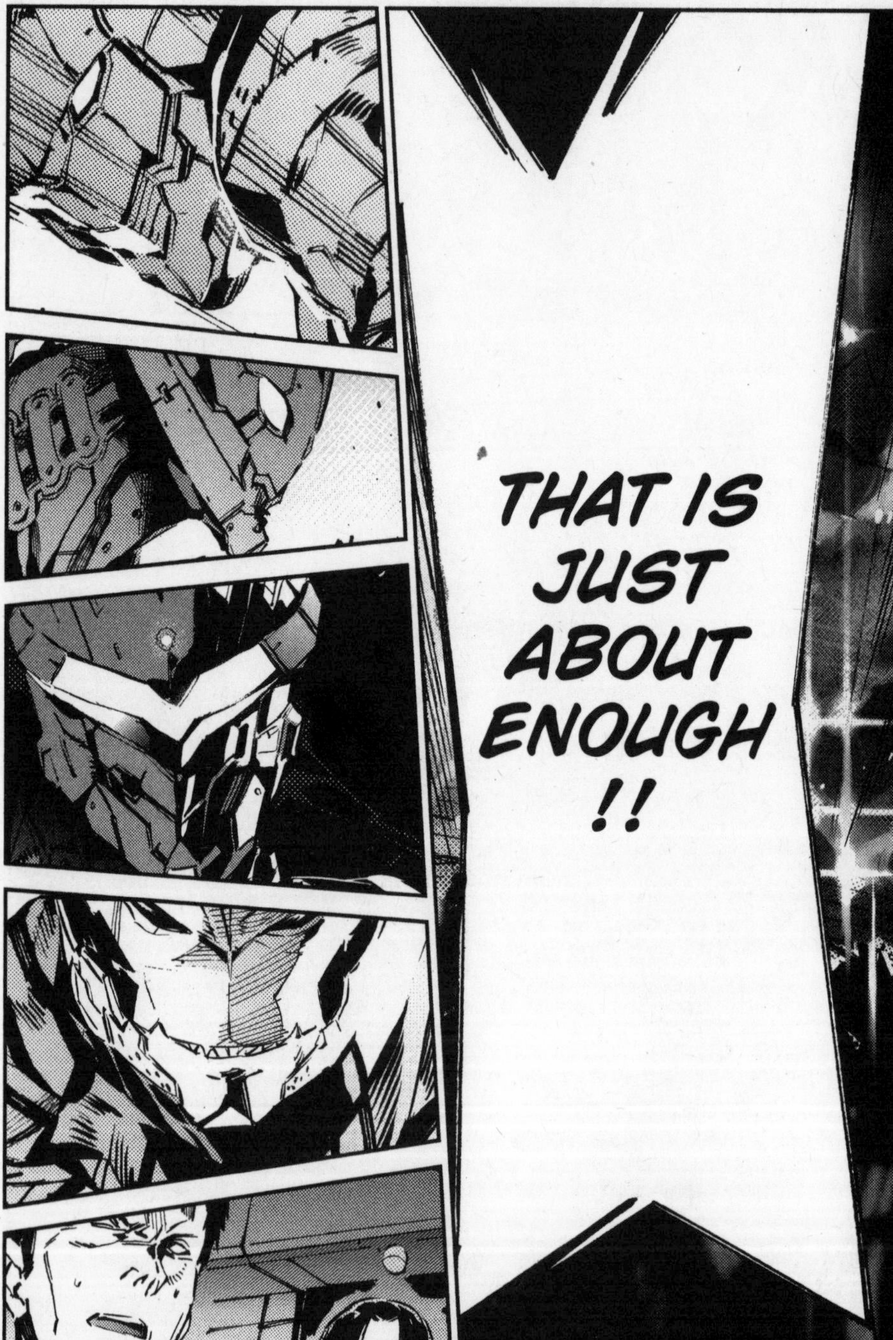
THAT IS JUST ABOUT ENOUGH!!

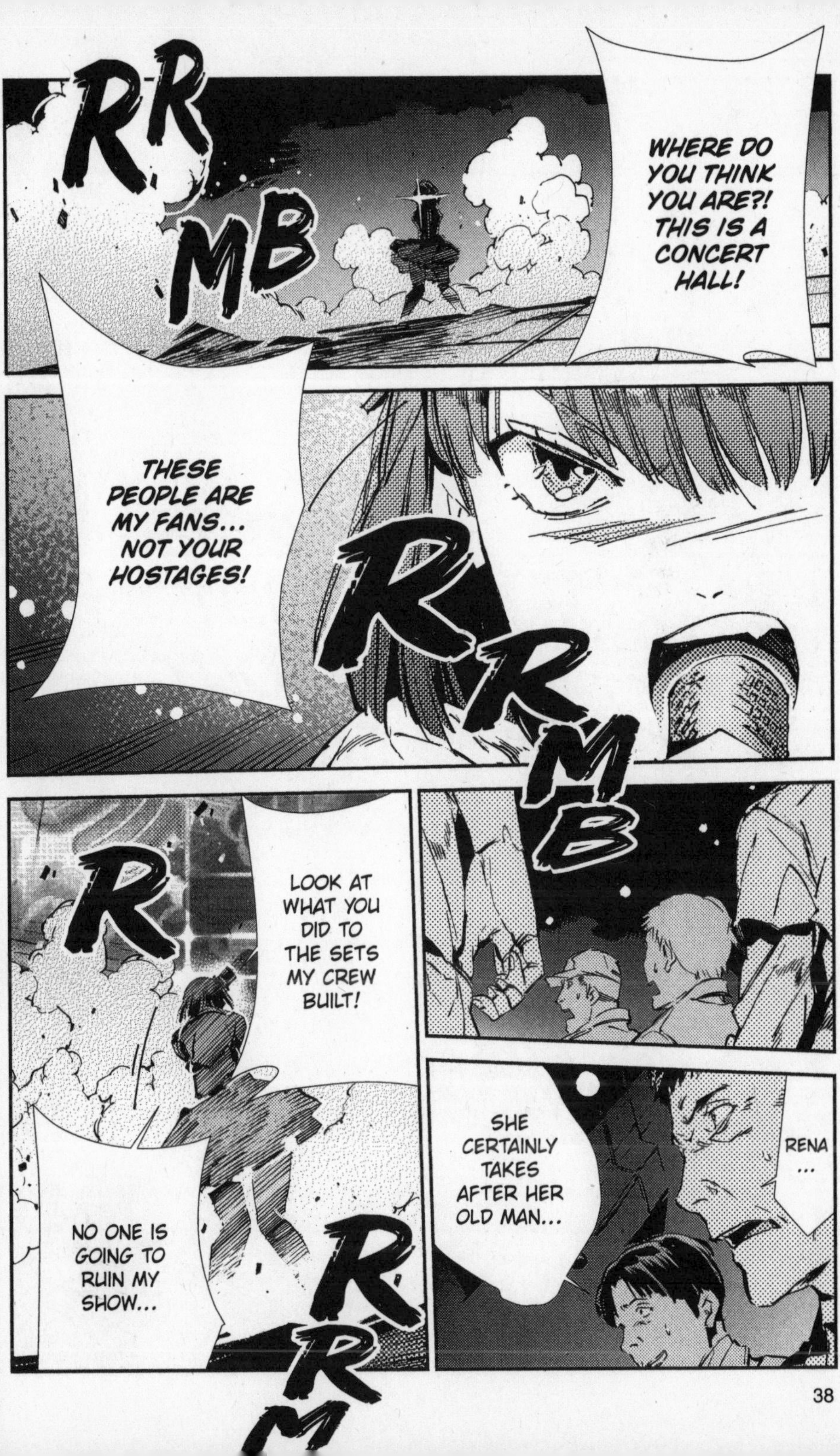
WHERE DO YOU THINK YOU ARE?! THIS IS A CONCERT HALL!
RRMB
THESE PEOPLE ARE MY FANS... NOT YOUR HOSTAGES!
RRRMB
RENA...
SHE CERTAINLY TAKES AFTER HER OLD MAN...
LOOK AT WHAT YOU DID TO THE SETS MY CREW BUILT!
R
NO ONE IS GOING TO RUIN MY SHOW...
RRM

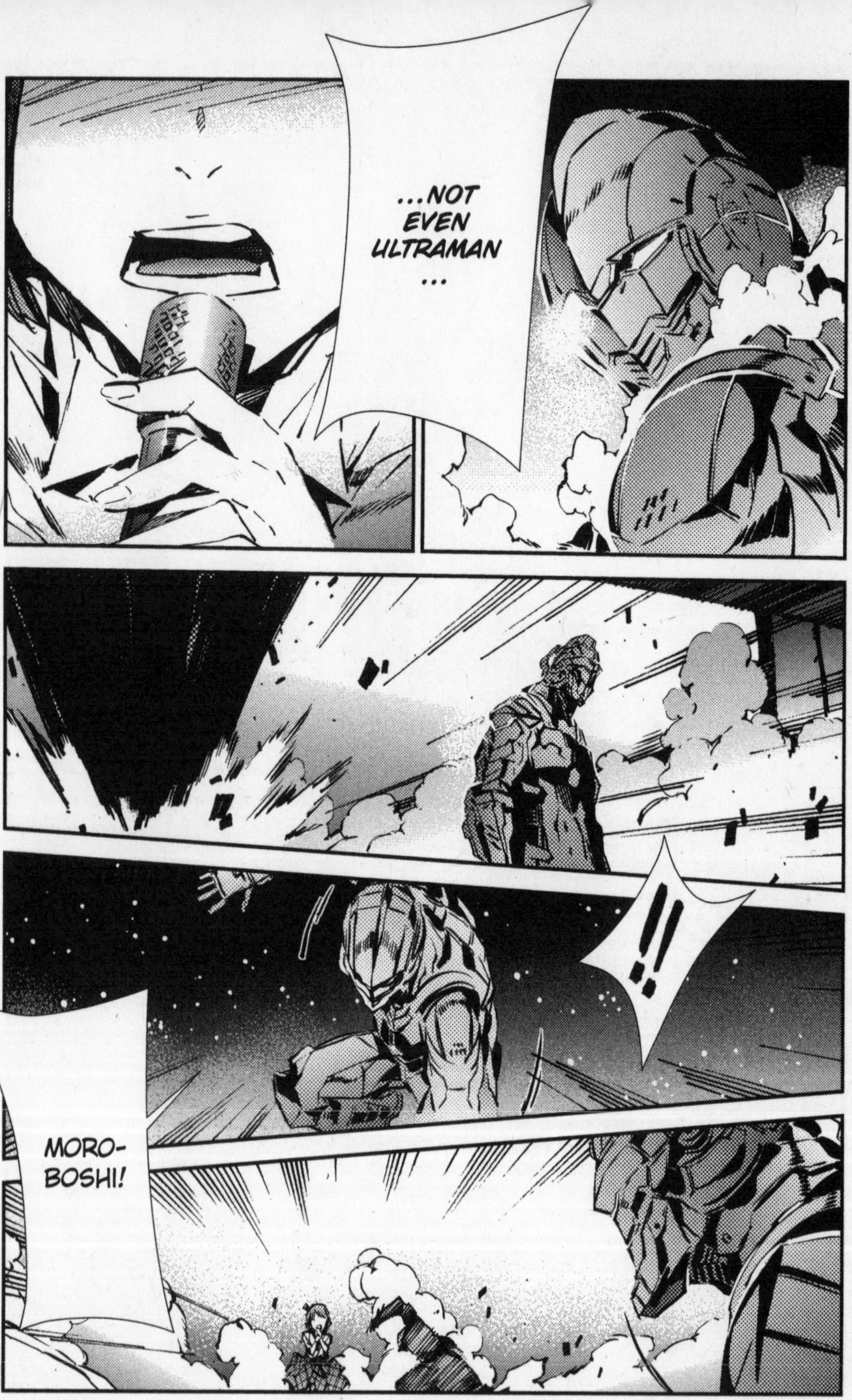
...NOT EVEN ULTRAMAN ...
!!
MORO-BOSHI!

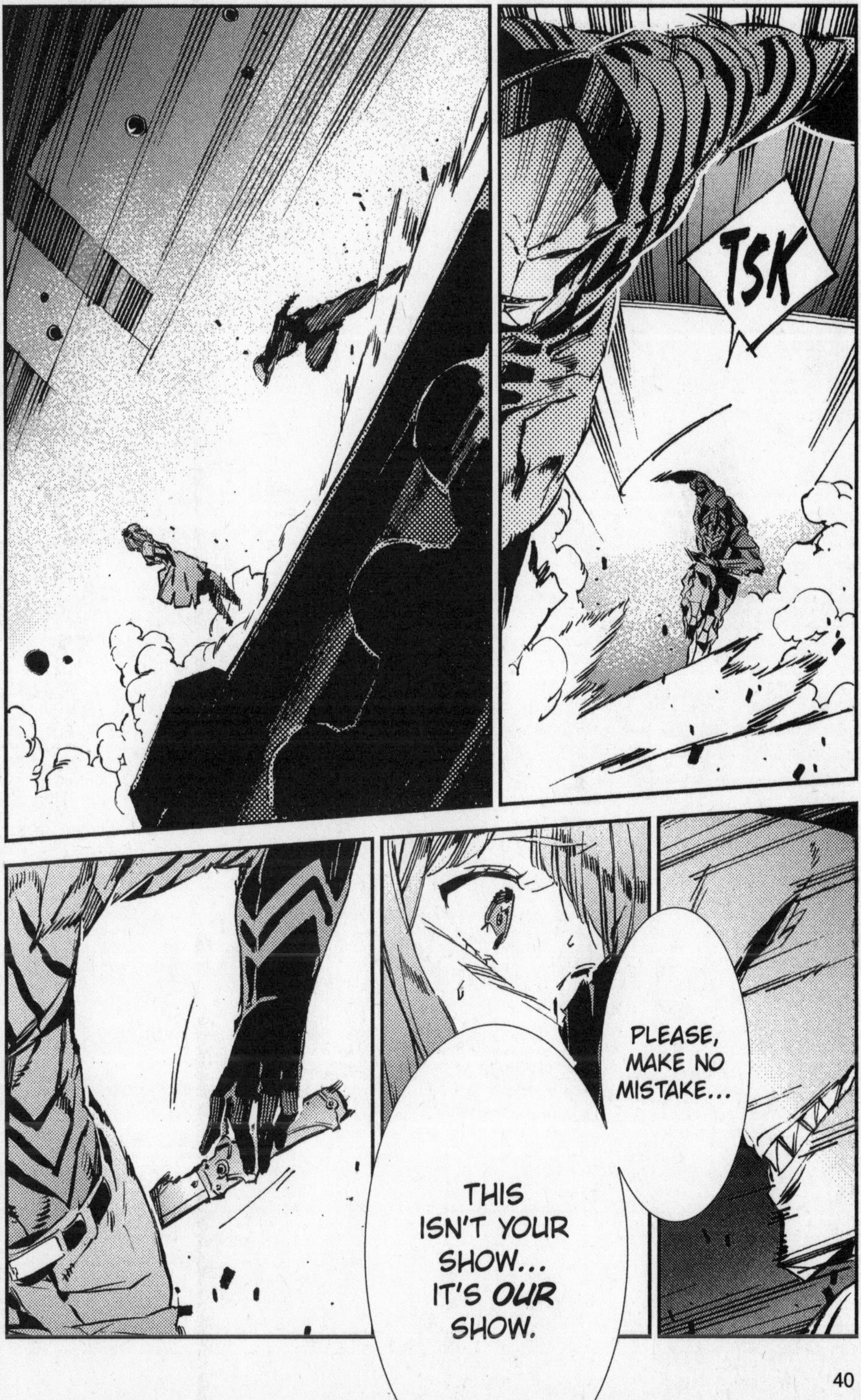
TSK
PLEASE, MAKE NO MISTAKE...
THIS ISN'T YOUR SHOW... IT'S *OUR* SHOW.

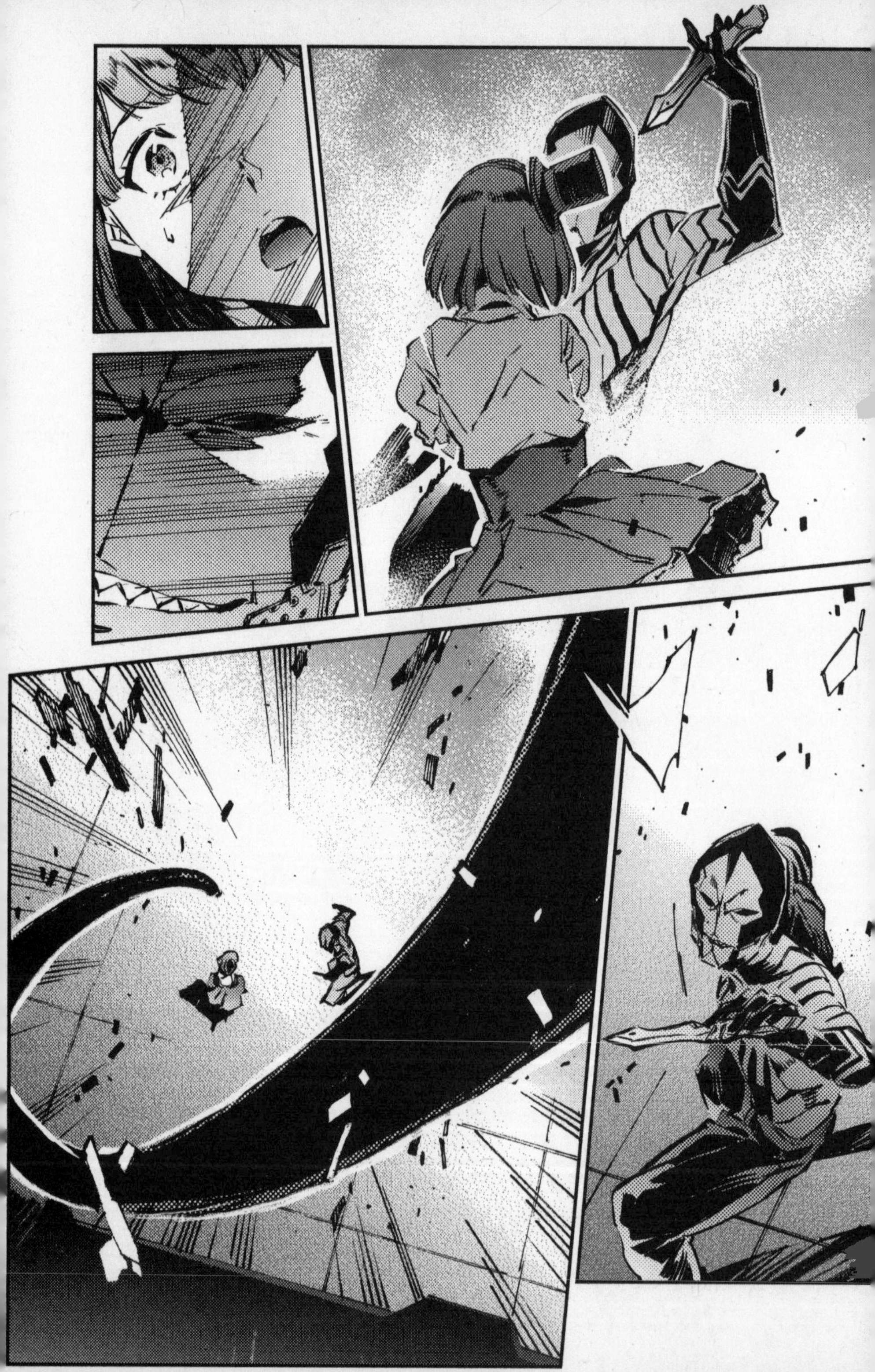

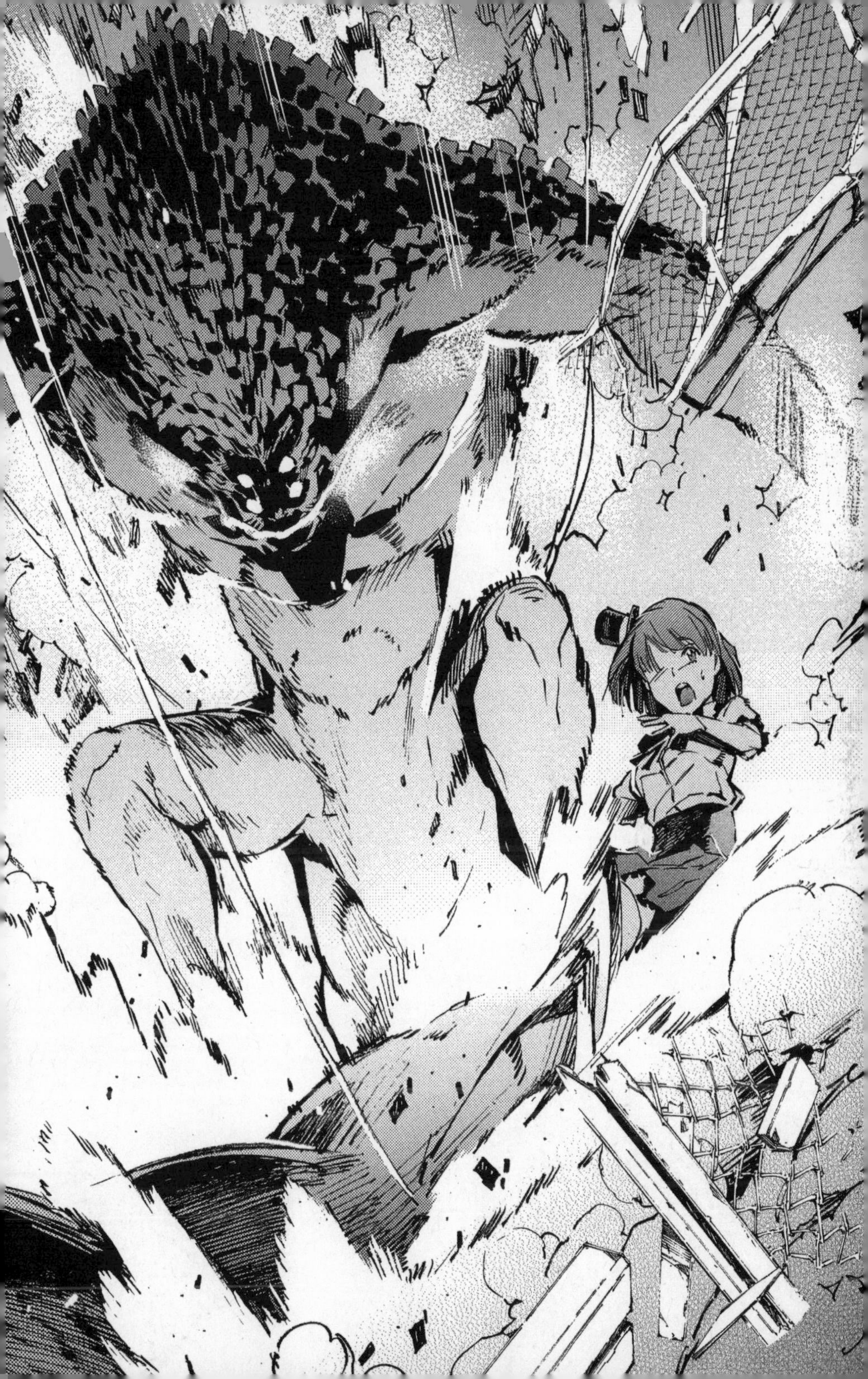

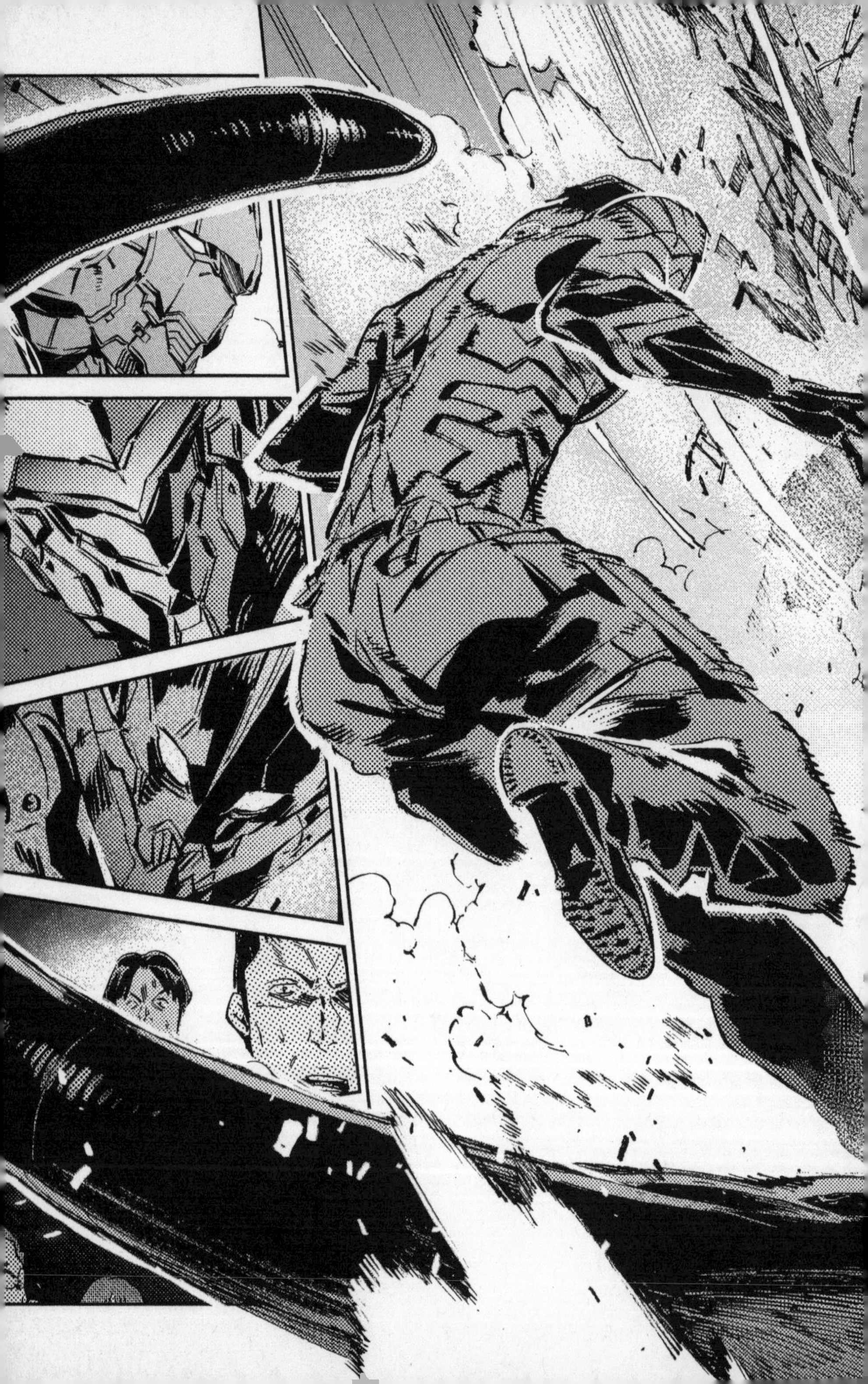

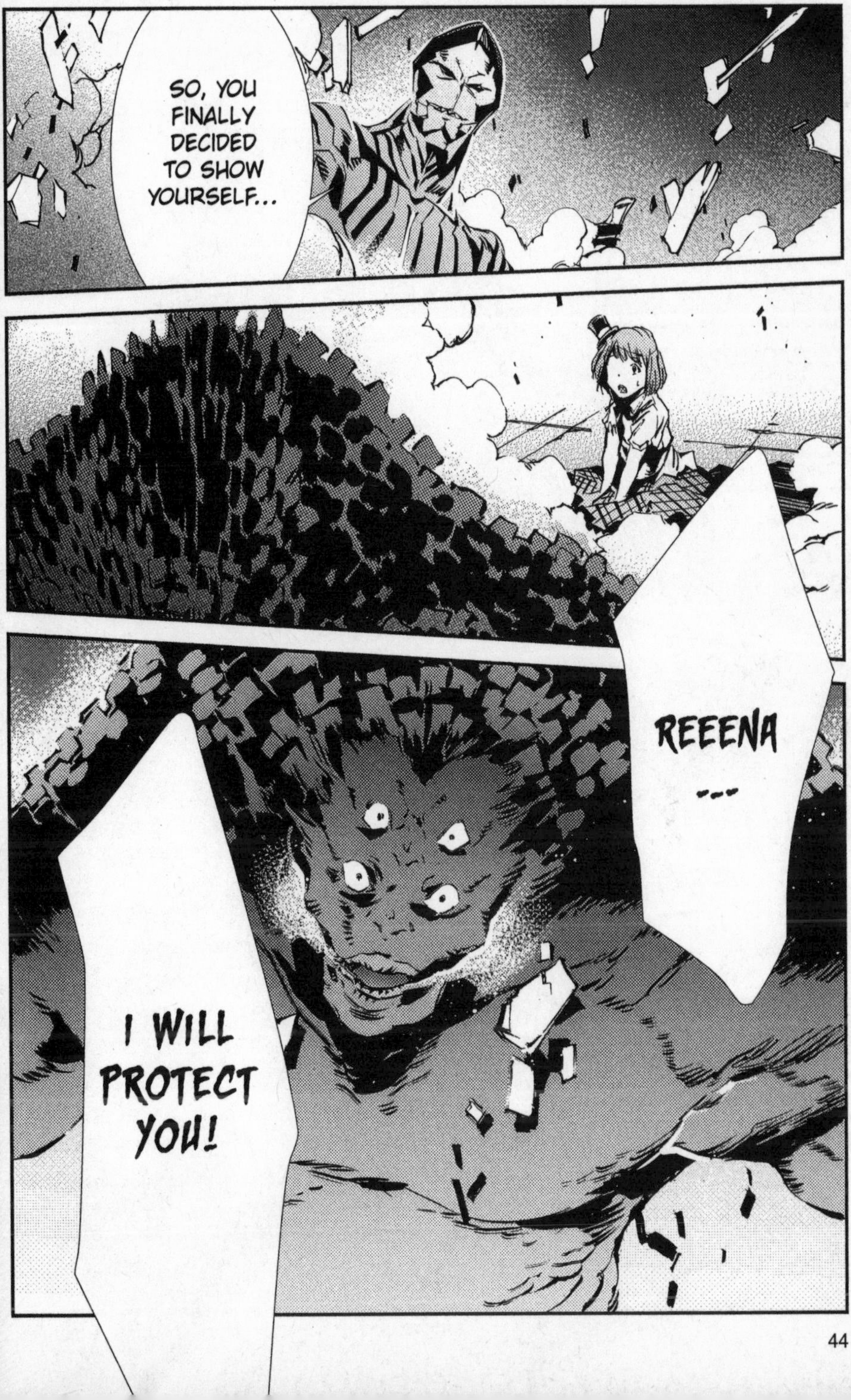
SO, YOU FINALLY DECIDED TO SHOW YOURSELF...
REEENA ...
I WILL PROTECT YOU!

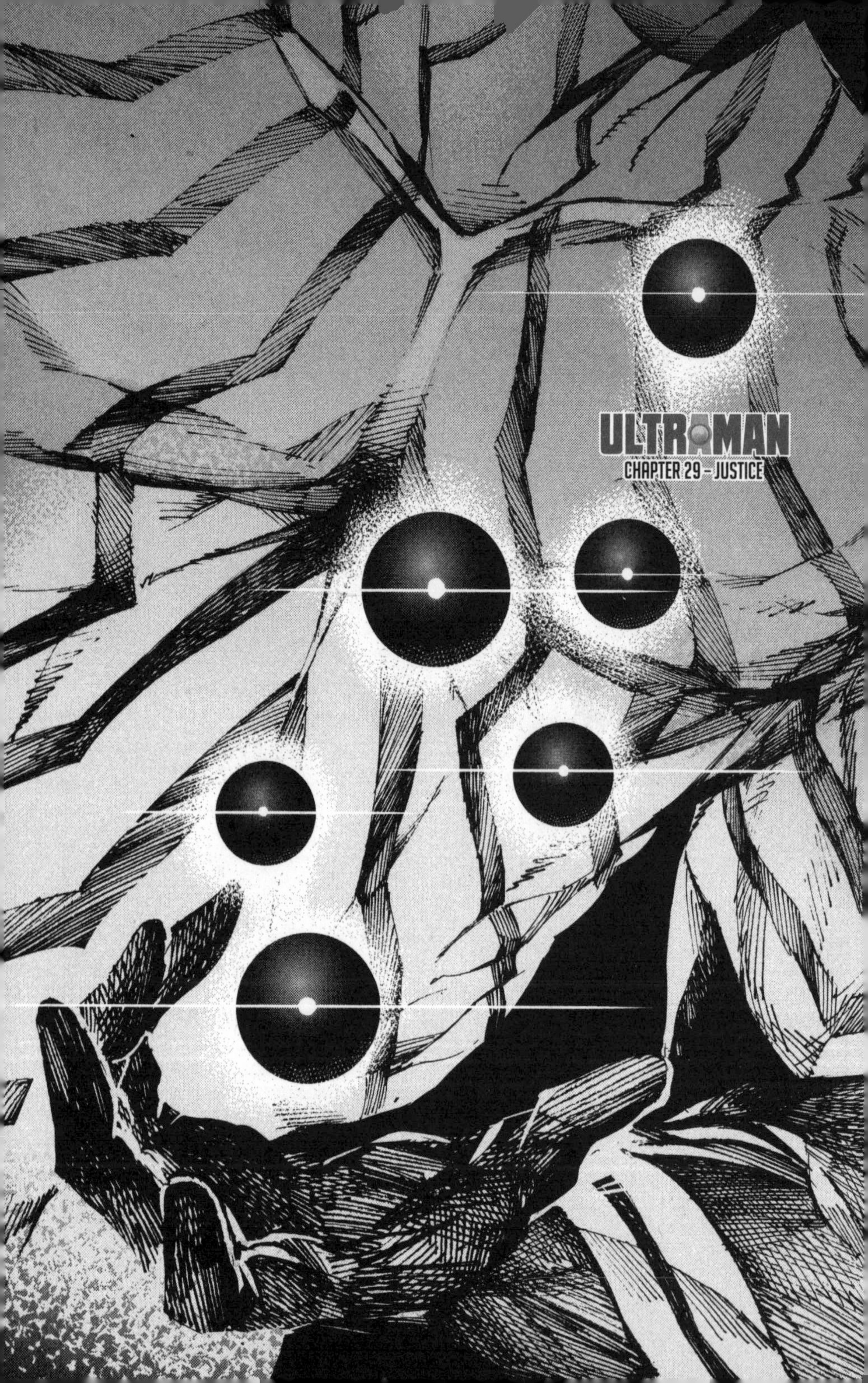
ULTRAMAN
CHAPTER 29 – JUSTICE

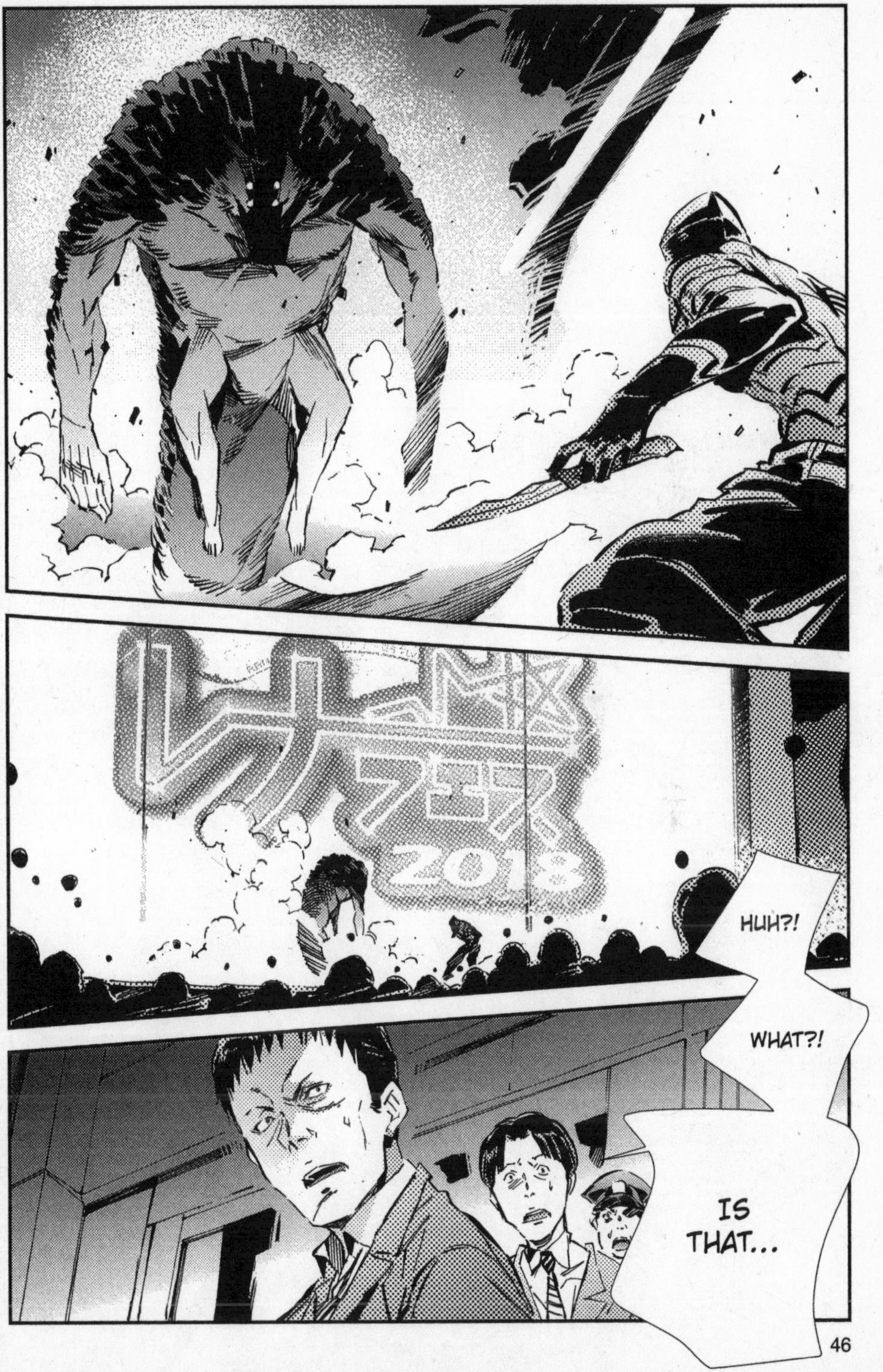
2018
HUH?!
WHAT?!
IS THAT...

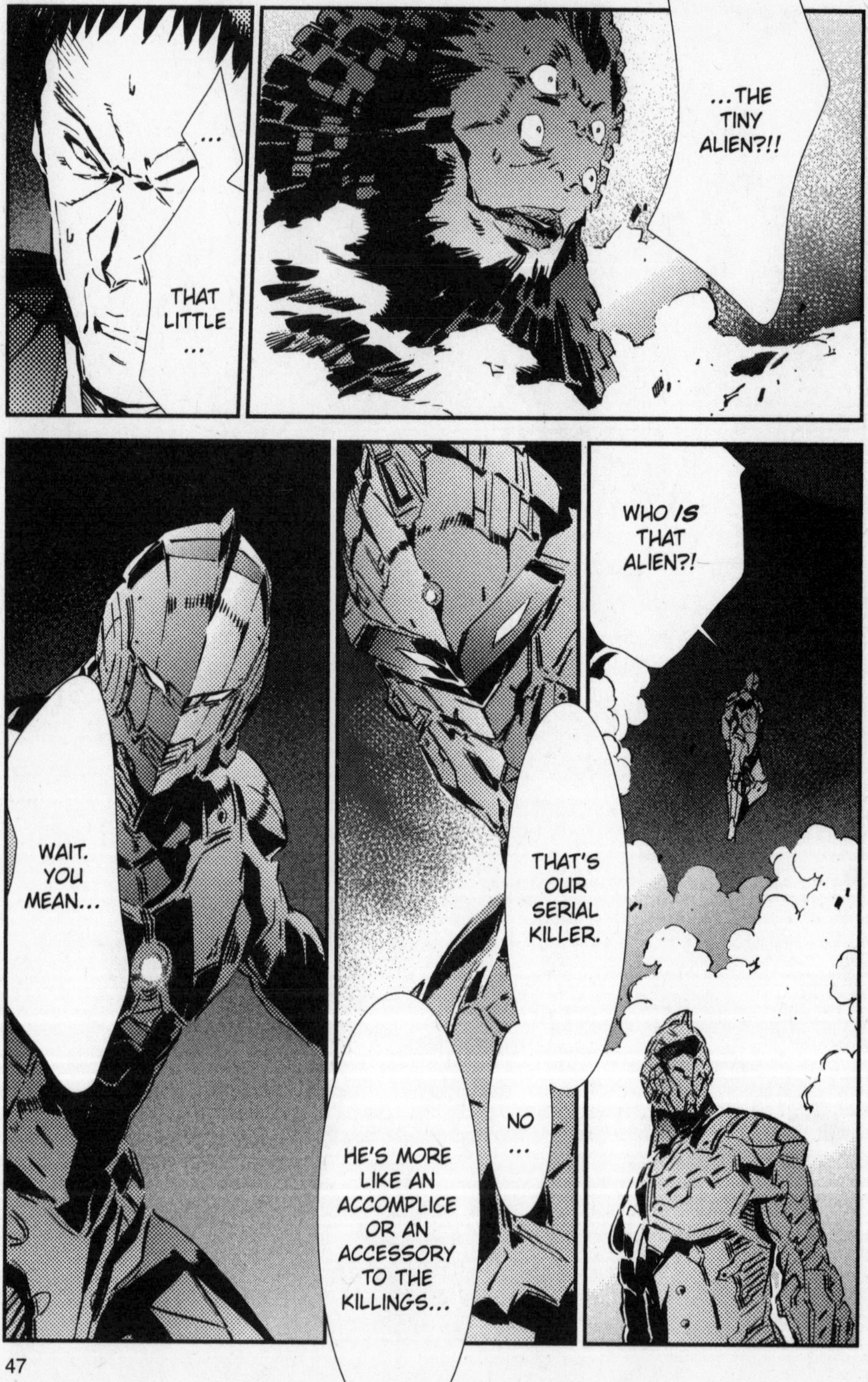
...THE TINY ALIEN?!!
...
THAT LITTLE ...
WHO *IS* THAT ALIEN?!
THAT'S OUR SERIAL KILLER.
NO ...
HE'S MORE LIKE AN ACCOMPLICE OR AN ACCESSORY TO THE KILLINGS...
WAIT. YOU MEAN...

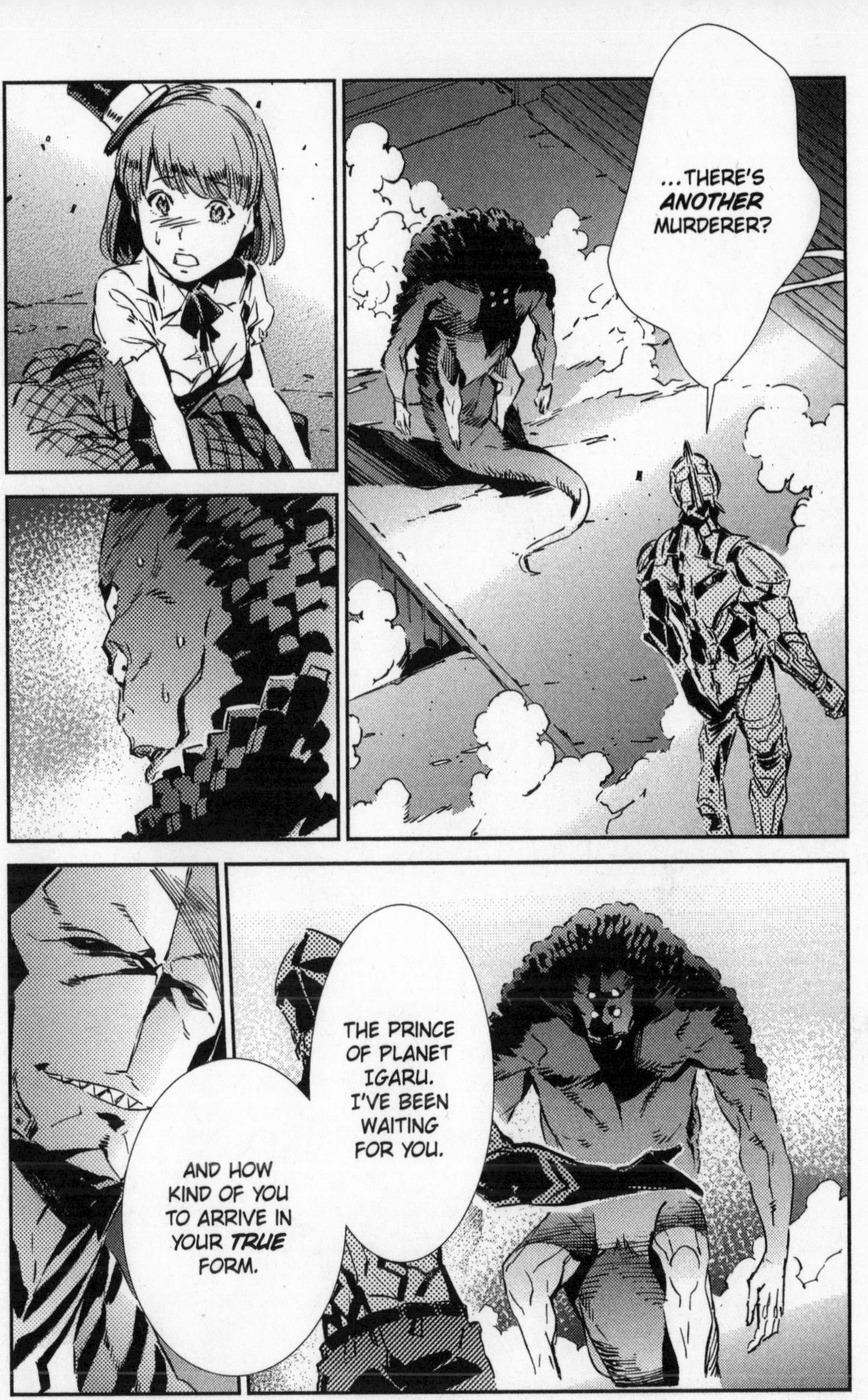
...THERE'S ANOTHER MURDERER?
THE PRINCE OF PLANET IGARU. I'VE BEEN WAITING FOR YOU.
AND HOW KIND OF YOU TO ARRIVE IN YOUR TRUE FORM.

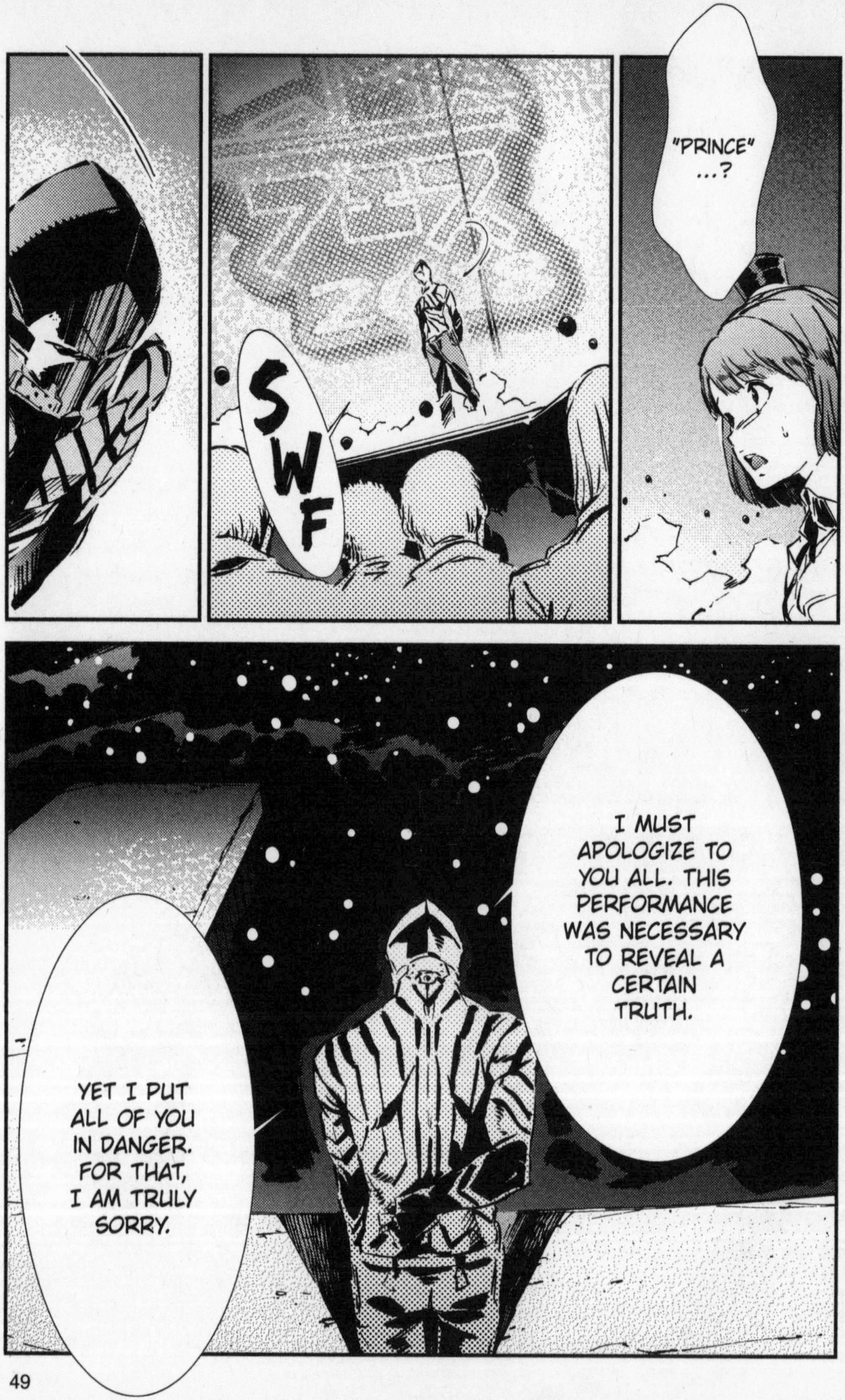
"PRINCE" ...?
SWF
I MUST APOLOGIZE TO YOU ALL. THIS PERFORMANCE WAS NECESSARY TO REVEAL A CERTAIN TRUTH.
YET I PUT ALL OF YOU IN DANGER. FOR THAT, I AM TRULY SORRY.

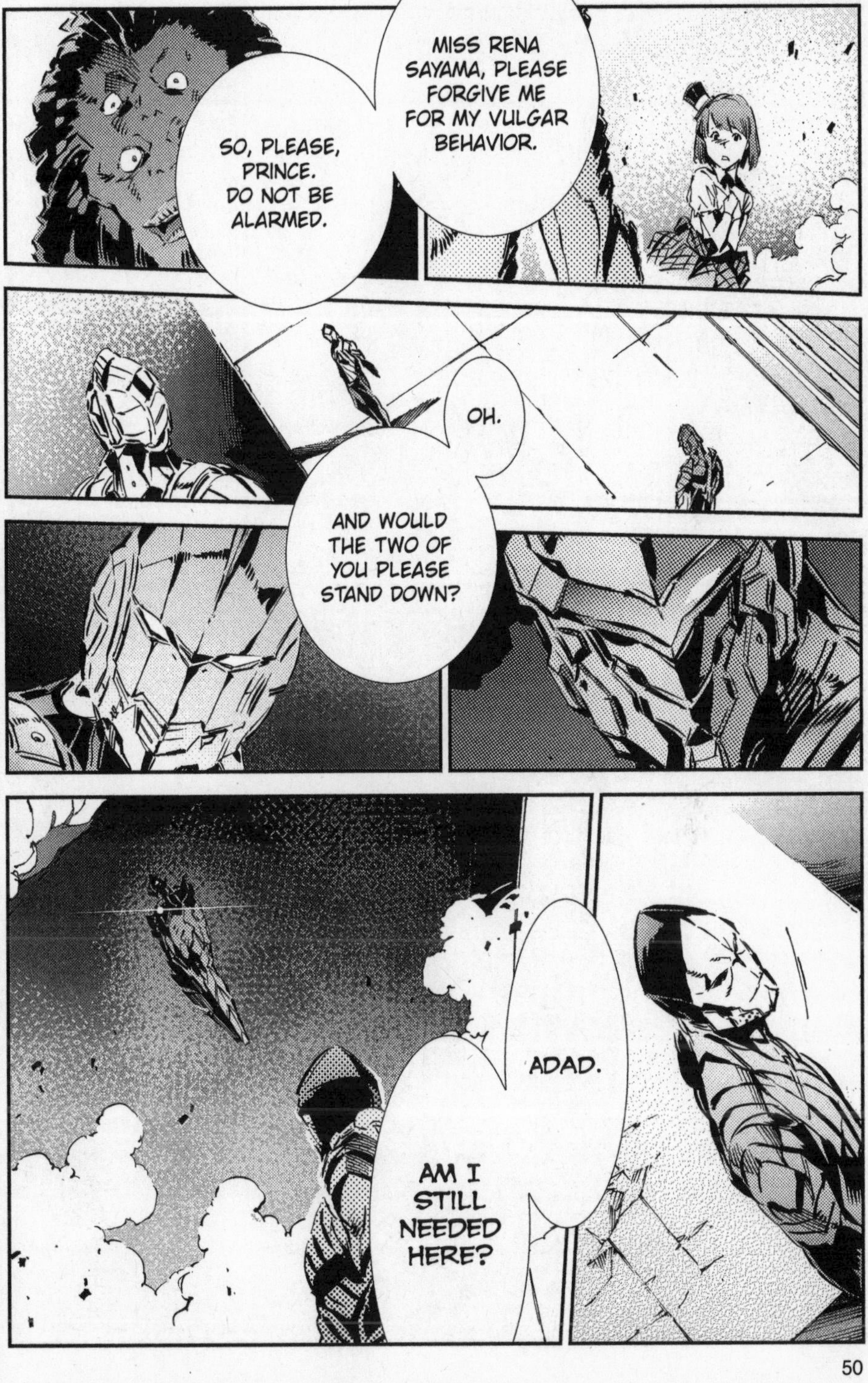
MISS RENA SAYAMA, PLEASE FORGIVE ME FOR MY VULGAR BEHAVIOR.
SO, PLEASE, PRINCE. DO NOT BE ALARMED.
OH.
AND WOULD THE TWO OF YOU PLEASE STAND DOWN?
ADAD.
AM I STILL NEEDED HERE?

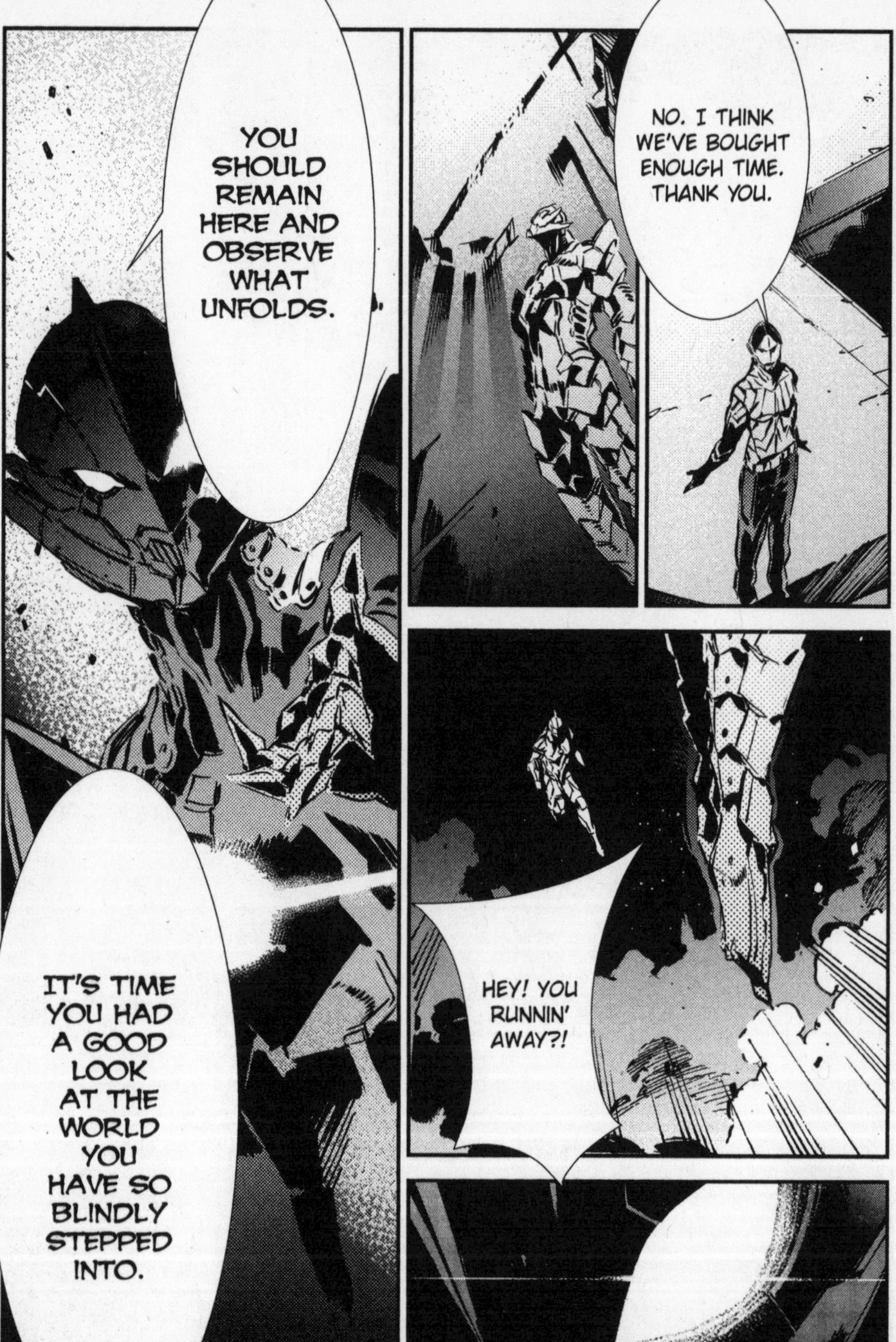
NO. I THINK WE'VE BOUGHT ENOUGH TIME. THANK YOU.
HEY! YOU RUNNIN' AWAY?!
YOU SHOULD REMAIN HERE AND OBSERVE WHAT UNFOLDS.
IT'S TIME YOU HAD A GOOD LOOK AT THE WORLD YOU HAVE SO BLINDLY STEPPED INTO.

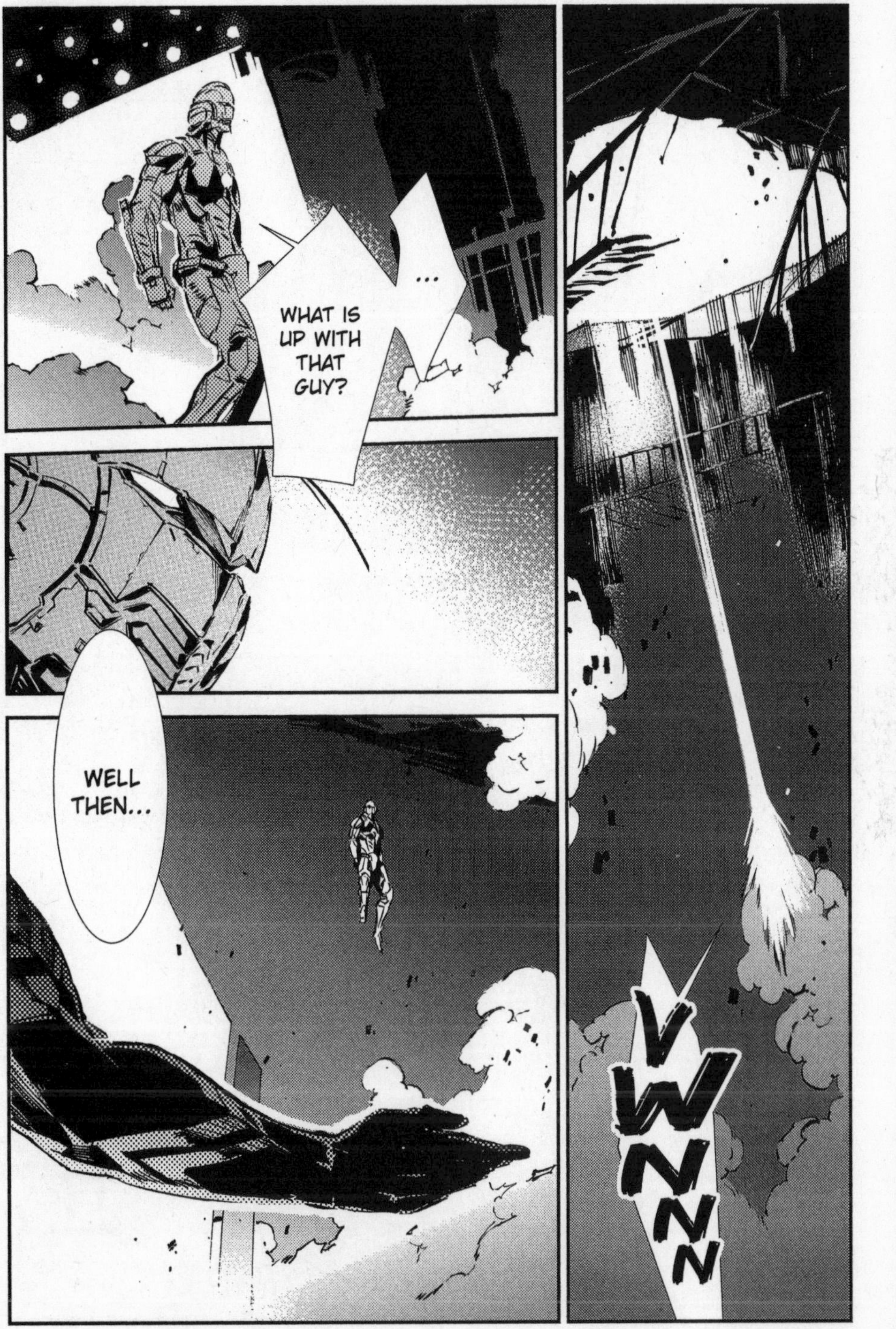
VWNNN
...
WHAT IS UP WITH THAT GUY?
WELL THEN...

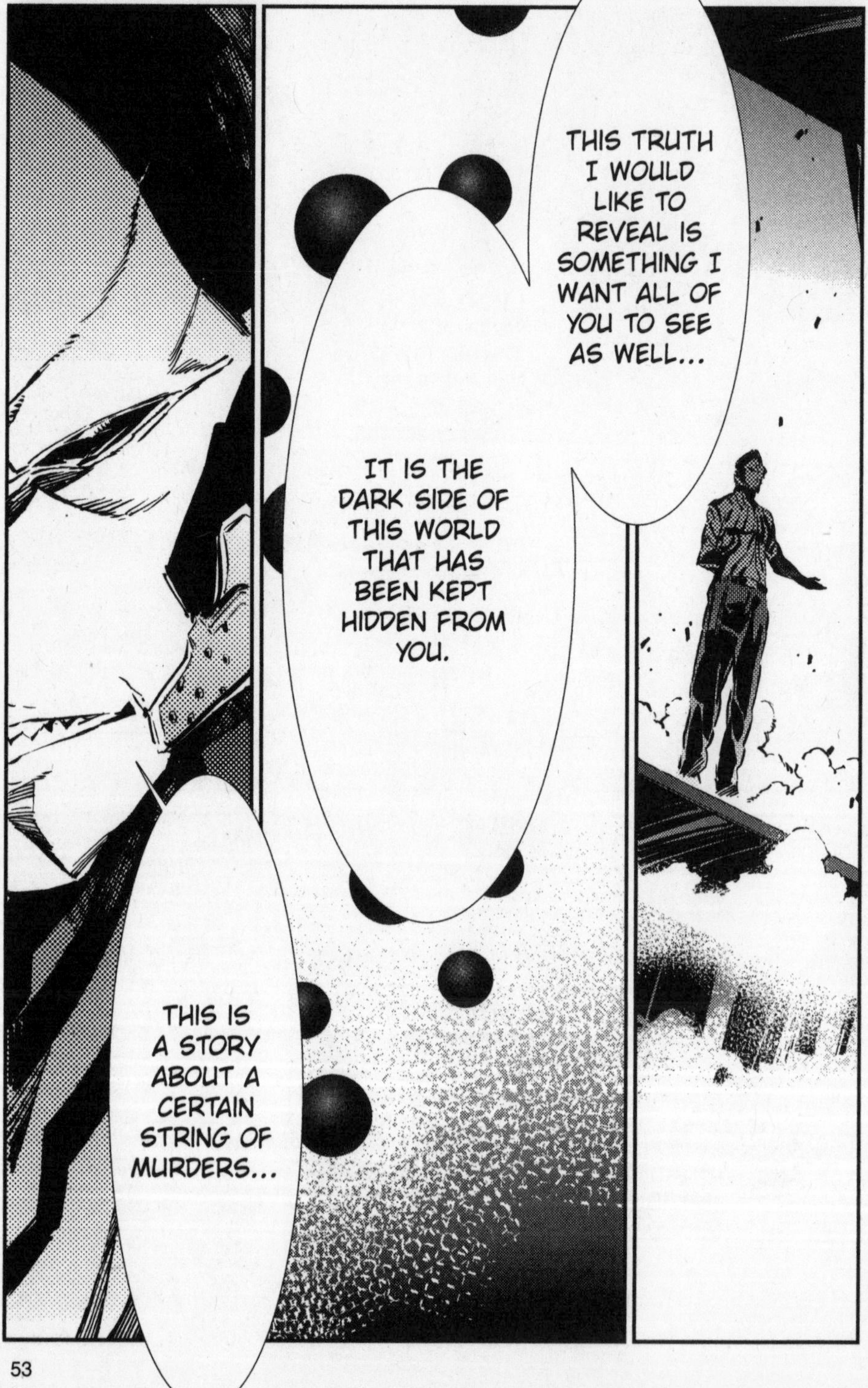
THIS TRUTH I WOULD LIKE TO REVEAL IS SOMETHING I WANT ALL OF YOU TO SEE AS WELL...
IT IS THE DARK SIDE OF THIS WORLD THAT HAS BEEN KEPT HIDDEN FROM YOU.
THIS IS A STORY ABOUT A CERTAIN STRING OF MURDERS...

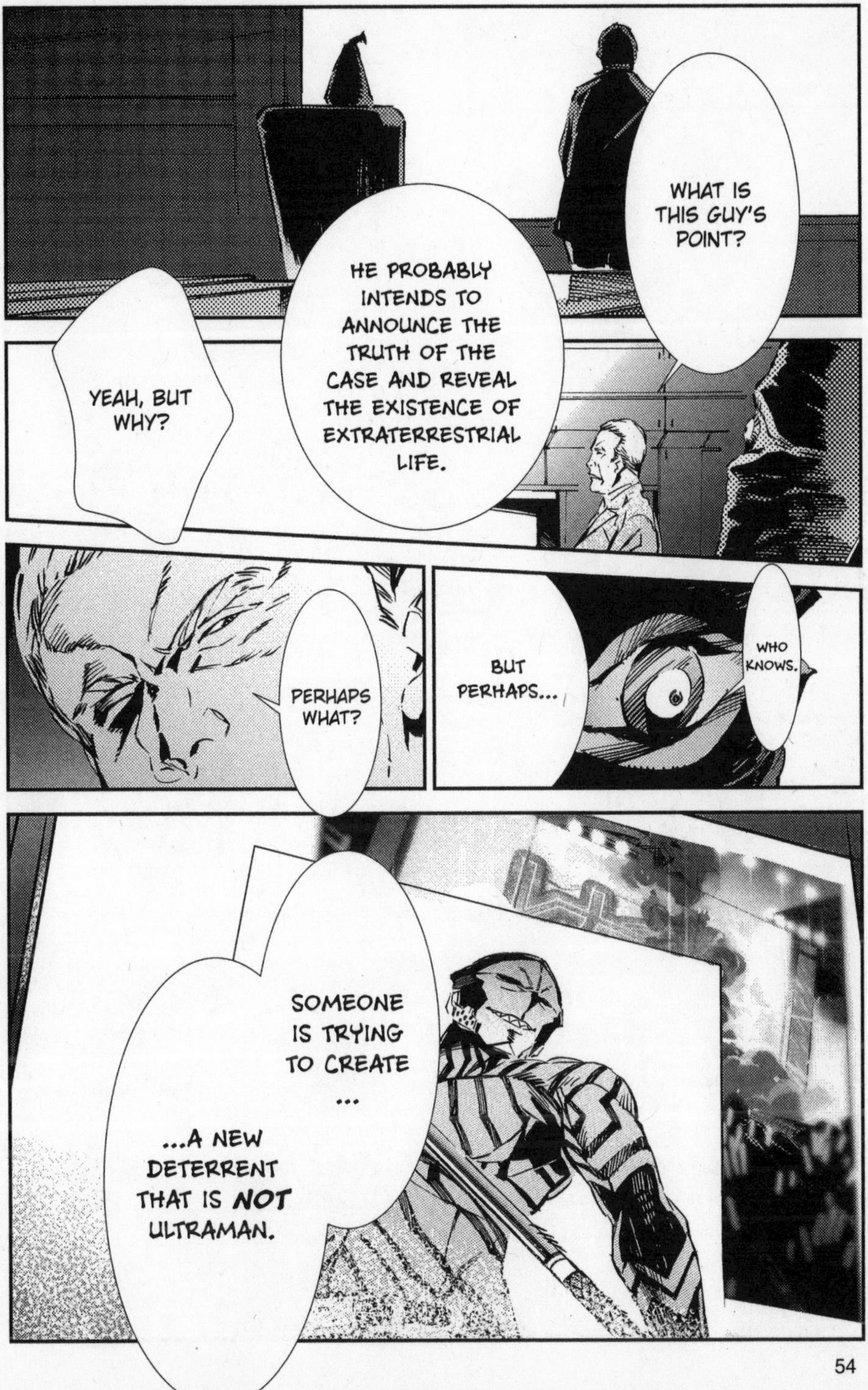
WHAT IS THIS GUY'S POINT?
HE PROBABLY INTENDS TO ANNOUNCE THE TRUTH OF THE CASE AND REVEAL THE EXISTENCE OF EXTRATERRESTRIAL LIFE.
YEAH, BUT WHY?
WHO KNOWS.
BUT PERHAPS...
PERHAPS WHAT?
SOMEONE IS TRYING TO CREATE ...
...A NEW DETERRENT THAT IS ***NOT*** ULTRAMAN.

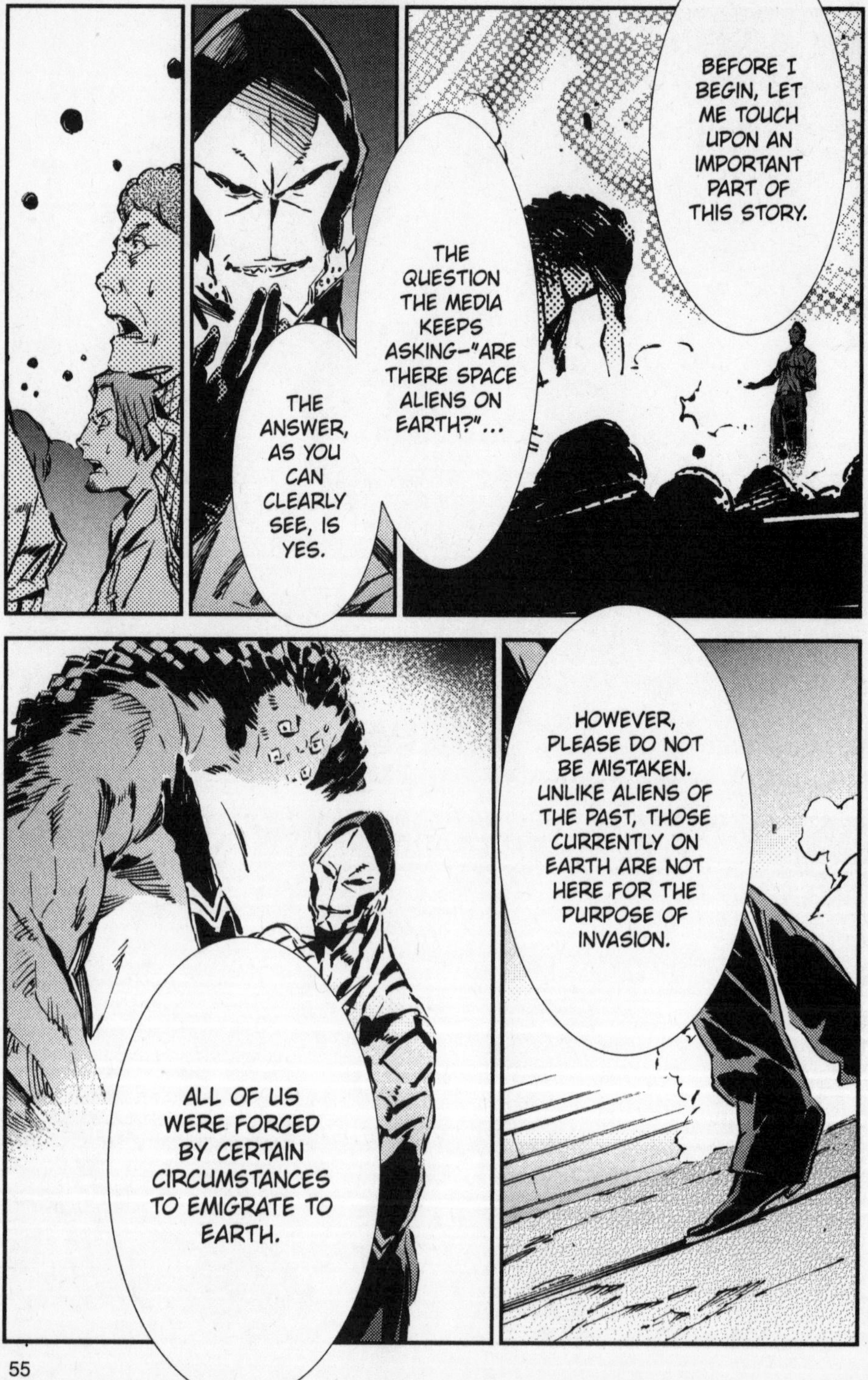
BEFORE I BEGIN, LET ME TOUCH UPON AN IMPORTANT PART OF THIS STORY.
THE QUESTION THE MEDIA KEEPS ASKING--"ARE THERE SPACE ALIENS ON EARTH?"...
THE ANSWER, AS YOU CAN CLEARLY SEE, IS YES.
HOWEVER, PLEASE DO NOT BE MISTAKEN. UNLIKE ALIENS OF THE PAST, THOSE CURRENTLY ON EARTH ARE NOT HERE FOR THE PURPOSE OF INVASION.
ALL OF US WERE FORCED BY CERTAIN CIRCUMSTANCES TO EMIGRATE TO EARTH.

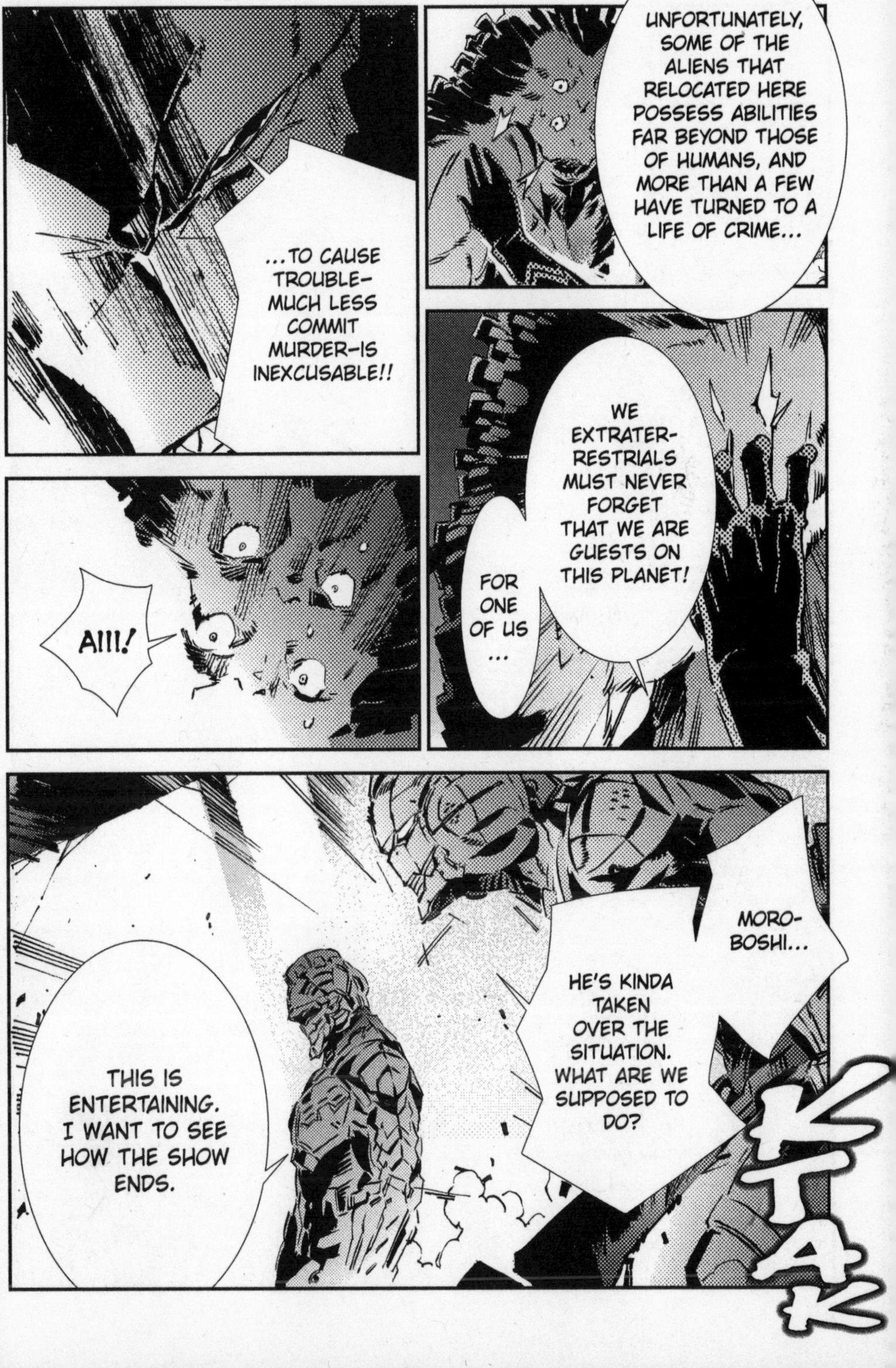
UNFORTUNATELY, SOME OF THE ALIENS THAT RELOCATED HERE POSSESS ABILITIES FAR BEYOND THOSE OF HUMANS, AND MORE THAN A FEW HAVE TURNED TO A LIFE OF CRIME...
WE EXTRATER-RESTRIALS MUST NEVER FORGET THAT WE ARE GUESTS ON THIS PLANET!
FOR ONE OF US ...
...TO CAUSE TROUBLE—MUCH LESS COMMIT MURDER—IS INEXCUSABLE!!
AIII!
MORO-BOSHI...
HE'S KINDA TAKEN OVER THE SITUATION. WHAT ARE WE SUPPOSED TO DO?
THIS IS ENTERTAINING. I WANT TO SEE HOW THE SHOW ENDS.
KTAK

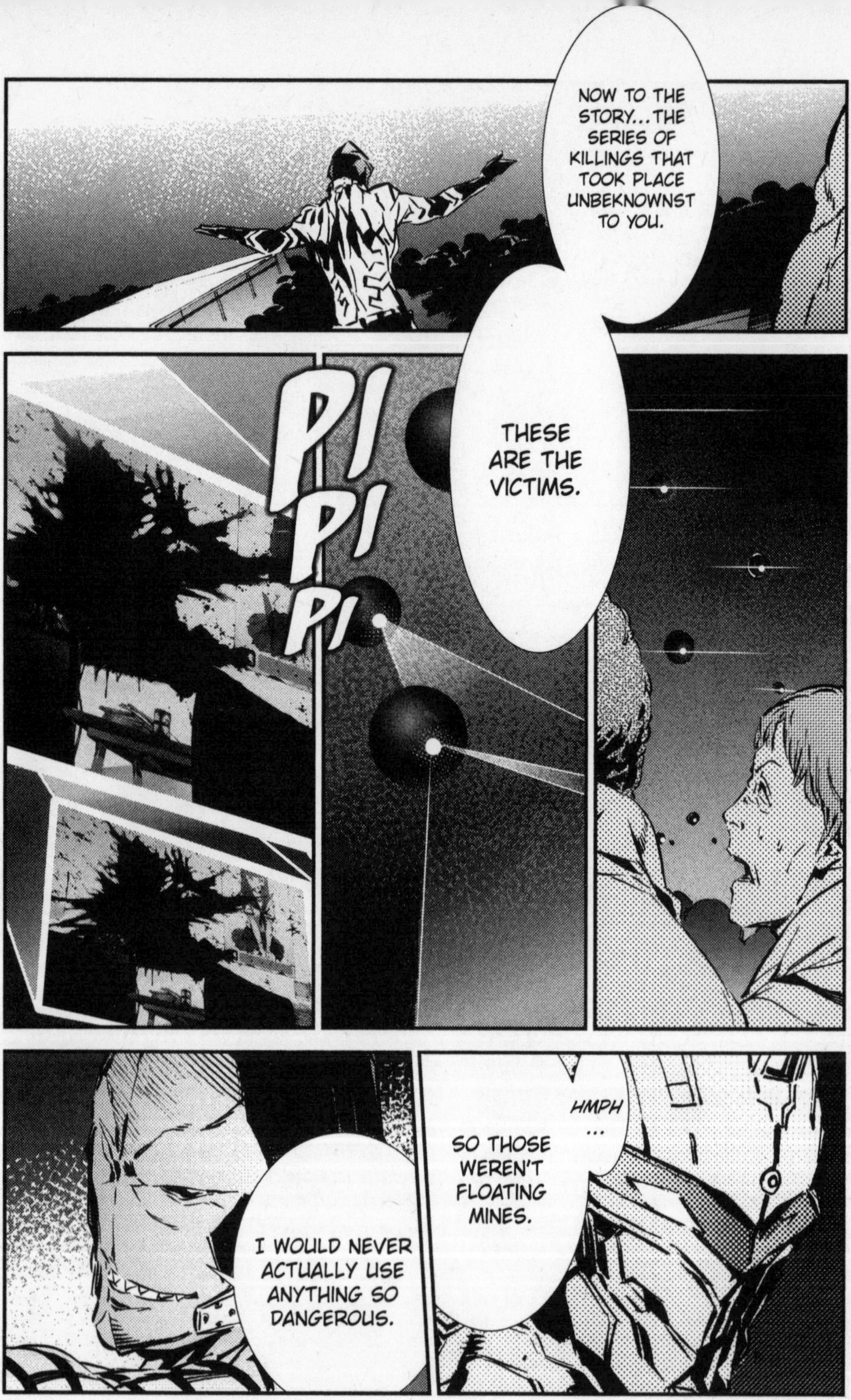
NOW TO THE STORY...THE SERIES OF KILLINGS THAT TOOK PLACE UNBEKNOWNST TO YOU.
THESE ARE THE VICTIMS.
PI PI PI
HMPH ...
SO THOSE WEREN'T FLOATING MINES.
I WOULD NEVER ACTUALLY USE ANYTHING SO DANGEROUS.

SIR, THIS INFORMATION ...
YEAH.
ONLY US AND THE SCIENCE PATROL SHOULD HAVE IT.
ALL THE VICTIMS HAD SOMETHING IN COMMON. THAT WAS WHAT DROVE THE KILLER TO COMMIT THE MURDERS.
Planet R
Official Blog of Rena
WHAT DID THEY HAVE IN COMMON...?
ALL THE VICTIMS HAD POSTED DISPARAGING COMMENTS ON THE INTERNET ABOUT THIS YOUNG WOMAN!
HUH?

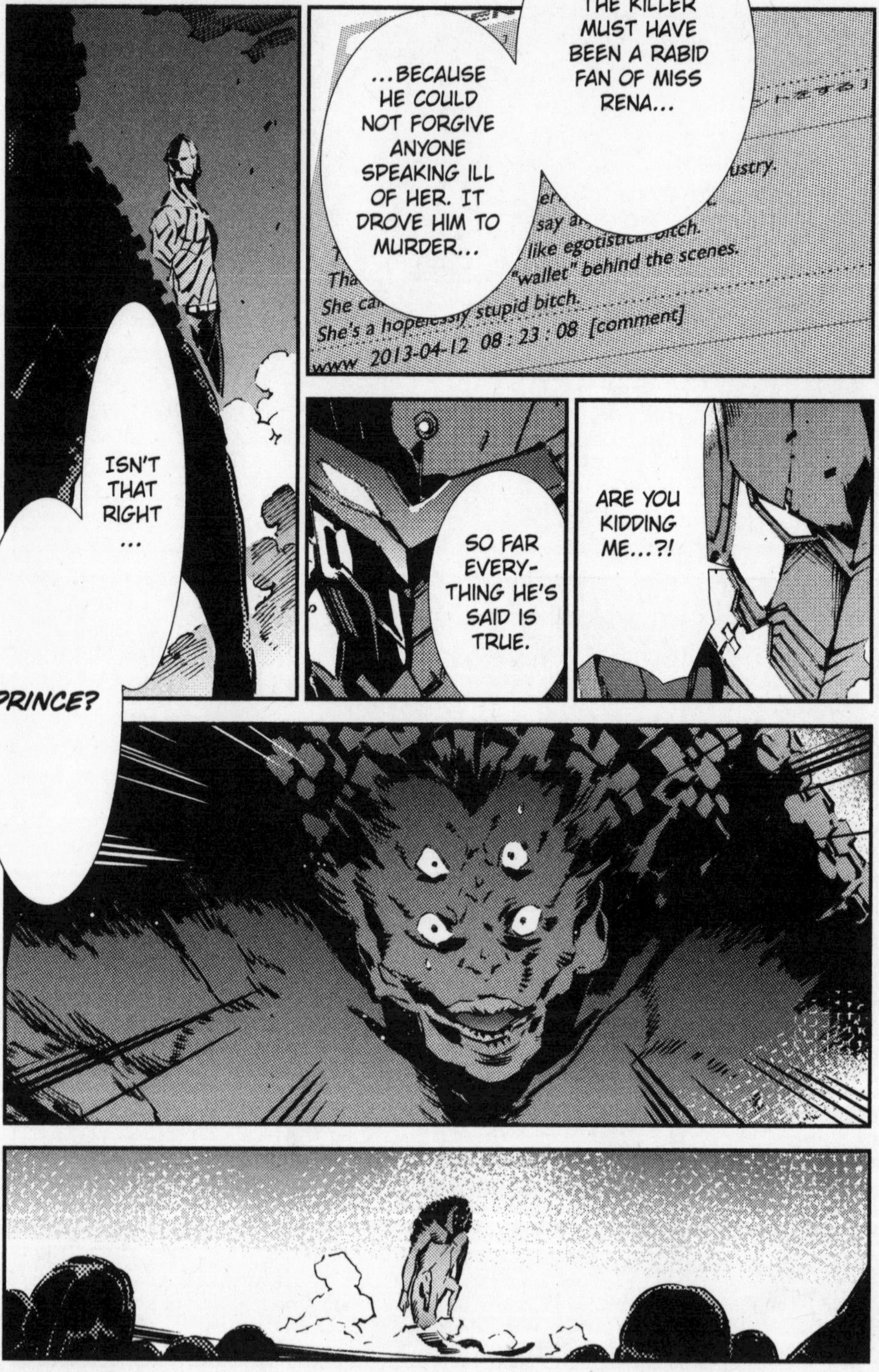
THE KILLER MUST HAVE BEEN A RABID FAN OF MISS RENA...
...BECAUSE HE COULD NOT FORGIVE ANYONE SPEAKING ILL OF HER. IT DROVE HIM TO MURDER...
like egotistical bitch.
"wallet" behind the scenes.
She's a hopelessly stupid bitch.
www 2013-04-12 08 : 23 : 08 [comment]
ARE YOU KIDDING ME...?!
SO FAR EVERY-THING HE'S SAID IS TRUE.
ISN'T THAT RIGHT ...
PRINCE?

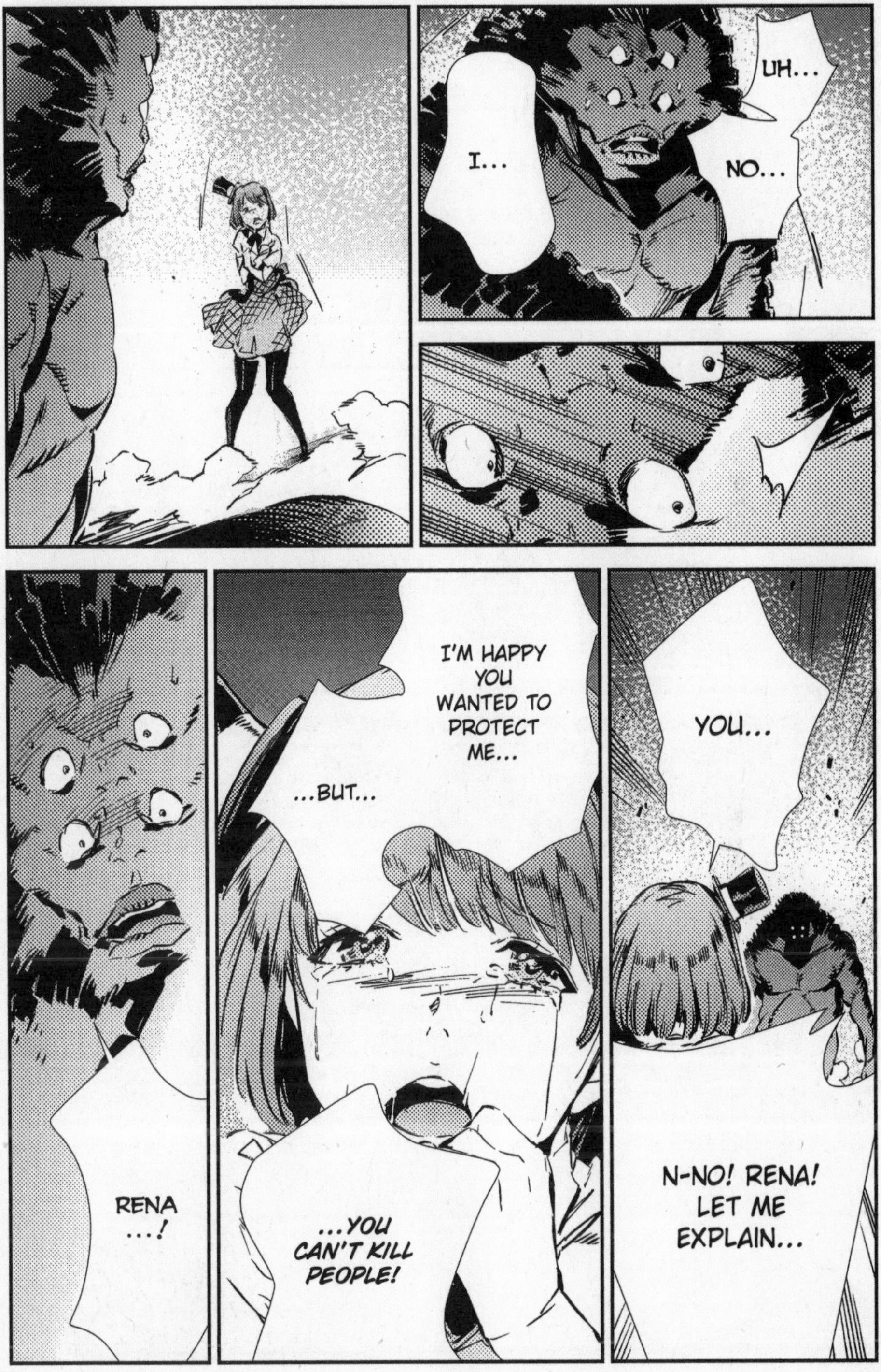
UH…
NO…
I…
YOU…
N-NO! RENA! LET ME EXPLAIN…
I'M HAPPY YOU WANTED TO PROTECT ME…
…BUT…
…YOU CAN'T KILL PEOPLE!
RENA …!

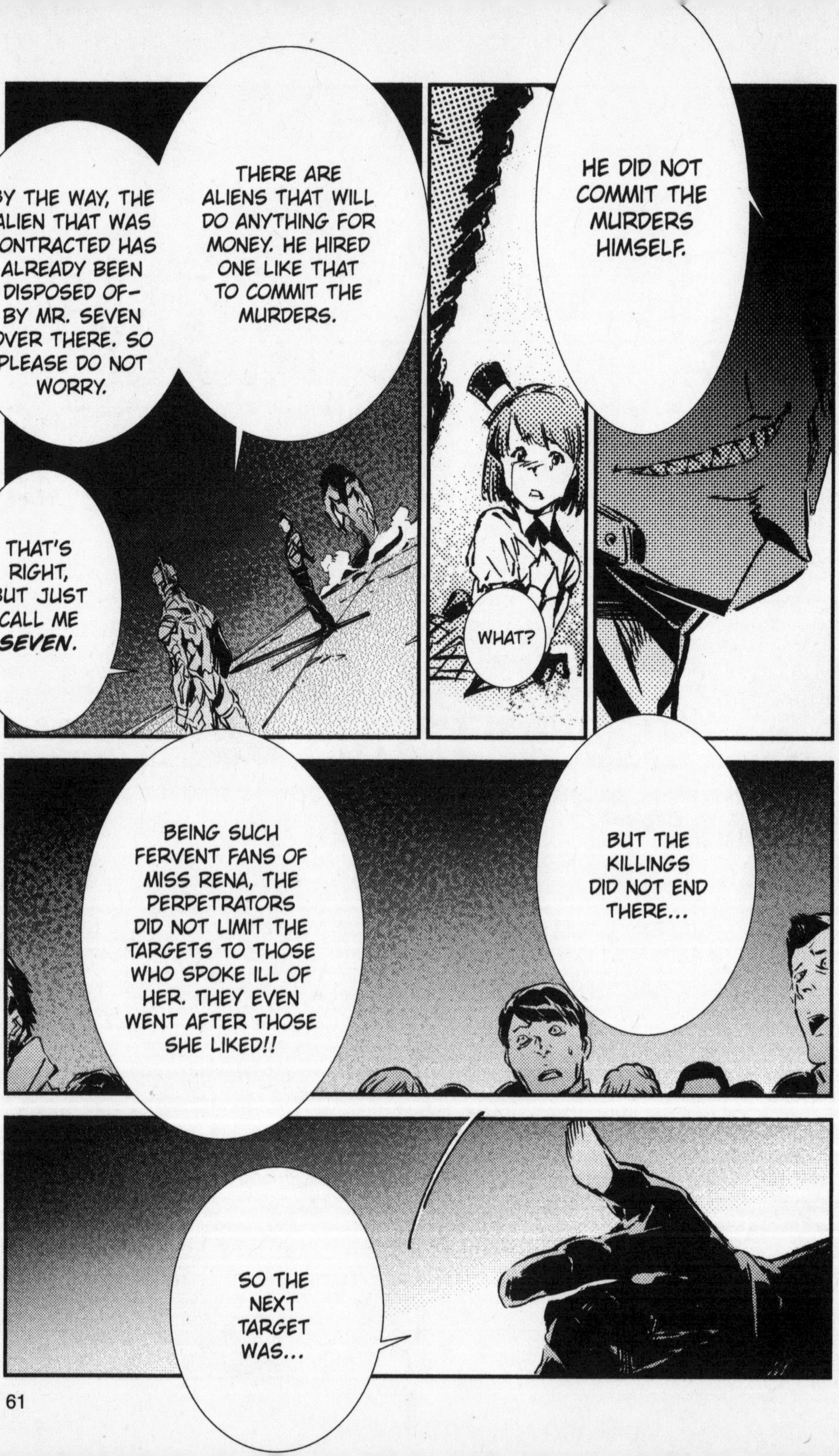
HE DID NOT COMMIT THE MURDERS HIMSELF.
WHAT?
THERE ARE ALIENS THAT WILL DO ANYTHING FOR MONEY. HE HIRED ONE LIKE THAT TO COMMIT THE MURDERS.
BY THE WAY, THE ALIEN THAT WAS CONTRACTED HAS ALREADY BEEN DISPOSED OF— BY MR. SEVEN OVER THERE. SO PLEASE DO NOT WORRY.
THAT'S RIGHT, BUT JUST CALL ME ***SEVEN***.
BUT THE KILLINGS DID NOT END THERE...
BEING SUCH FERVENT FANS OF MISS RENA, THE PERPETRATORS DID NOT LIMIT THE TARGETS TO THOSE WHO SPOKE ILL OF HER. THEY EVEN WENT AFTER THOSE SHE LIKED!!
SO THE NEXT TARGET WAS...

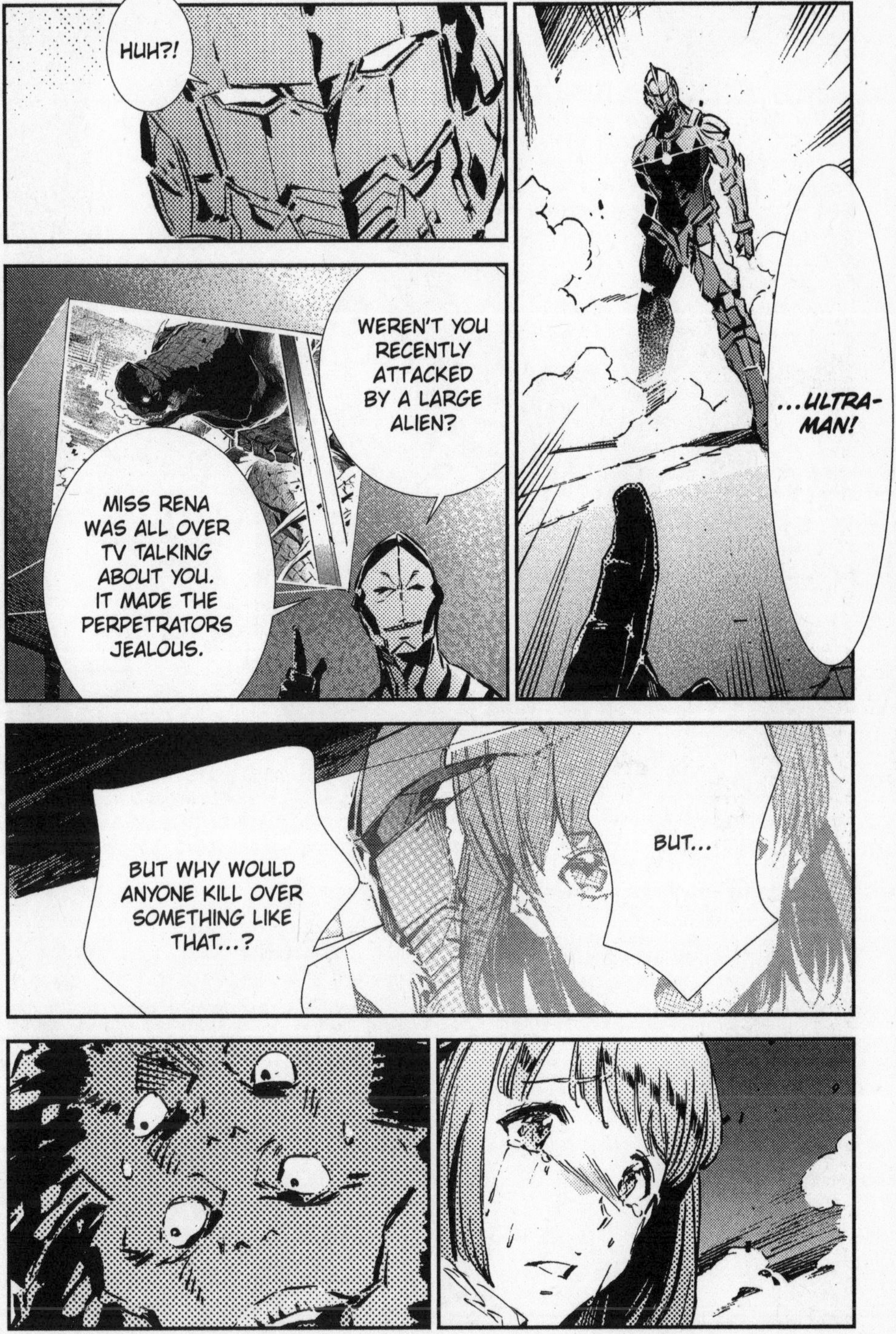
...ULTRA-MAN!
HUH?!
WEREN'T YOU RECENTLY ATTACKED BY A LARGE ALIEN?
MISS RENA WAS ALL OVER TV TALKING ABOUT YOU. IT MADE THE PERPETRATORS JEALOUS.
BUT...
BUT WHY WOULD ANYONE KILL OVER SOMETHING LIKE THAT...?

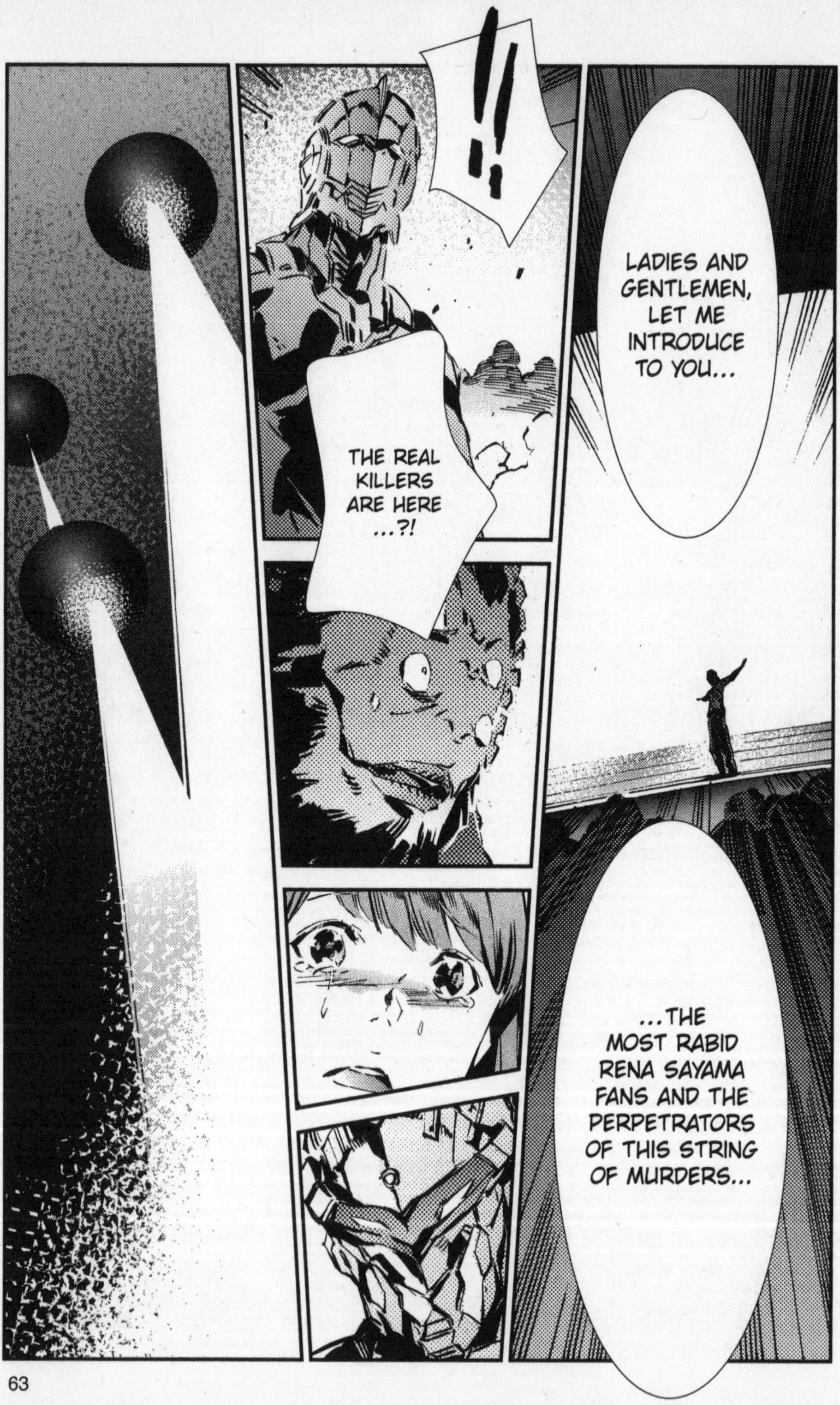
LADIES AND GENTLEMEN, LET ME INTRODUCE TO YOU...
...THE MOST RABID RENA SAYAMA FANS AND THE PERPETRATORS OF THIS STRING OF MURDERS...
!!
THE REAL KILLERS ARE HERE ...?!

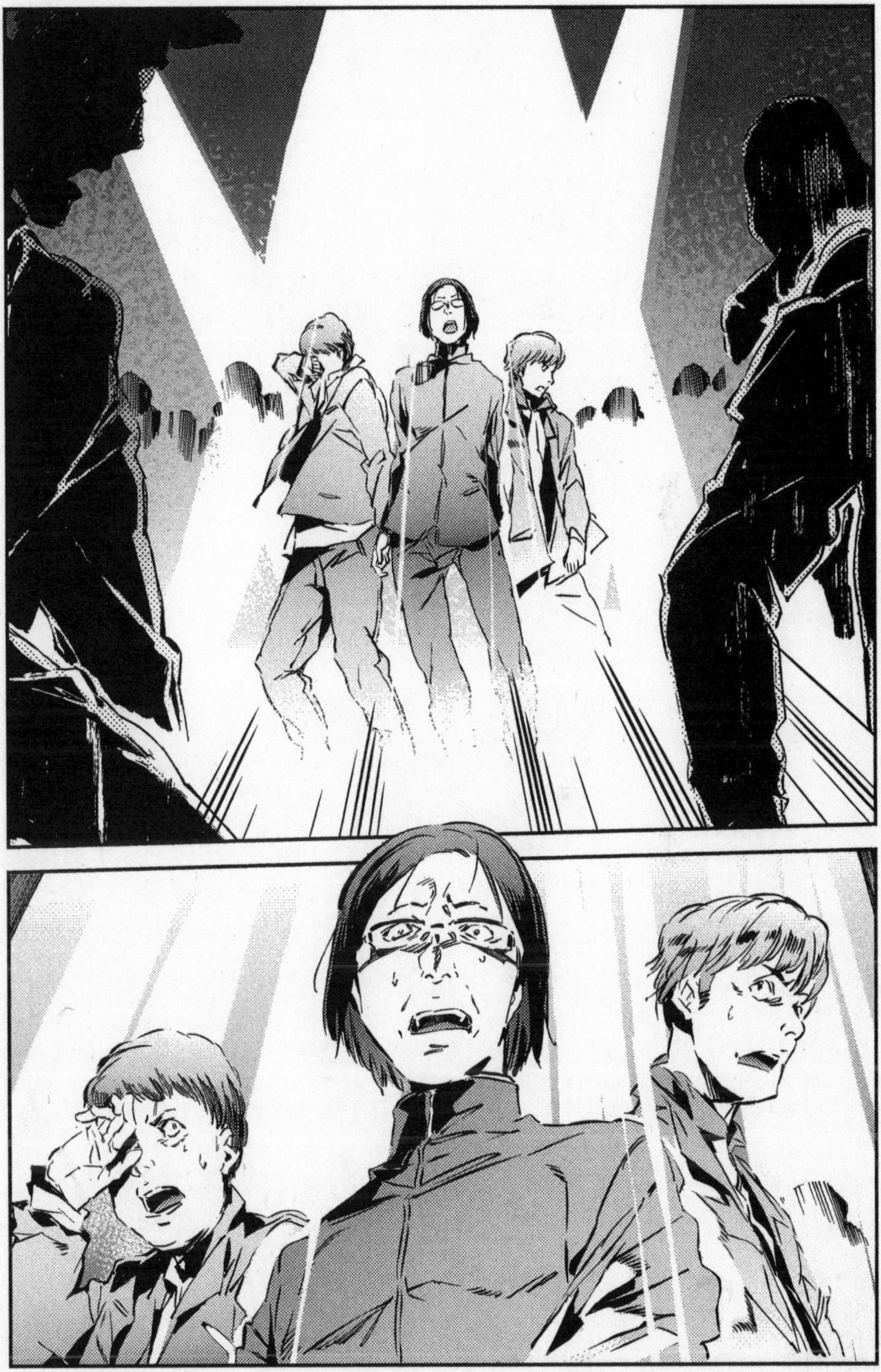

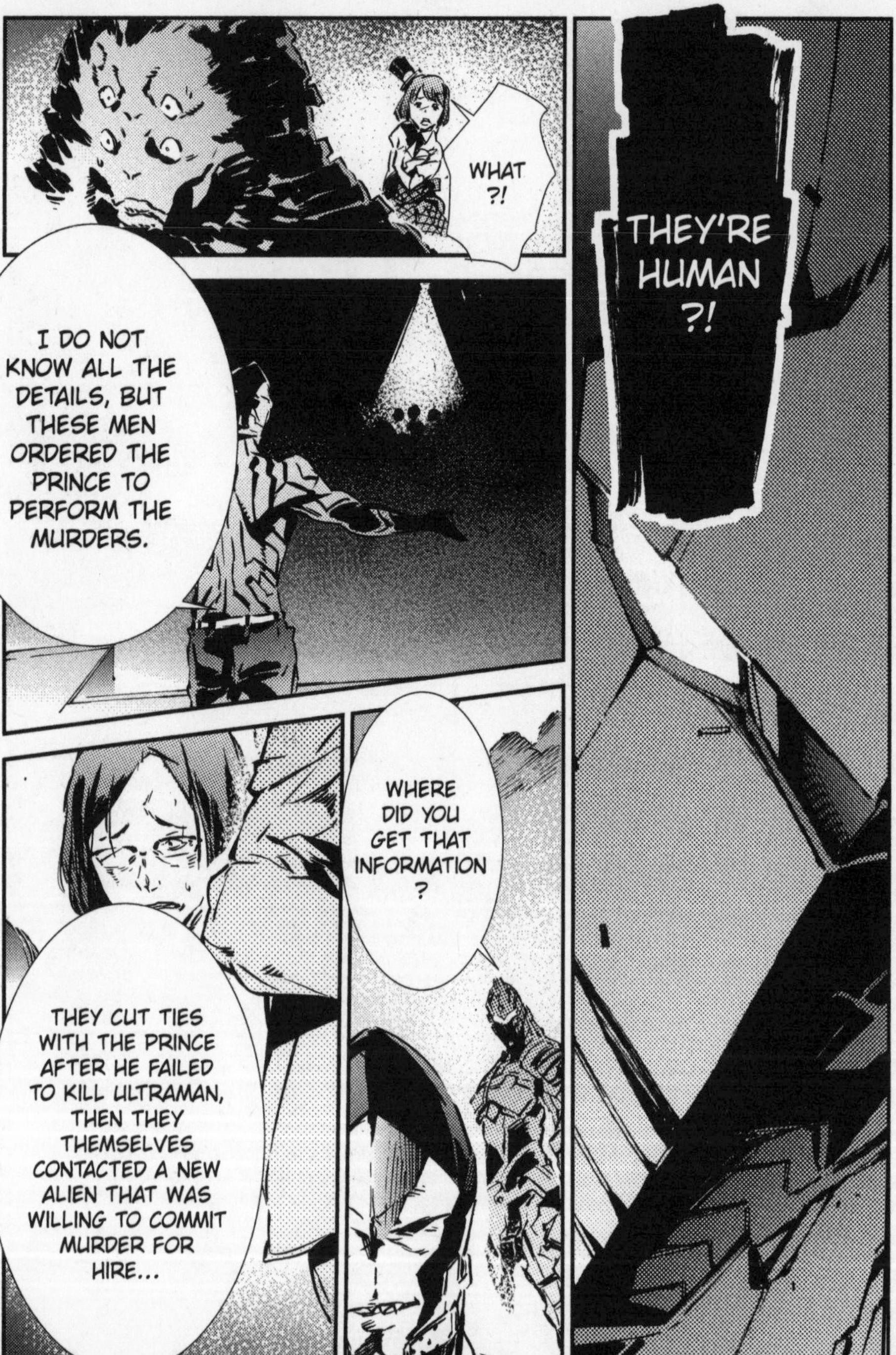
THEY'RE HUMAN ?!
WHAT ?!
I DO NOT KNOW ALL THE DETAILS, BUT THESE MEN ORDERED THE PRINCE TO PERFORM THE MURDERS.
WHERE DID YOU GET THAT INFORMATION ?
THEY CUT TIES WITH THE PRINCE AFTER HE FAILED TO KILL ULTRAMAN, THEN THEY THEMSELVES CONTACTED A NEW ALIEN THAT WAS WILLING TO COMMIT MURDER FOR HIRE...

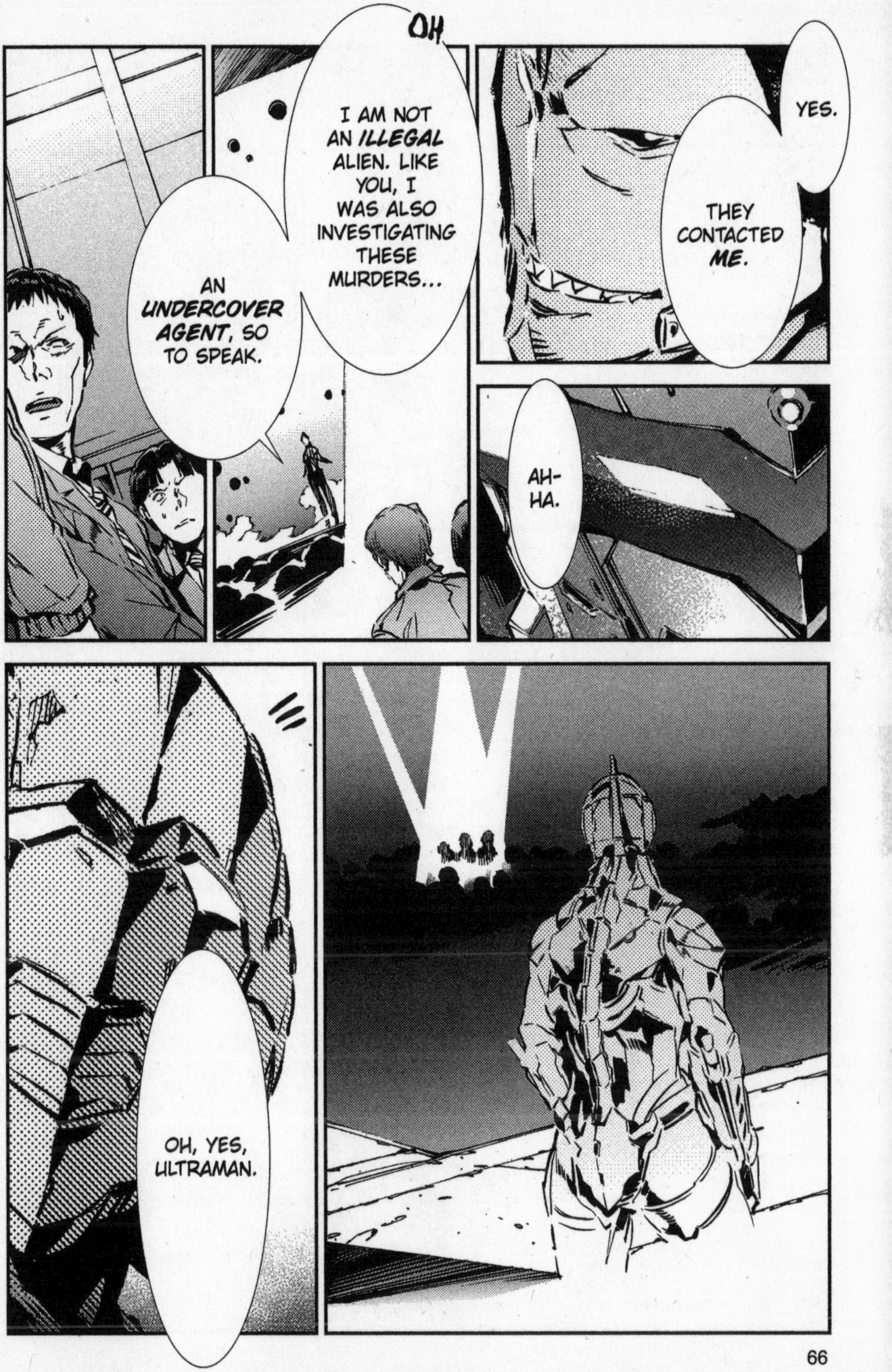
YES.
THEY CONTACTED **ME**.
AH-HA.
OH
I AM NOT AN ***ILLEGAL*** ALIEN. LIKE YOU, I WAS ALSO INVESTIGATING THESE MURDERS...
AN ***UNDERCOVER AGENT***, SO TO SPEAK.
OH, YES, ULTRAMAN.

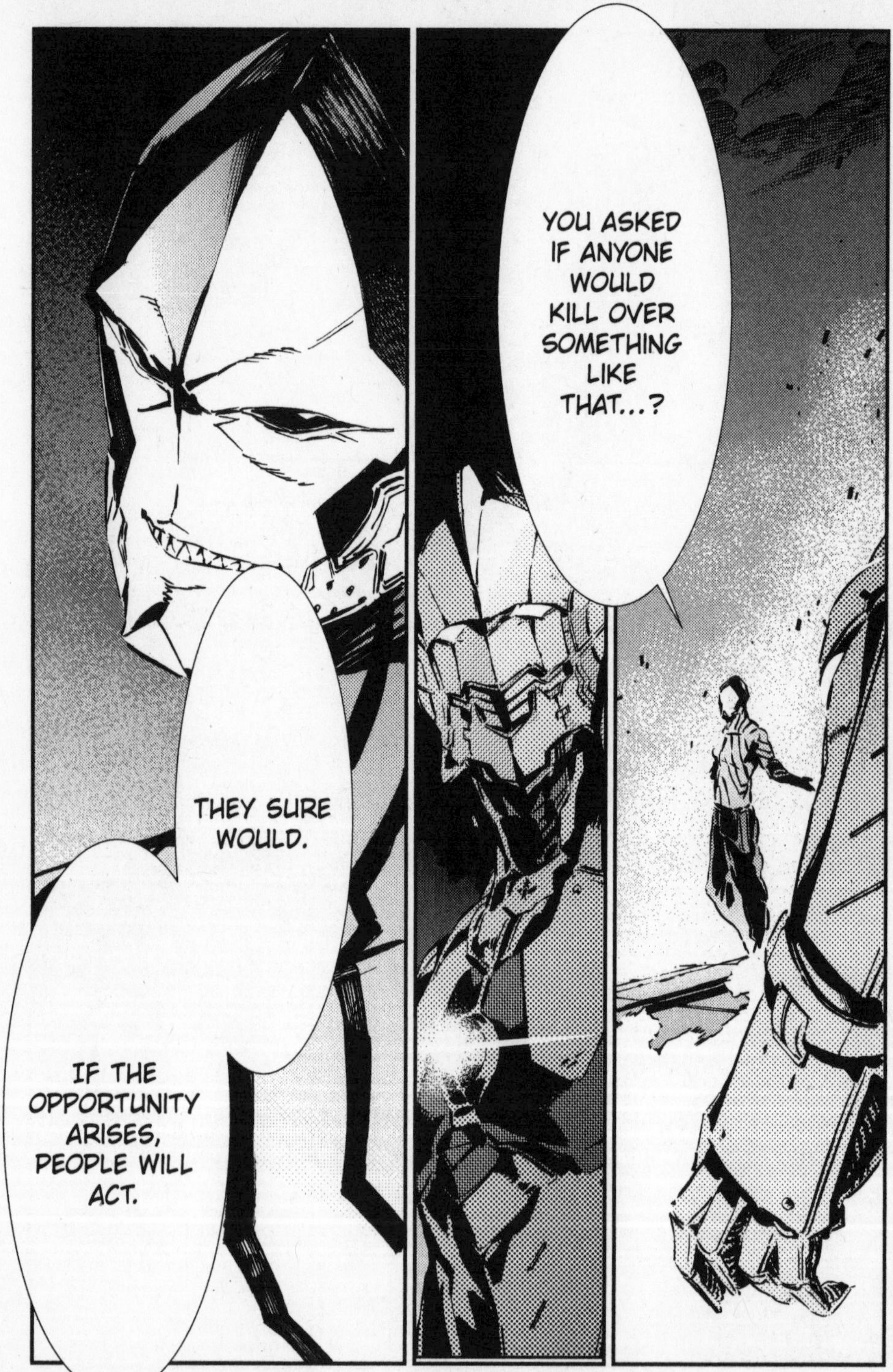
YOU ASKED IF ANYONE WOULD KILL OVER SOMETHING LIKE THAT...?
THEY SURE WOULD.
IF THE OPPORTUNITY ARISES, PEOPLE WILL ACT.

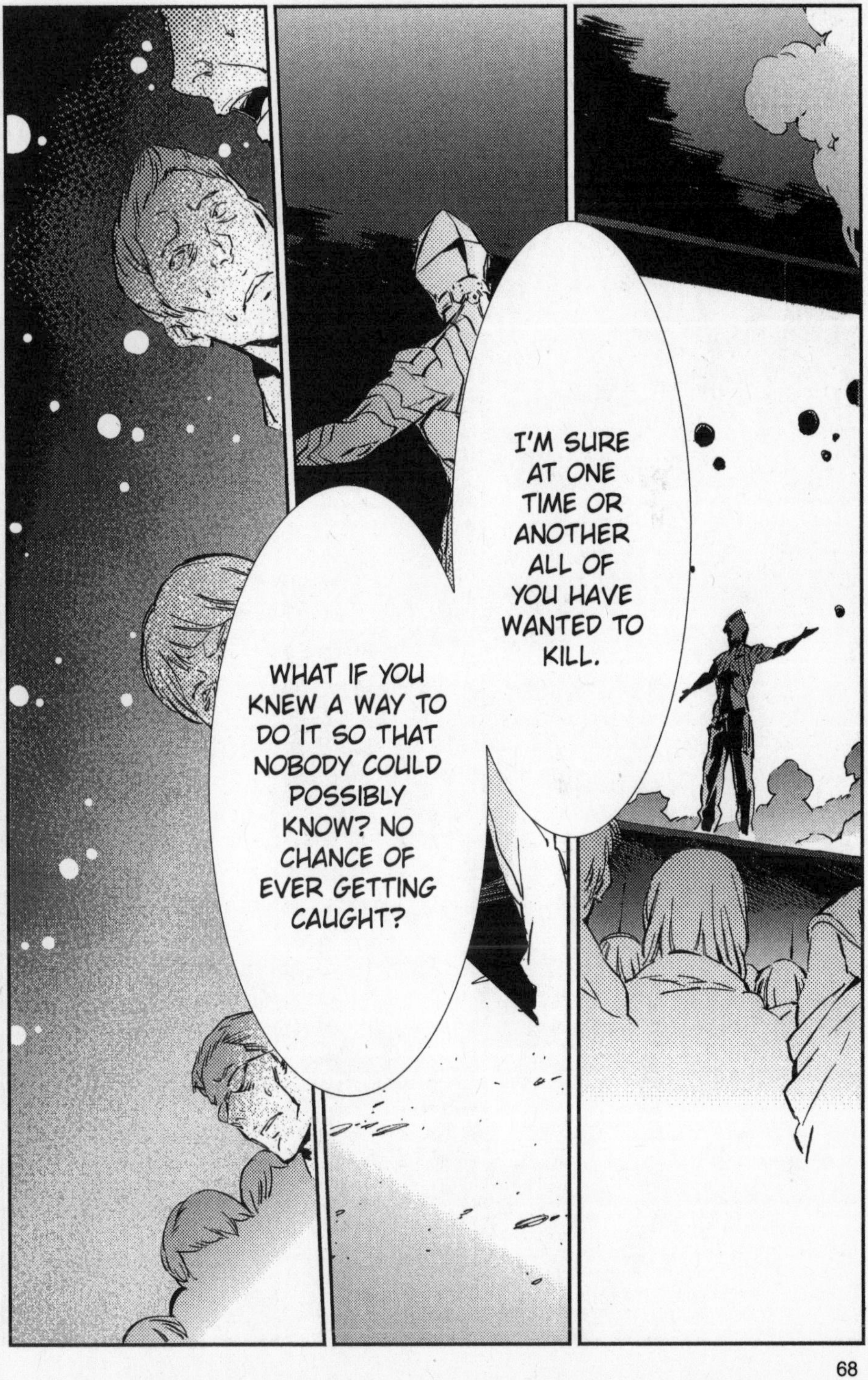
I'M SURE AT ONE TIME OR ANOTHER ALL OF YOU HAVE WANTED TO KILL.
WHAT IF YOU KNEW A WAY TO DO IT SO THAT NOBODY COULD POSSIBLY KNOW? NO CHANCE OF EVER GETTING CAUGHT?

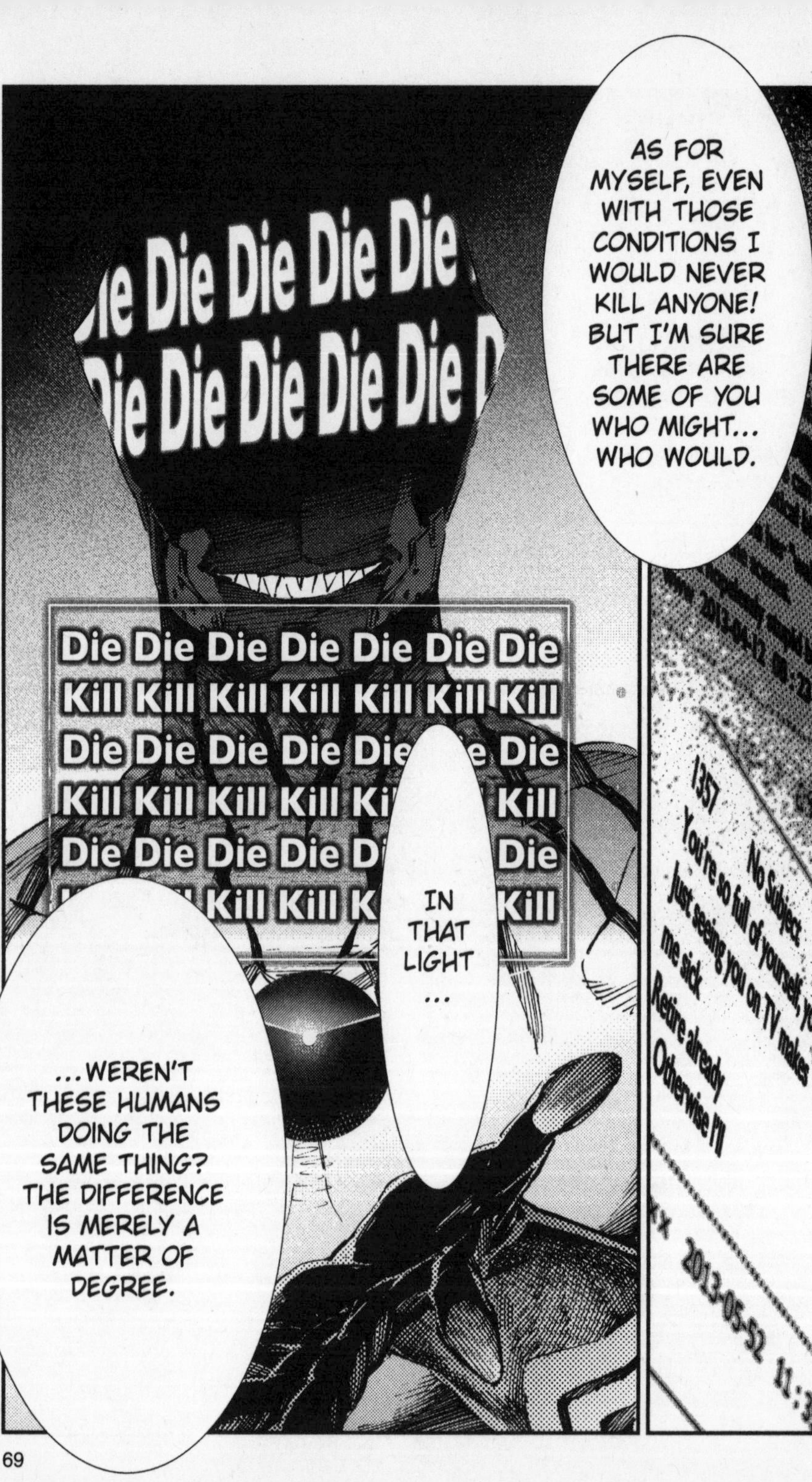
AS FOR MYSELF, EVEN WITH THOSE CONDITIONS I WOULD NEVER KILL ANYONE! BUT I'M SURE THERE ARE SOME OF YOU WHO MIGHT... WHO WOULD.
1357
No Subject
You're so full of yourself, you bitch
just seeing you on TV makes me sick
Retire already
Otherwise I'll
2013-05-52 11:35
Die Die Die Die Die
Die Die Die Die Die Die Die
Kill Kill Kill Kill Kill Kill Kill
IN THAT LIGHT ...
...WEREN'T THESE HUMANS DOING THE SAME THING? THE DIFFERENCE IS MERELY A MATTER OF DEGREE.

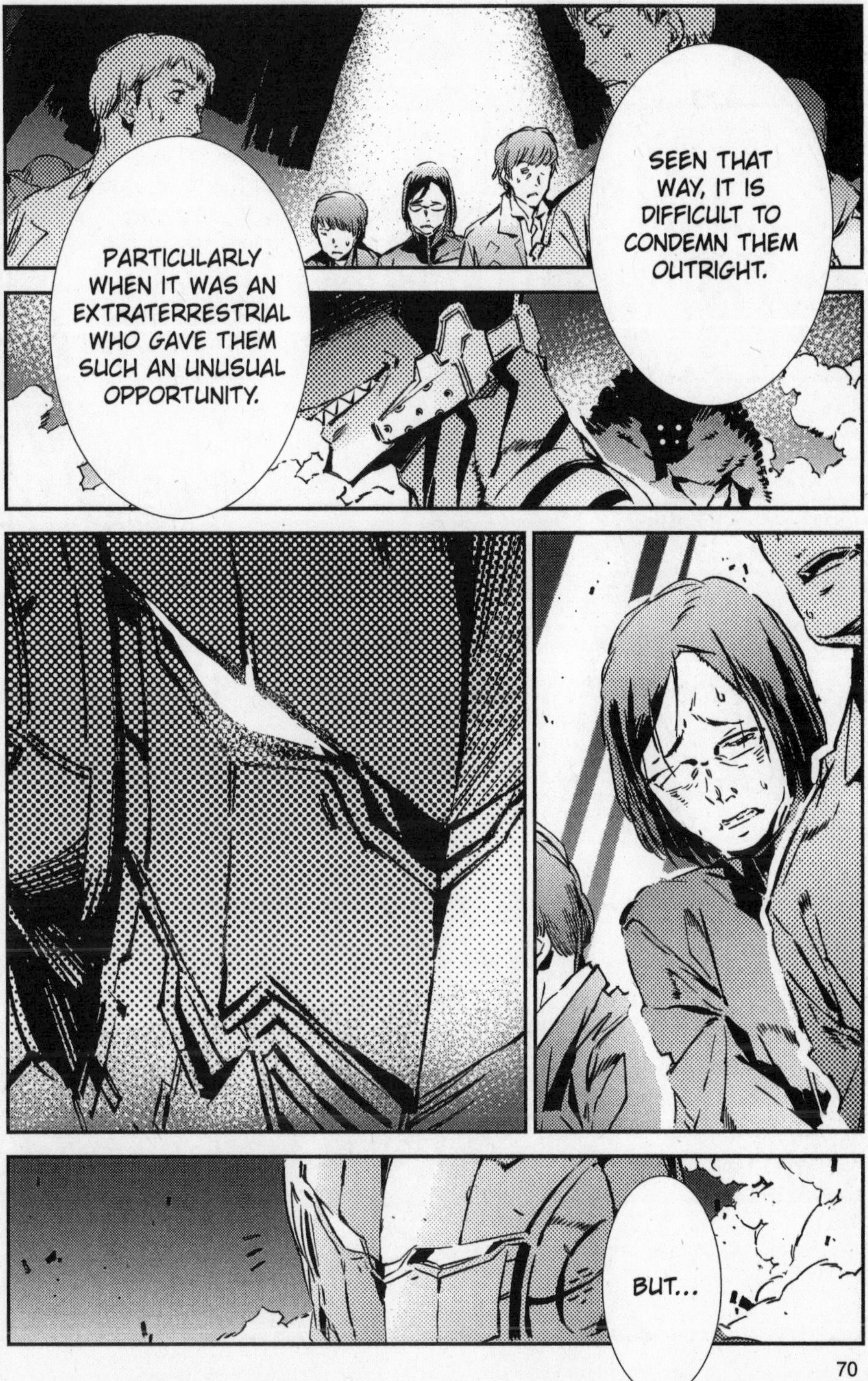
SEEN THAT WAY, IT IS DIFFICULT TO CONDEMN THEM OUTRIGHT.
PARTICULARLY WHEN IT WAS AN EXTRATERRESTRIAL WHO GAVE THEM SUCH AN UNUSUAL OPPORTUNITY.
BUT...

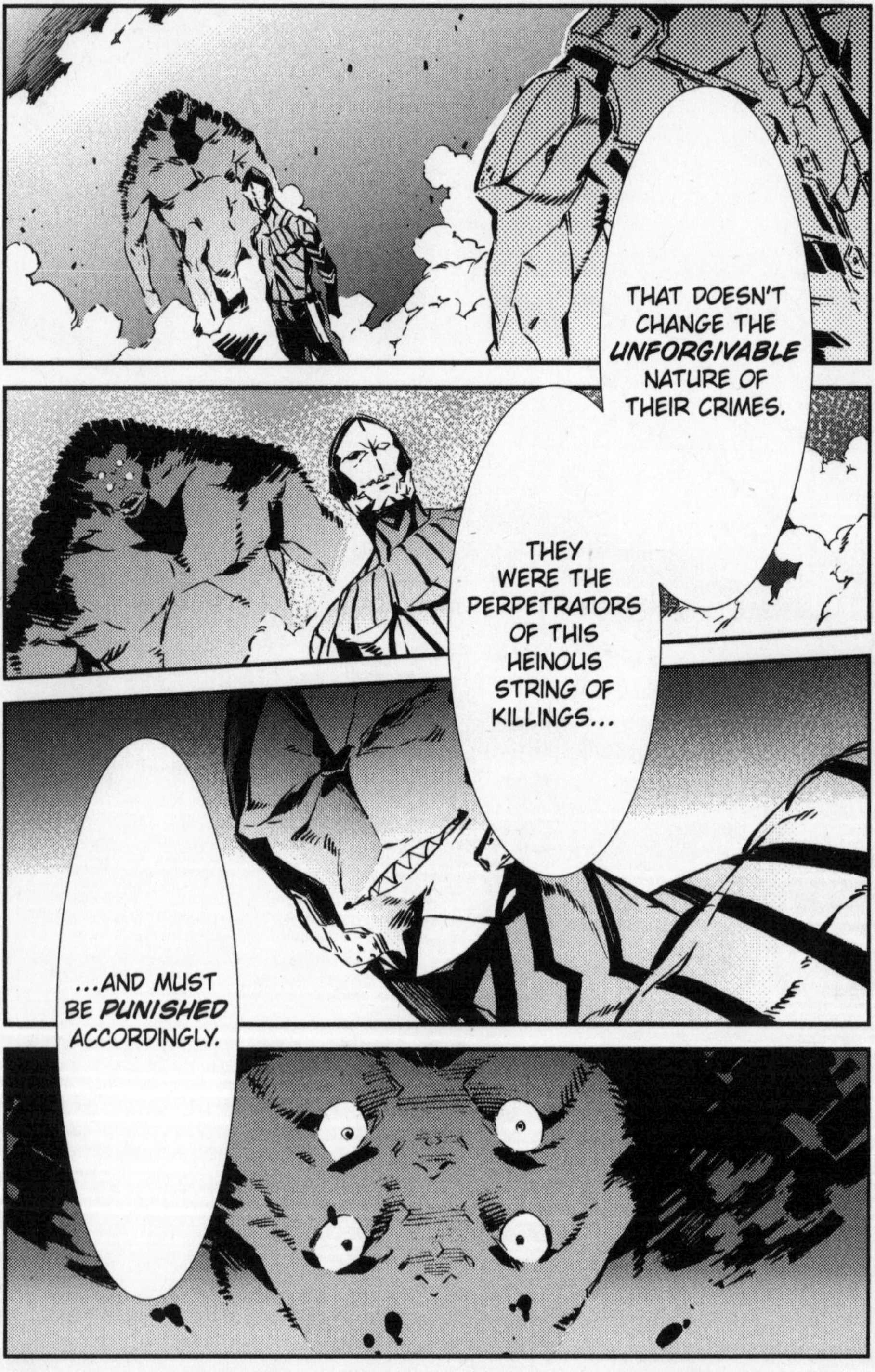
THAT DOESN'T CHANGE THE ***UNFORGIVABLE*** NATURE OF THEIR CRIMES.
THEY WERE THE PERPETRATORS OF THIS HEINOUS STRING OF KILLINGS...
...AND MUST BE ***PUNISHED*** ACCORDINGLY.

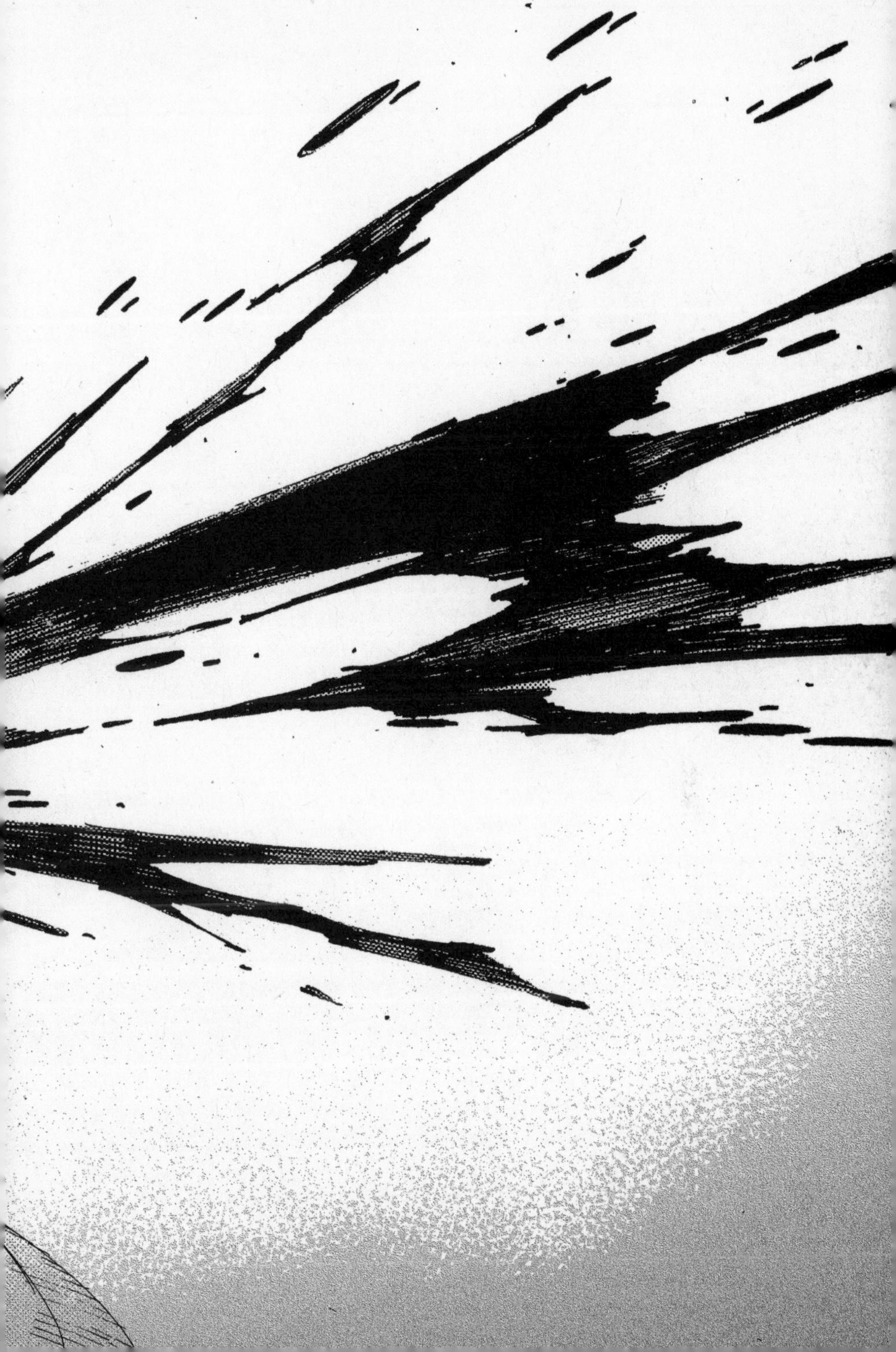

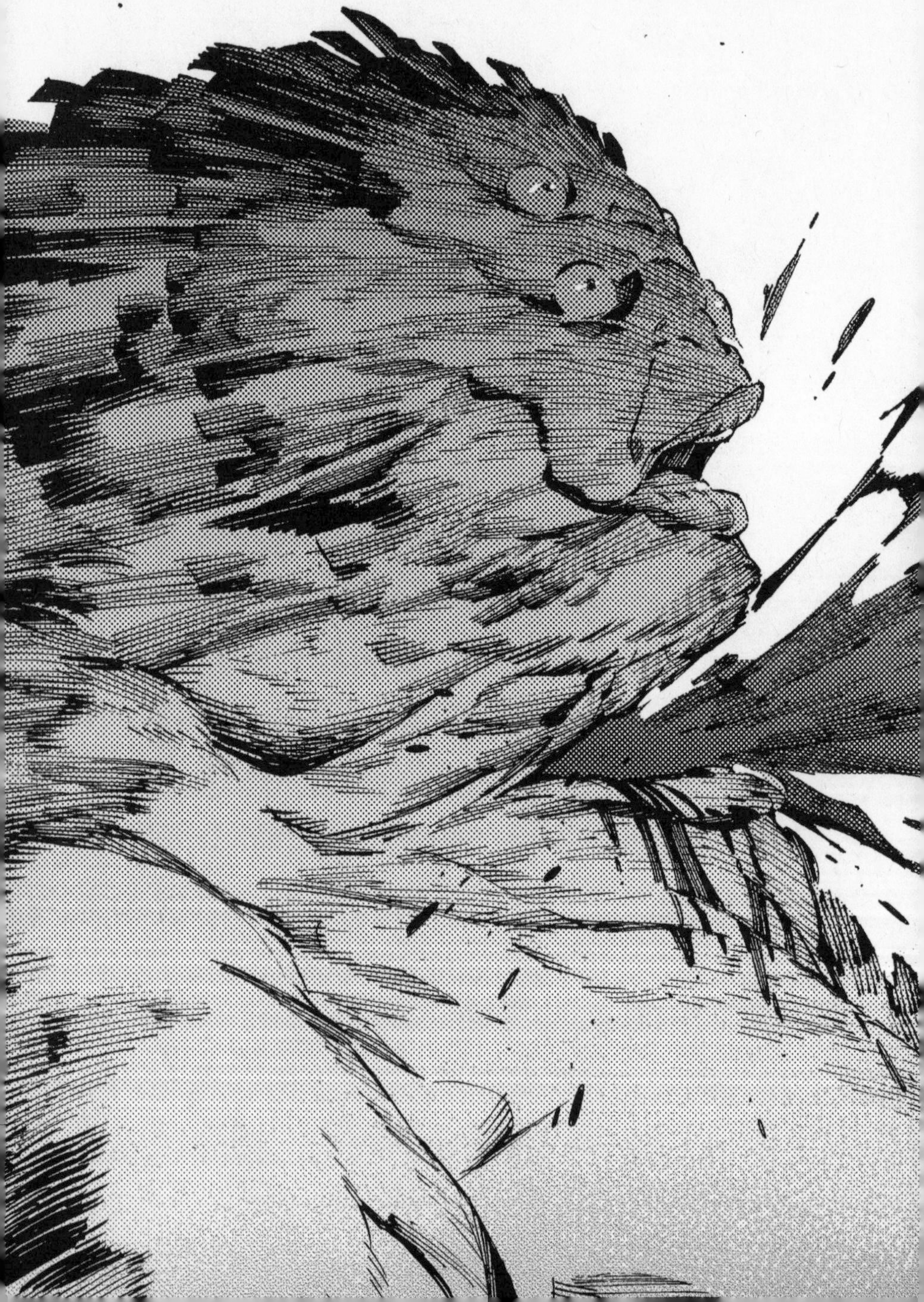

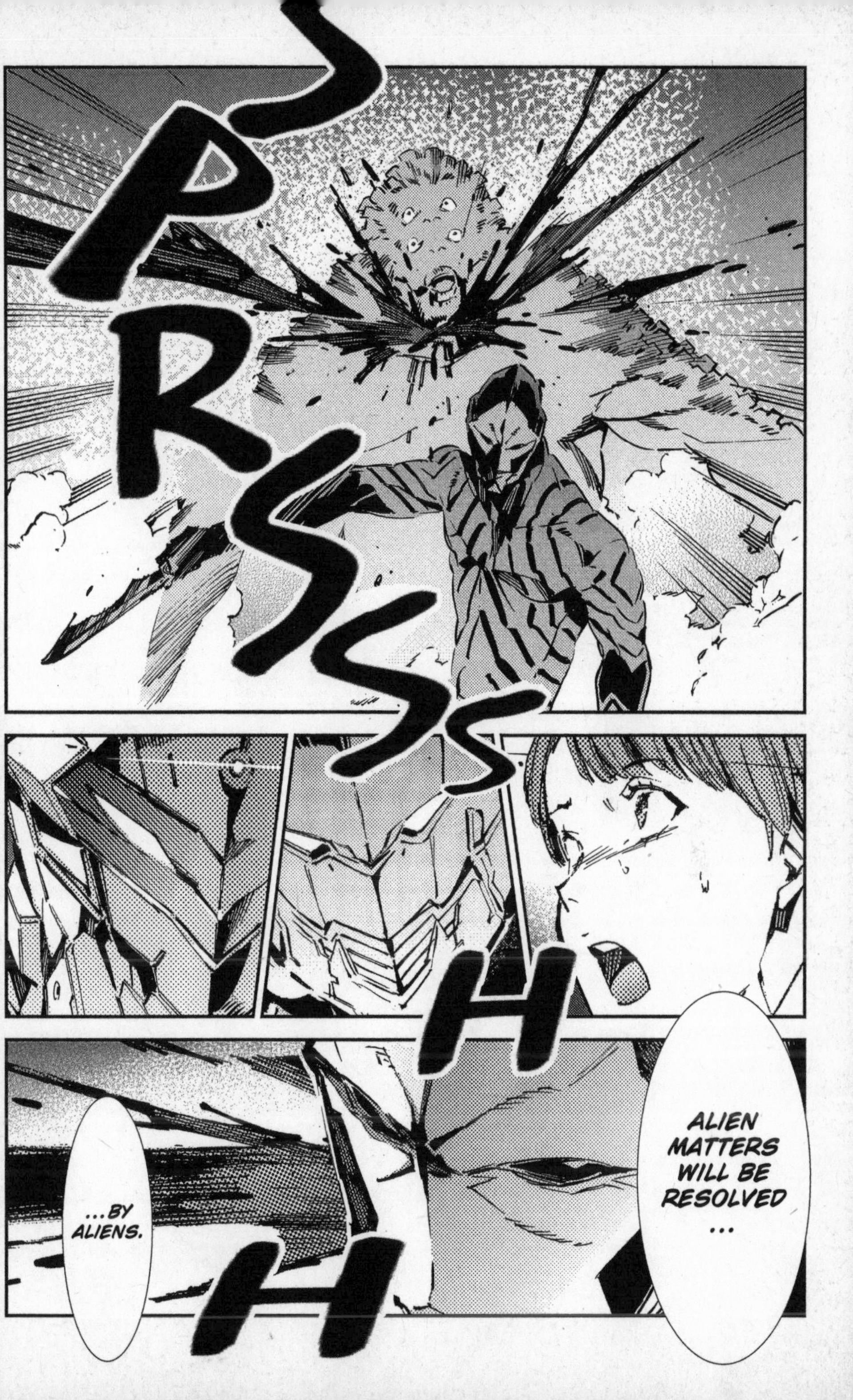
PRSSSHH
ALIEN MATTERS WILL BE RESOLVED ...
...BY ALIENS.

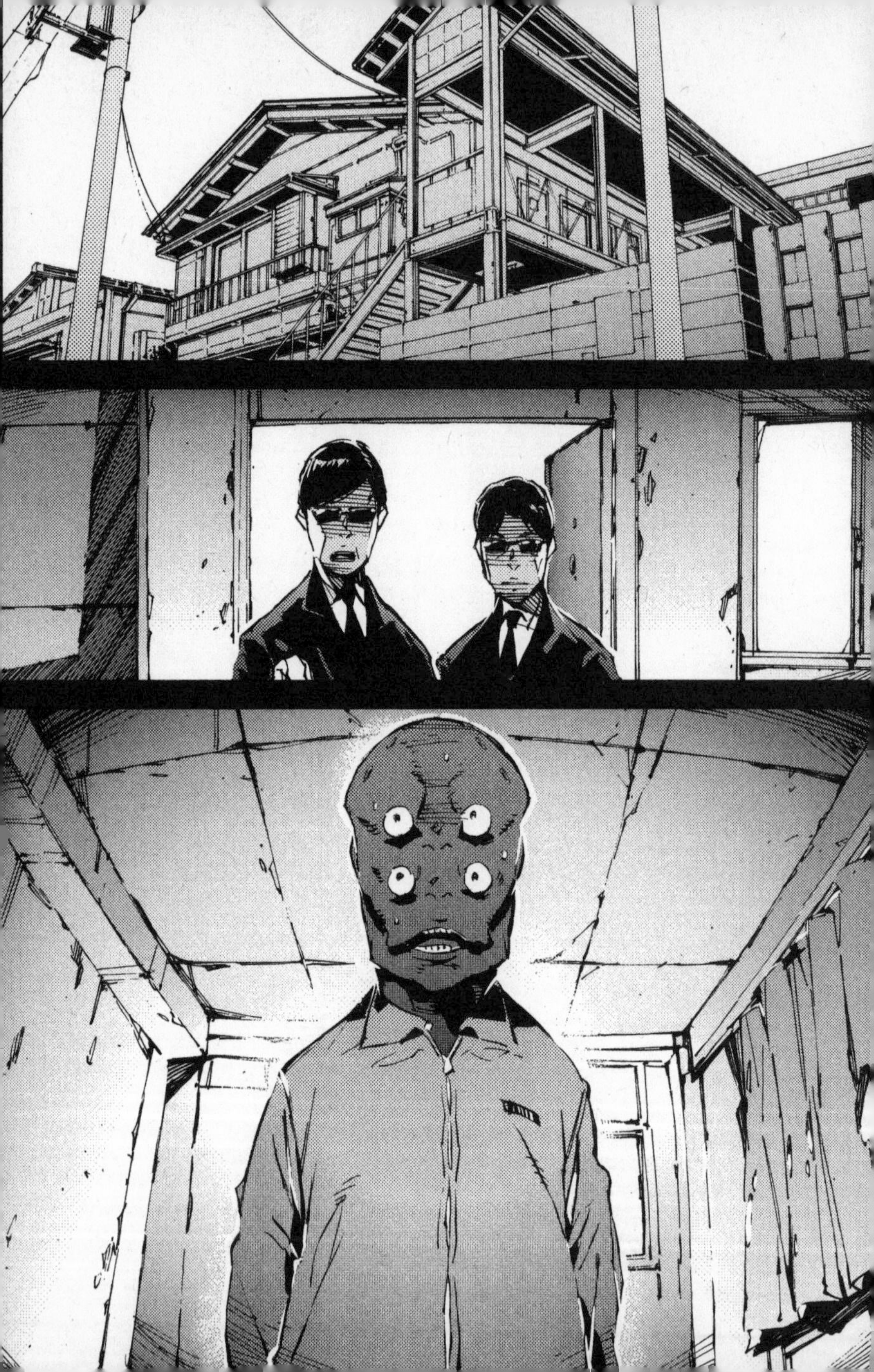

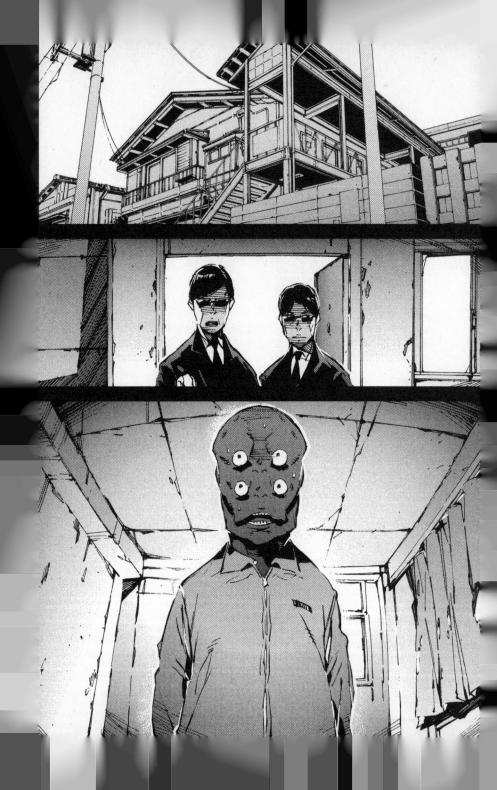

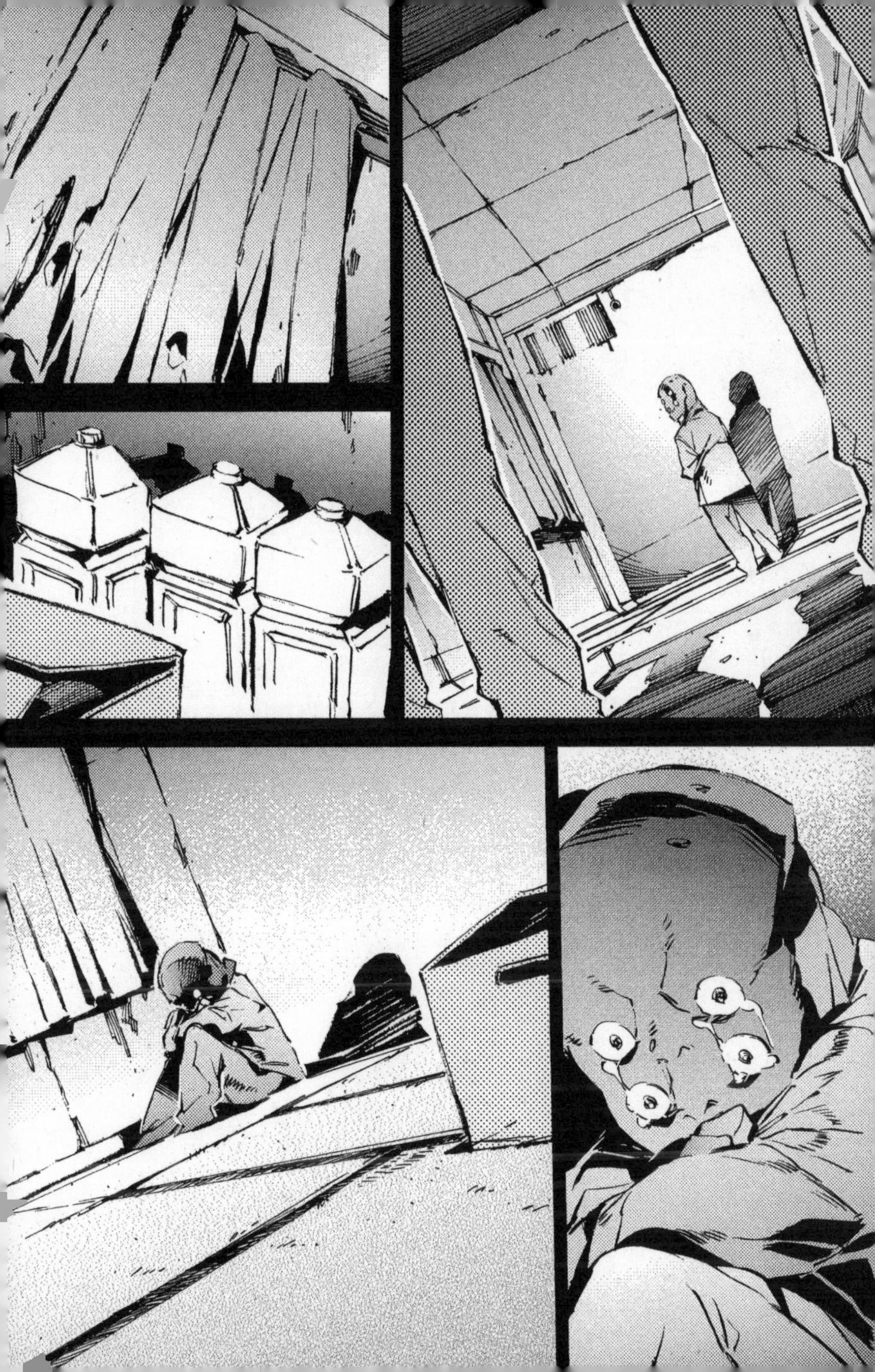

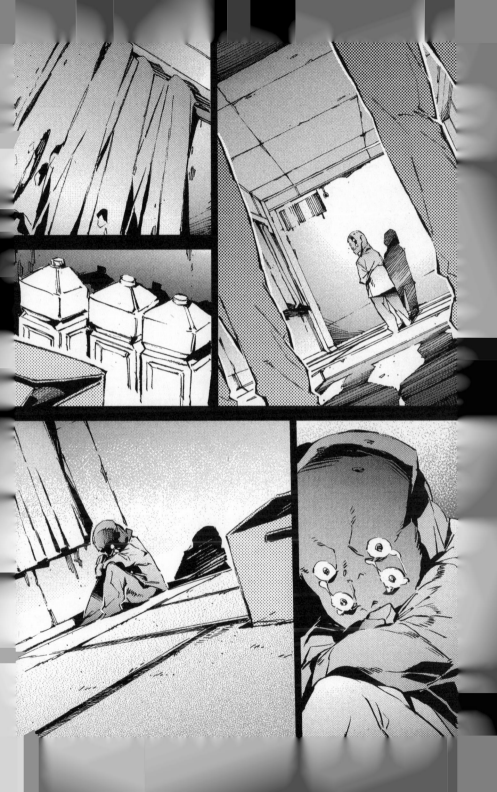

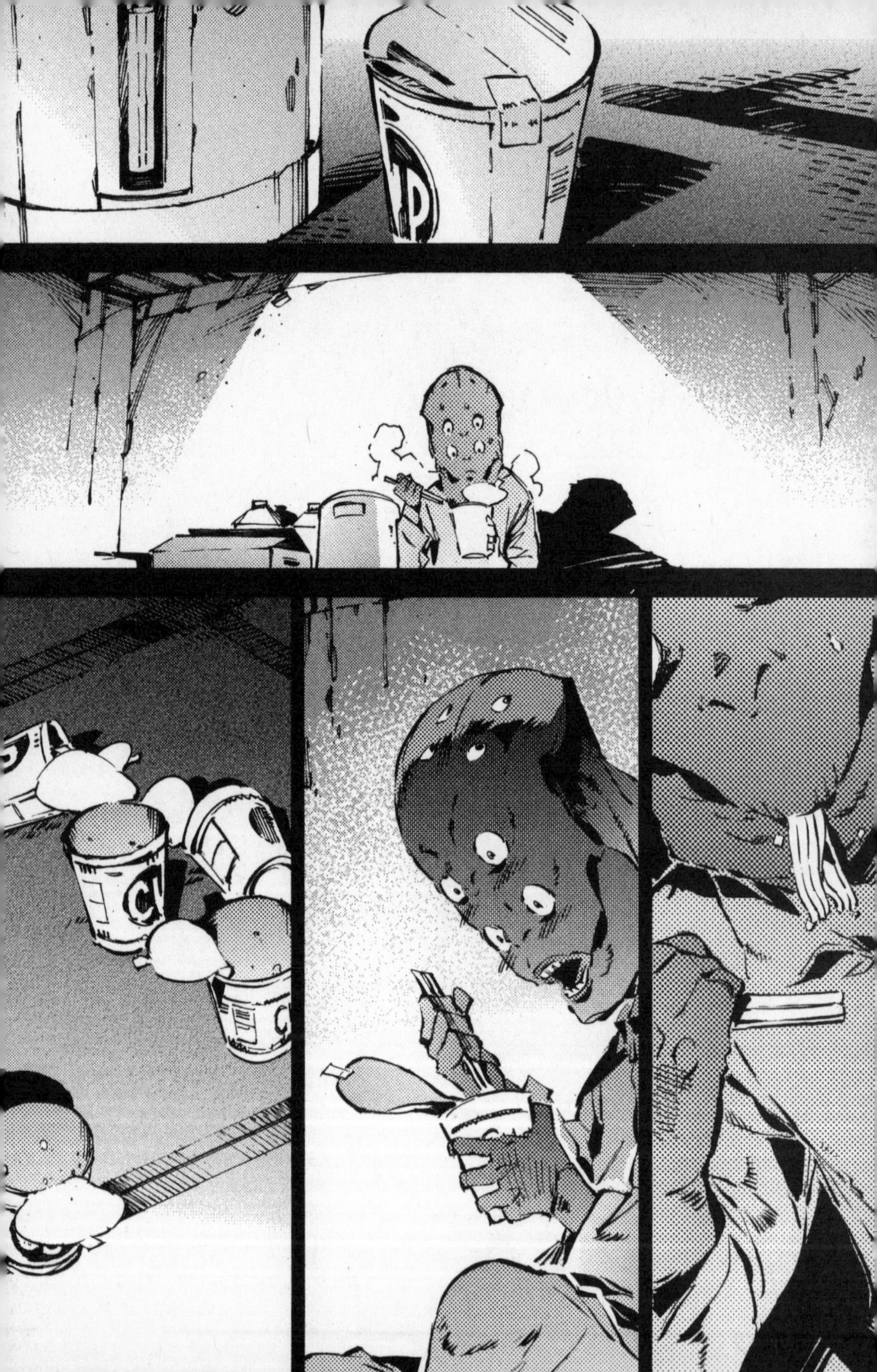

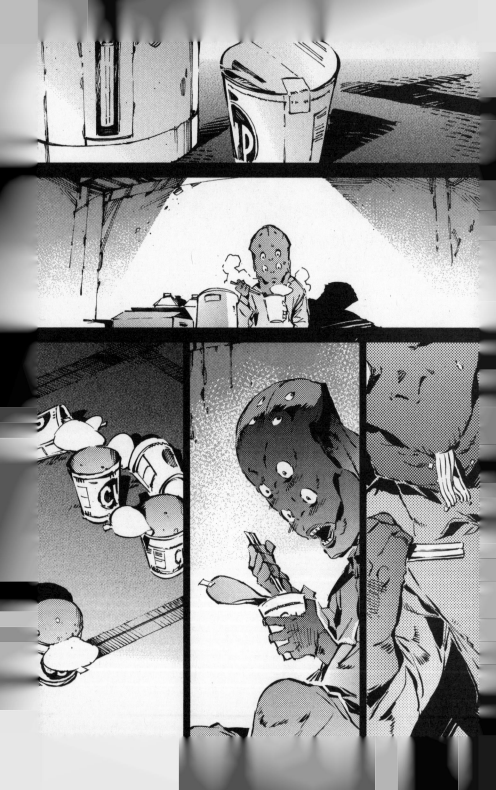

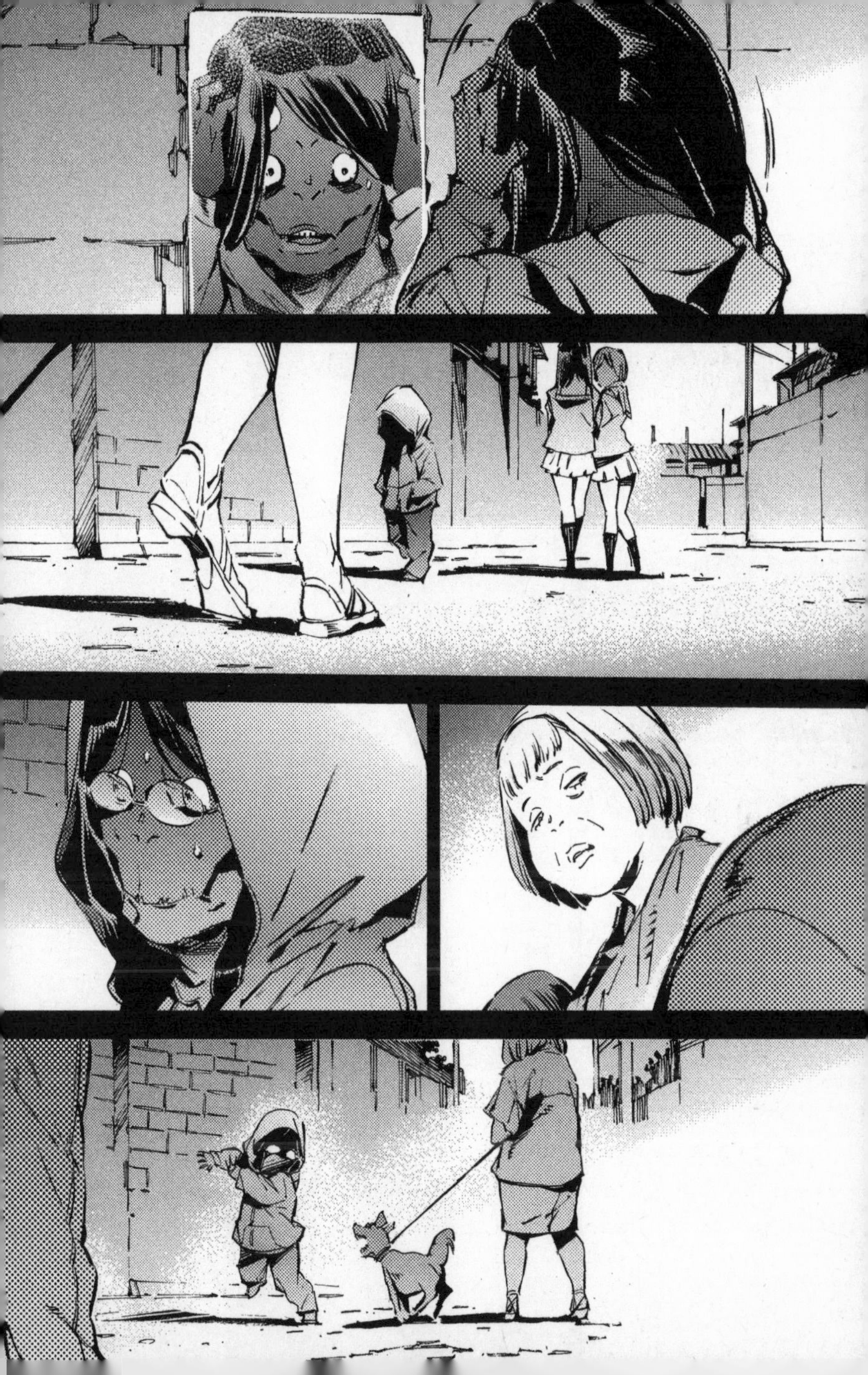

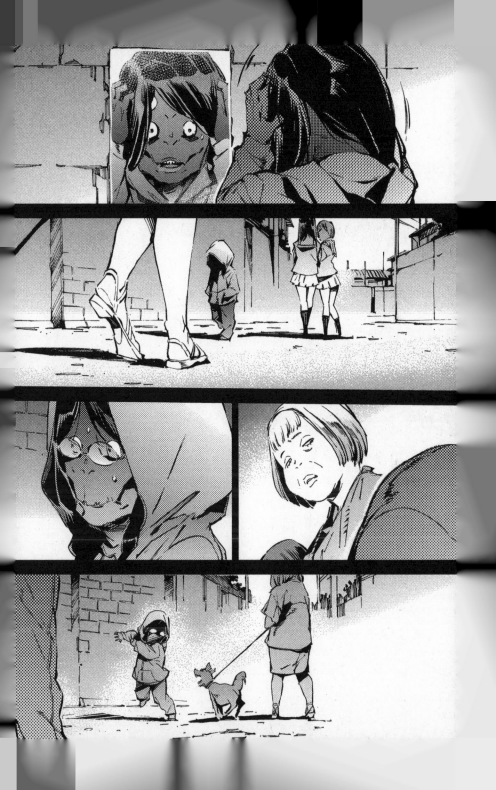

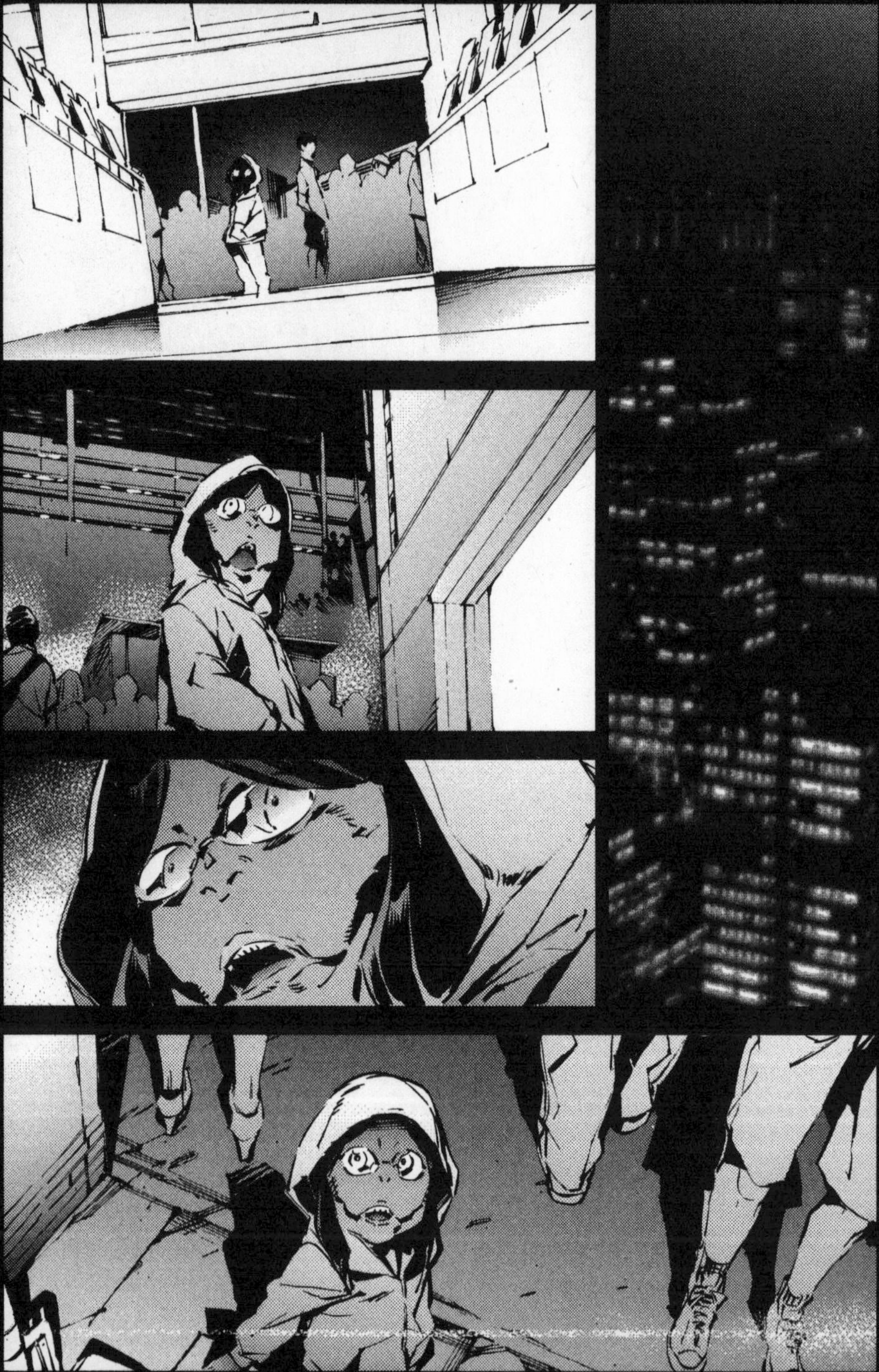

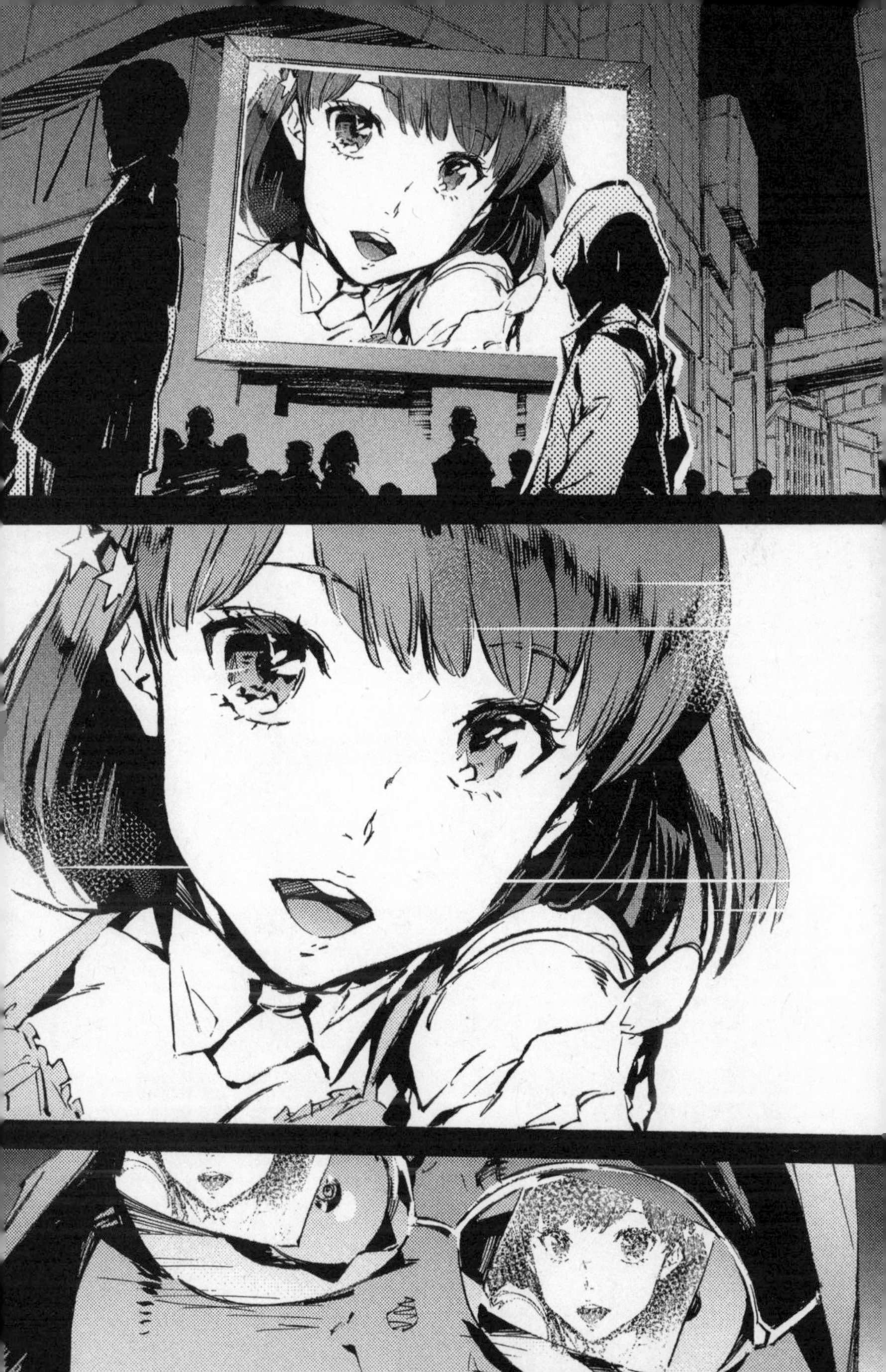

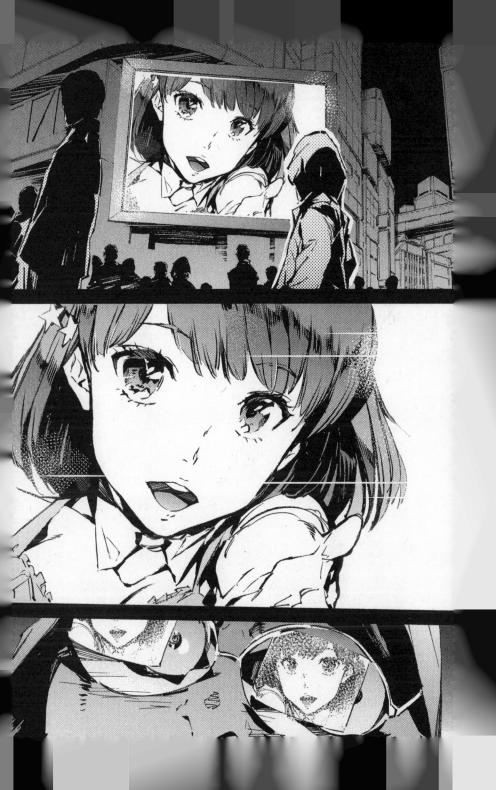

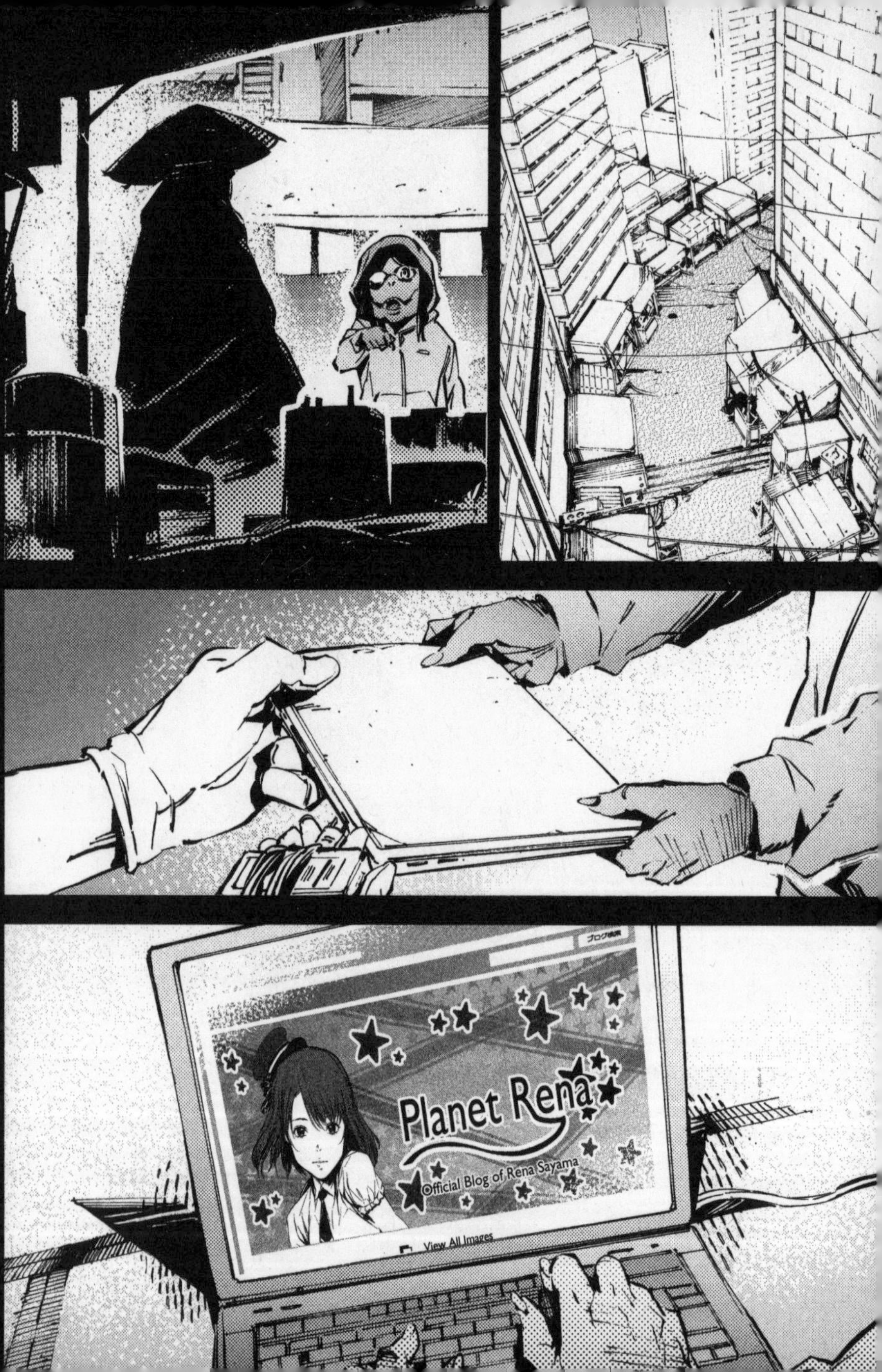
Planet Rena
Official Blog of Rena Sayama
View All Images

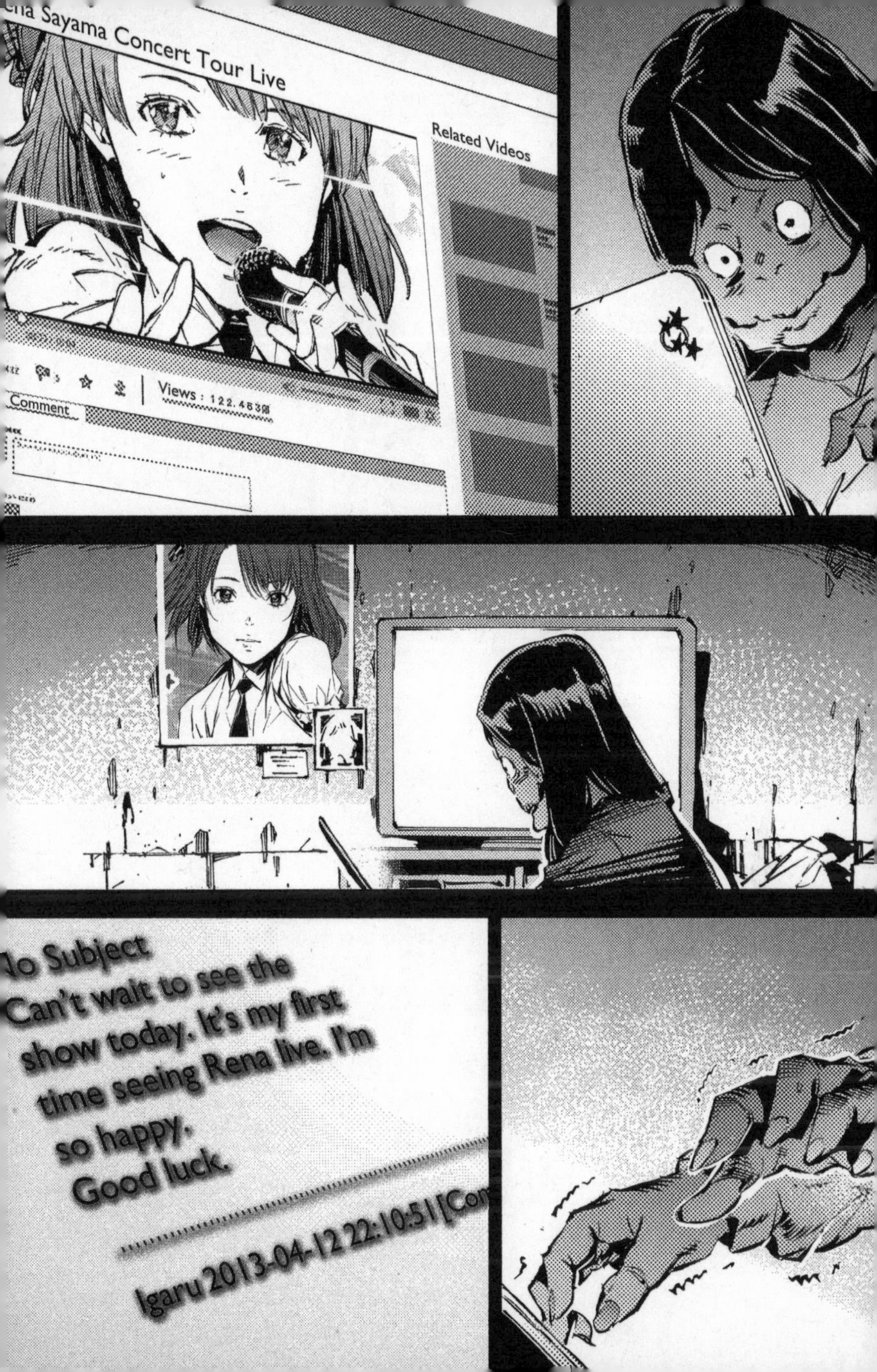
ena Sayama Concert Tour Live
Related Videos
Views : 122,463
Comment
o Subject
Can't wait to see the show today. It's my first time seeing Rena live. I'm so happy.
Good luck.
Igaru 2013-04-12 22:10:51 [Co

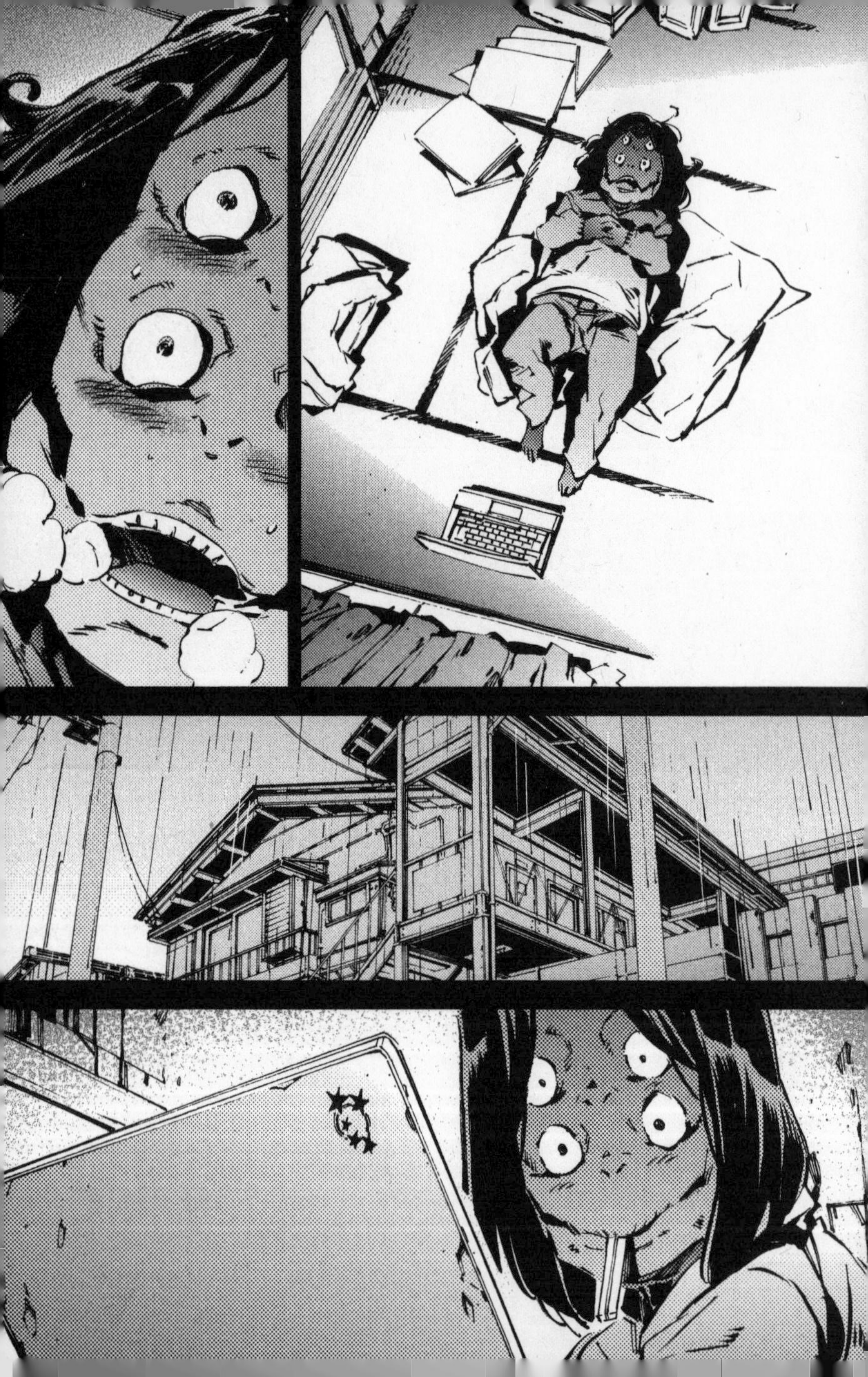

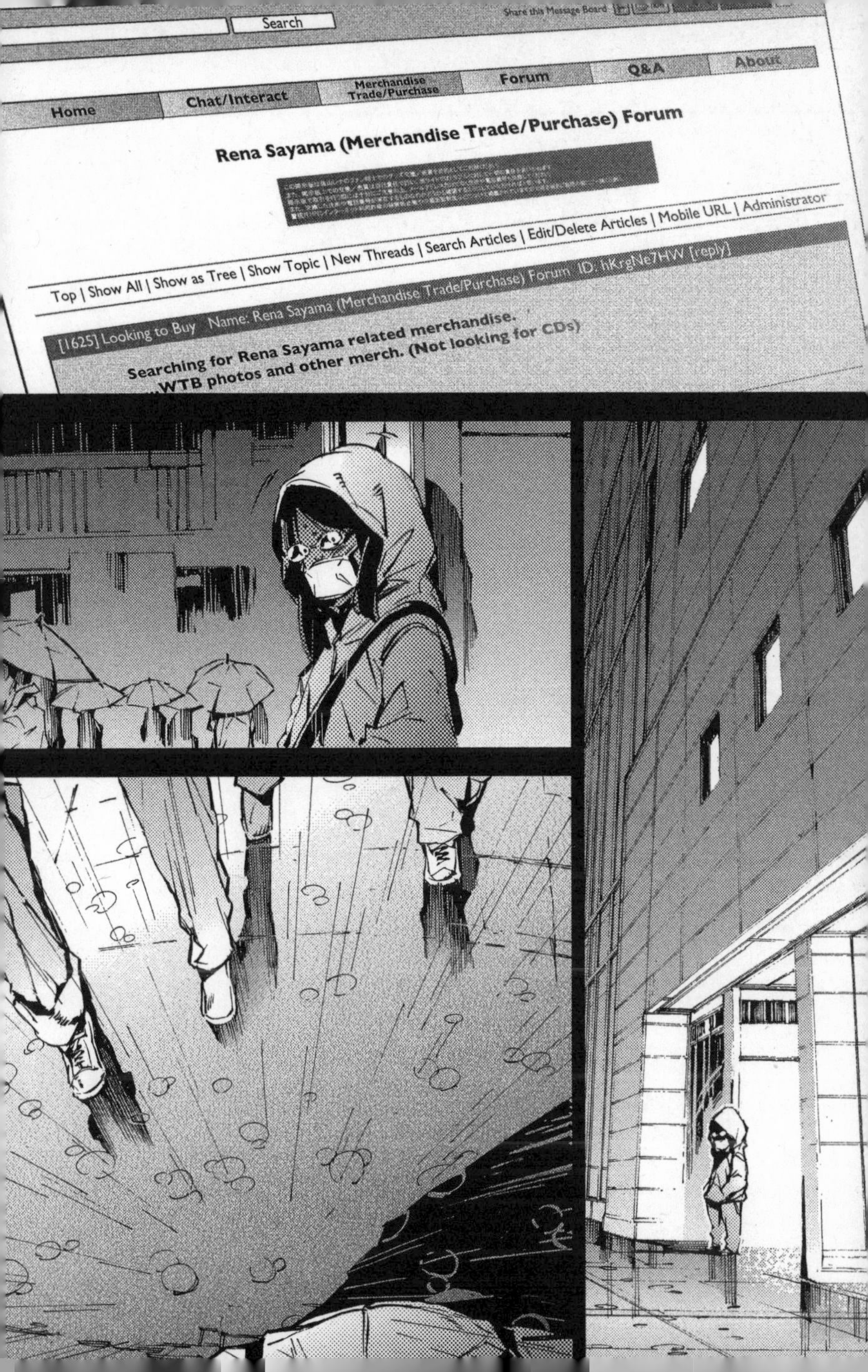

Search
Share this Message Board
Home
Chat/Interact
Merchandise Trade/Purchase
Forum
Q&A
About
Rena Sayama (Merchandise Trade/Purchase) Forum
Top | Show All | Show as Tree | Show Topic | New Threads | Search Articles | Edit/Delete Articles | Mobile URL | Administrator
[1625] Looking to Buy Name: Rena Sayama (Merchandise Trade/Purchase) Forum ID: hKrgNe7HW [reply]
Searching for Rena Sayama related merchandise.
WTB photos and other merch. (Not looking for CDs)

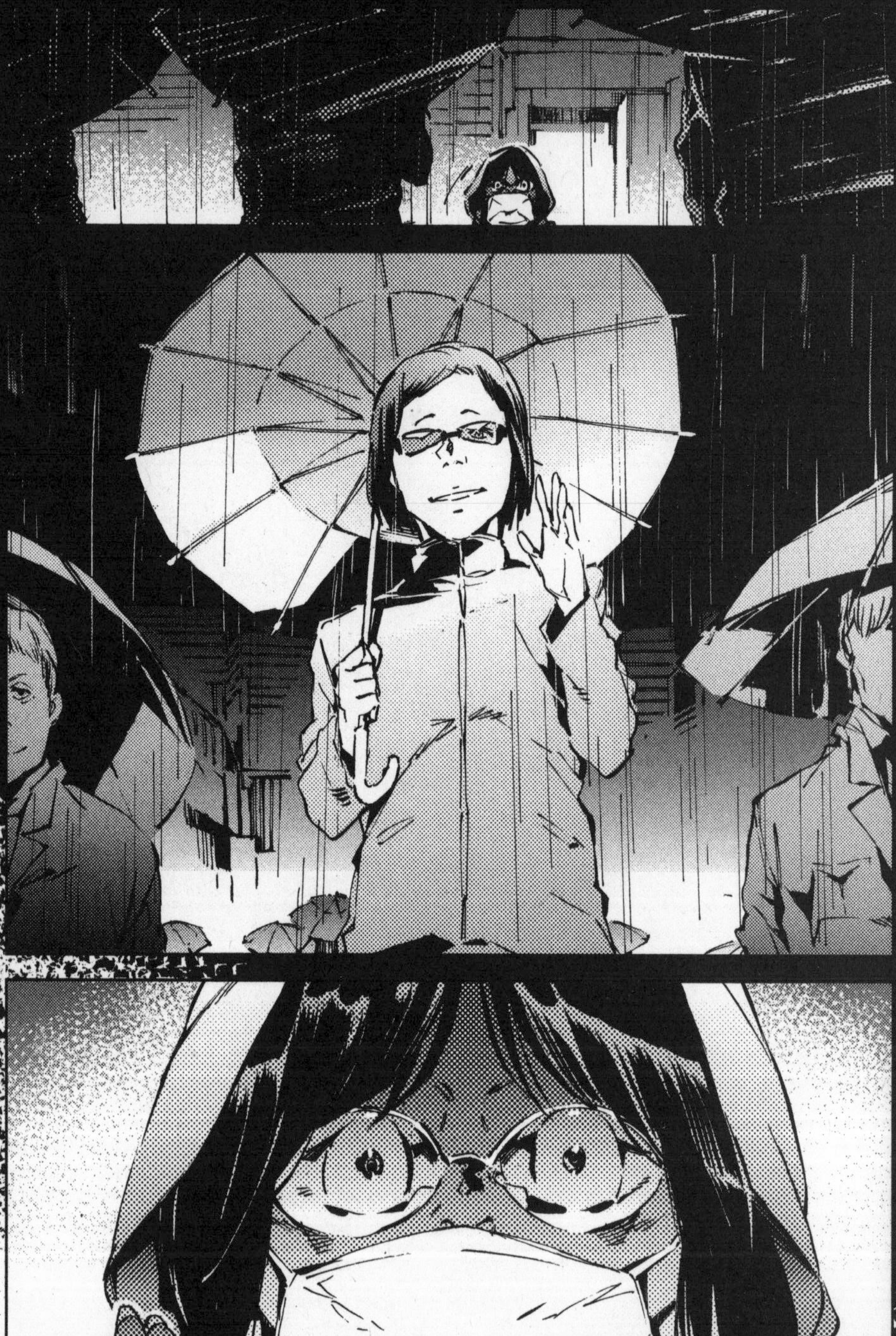

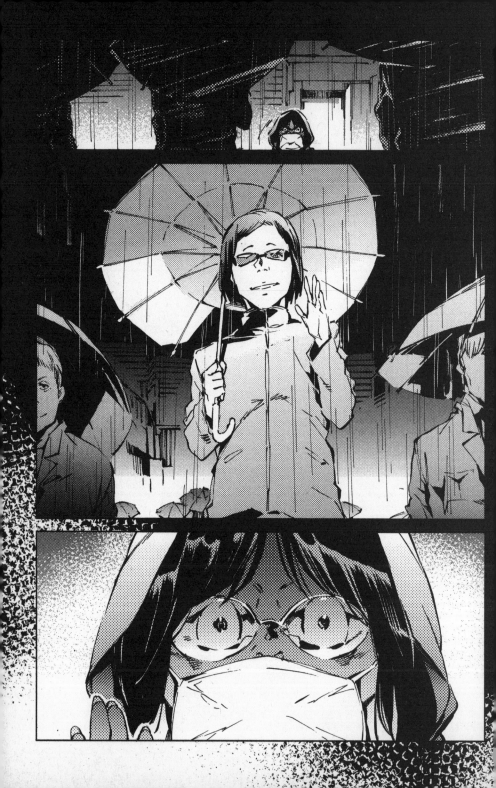

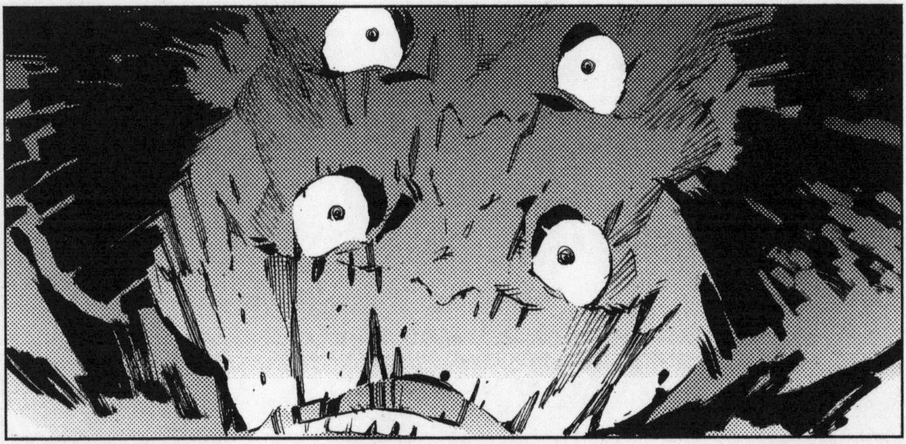
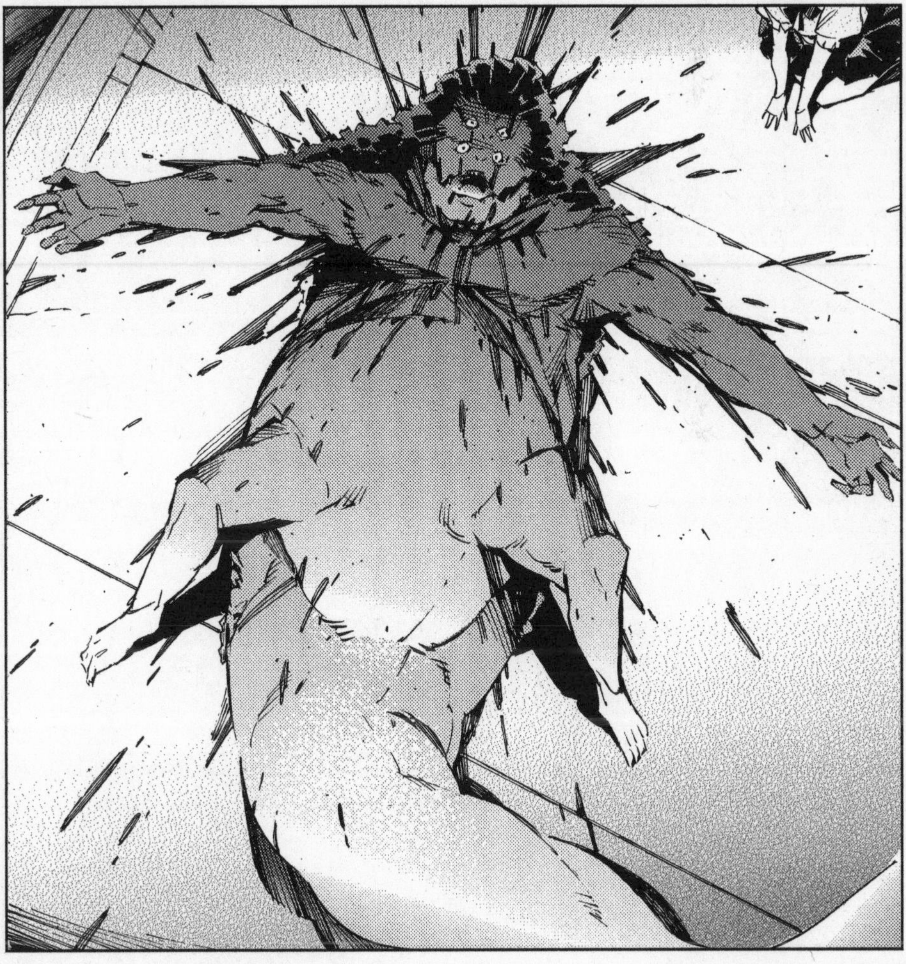

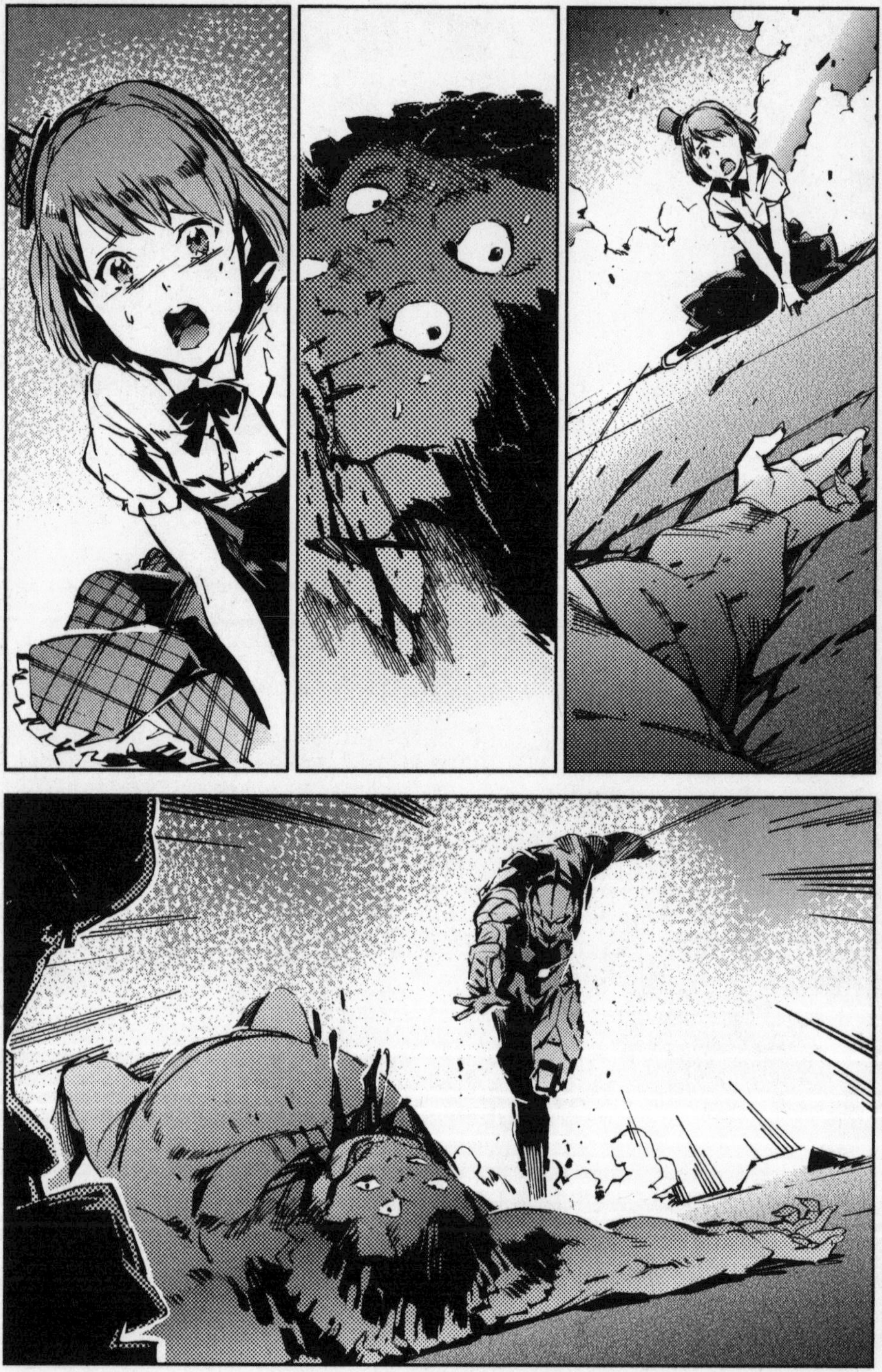

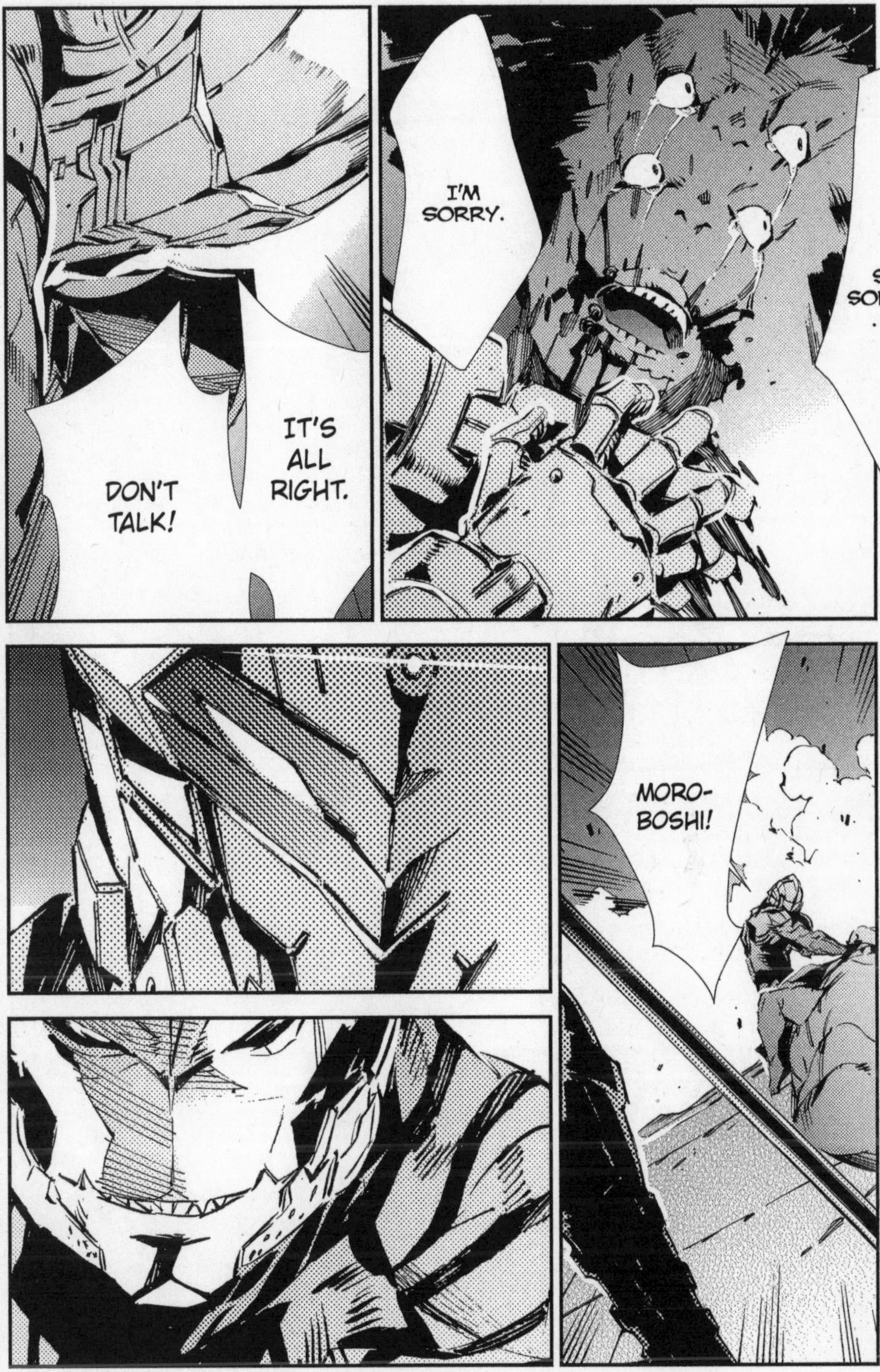
S-SORRY...
I'M SORRY.
IT'S ALL RIGHT.
DON'T TALK!
MORO-BOSHI!

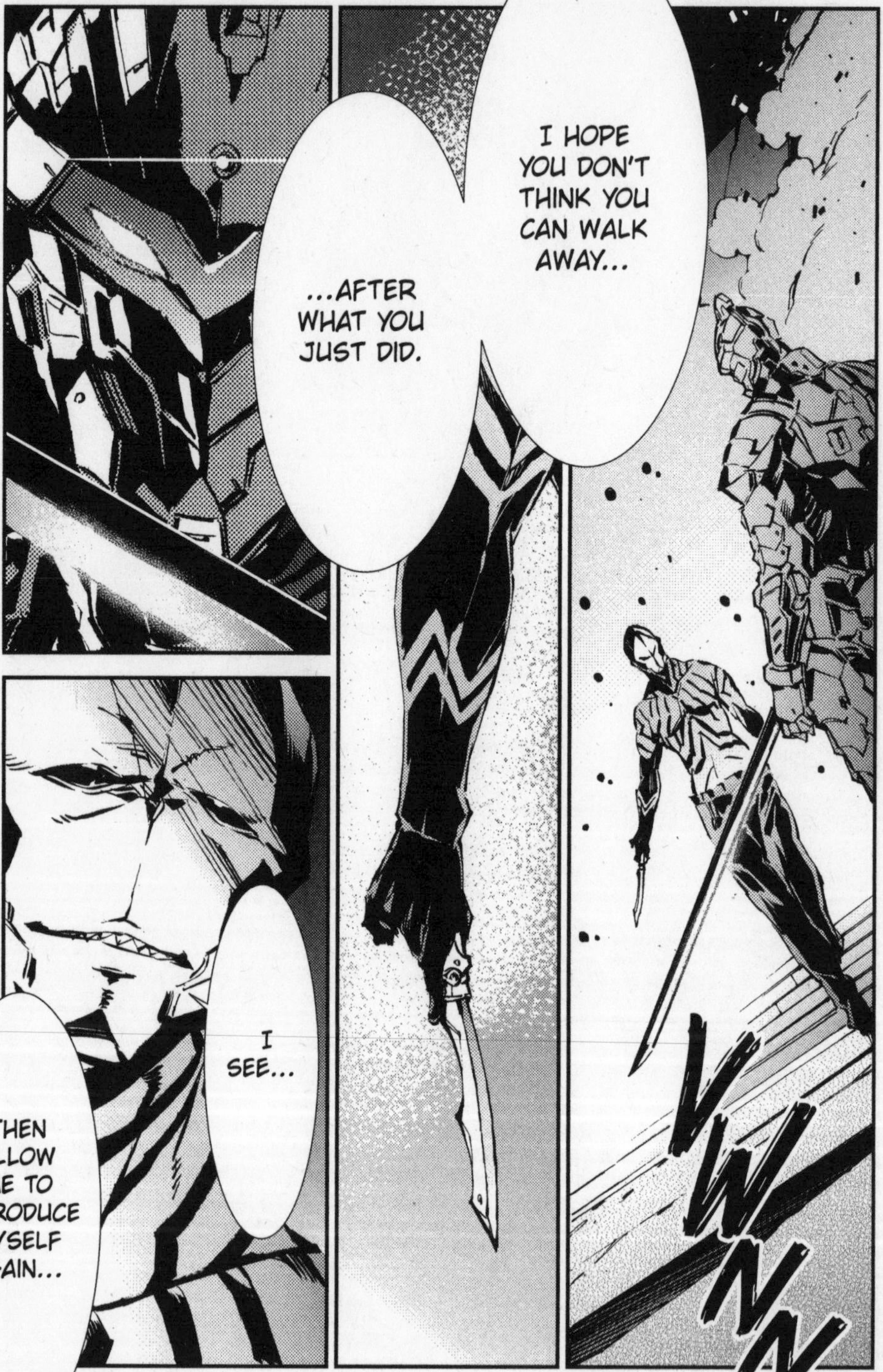
VWNN
I HOPE YOU DON'T THINK YOU CAN WALK AWAY...
...AFTER WHAT YOU JUST DID.
I SEE...
THEN ALLOW ME TO INTRODUCE MYSELF AGAIN...

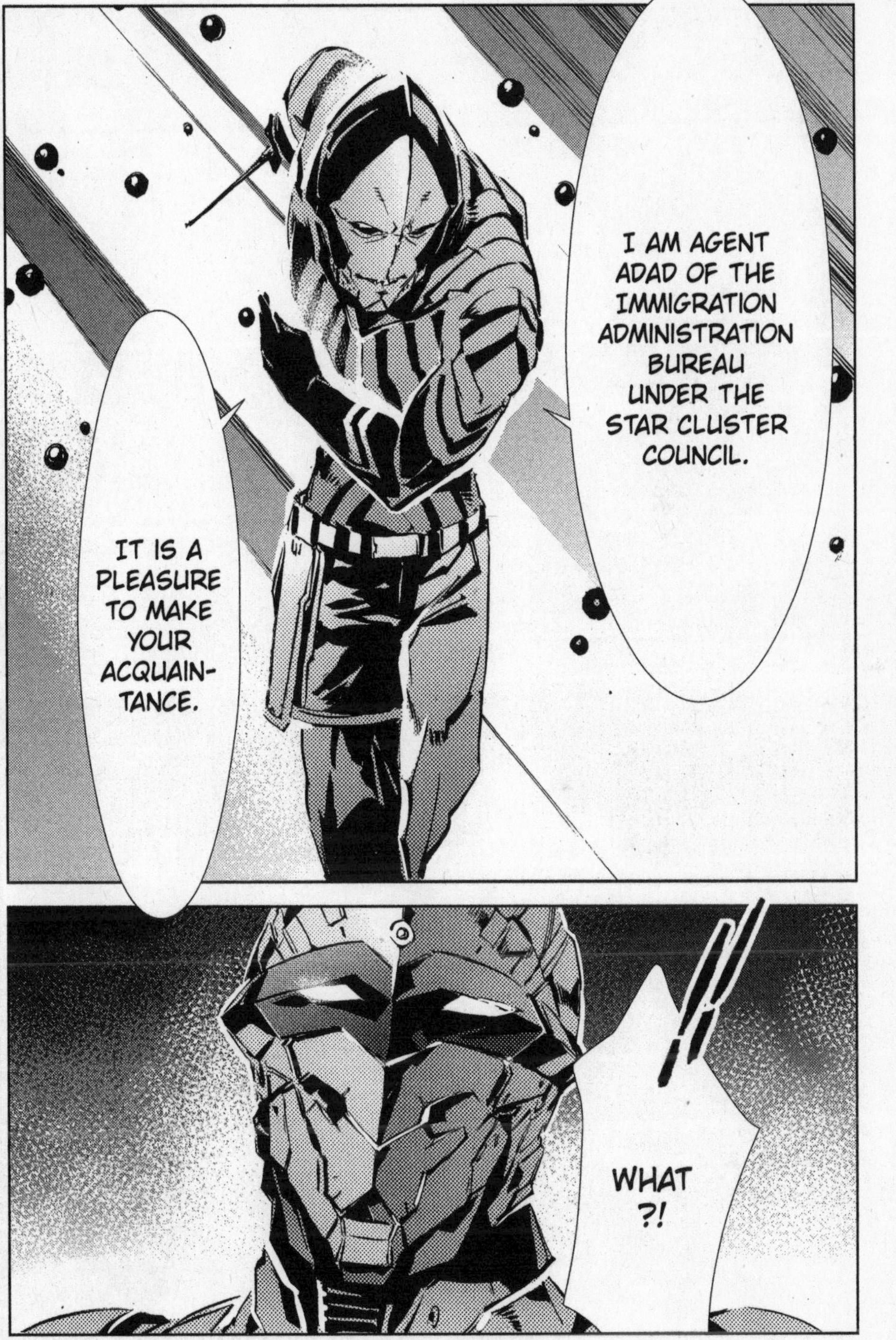
I AM AGENT ADAD OF THE IMMIGRATION ADMINISTRATION BUREAU UNDER THE STAR CLUSTER COUNCIL.
IT IS A PLEASURE TO MAKE YOUR ACQUAIN-TANCE.
WHAT ?!

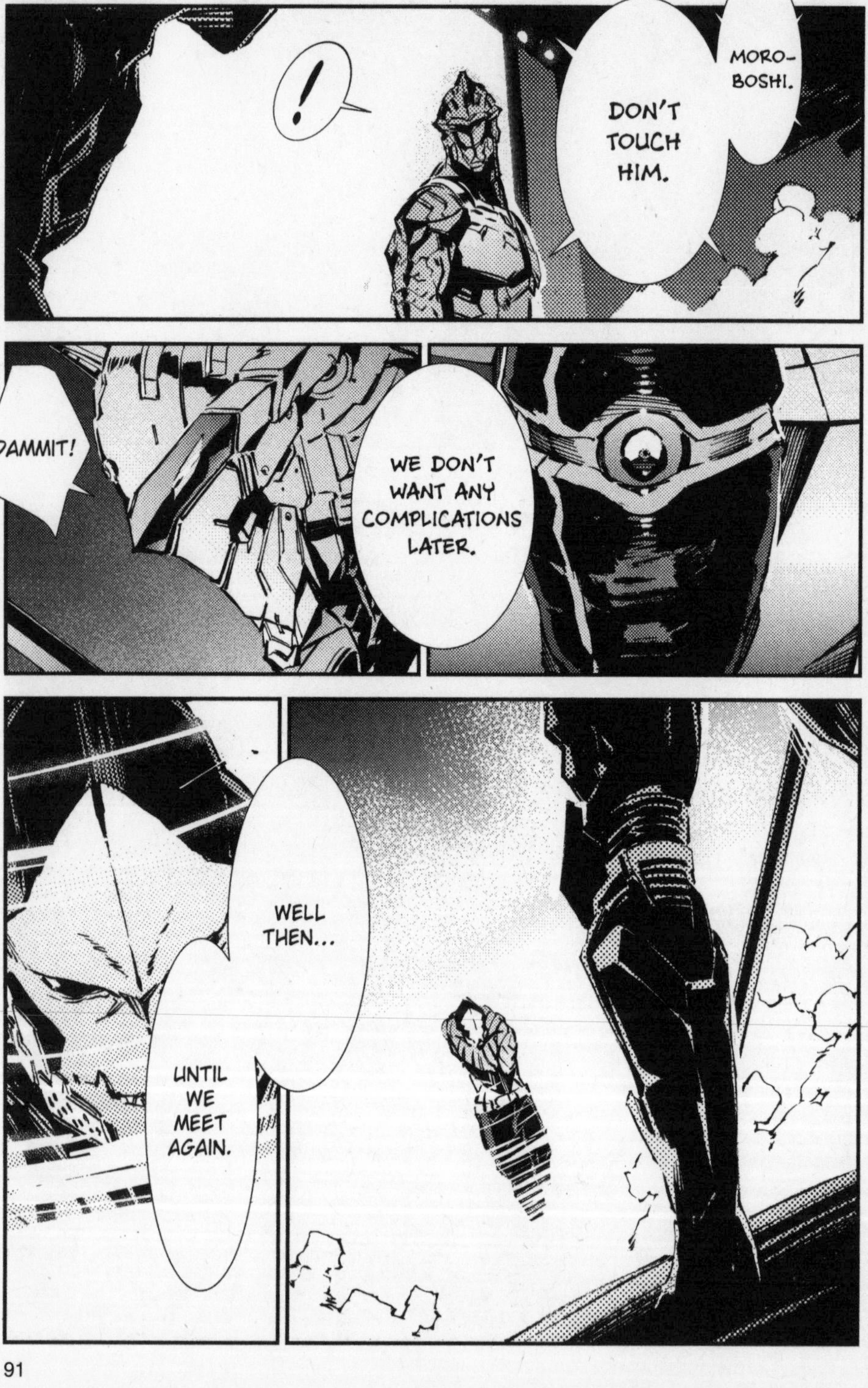
MORO-BOSHI.
DON'T TOUCH HIM.
!
WE DON'T WANT ANY COMPLICATIONS LATER.
DAMMIT!
WELL THEN...
UNTIL WE MEET AGAIN.

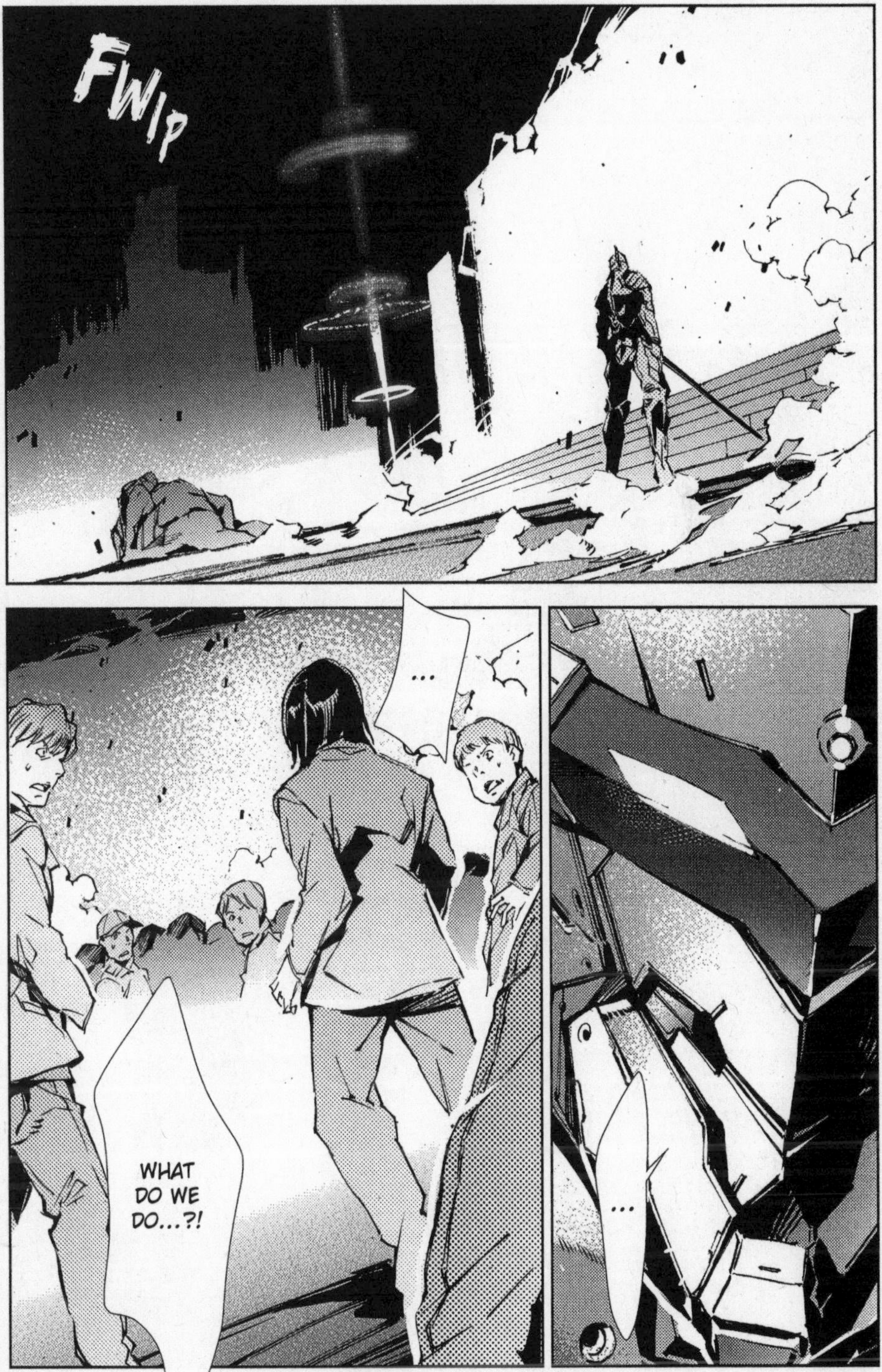

FWIP
...
...
WHAT DO WE DO...?!

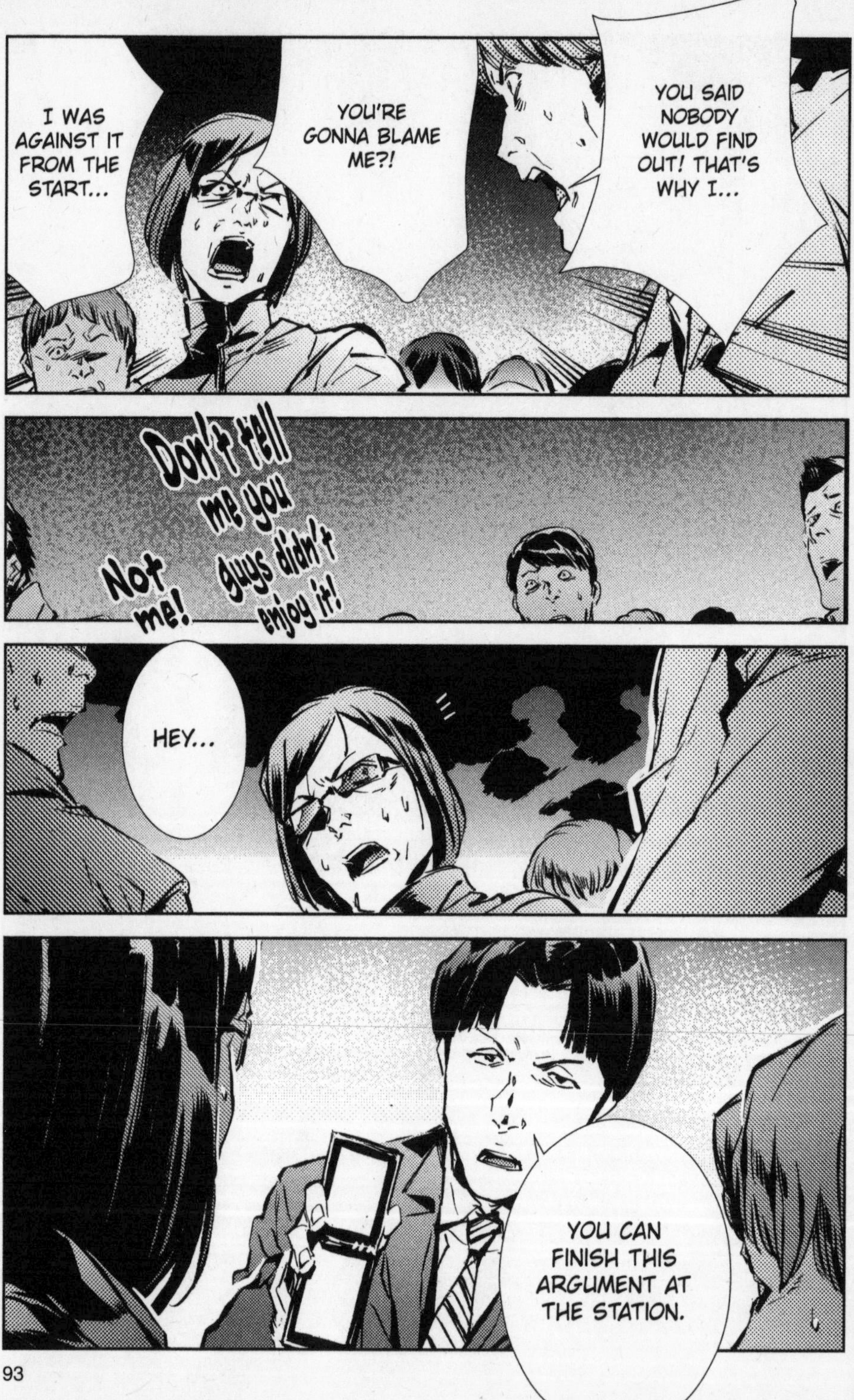
YOU SAID NOBODY WOULD FIND OUT! THAT'S WHY I...
YOU'RE GONNA BLAME ME?!
I WAS AGAINST IT FROM THE START...
Don't tell me you guys didn't enjoy it!
Not me!
HEY...
YOU CAN FINISH THIS ARGUMENT AT THE STATION.

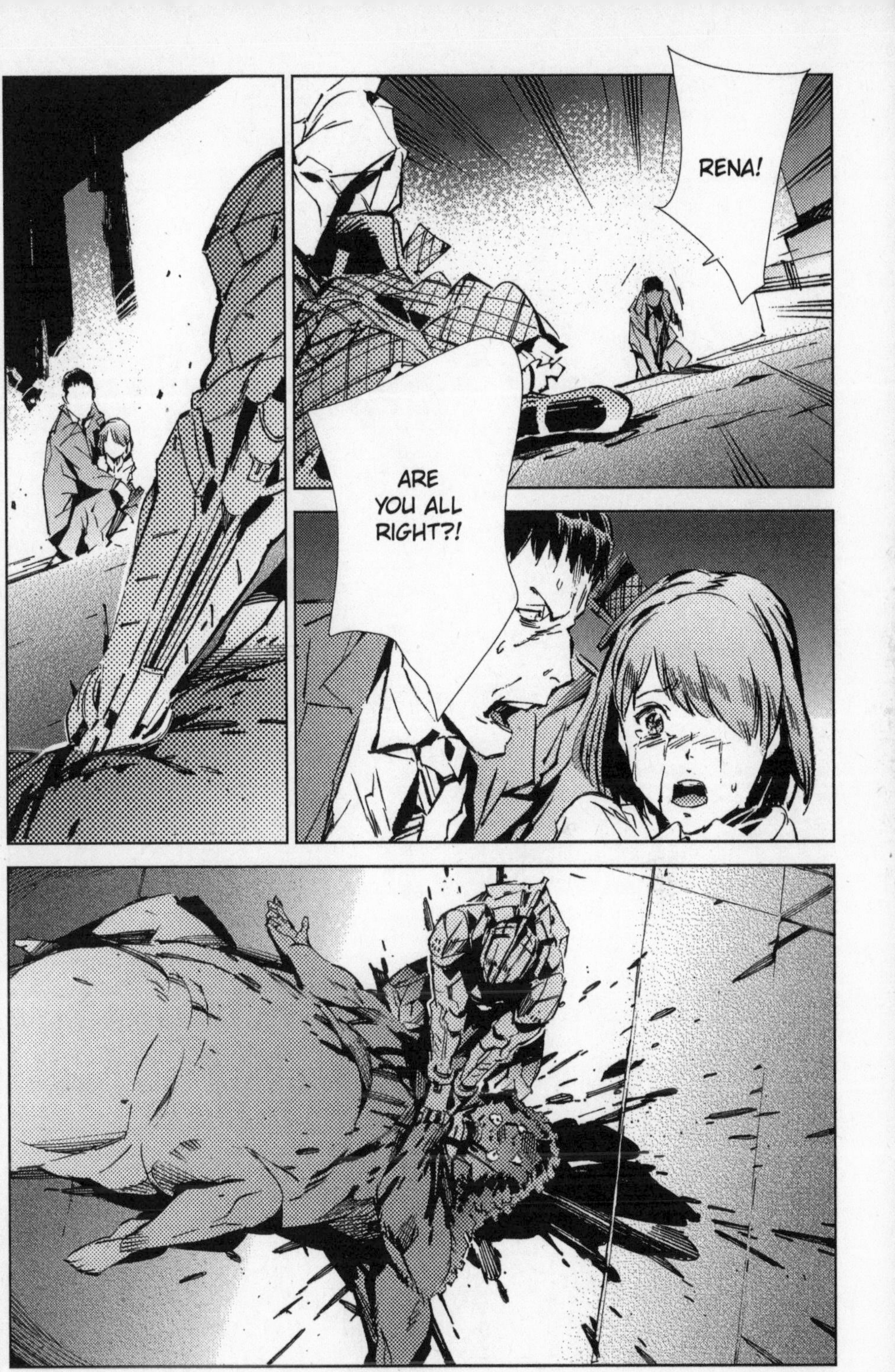
RENA!
ARE YOU ALL RIGHT?!

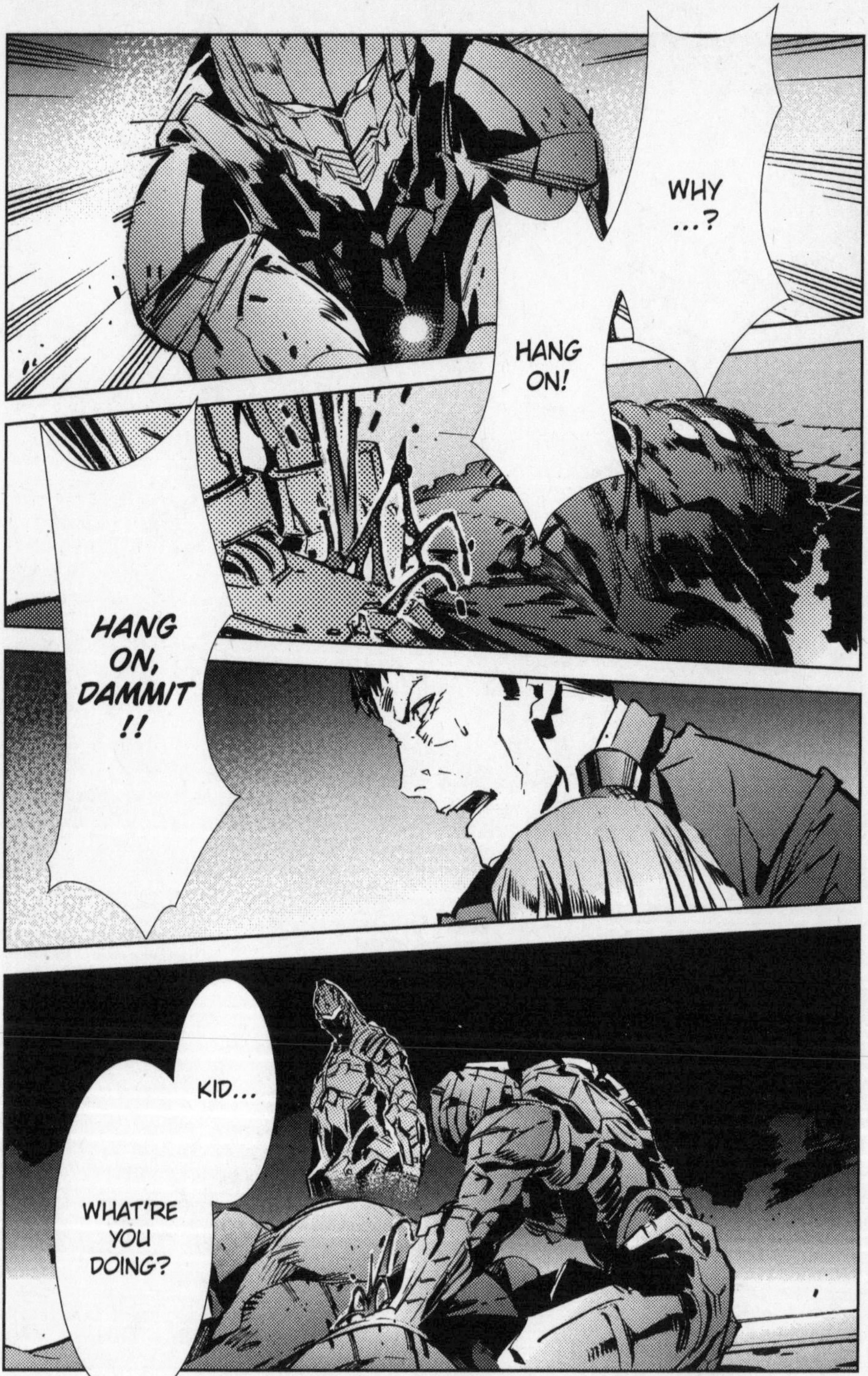
WHY ...?
HANG ON!
HANG ON, DAMMIT !!
KID...
WHAT'RE YOU DOING?

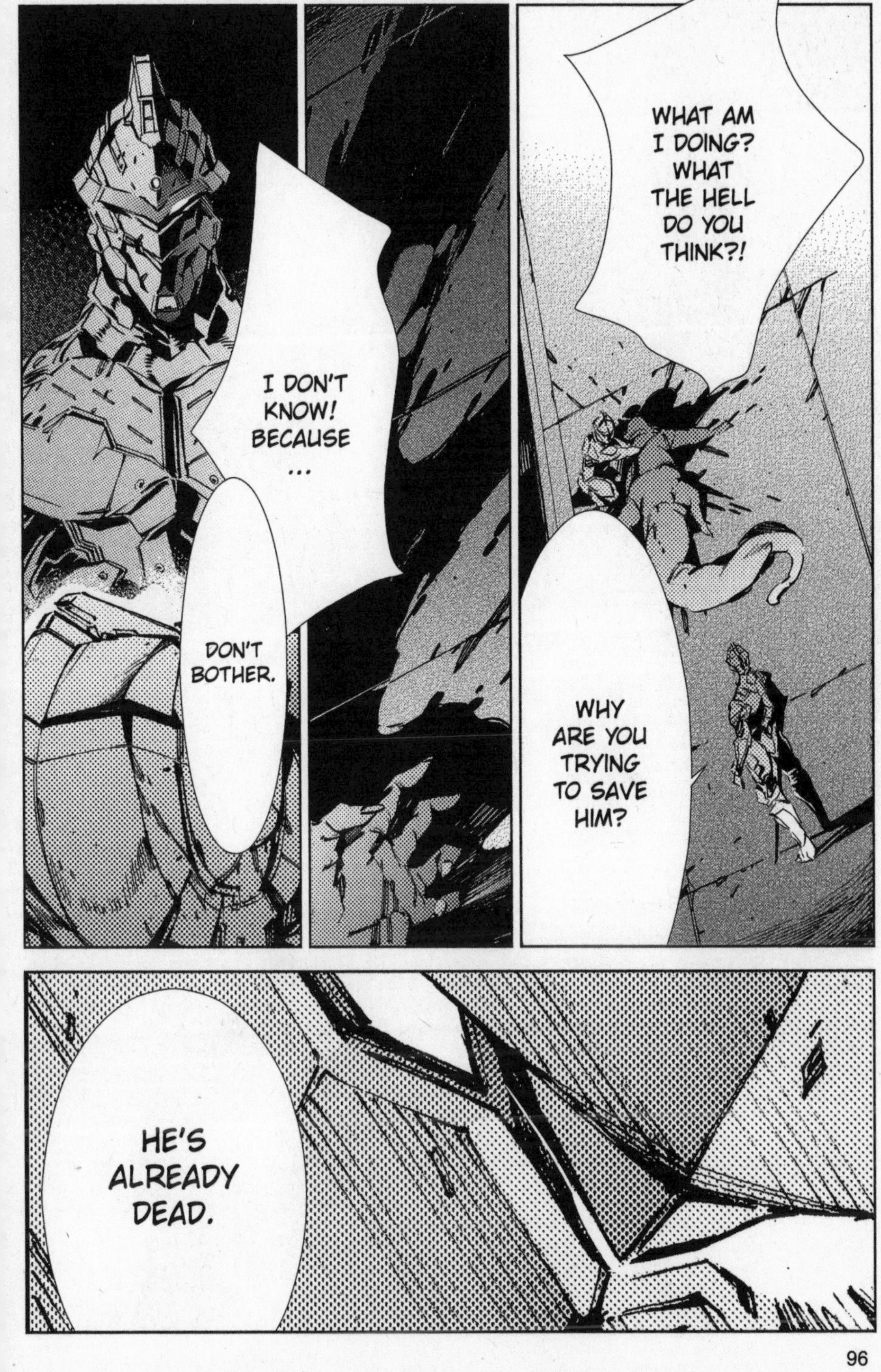
WHAT AM I DOING? WHAT THE HELL DO YOU THINK?!
WHY ARE YOU TRYING TO SAVE HIM?
I DON'T KNOW! BECAUSE ...
DON'T BOTHER.
HE'S ALREADY DEAD.

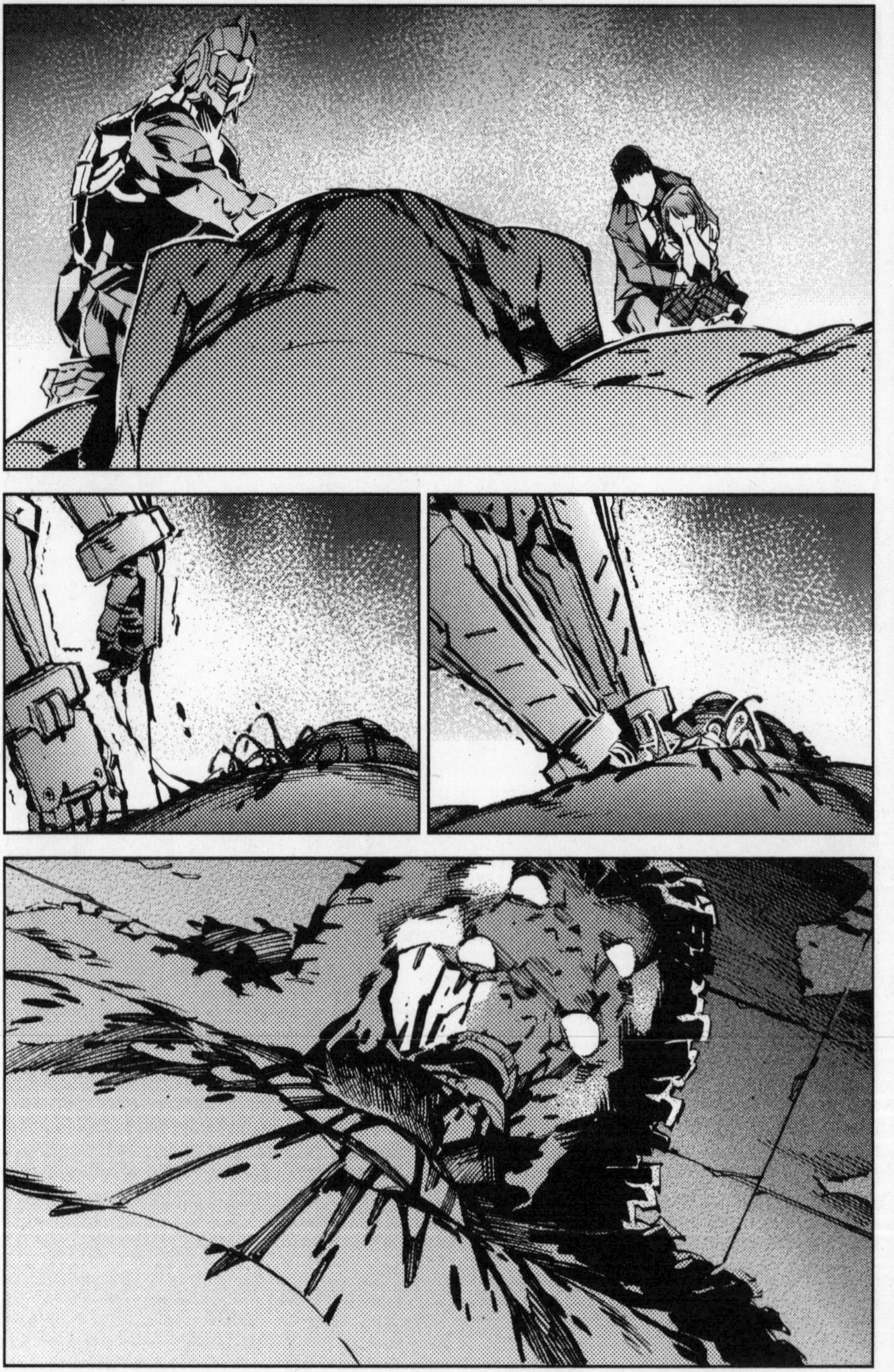

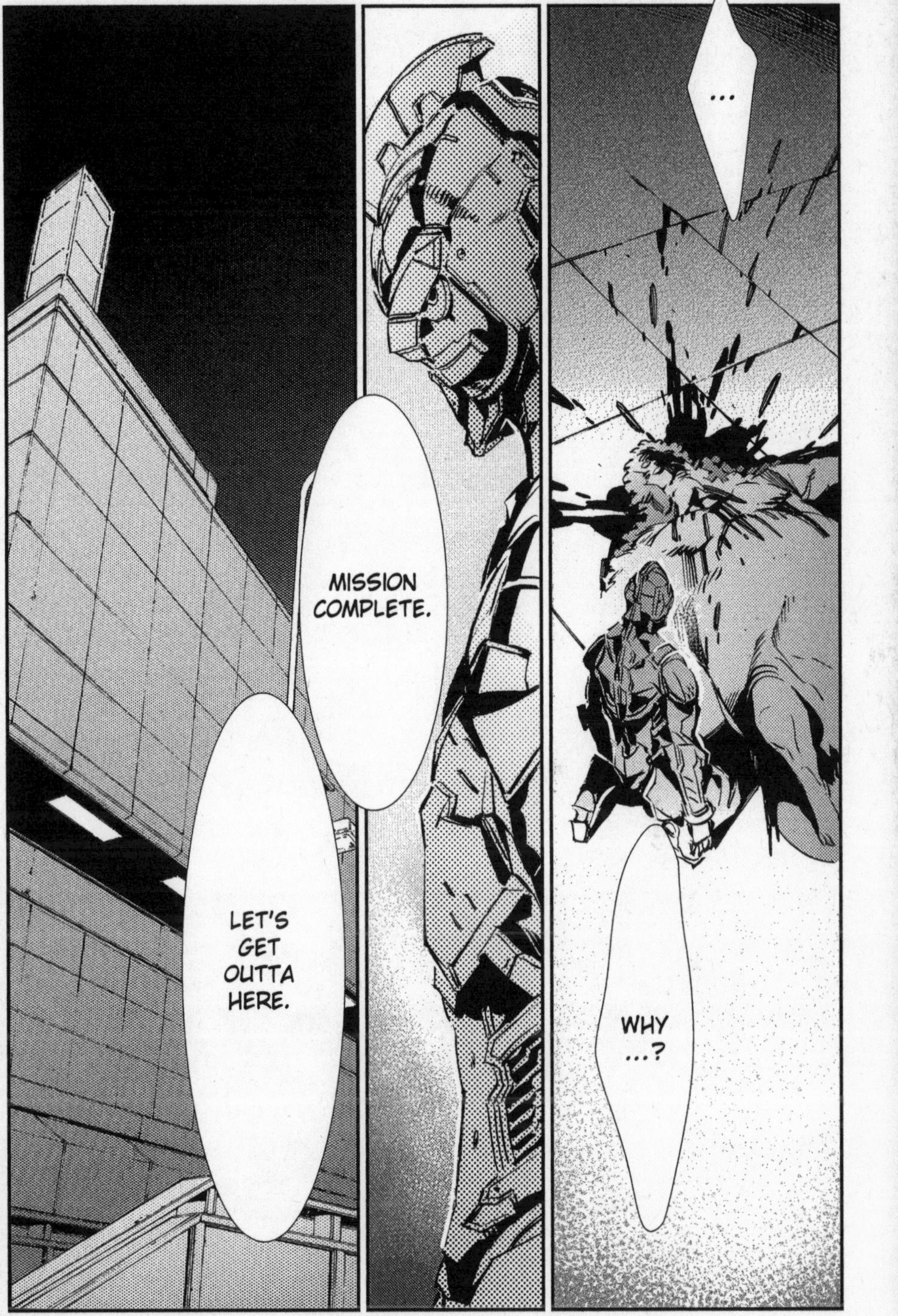
...
WHY ...?
MISSION COMPLETE.
LET'S GET OUTTA HERE.

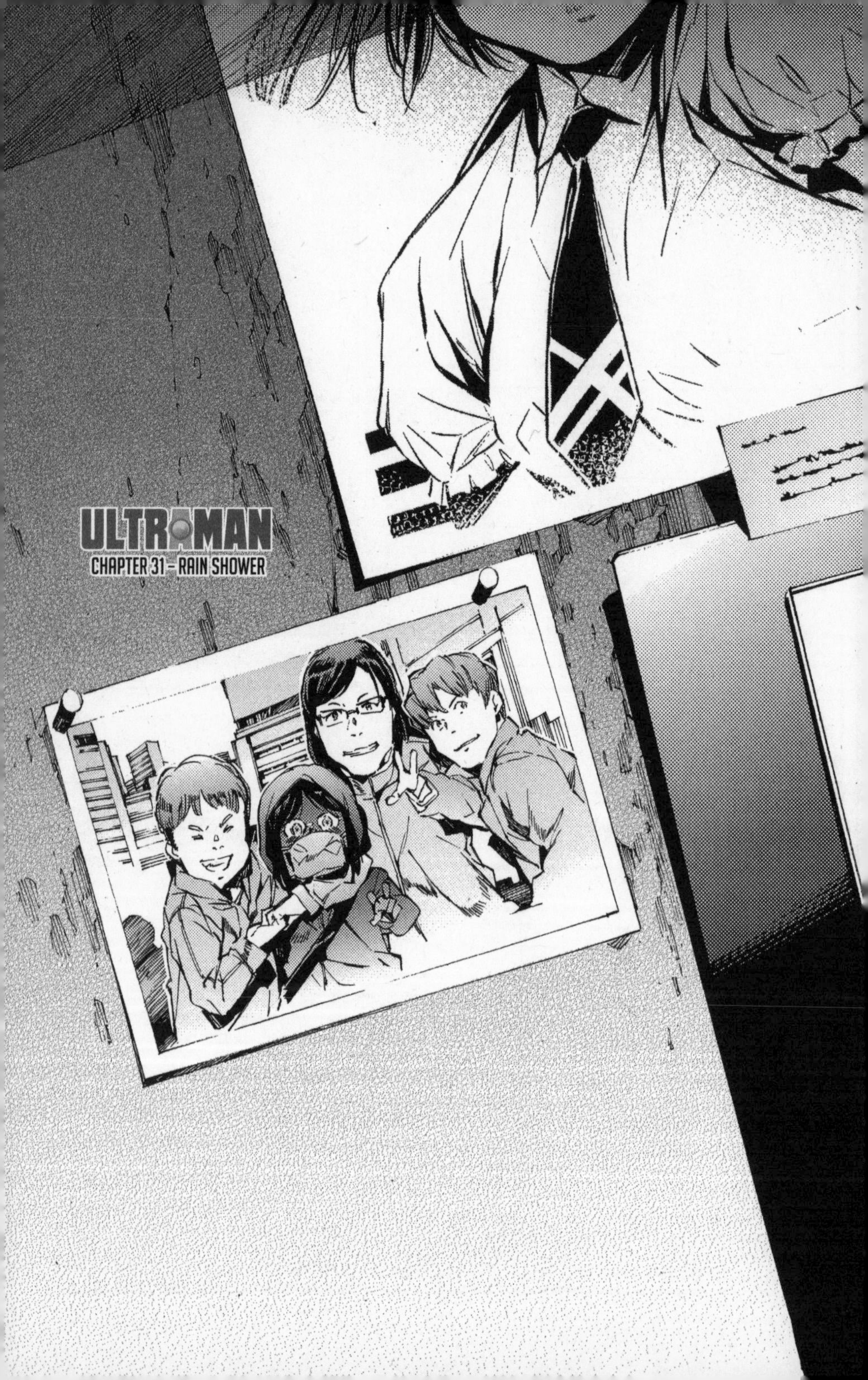
ULTRAMAN
CHAPTER 31 - RAIN SHOWER

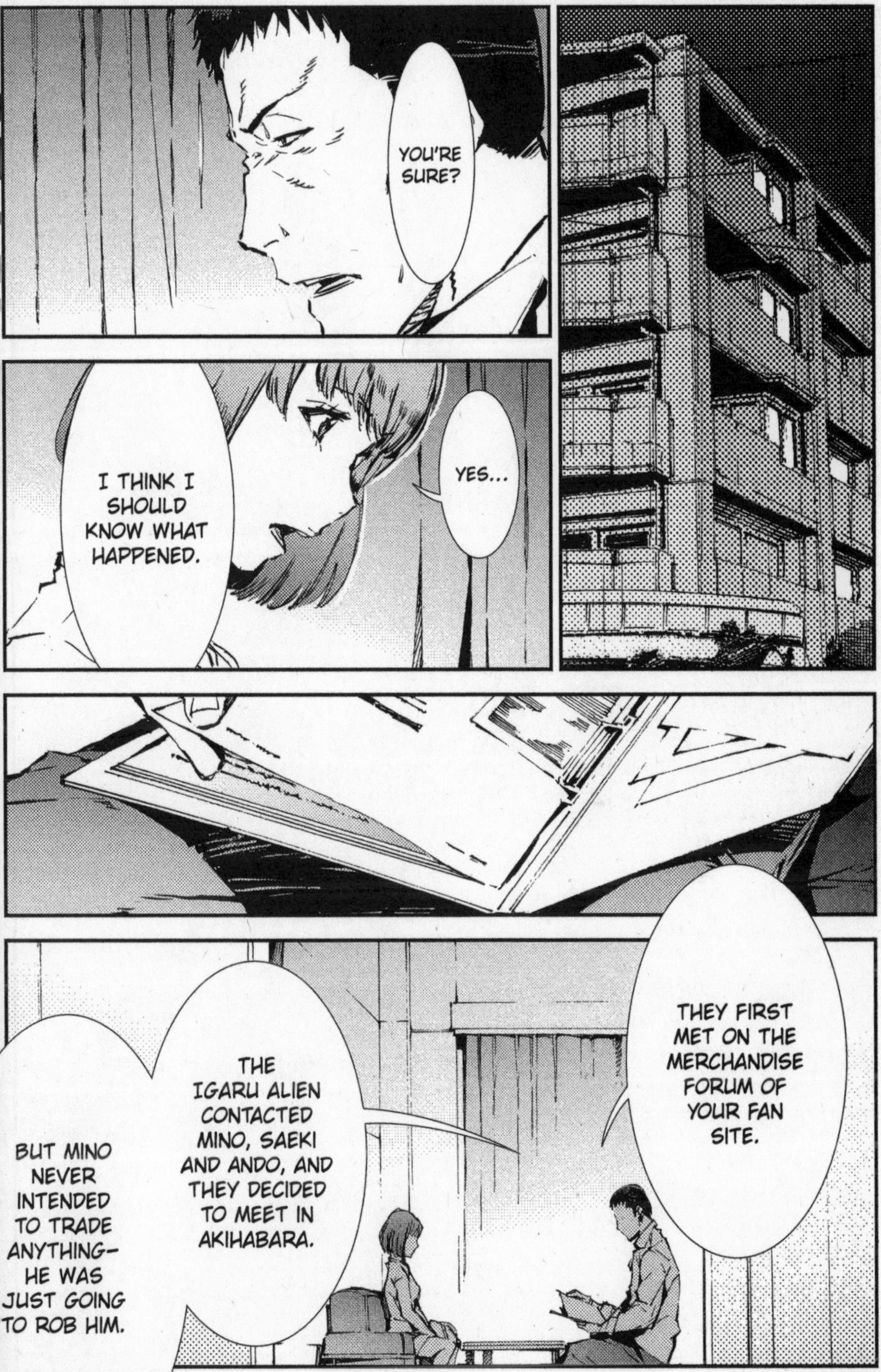
YOU'RE SURE?
YES...
I THINK I SHOULD KNOW WHAT HAPPENED.
THEY FIRST MET ON THE MERCHANDISE FORUM OF YOUR FAN SITE.
THE IGARU ALIEN CONTACTED MINO, SAEKI AND ANDO, AND THEY DECIDED TO MEET IN AKIHABARA.
BUT MINO NEVER INTENDED TO TRADE ANYTHING—HE WAS JUST GOING TO ROB HIM.

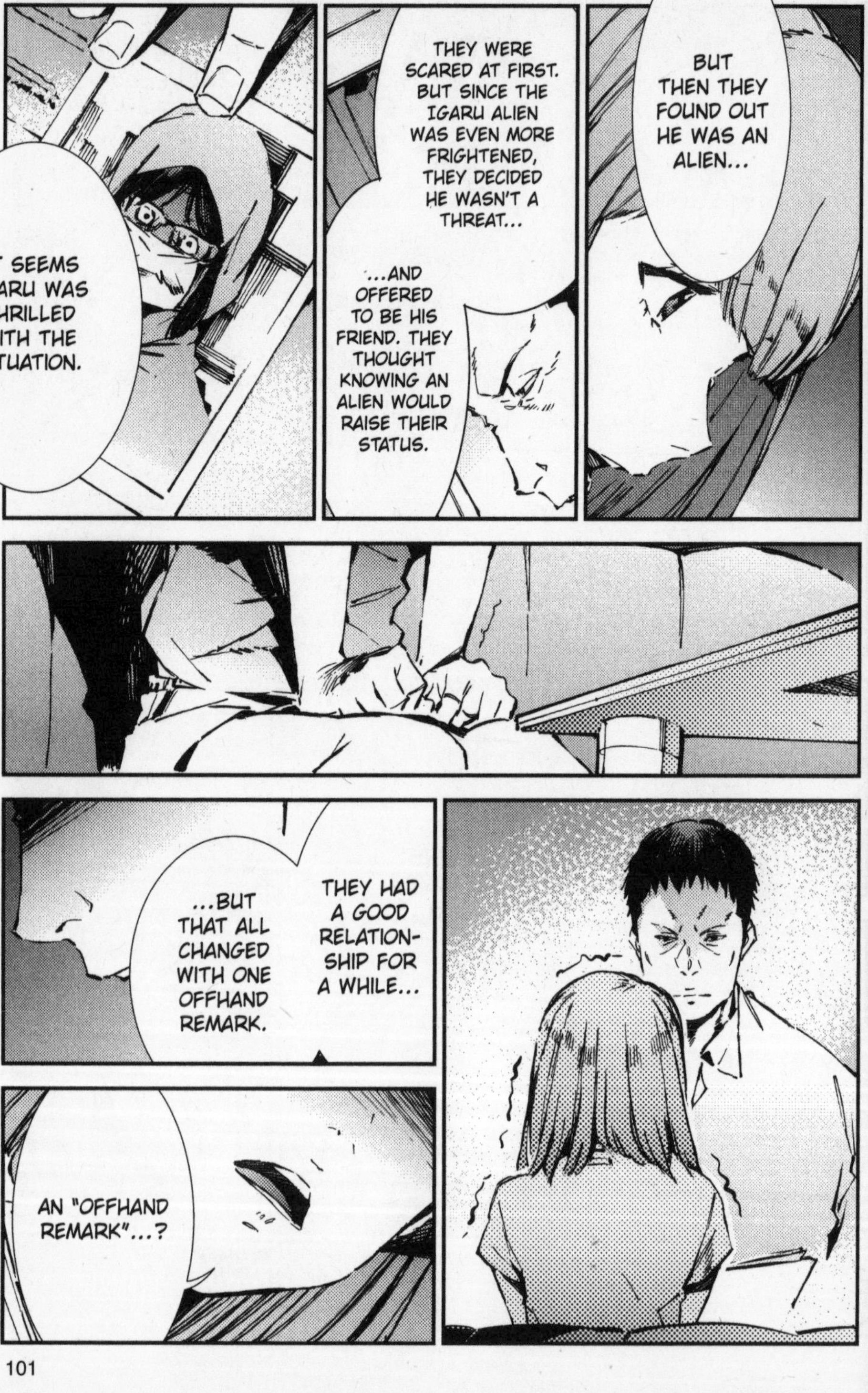
BUT THEN THEY FOUND OUT HE WAS AN ALIEN...
THEY WERE SCARED AT FIRST. BUT SINCE THE IGARU ALIEN WAS EVEN MORE FRIGHTENED, THEY DECIDED HE WASN'T A THREAT...
...AND OFFERED TO BE HIS FRIEND. THEY THOUGHT KNOWING AN ALIEN WOULD RAISE THEIR STATUS.
IT SEEMS IGARU WAS THRILLED WITH THE SITUATION.
THEY HAD A GOOD RELATION-SHIP FOR A WHILE...
...BUT THAT ALL CHANGED WITH ONE OFFHAND REMARK.
AN "OFFHAND REMARK"...?

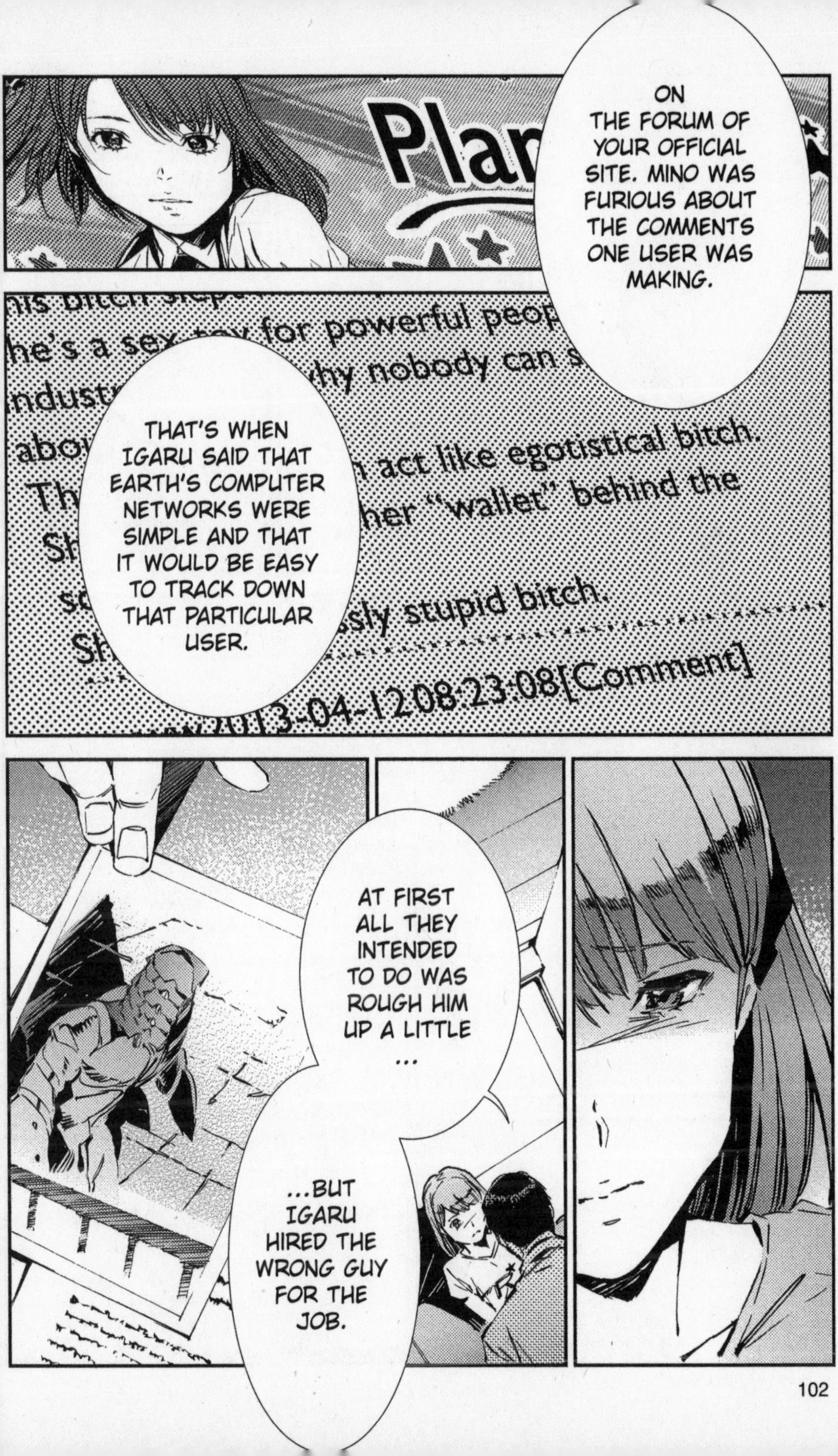
ON THE FORUM OF YOUR OFFICIAL SITE. MINO WAS FURIOUS ABOUT THE COMMENTS ONE USER WAS MAKING.
THAT'S WHEN IGARU SAID THAT EARTH'S COMPUTER NETWORKS WERE SIMPLE AND THAT IT WOULD BE EASY TO TRACK DOWN THAT PARTICULAR USER.
AT FIRST ALL THEY INTENDED TO DO WAS ROUGH HIM UP A LITTLE ...
...BUT IGARU HIRED THE WRONG GUY FOR THE JOB.

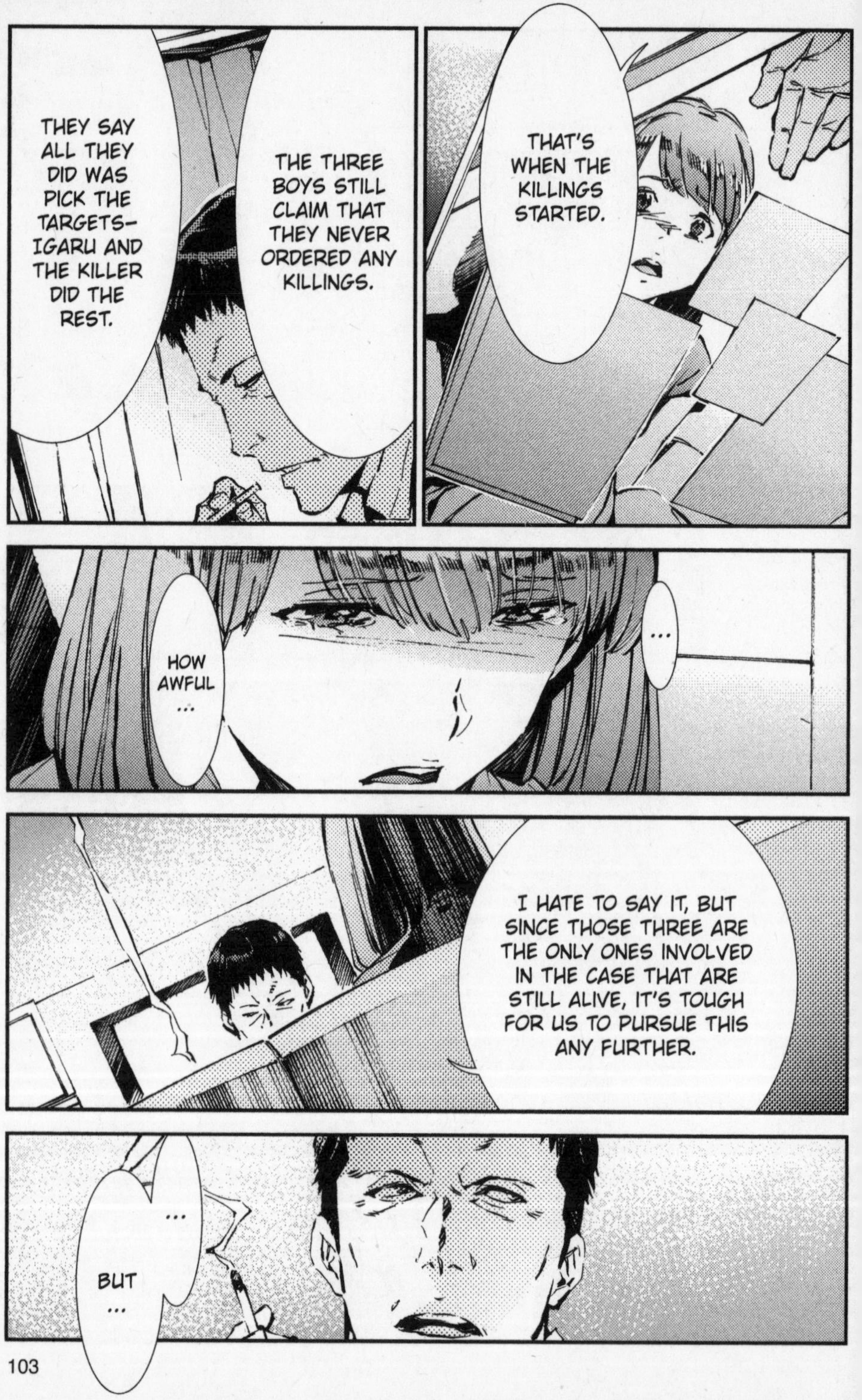
THAT'S WHEN THE KILLINGS STARTED.
THE THREE BOYS STILL CLAIM THAT THEY NEVER ORDERED ANY KILLINGS.
THEY SAY ALL THEY DID WAS PICK THE TARGETS— IGARU AND THE KILLER DID THE REST.
...
HOW AWFUL ...
I HATE TO SAY IT, BUT SINCE THOSE THREE ARE THE ONLY ONES INVOLVED IN THE CASE THAT ARE STILL ALIVE, IT'S TOUGH FOR US TO PURSUE THIS ANY FURTHER.
...
BUT ...

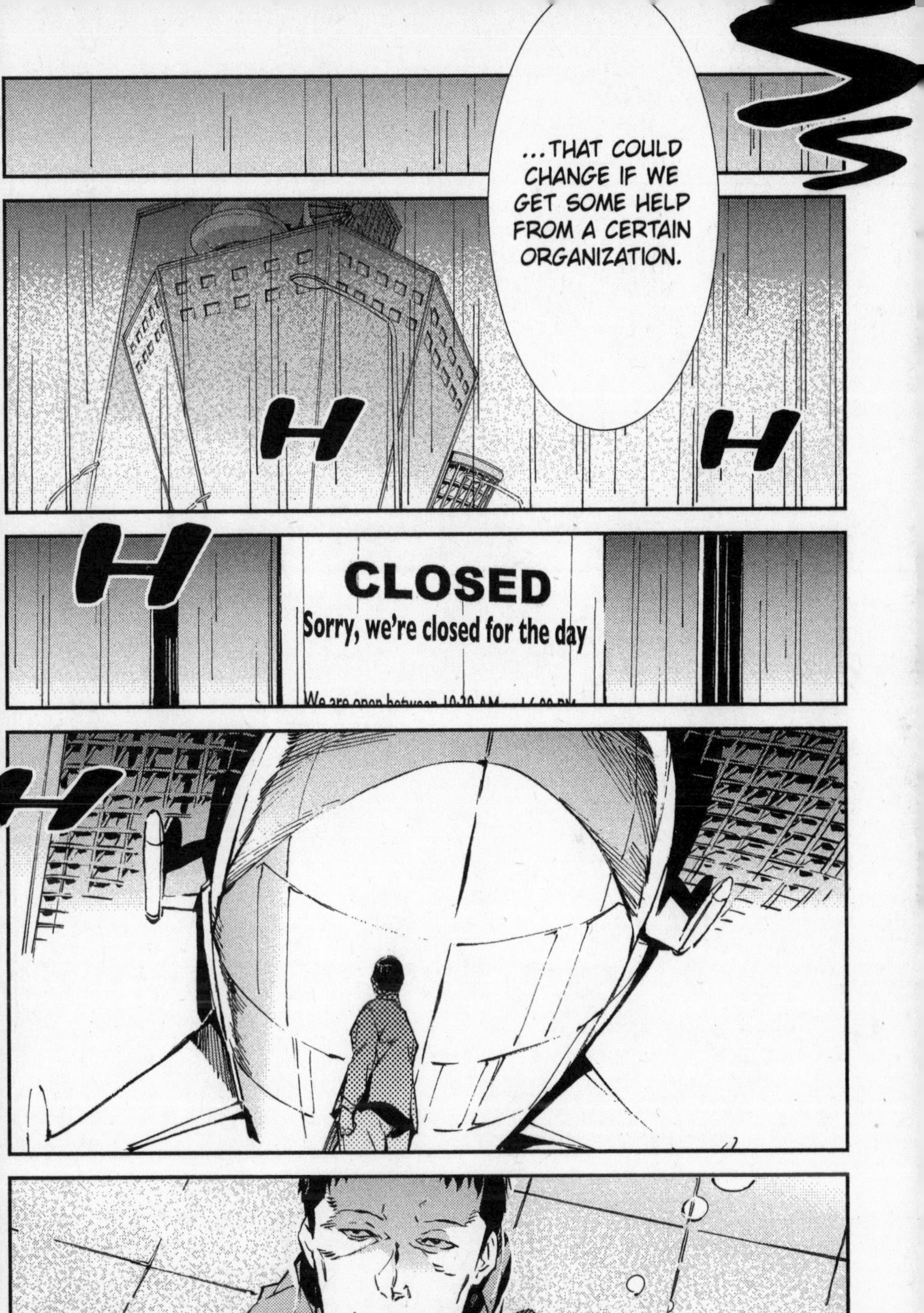
...THAT COULD CHANGE IF WE GET SOME HELP FROM A CERTAIN ORGANIZATION.
H
H
H
CLOSED
Sorry, we're closed for the day
H

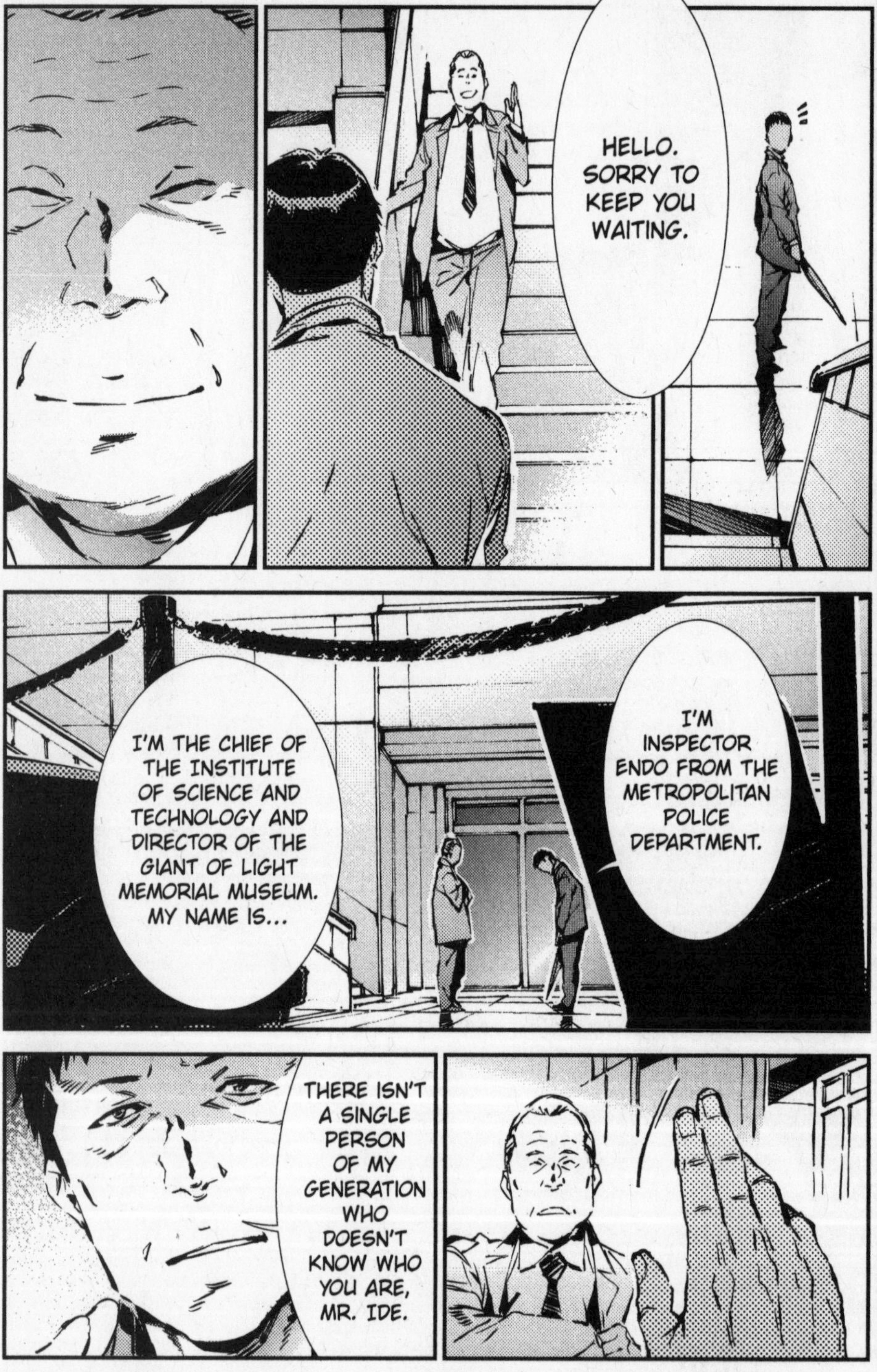
HELLO. SORRY TO KEEP YOU WAITING.
I'M INSPECTOR ENDO FROM THE METROPOLITAN POLICE DEPARTMENT.
I'M THE CHIEF OF THE INSTITUTE OF SCIENCE AND TECHNOLOGY AND DIRECTOR OF THE GIANT OF LIGHT MEMORIAL MUSEUM. MY NAME IS...
THERE ISN'T A SINGLE PERSON OF MY GENERATION WHO DOESN'T KNOW WHO YOU ARE, MR. IDE.

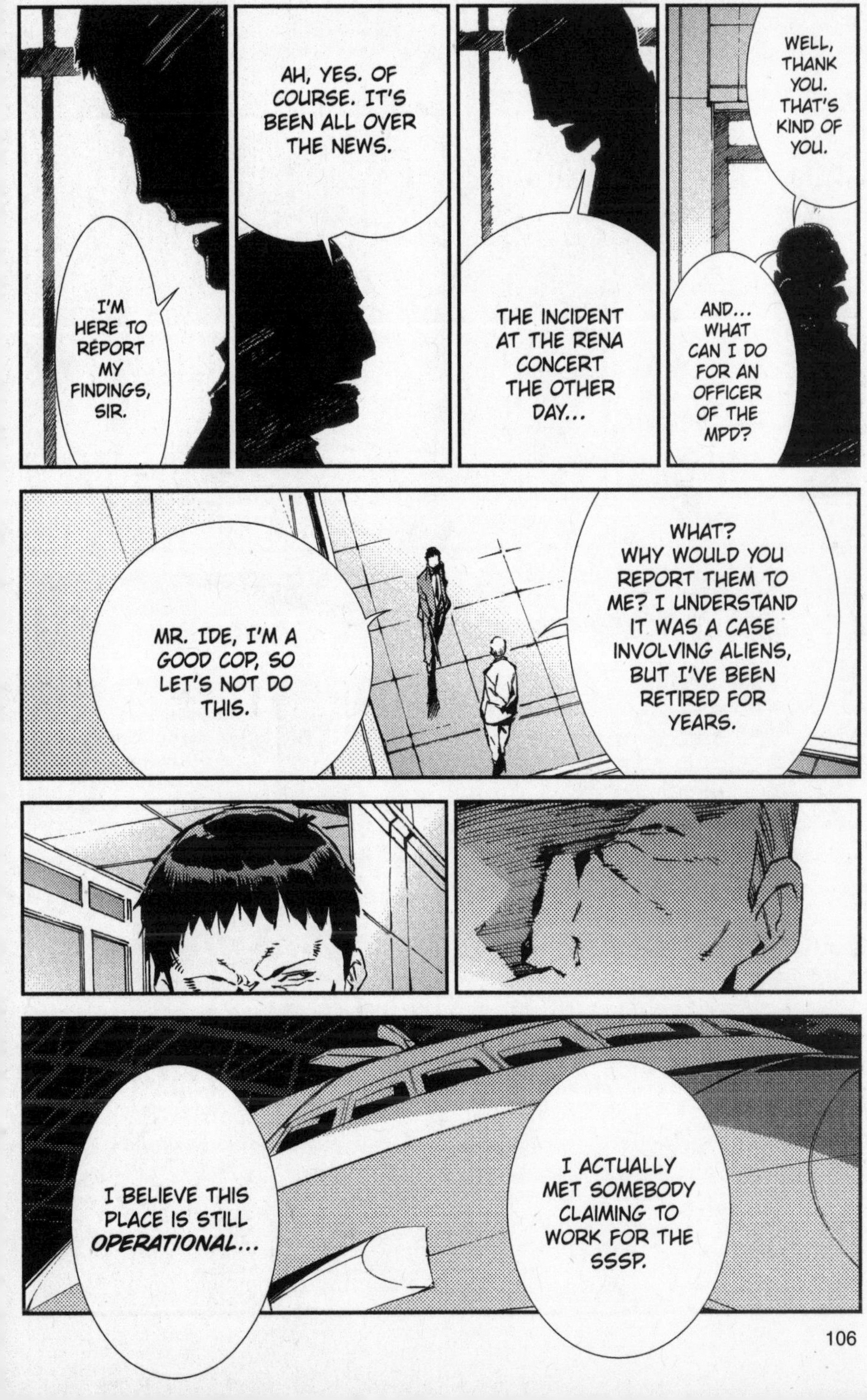
WELL, THANK YOU. THAT'S KIND OF YOU.
AND... WHAT CAN I DO FOR AN OFFICER OF THE MPD?
THE INCIDENT AT THE RENA CONCERT THE OTHER DAY...
AH, YES. OF COURSE. IT'S BEEN ALL OVER THE NEWS.
I'M HERE TO REPORT MY FINDINGS, SIR.
WHAT? WHY WOULD YOU REPORT THEM TO ME? I UNDERSTAND IT WAS A CASE INVOLVING ALIENS, BUT I'VE BEEN RETIRED FOR YEARS.
MR. IDE, I'M A GOOD COP, SO LET'S NOT DO THIS.
I ACTUALLY MET SOMEBODY CLAIMING TO WORK FOR THE SSSP.
I BELIEVE THIS PLACE IS STILL *OPERATIONAL*...

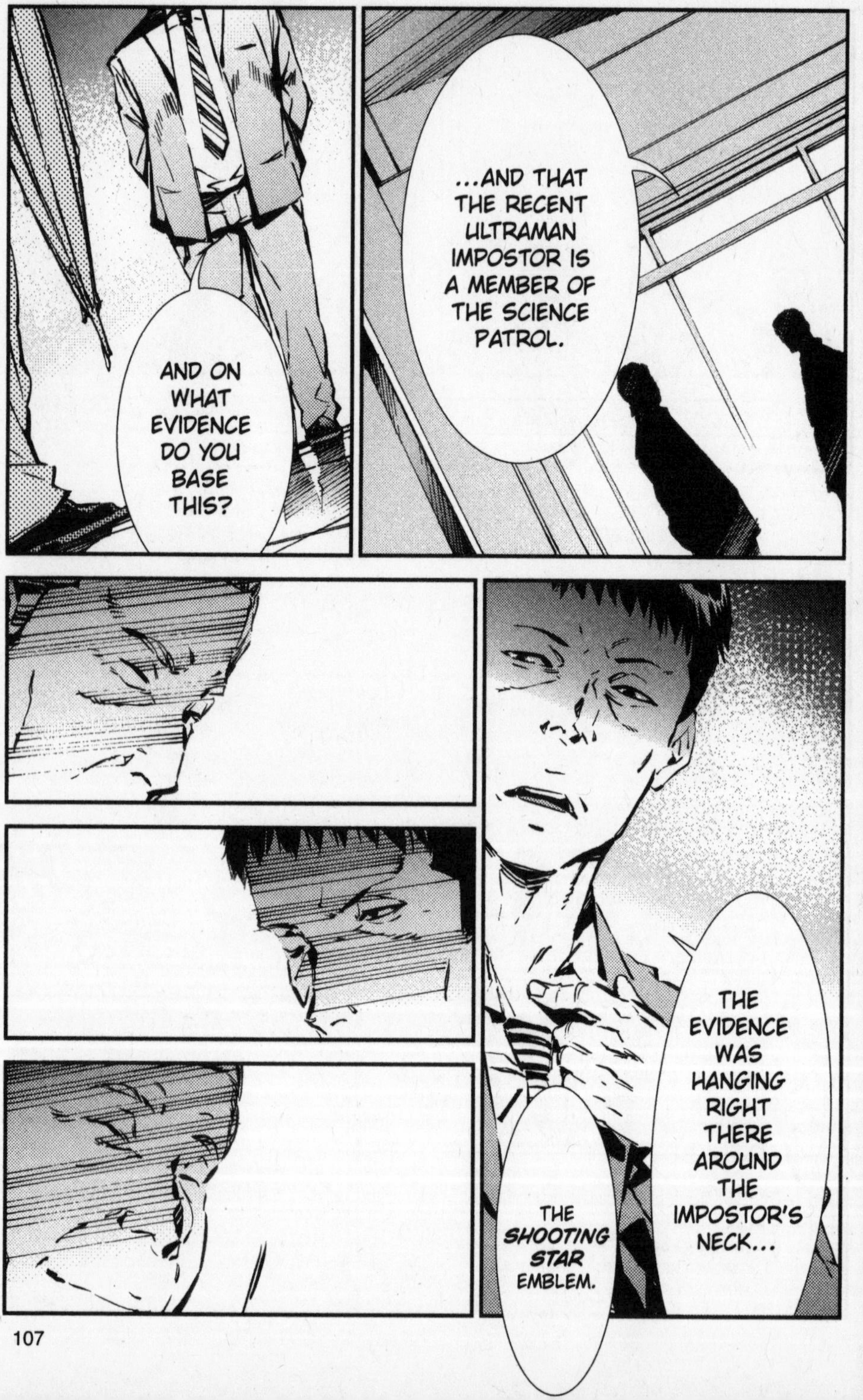
...AND THAT THE RECENT ULTRAMAN IMPOSTOR IS A MEMBER OF THE SCIENCE PATROL.
AND ON WHAT EVIDENCE DO YOU BASE THIS?
THE EVIDENCE WAS HANGING RIGHT THERE AROUND THE IMPOSTOR'S NECK...
THE *SHOOTING STAR* EMBLEM.

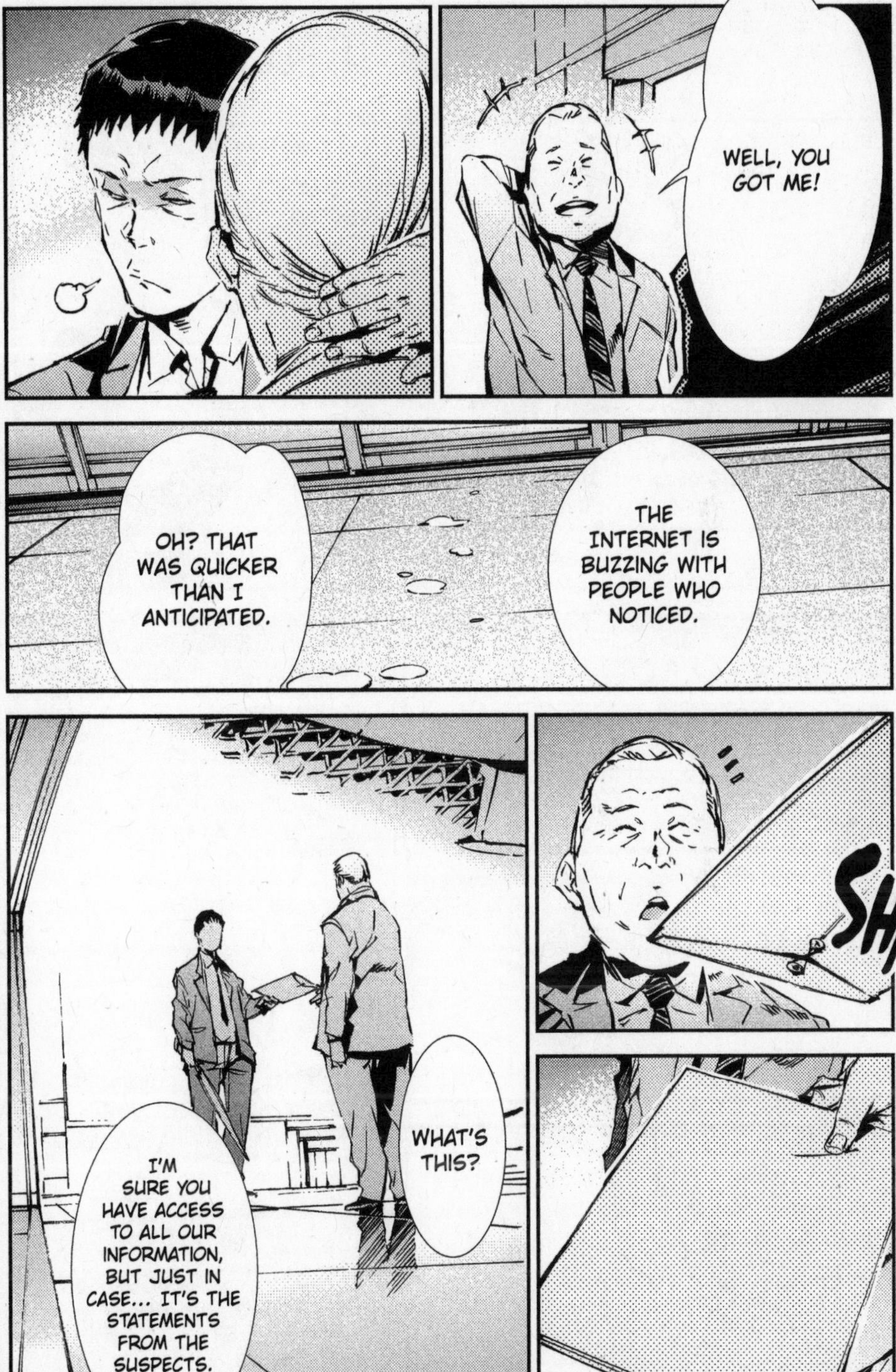
WELL, YOU GOT ME!
THE INTERNET IS BUZZING WITH PEOPLE WHO NOTICED.
OH? THAT WAS QUICKER THAN I ANTICIPATED.
SHF
WHAT'S THIS?
I'M SURE YOU HAVE ACCESS TO ALL OUR INFORMATION, BUT JUST IN CASE... IT'S THE STATEMENTS FROM THE SUSPECTS.

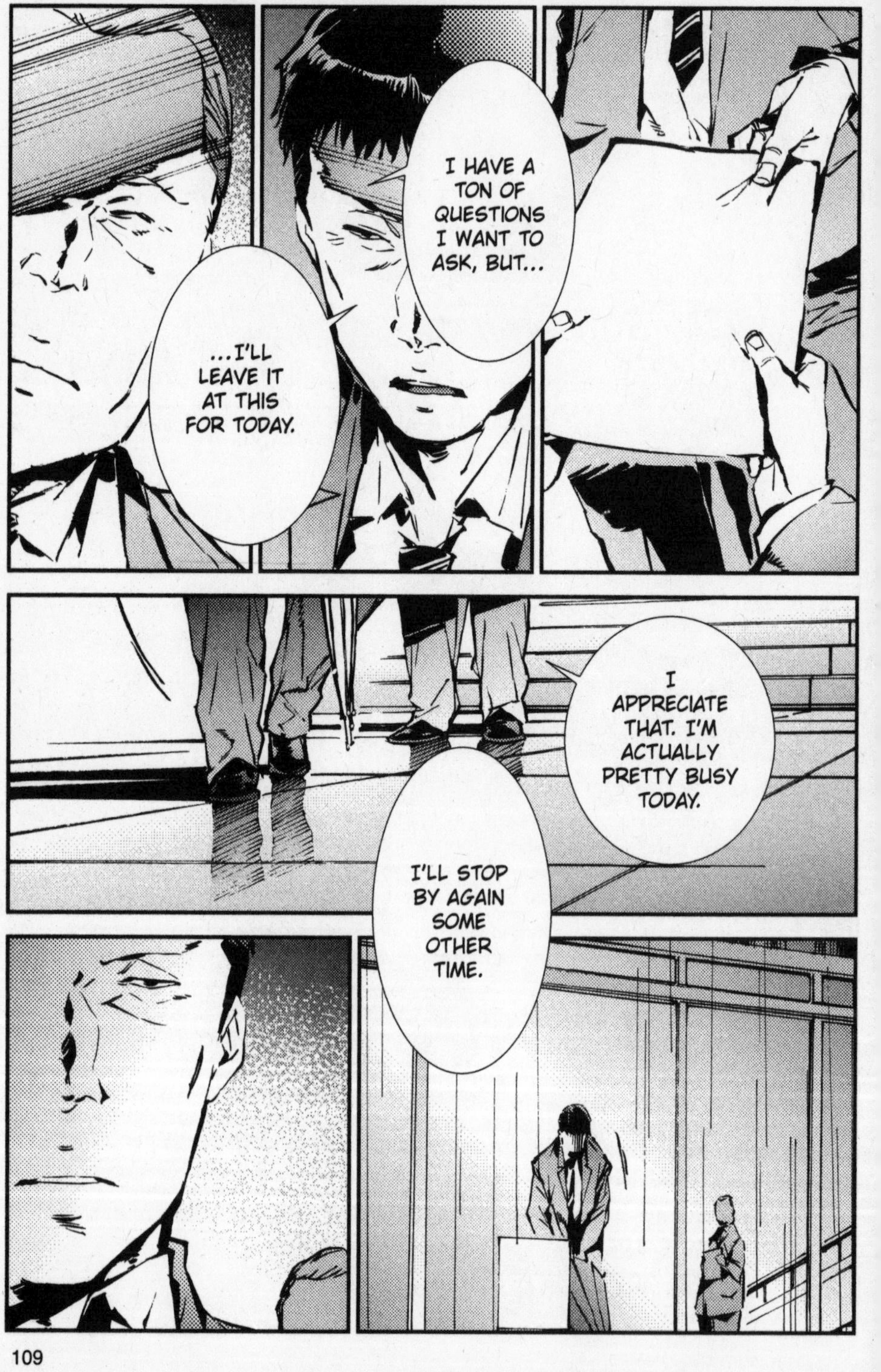
I HAVE A TON OF QUESTIONS I WANT TO ASK, BUT...
...I'LL LEAVE IT AT THIS FOR TODAY.
I APPRECIATE THAT. I'M ACTUALLY PRETTY BUSY TODAY.
I'LL STOP BY AGAIN SOME OTHER TIME.

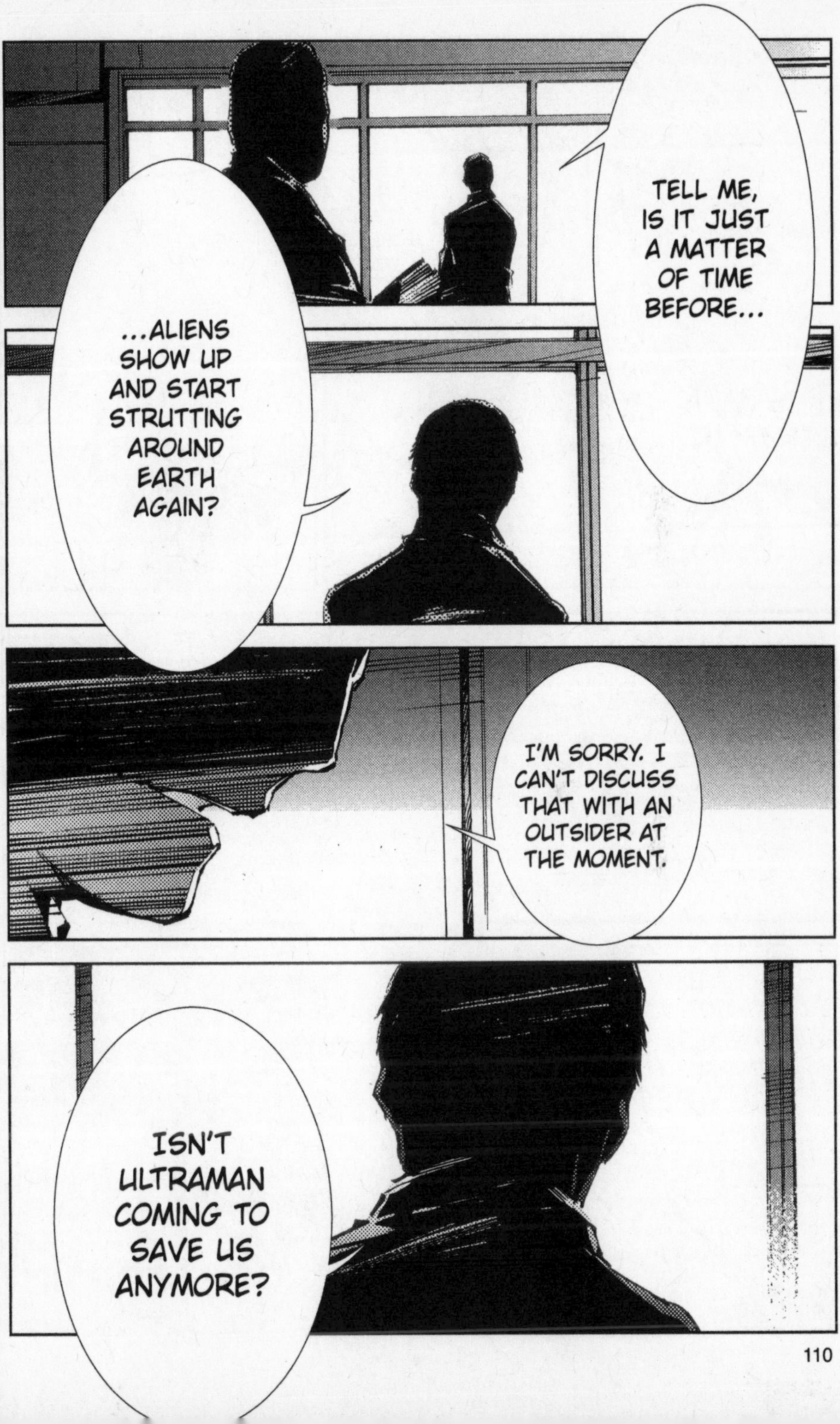
TELL ME, IS IT JUST A MATTER OF TIME BEFORE...
...ALIENS SHOW UP AND START STRUTTING AROUND EARTH AGAIN?
I'M SORRY. I CAN'T DISCUSS THAT WITH AN OUTSIDER AT THE MOMENT.
ISN'T ULTRAMAN COMING TO SAVE US ANYMORE?

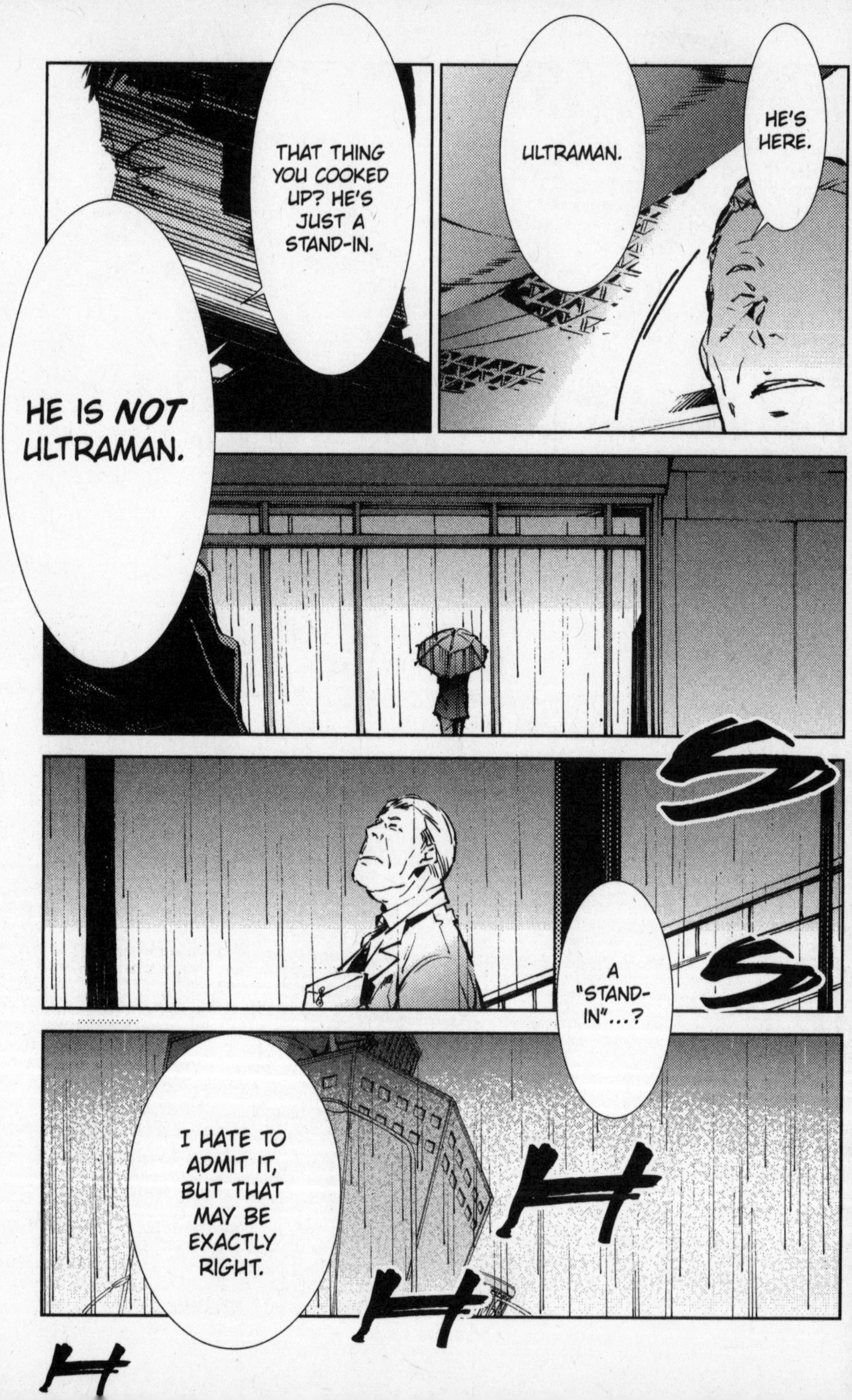
HE'S HERE.
ULTRAMAN.
THAT THING YOU COOKED UP? HE'S JUST A STAND-IN.
HE IS *NOT* ULTRAMAN.
S
S
A "STAND-IN"...?
I HATE TO ADMIT IT, BUT THAT MAY BE EXACTLY RIGHT.
H
H
H

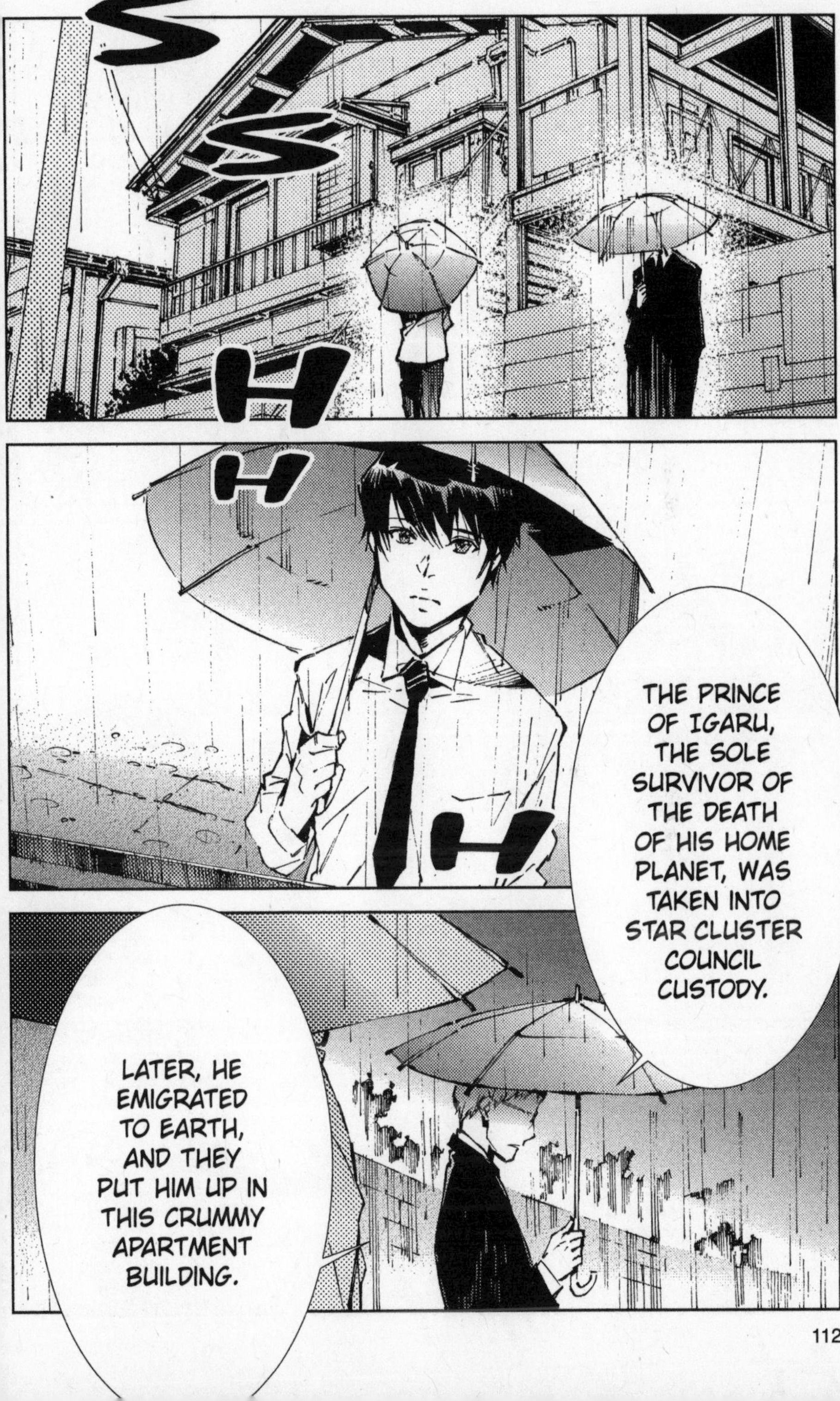
SHHH
THE PRINCE OF IGARU, THE SOLE SURVIVOR OF THE DEATH OF HIS HOME PLANET, WAS TAKEN INTO STAR CLUSTER COUNCIL CUSTODY.
LATER, HE EMIGRATED TO EARTH, AND THEY PUT HIM UP IN THIS CRUMMY APARTMENT BUILDING.

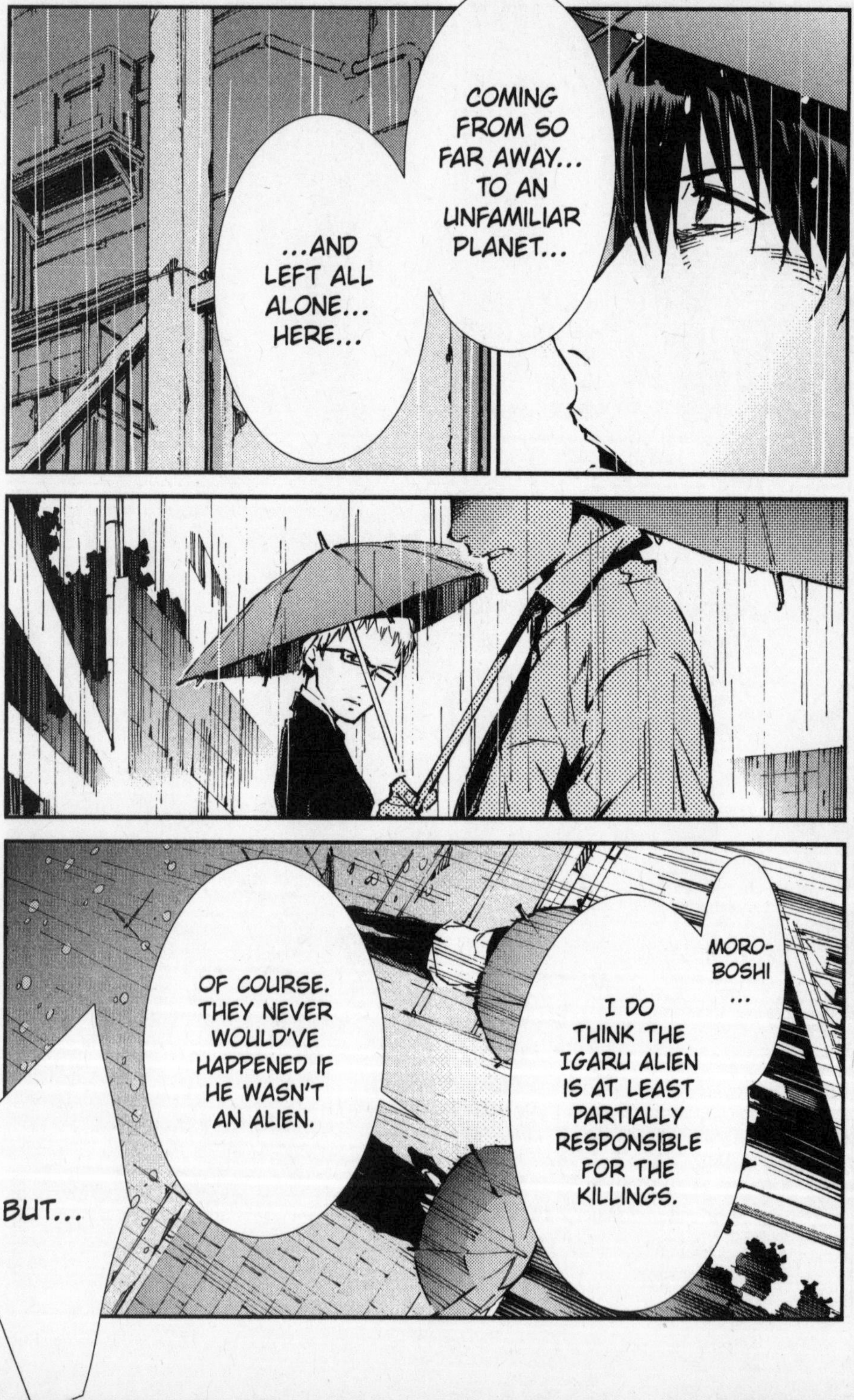
COMING FROM SO FAR AWAY... TO AN UNFAMILIAR PLANET...
...AND LEFT ALL ALONE... HERE...
MORO-BOSHI...
I DO THINK THE IGARU ALIEN IS AT LEAST PARTIALLY RESPONSIBLE FOR THE KILLINGS.
OF COURSE. THEY NEVER WOULD'VE HAPPENED IF HE WASN'T AN ALIEN.
BUT...

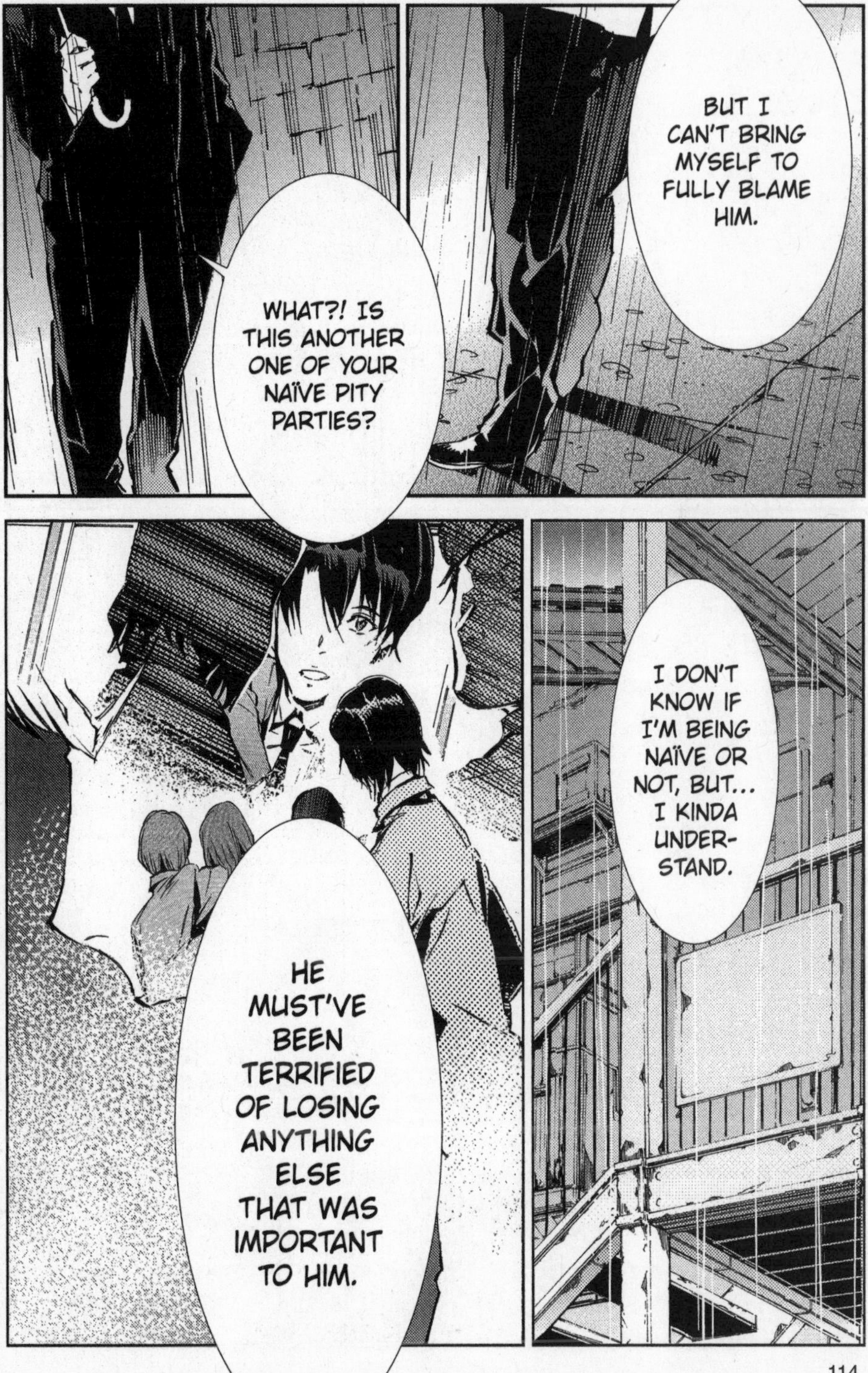
BUT I CAN'T BRING MYSELF TO FULLY BLAME HIM.
WHAT?! IS THIS ANOTHER ONE OF YOUR NAÏVE PITY PARTIES?
I DON'T KNOW IF I'M BEING NAÏVE OR NOT, BUT... I KINDA UNDER-STAND.
HE MUST'VE BEEN TERRIFIED OF LOSING ANYTHING ELSE THAT WAS IMPORTANT TO HIM.

THAT DOESN'T GIVE HIM THE RIGHT TO TAKE SOMETHING THAT'S IMPORTANT TO SOMEONE ELSE.
I KNOW ...
THAT'S WHY ...

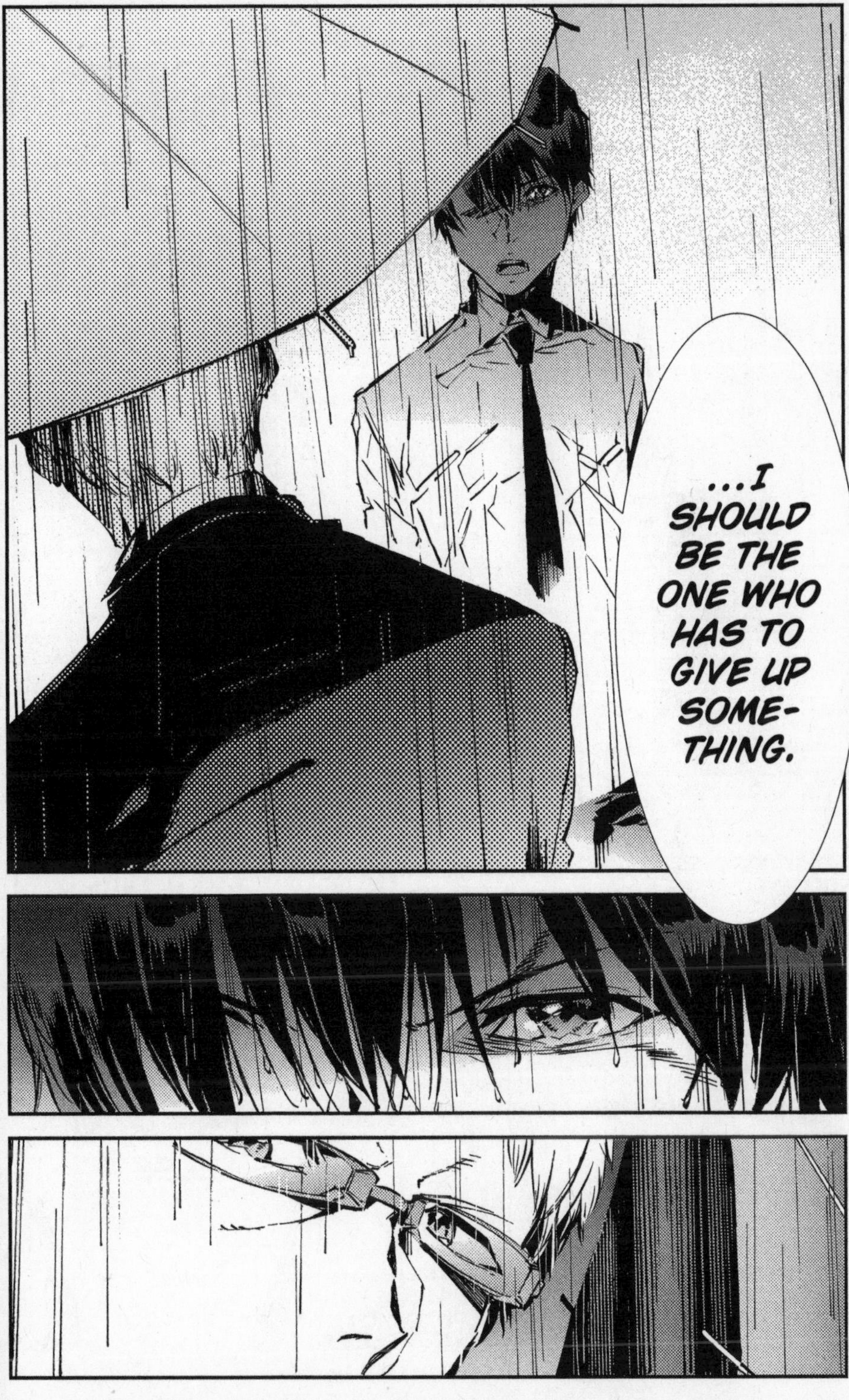
...I SHOULD BE THE ONE WHO HAS TO GIVE UP SOME-THING.

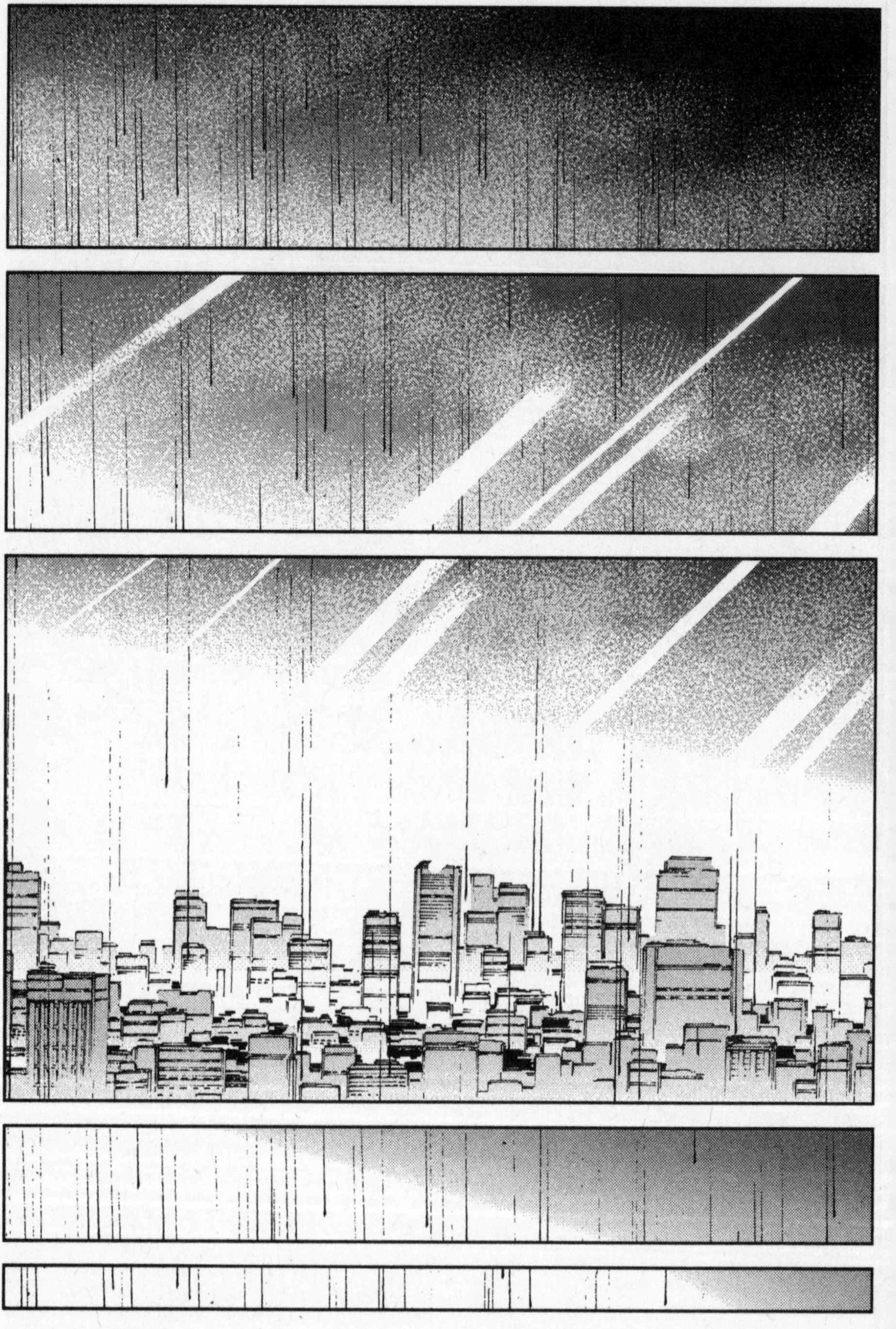

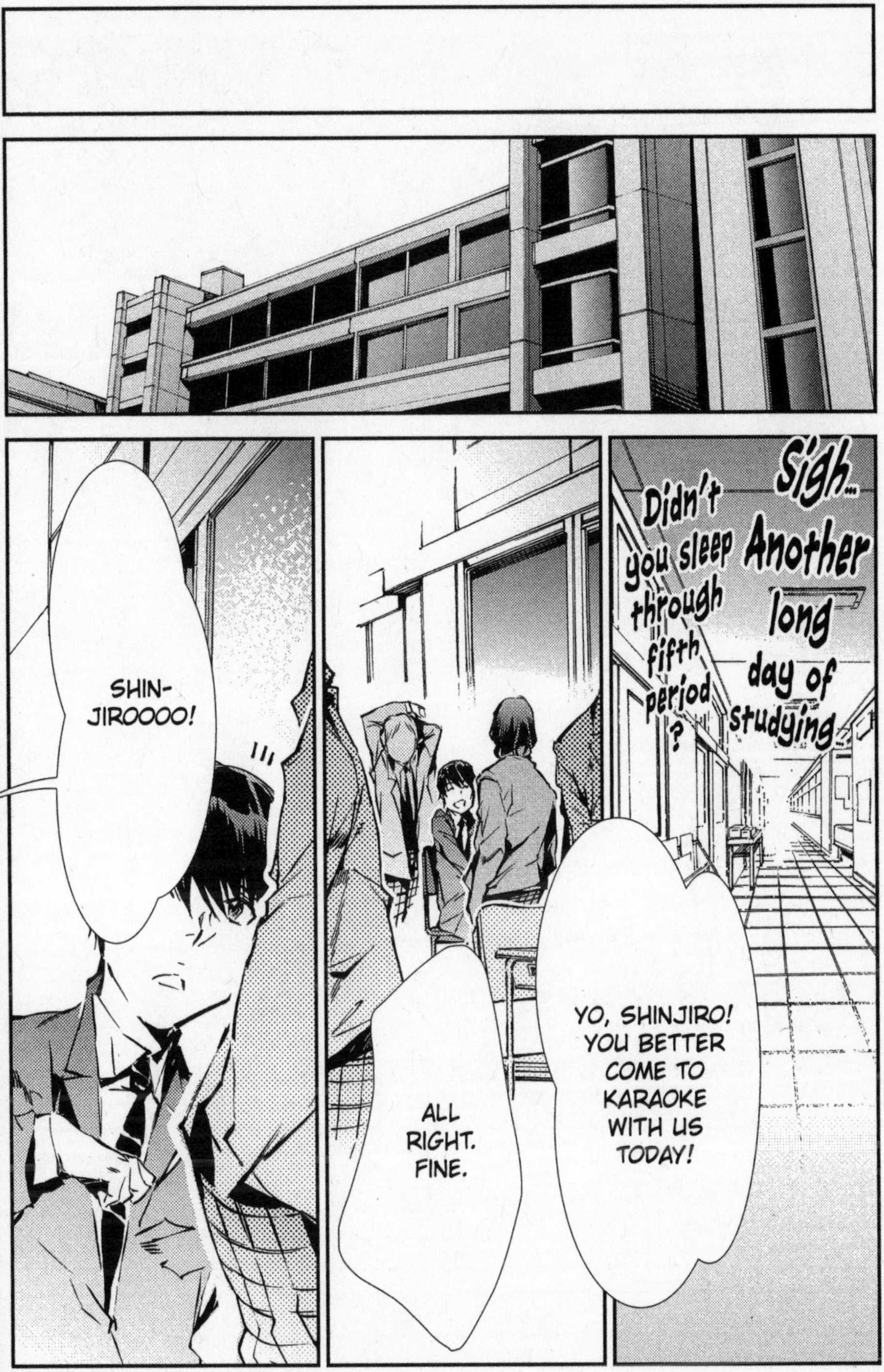
Sigh... Another long day of studying...
Didn't you sleep through fifth period?
YO, SHINJIRO! YOU BETTER COME TO KARAOKE WITH US TODAY!
ALL RIGHT. FINE.
SHIN-JIROOOO!

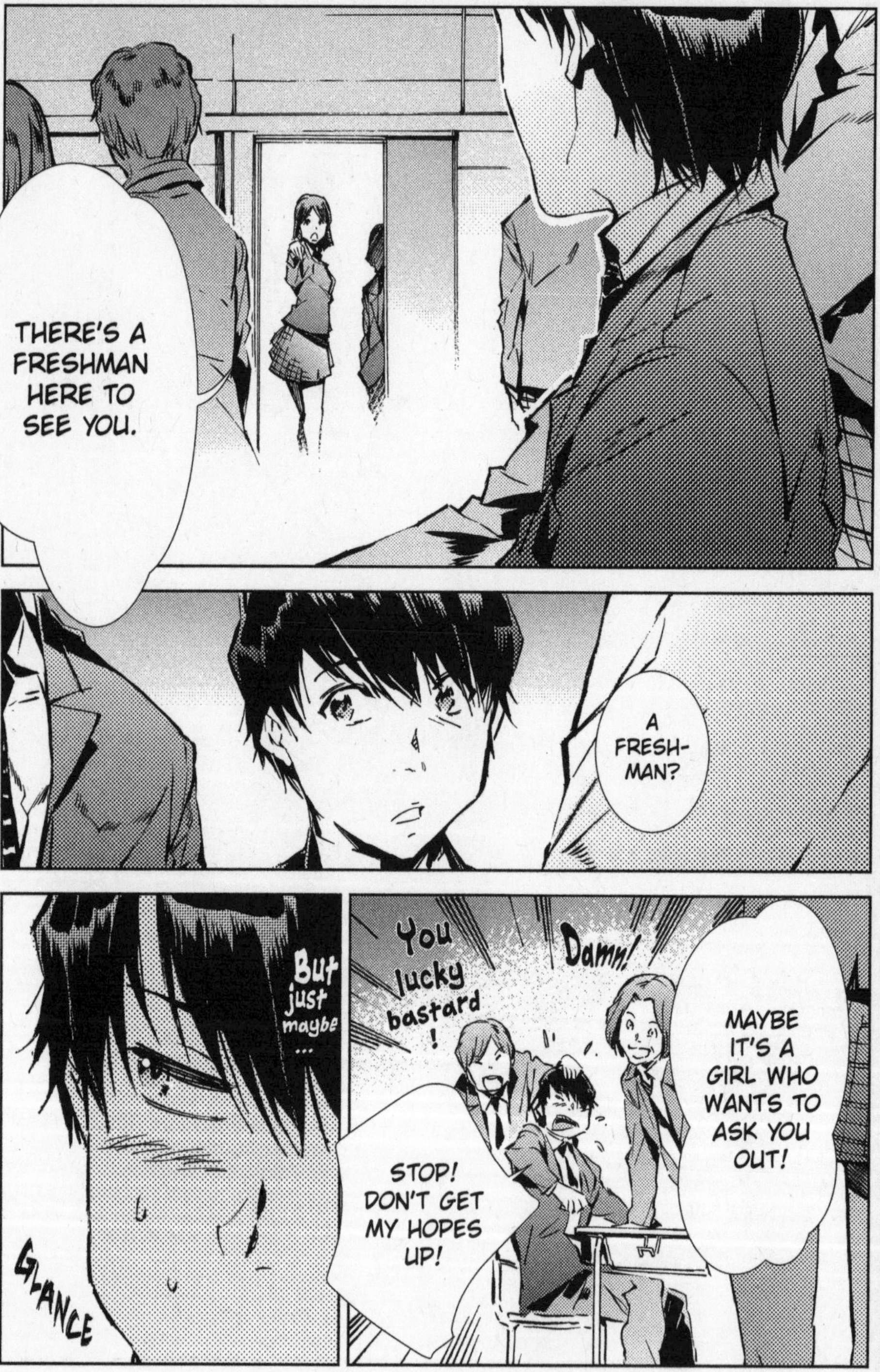
THERE'S A FRESHMAN HERE TO SEE YOU.
A FRESHMAN?
MAYBE IT'S A GIRL WHO WANTS TO ASK YOU OUT!
Damn!
You lucky bastard!
STOP! DON'T GET MY HOPES UP!
But just maybe...
GLANCE

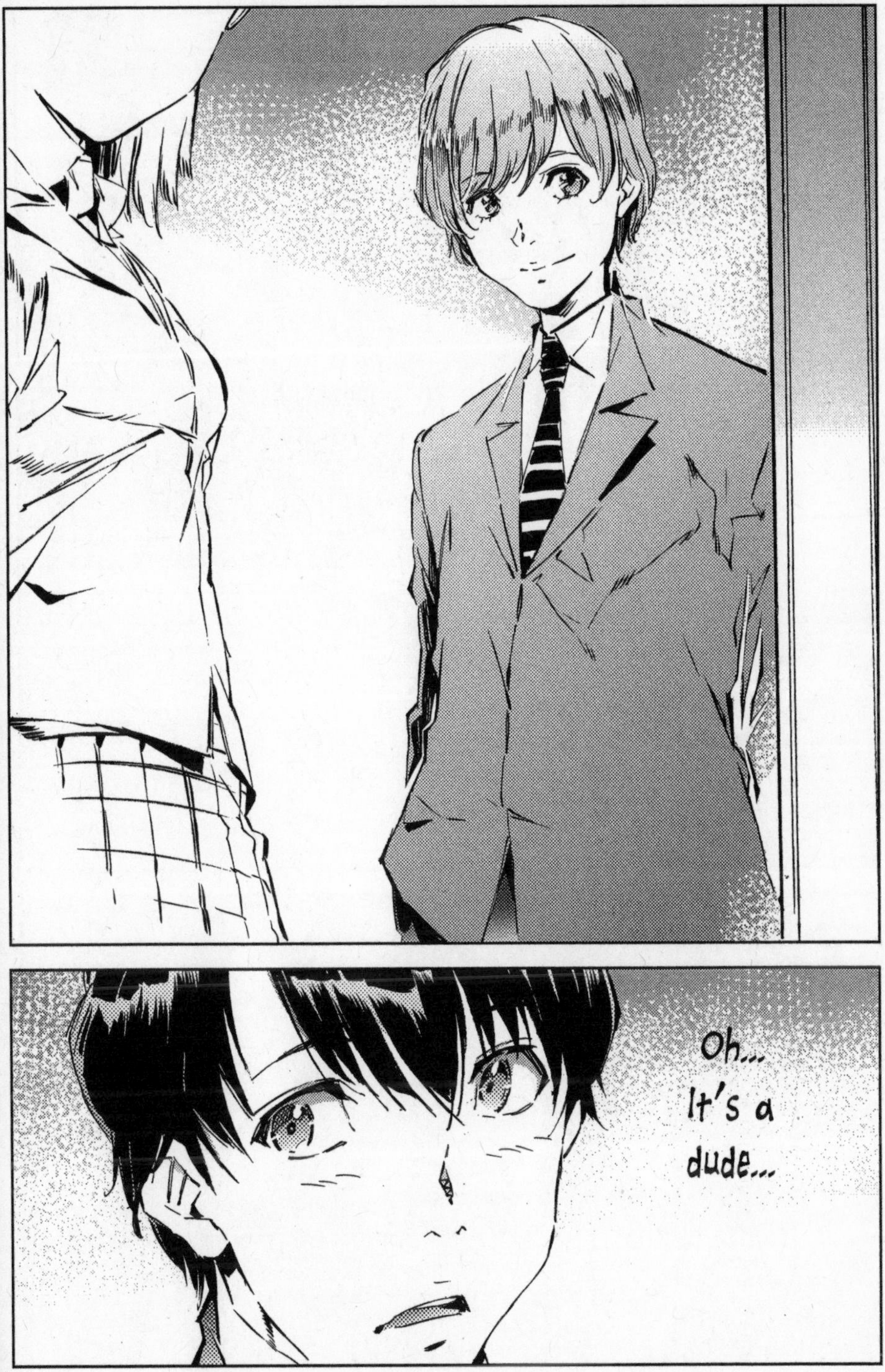
Oh... It's a dude...

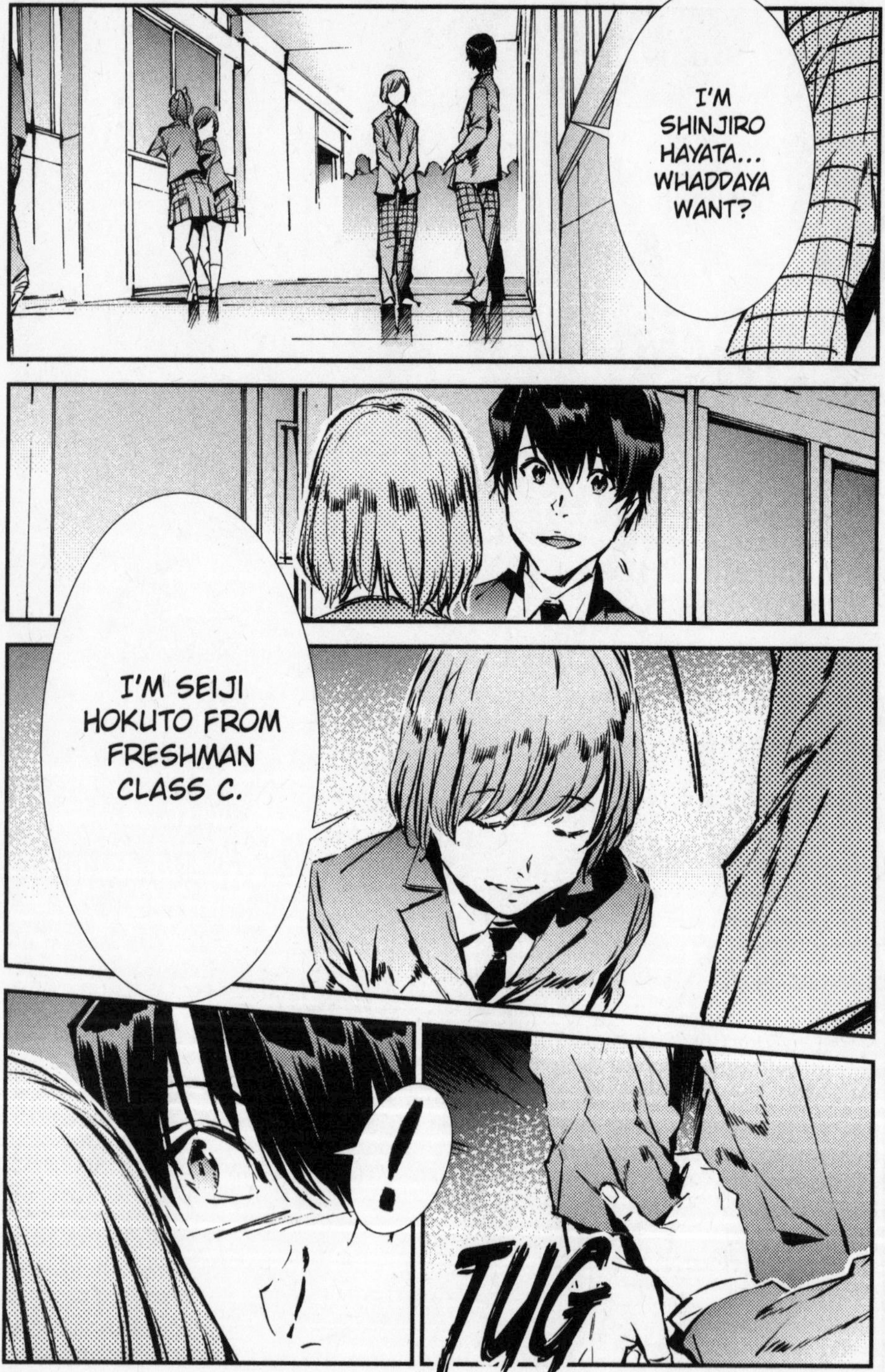
I'M SHINJIRO HAYATA... WHADDAYA WANT?
I'M SEIJI HOKUTO FROM FRESHMAN CLASS C.
TUG
!

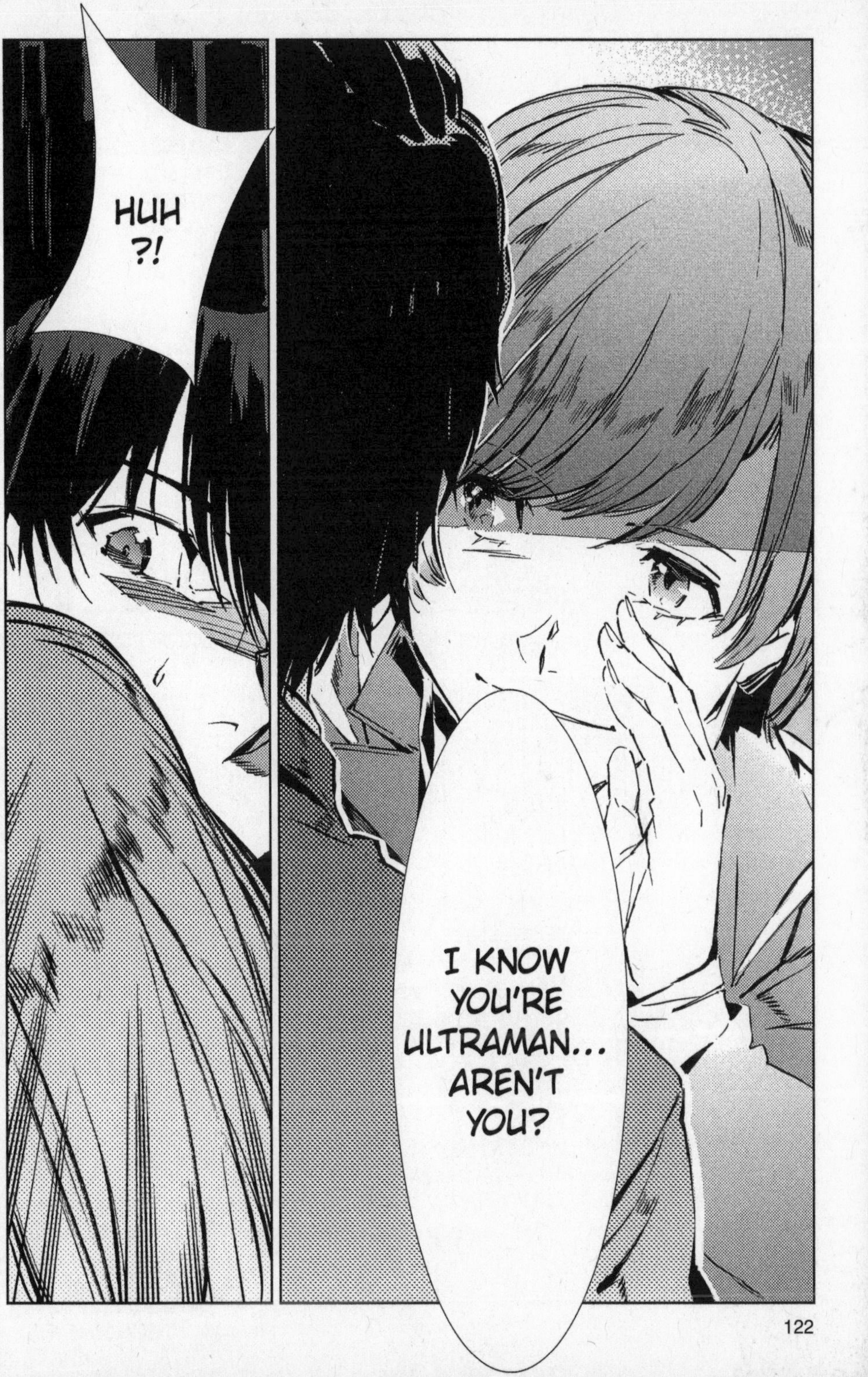
I KNOW YOU'RE ULTRAMAN... AREN'T YOU?
HUH ?!

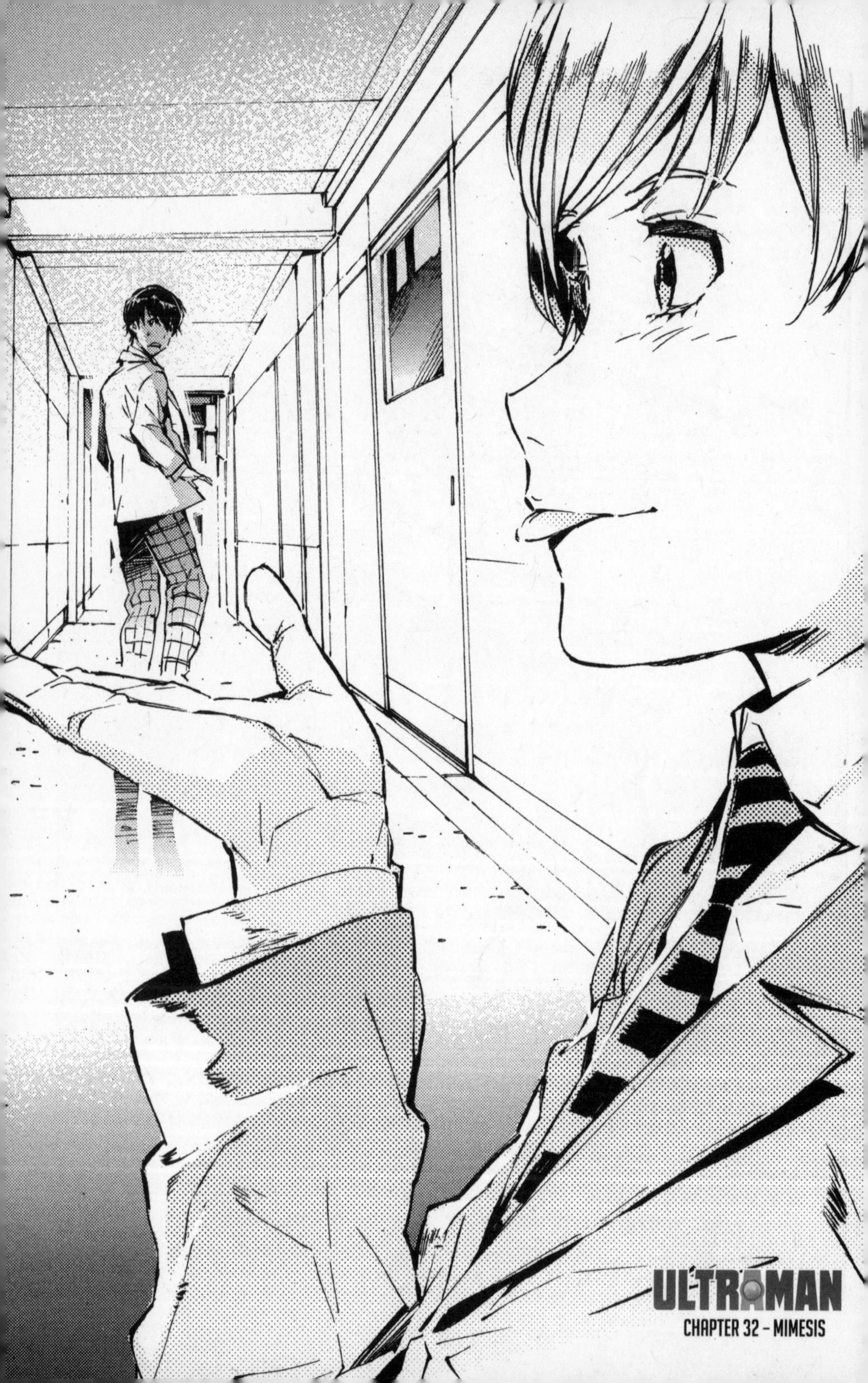
ULTRAMAN
CHAPTER 32 – MIMESIS

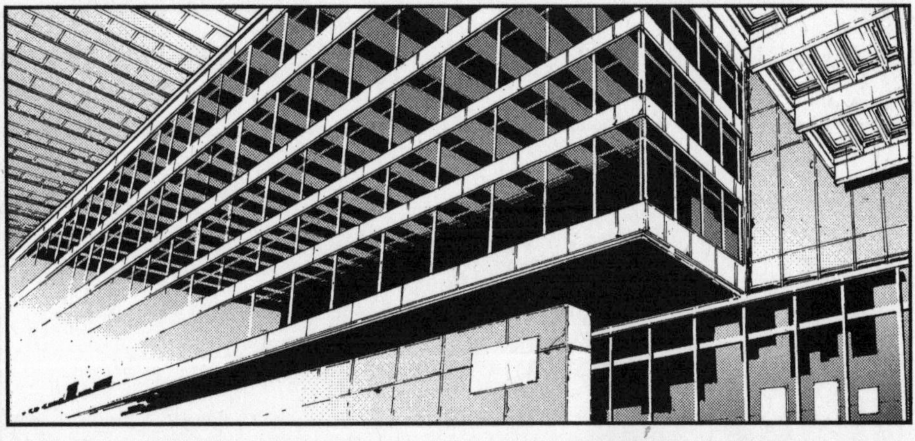
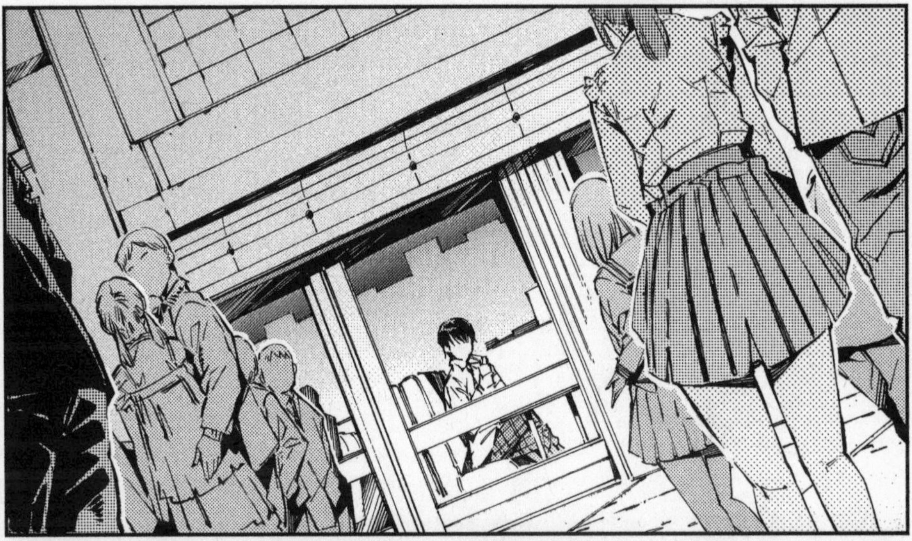
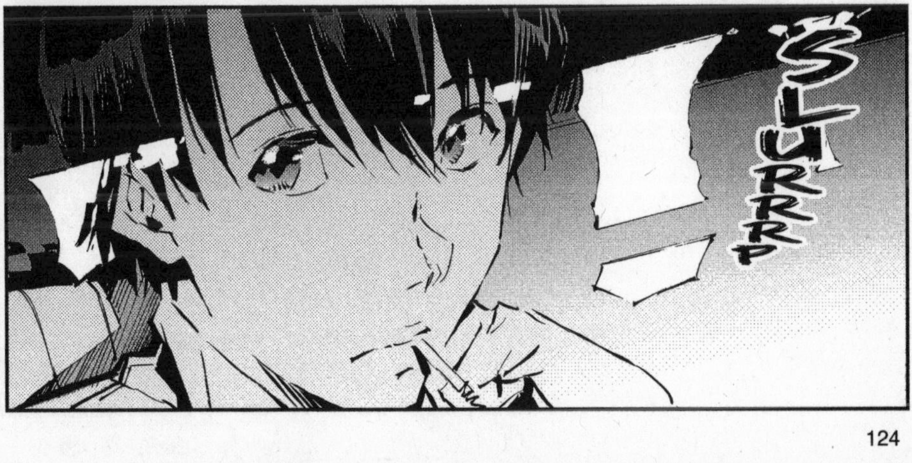
SLURRP

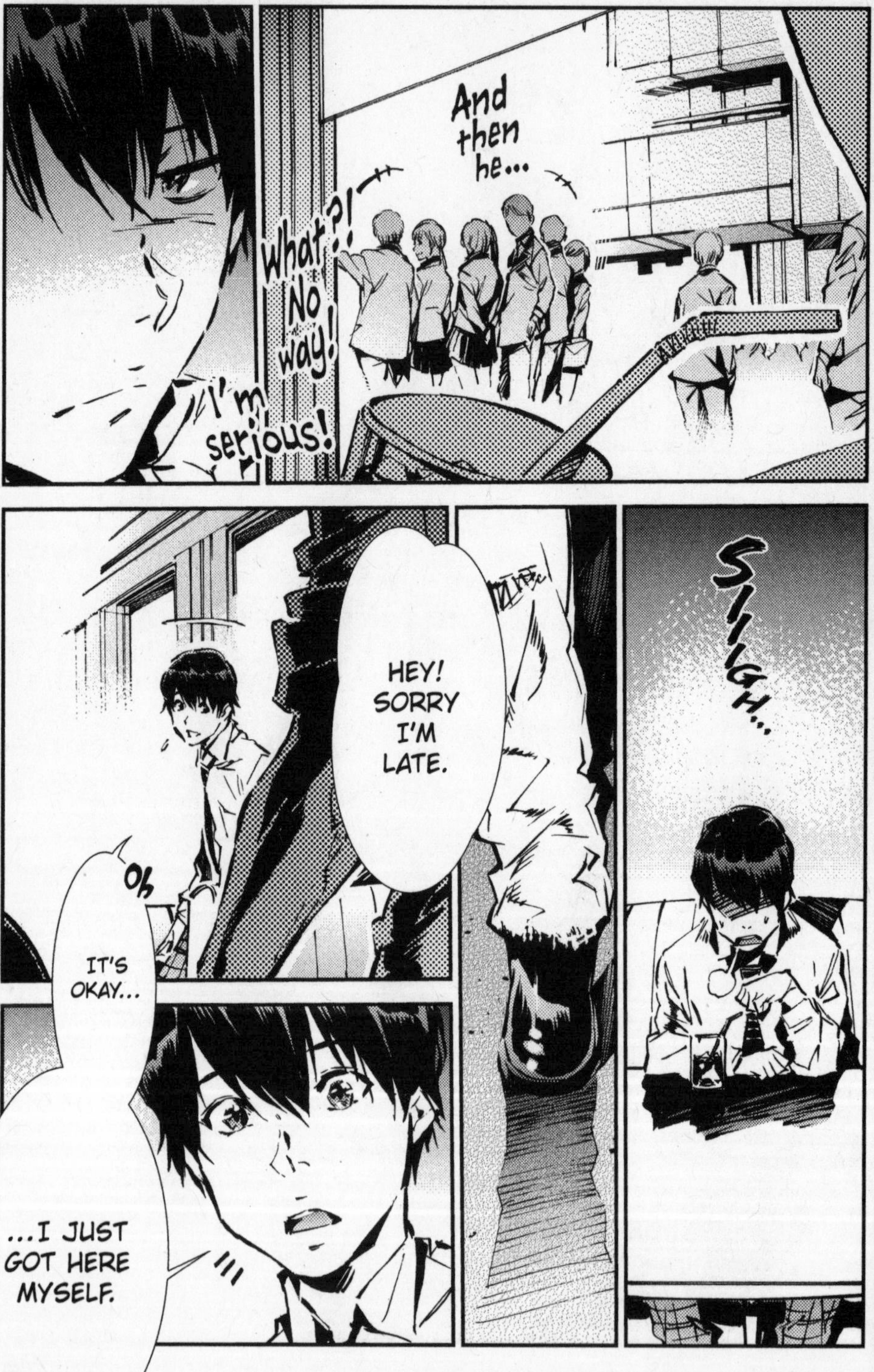
And then he...
What?! No way!
I'm serious!
SIIIGH...
HEY! SORRY I'M LATE.
Oh
IT'S OKAY... ...I JUST GOT HERE MYSELF.

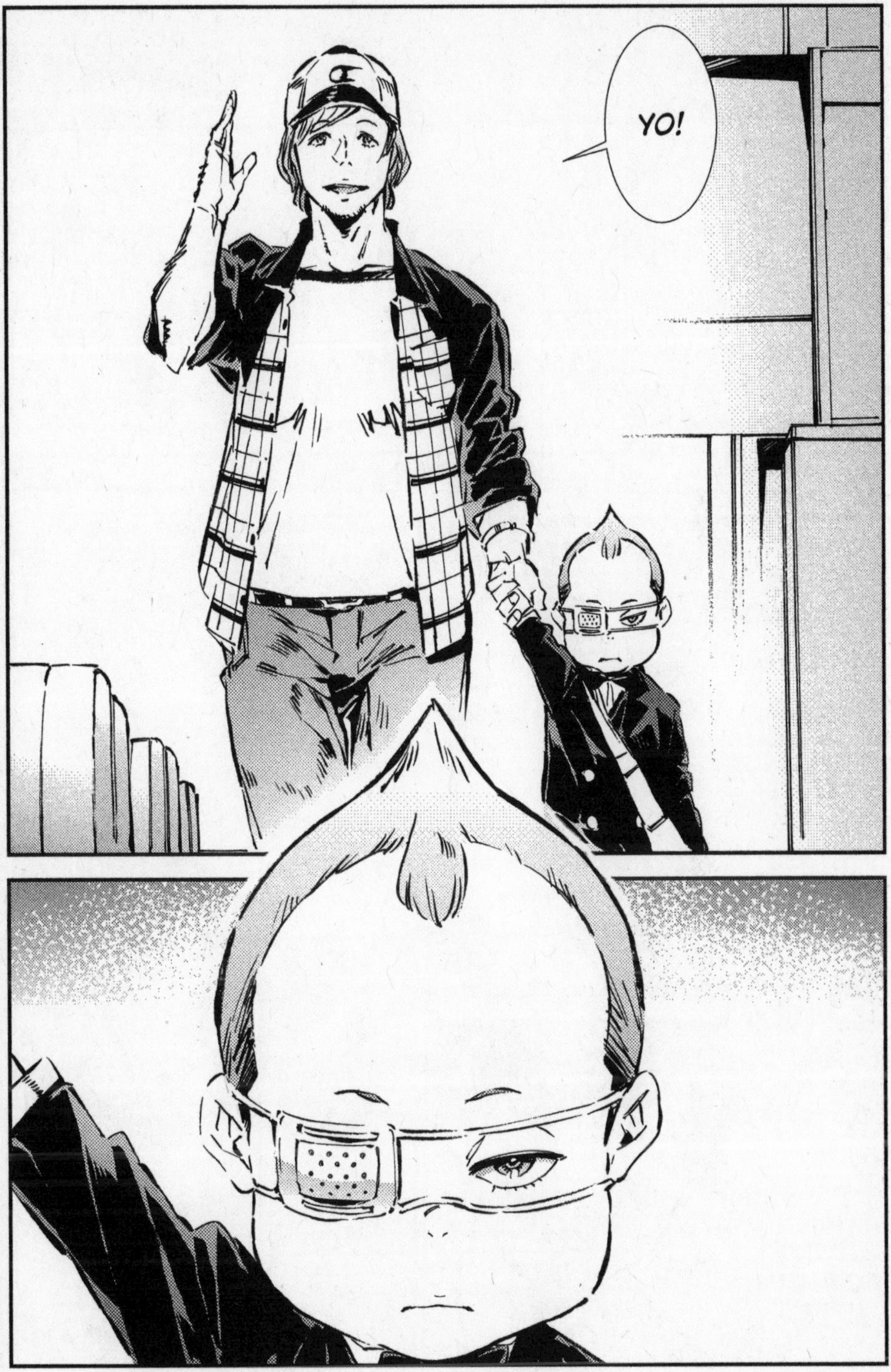
YO!

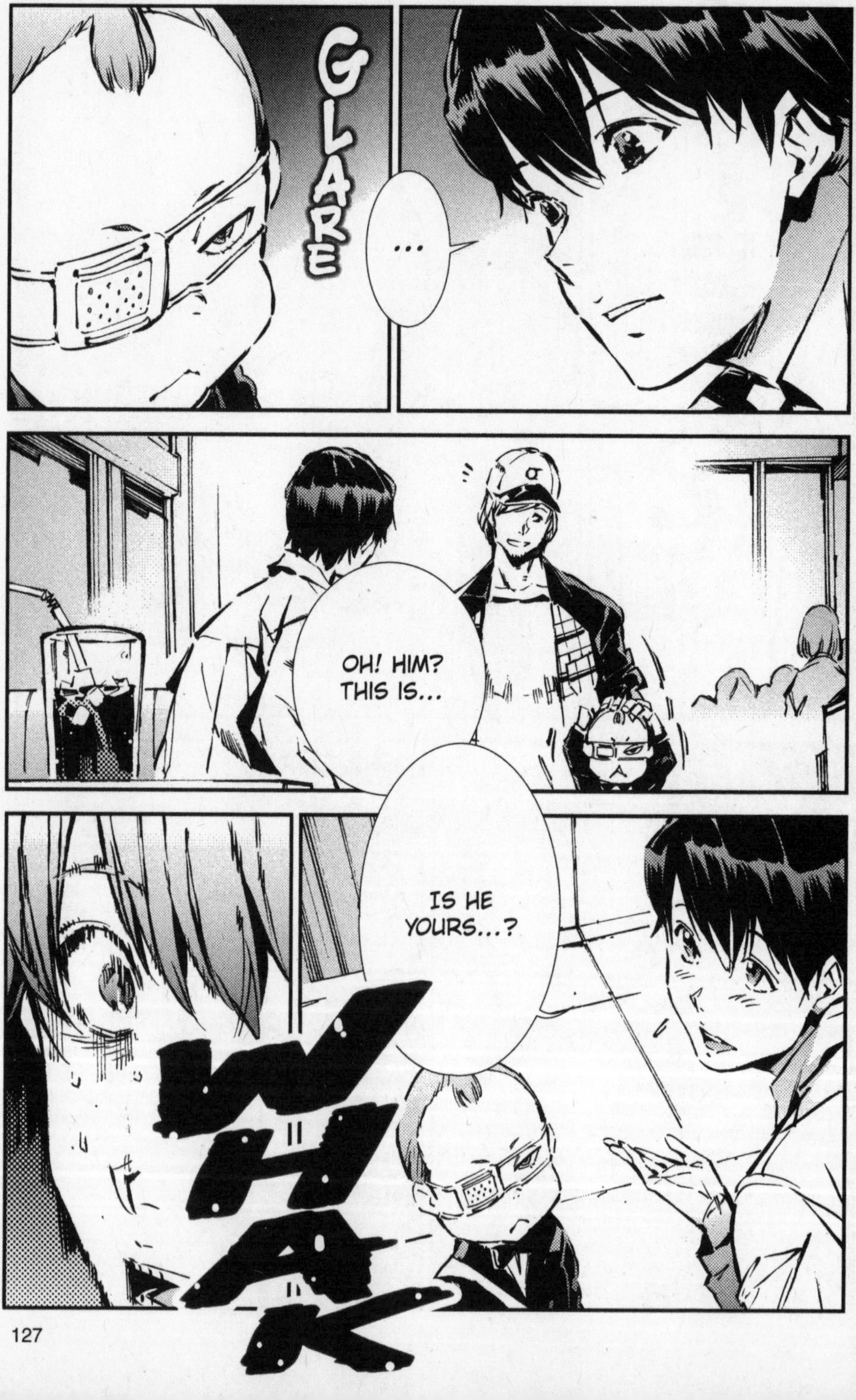
...
GLARE
OH! HIM? THIS IS...
IS HE YOURS...?
WHAK

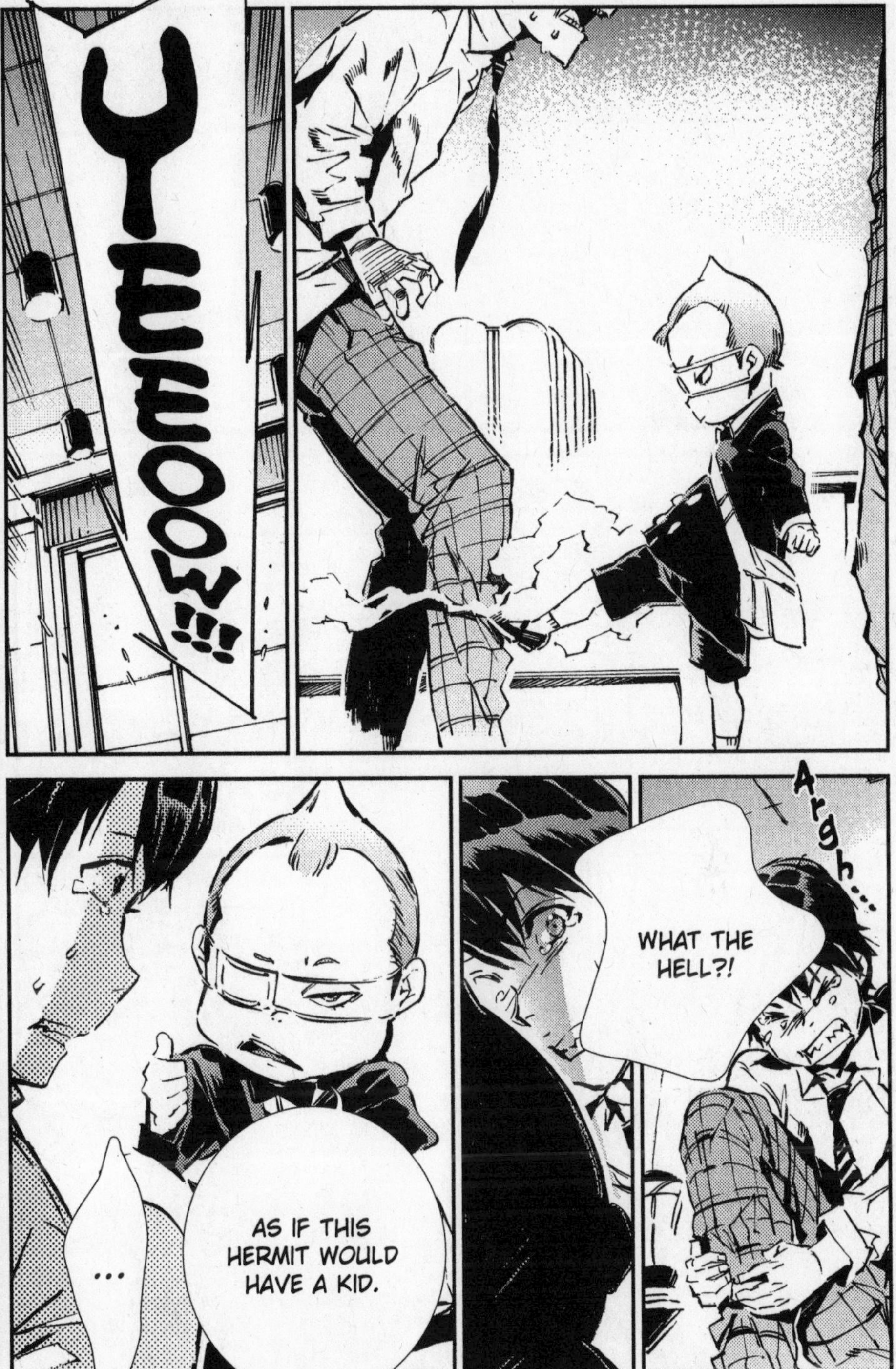
YEEEOOW!!!
Argh...
WHAT THE HELL?!
AS IF THIS HERMIT WOULD HAVE A KID.
...

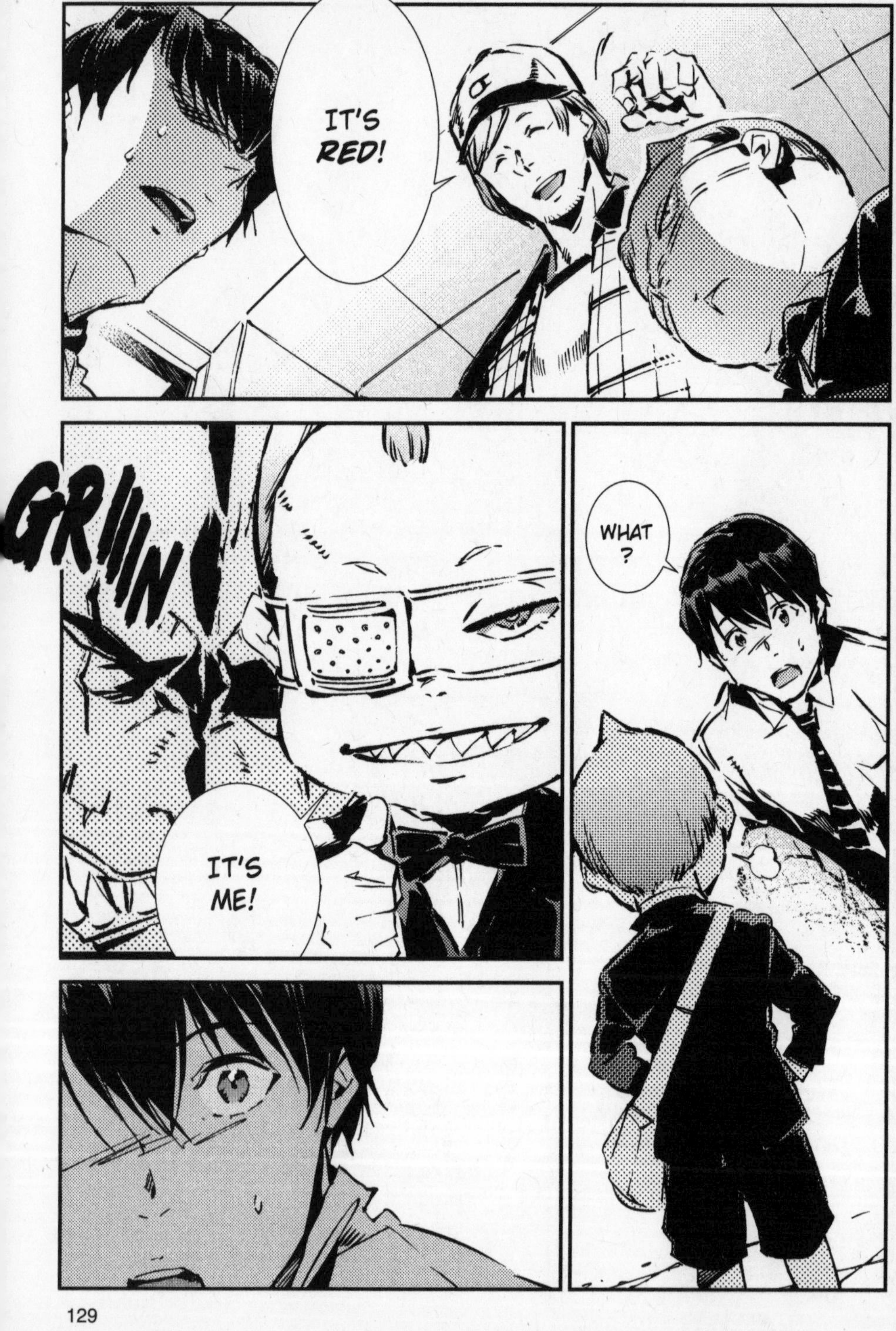
IT'S RED!
WHAT?
GRIIIN
IT'S ME!

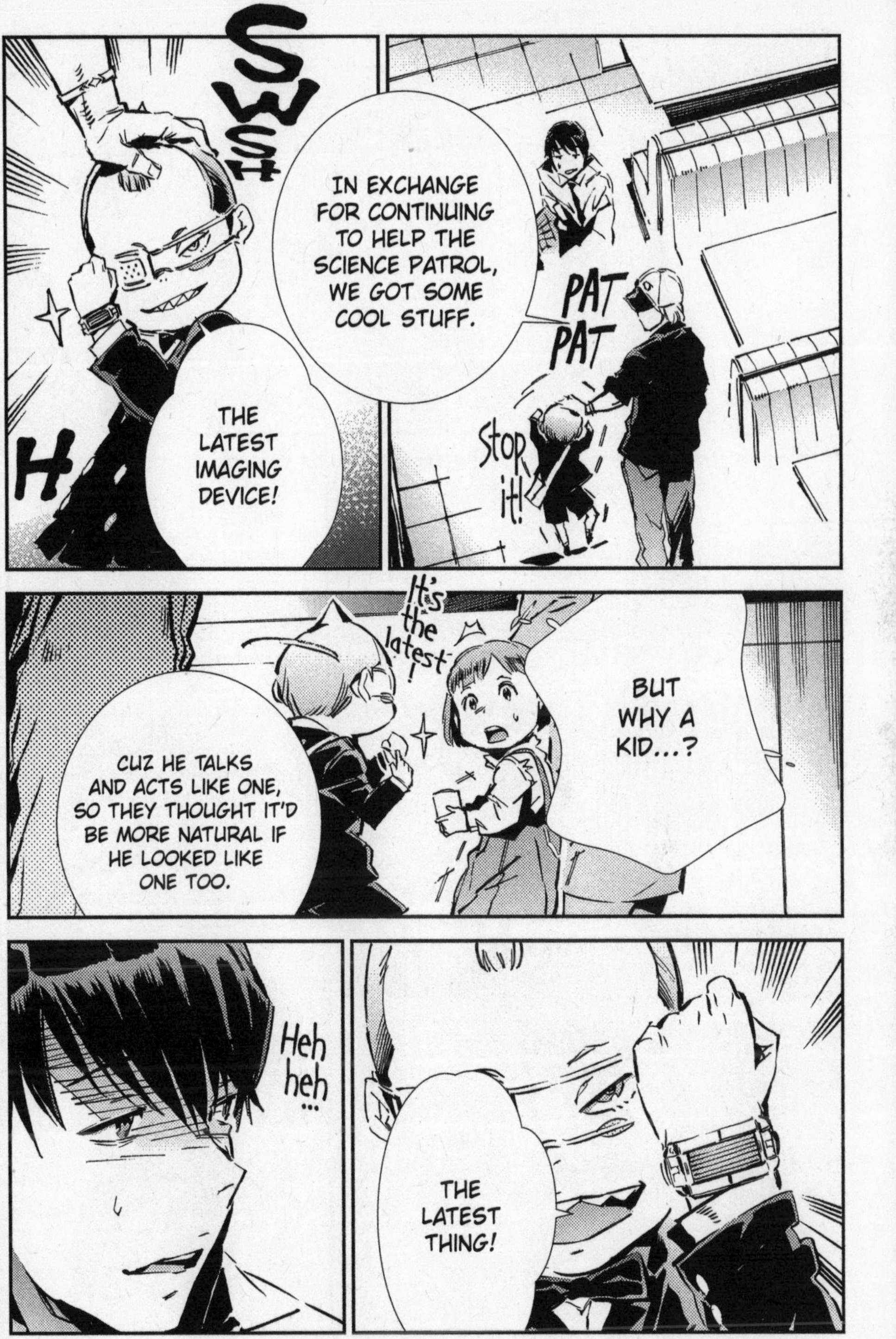
IN EXCHANGE FOR CONTINUING TO HELP THE SCIENCE PATROL, WE GOT SOME COOL STUFF.
PAT PAT
Stop it!
SWSH
THE LATEST IMAGING DEVICE!
H
BUT WHY A KID...?
It's the latest!
CUZ HE TALKS AND ACTS LIKE ONE, SO THEY THOUGHT IT'D BE MORE NATURAL IF HE LOOKED LIKE ONE TOO.
THE LATEST THING!
Heh heh...

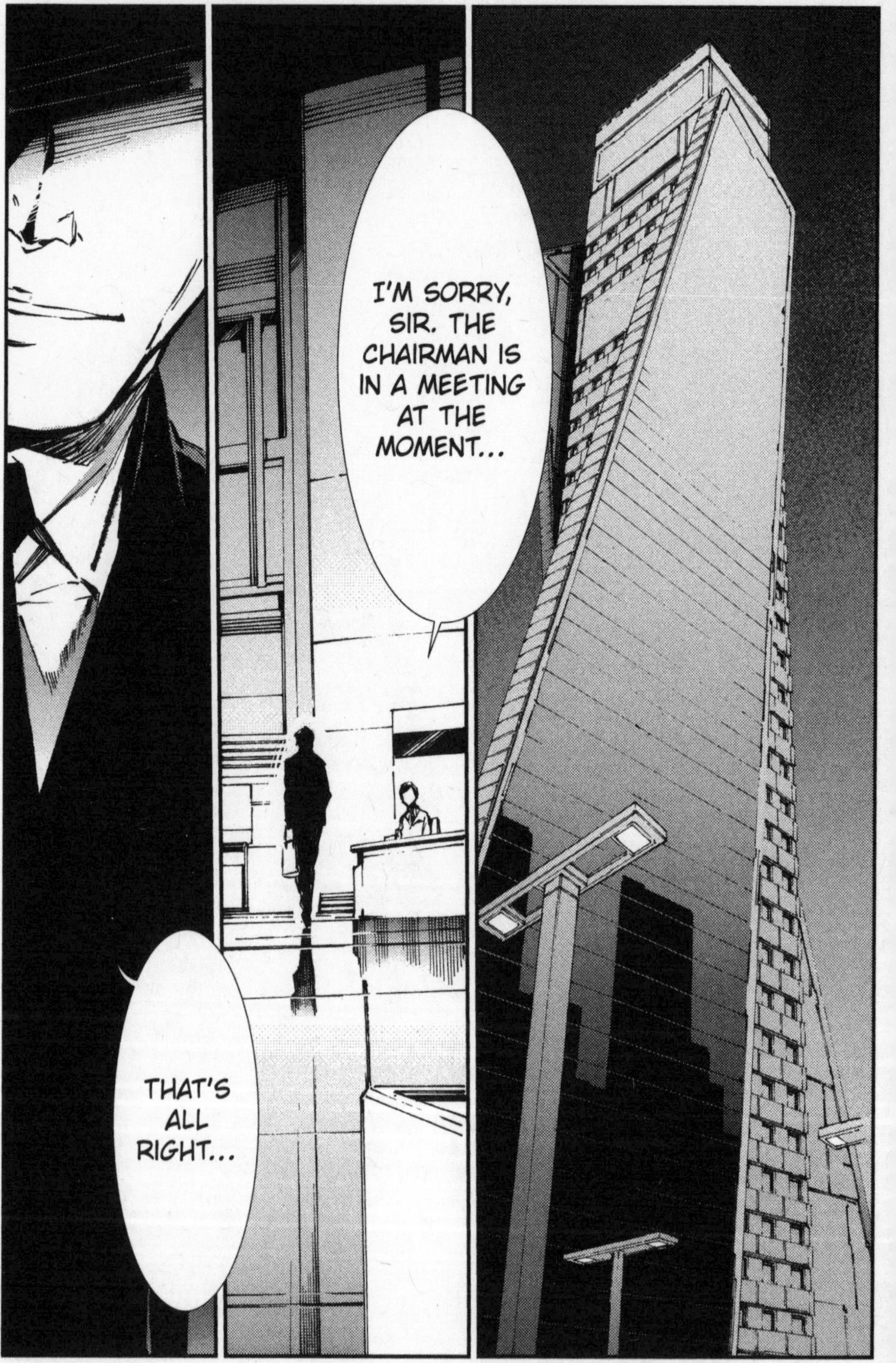
I'M SORRY, SIR. THE CHAIRMAN IS IN A MEETING AT THE MOMENT...
THAT'S ALL RIGHT...

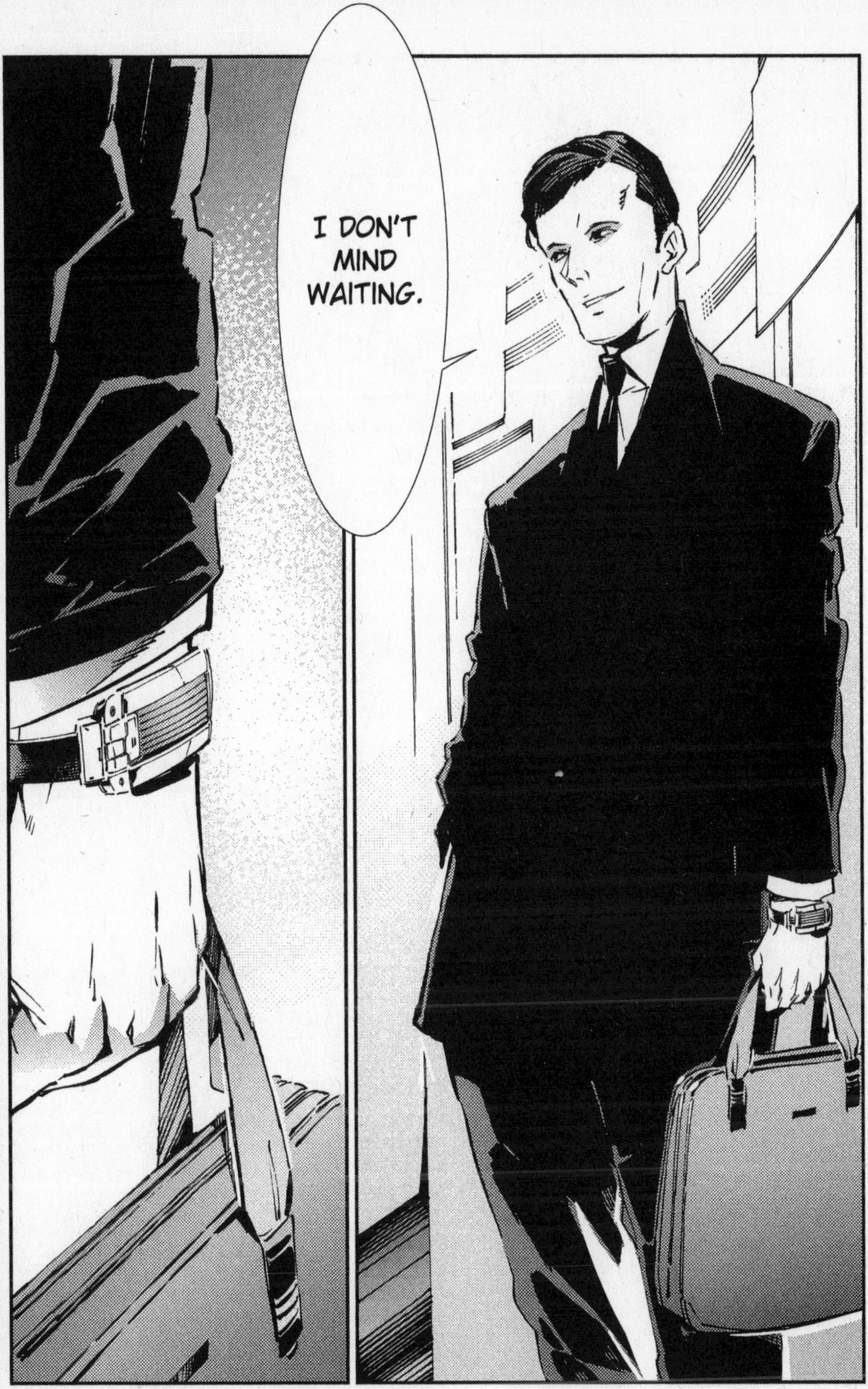
I DON'T MIND WAITING.

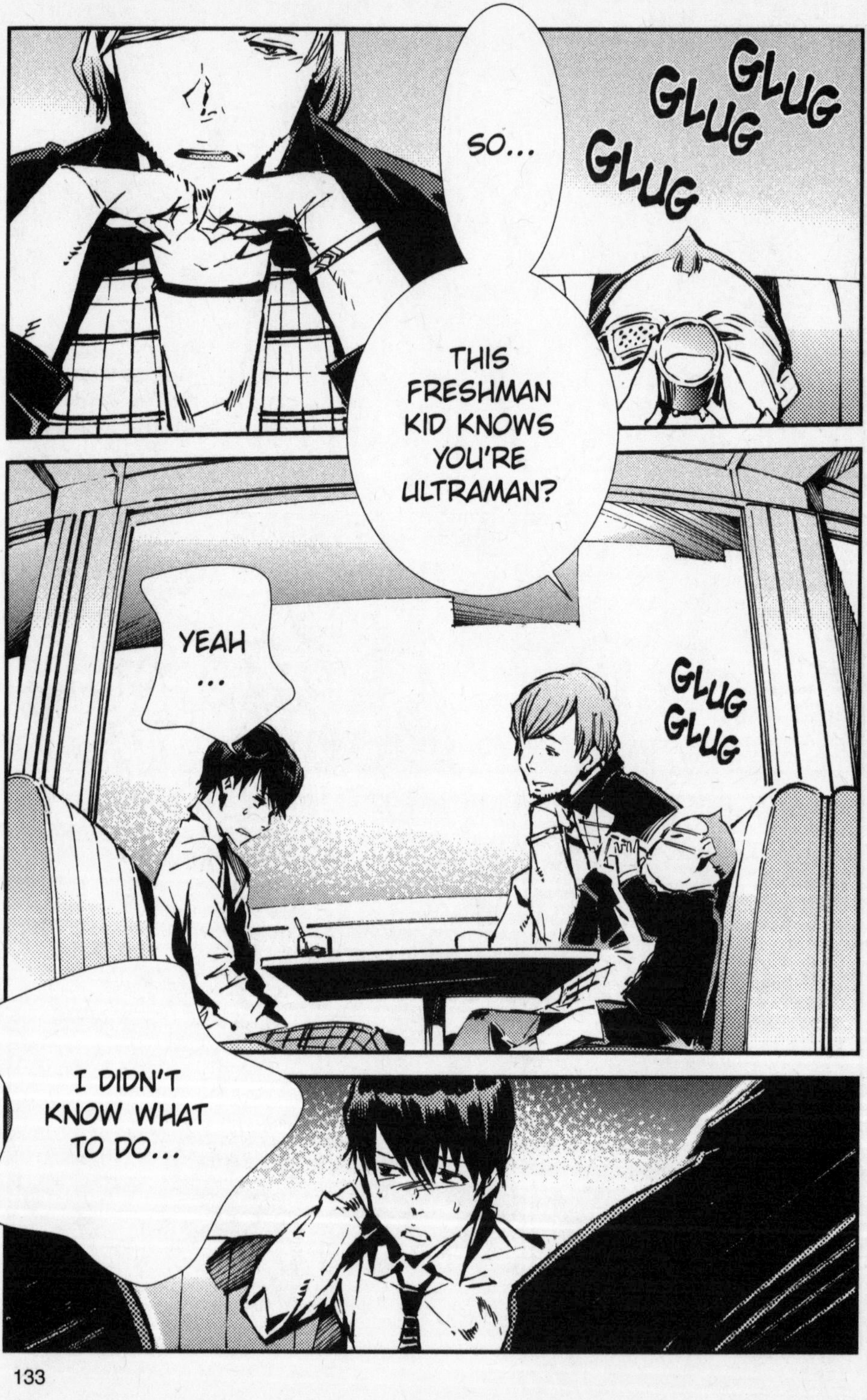
GLUG GLUG GLUG
SO...
THIS FRESHMAN KID KNOWS YOU'RE ULTRAMAN?
GLUG GLUG
YEAH ...
I DIDN'T KNOW WHAT TO DO...

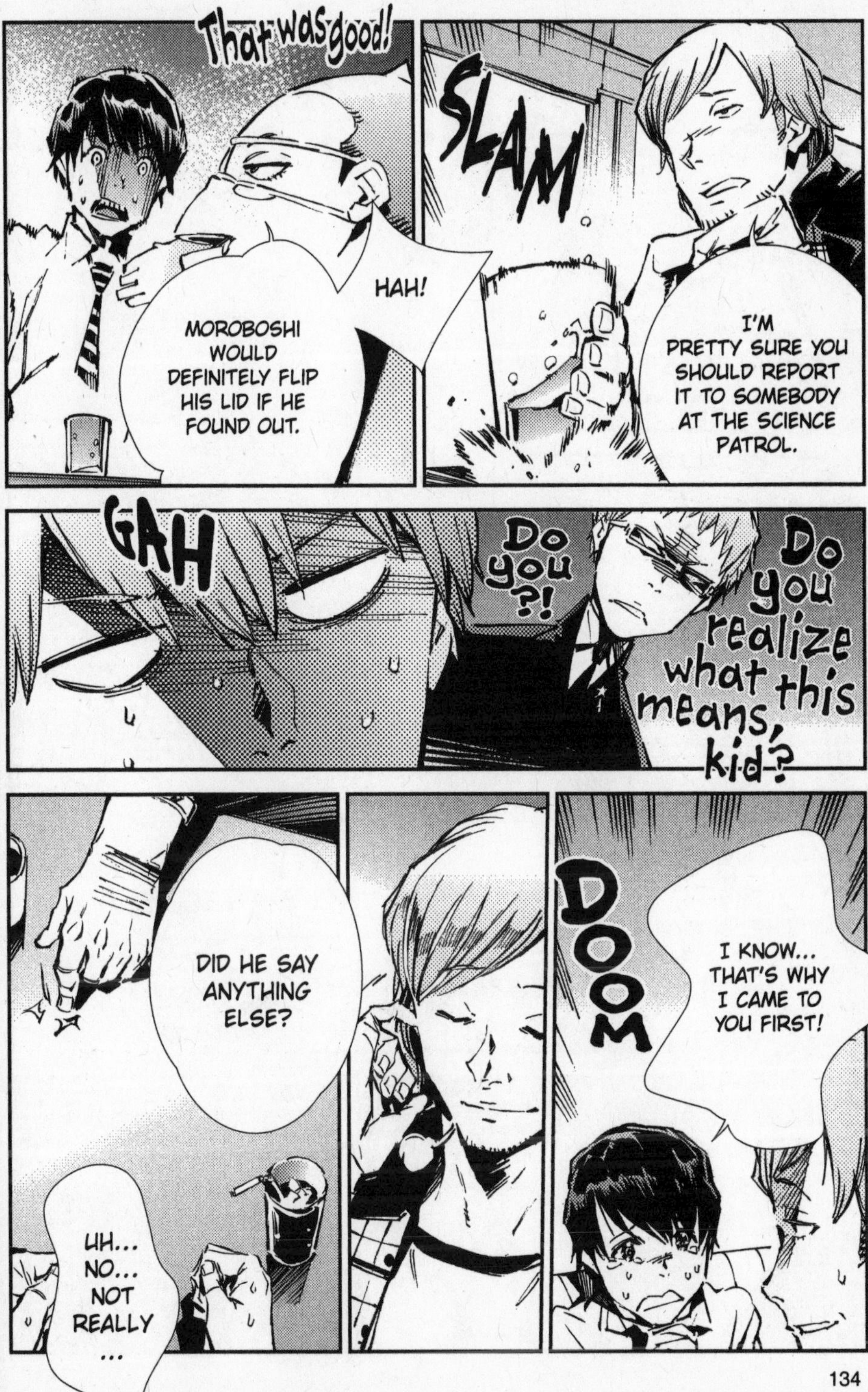

SLAM
I'M PRETTY SURE YOU SHOULD REPORT IT TO SOMEBODY AT THE SCIENCE PATROL.
That was good!
HAH!
MOROBOSHI WOULD DEFINITELY FLIP HIS LID IF HE FOUND OUT.
Do you realize what this means, kid?
Do you?!
GAH
DOOM
I KNOW... THAT'S WHY I CAME TO YOU FIRST!
DID HE SAY ANYTHING ELSE?
UH... NO... NOT REALLY ...

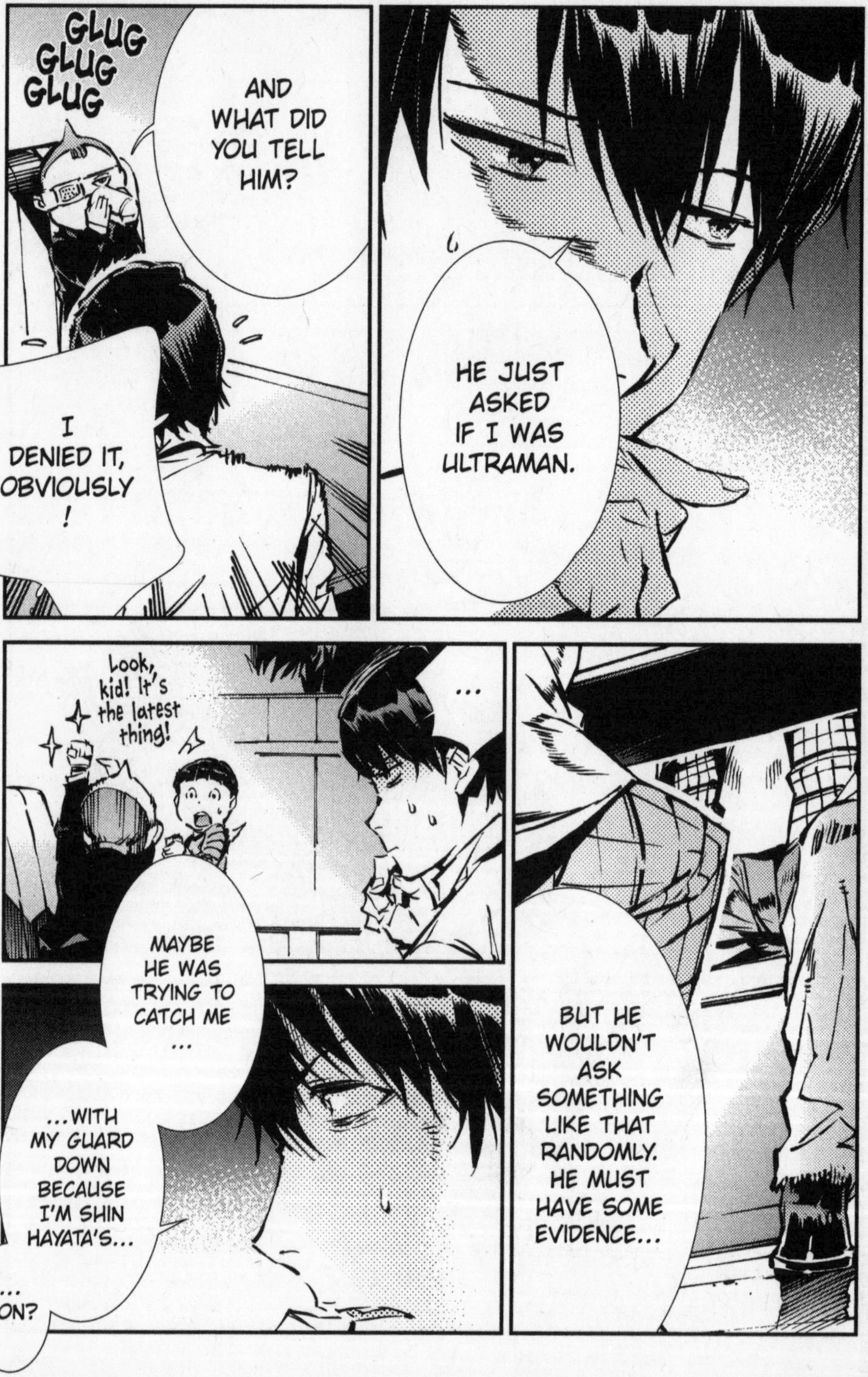
HE JUST ASKED IF I WAS ULTRAMAN.
AND WHAT DID YOU TELL HIM?
GLUG GLUG GLUG
I DENIED IT, OBVIOUSLY!
BUT HE WOULDN'T ASK SOMETHING LIKE THAT RANDOMLY. HE MUST HAVE SOME EVIDENCE...
...
Look, kid! It's the latest thing!
MAYBE HE WAS TRYING TO CATCH ME...
...WITH MY GUARD DOWN BECAUSE I'M SHIN HAYATA'S...
...SON?

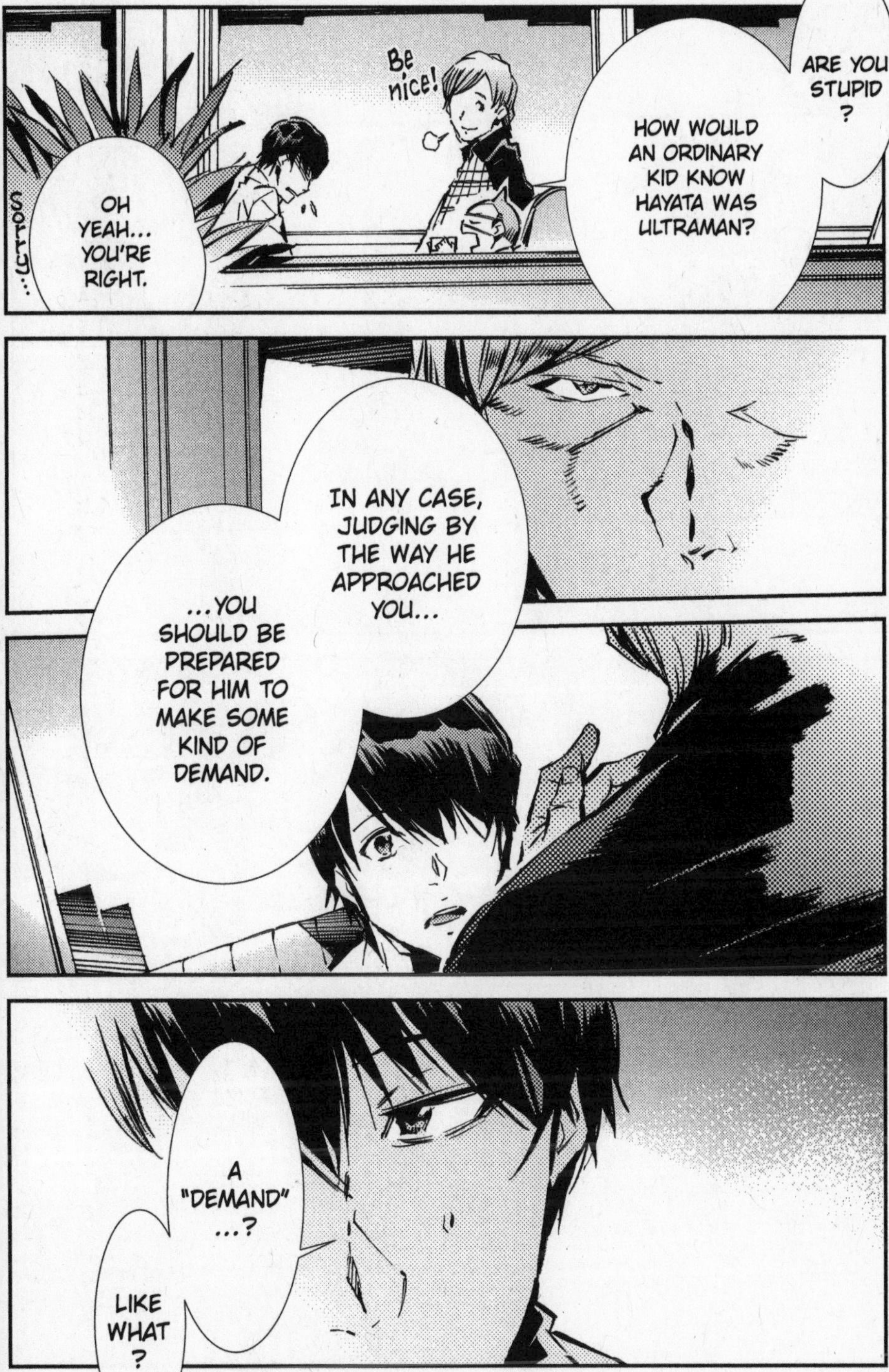
ARE YOU STUPID?
HOW WOULD AN ORDINARY KID KNOW HAYATA WAS ULTRAMAN?
Be nice!
OH YEAH... YOU'RE RIGHT.
Sorry...
IN ANY CASE, JUDGING BY THE WAY HE APPROACHED YOU...
...YOU SHOULD BE PREPARED FOR HIM TO MAKE SOME KIND OF DEMAND.
A "DEMAND"...?
LIKE WHAT?

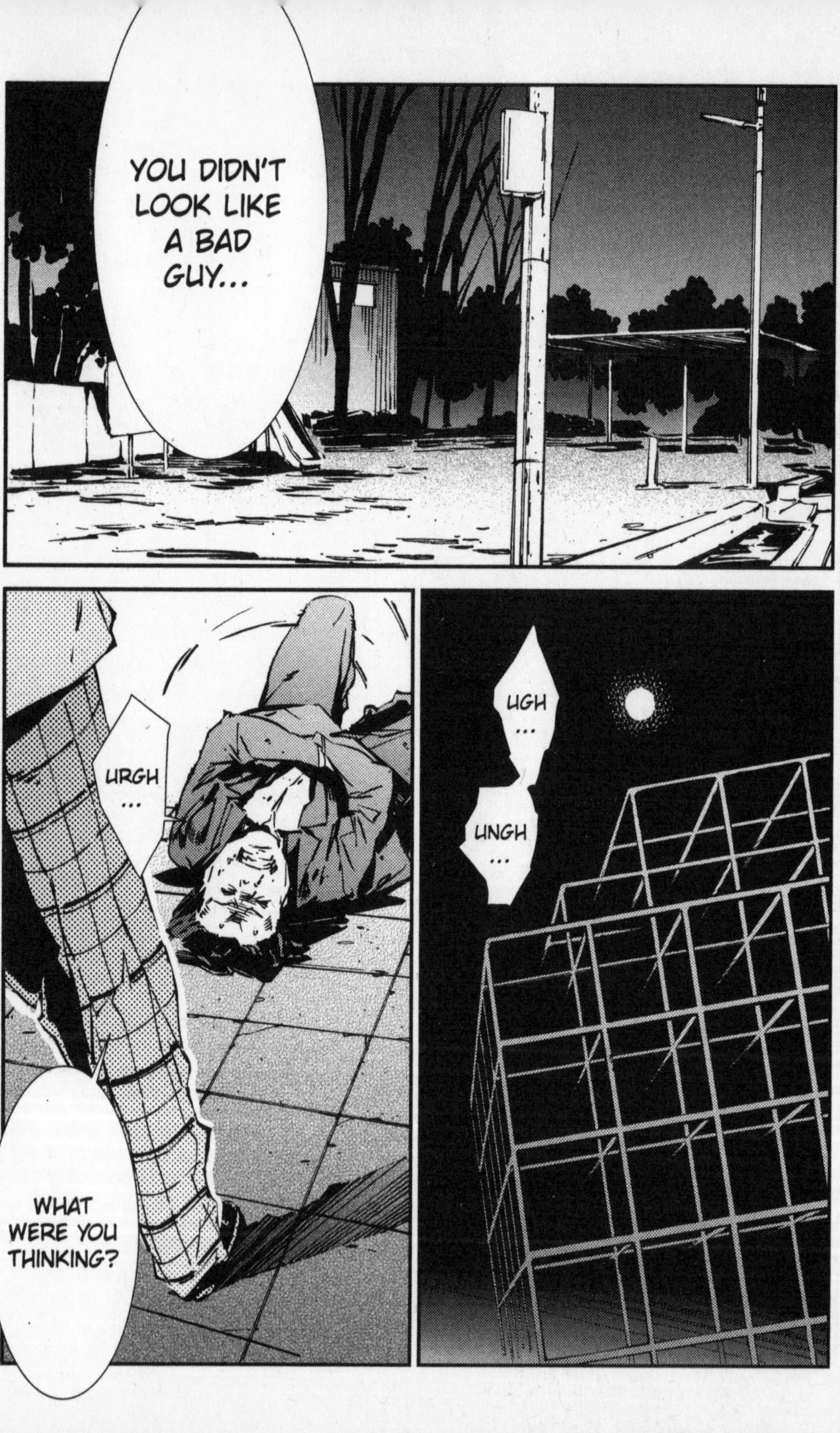
YOU DIDN'T LOOK LIKE A BAD GUY...
UGH ...
UNGH ...
URGH ...
WHAT WERE YOU THINKING?

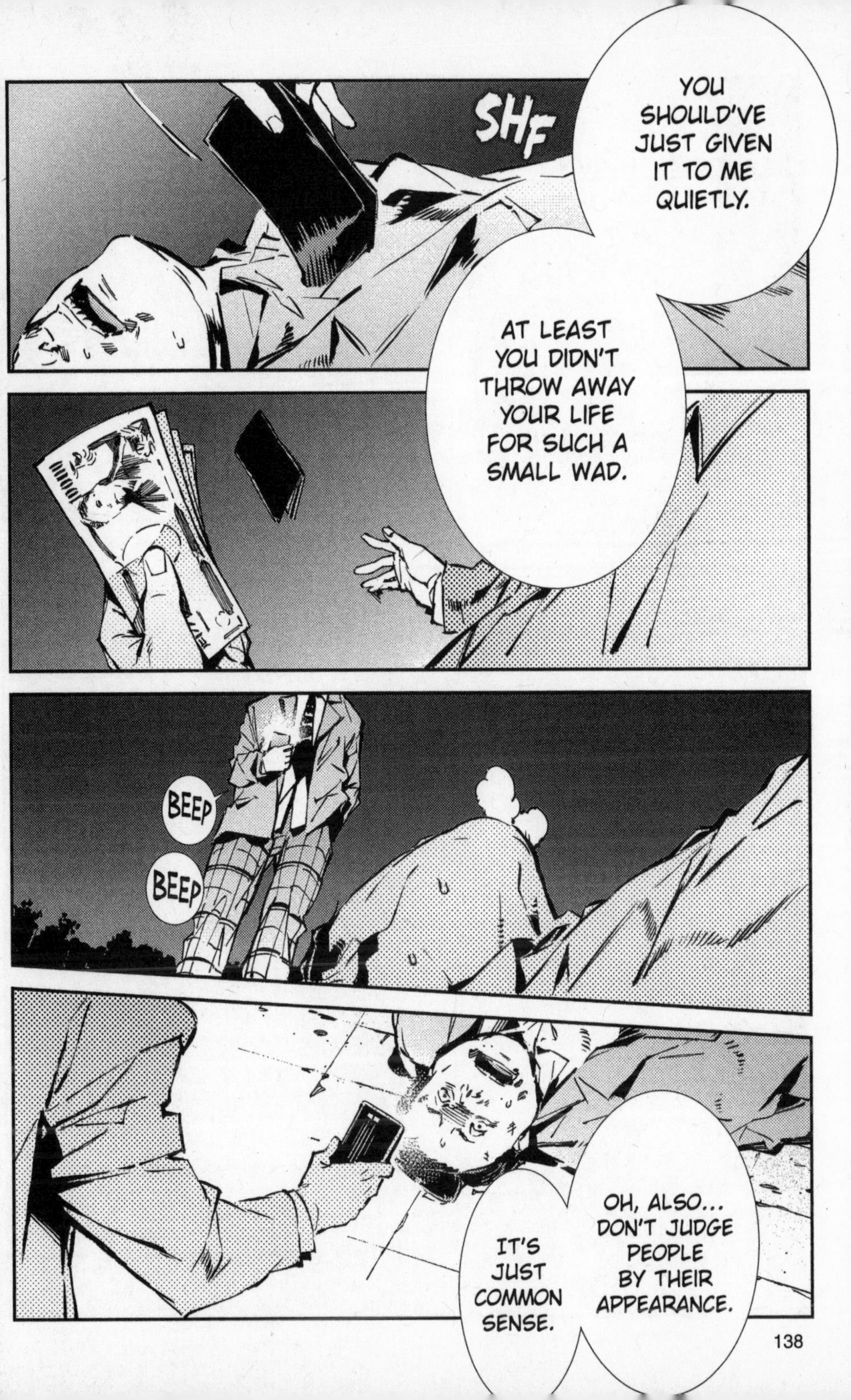
SHF
YOU SHOULD'VE JUST GIVEN IT TO ME QUIETLY.
AT LEAST YOU DIDN'T THROW AWAY YOUR LIFE FOR SUCH A SMALL WAD.
BEEP
BEEP
OH, ALSO... DON'T JUDGE PEOPLE BY THEIR APPEARANCE.
IT'S JUST COMMON SENSE.

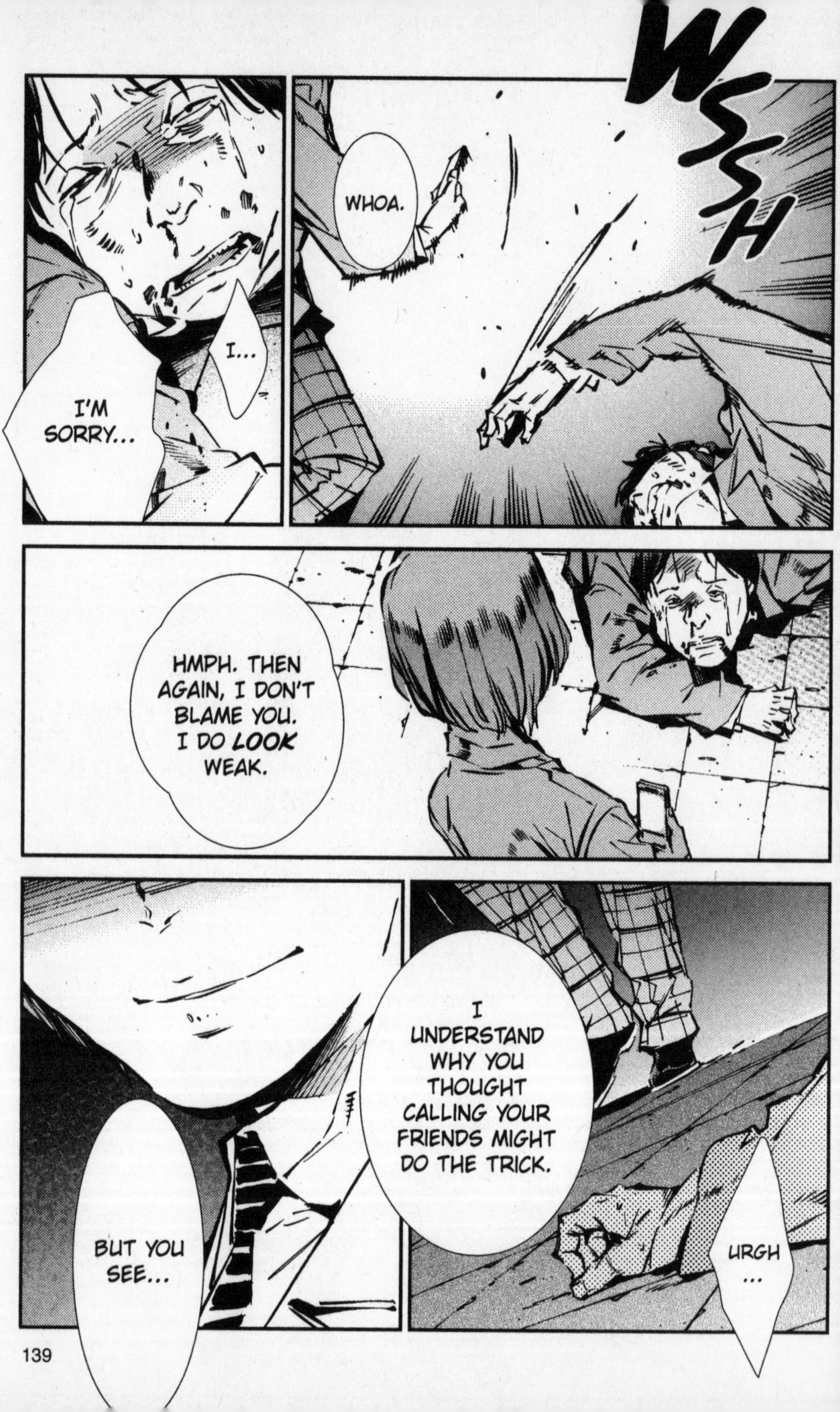
WSSH
WHOA.
I...
I'M SORRY...
HMPH. THEN AGAIN, I DON'T BLAME YOU. I DO *LOOK* WEAK.
I UNDERSTAND WHY YOU THOUGHT CALLING YOUR FRIENDS MIGHT DO THE TRICK.
URGH...
BUT YOU SEE...

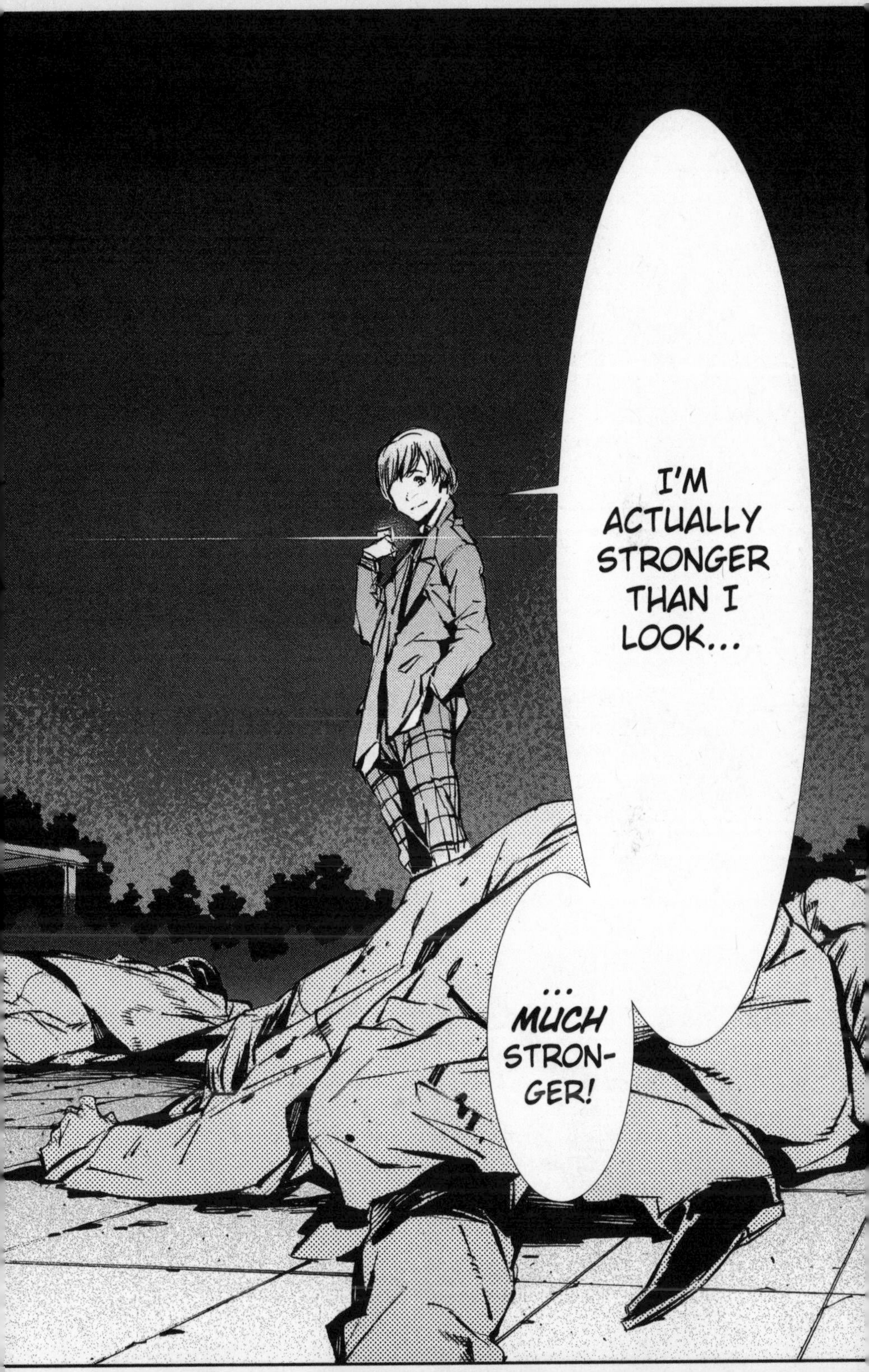
I'M ACTUALLY STRONGER THAN I LOOK...
... MUCH STRON-GER!

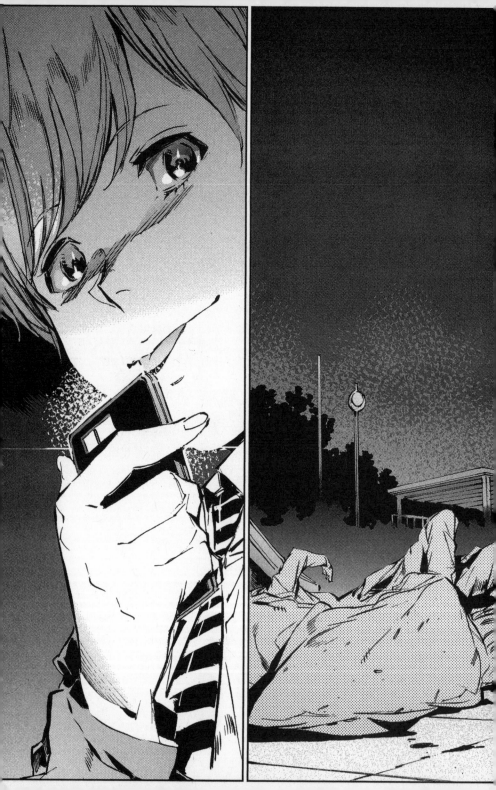

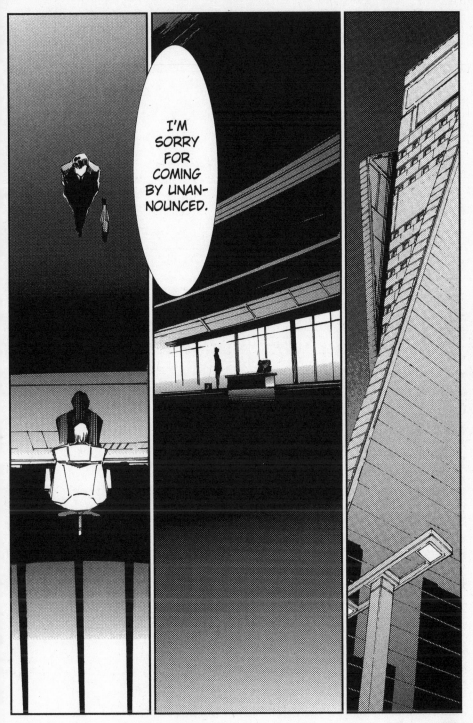

I'M SORRY FOR COMING BY UNAN-NOUNCED.

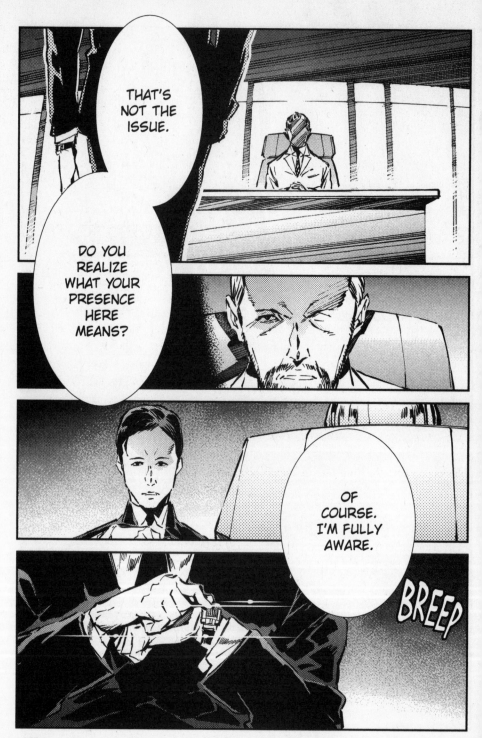

143

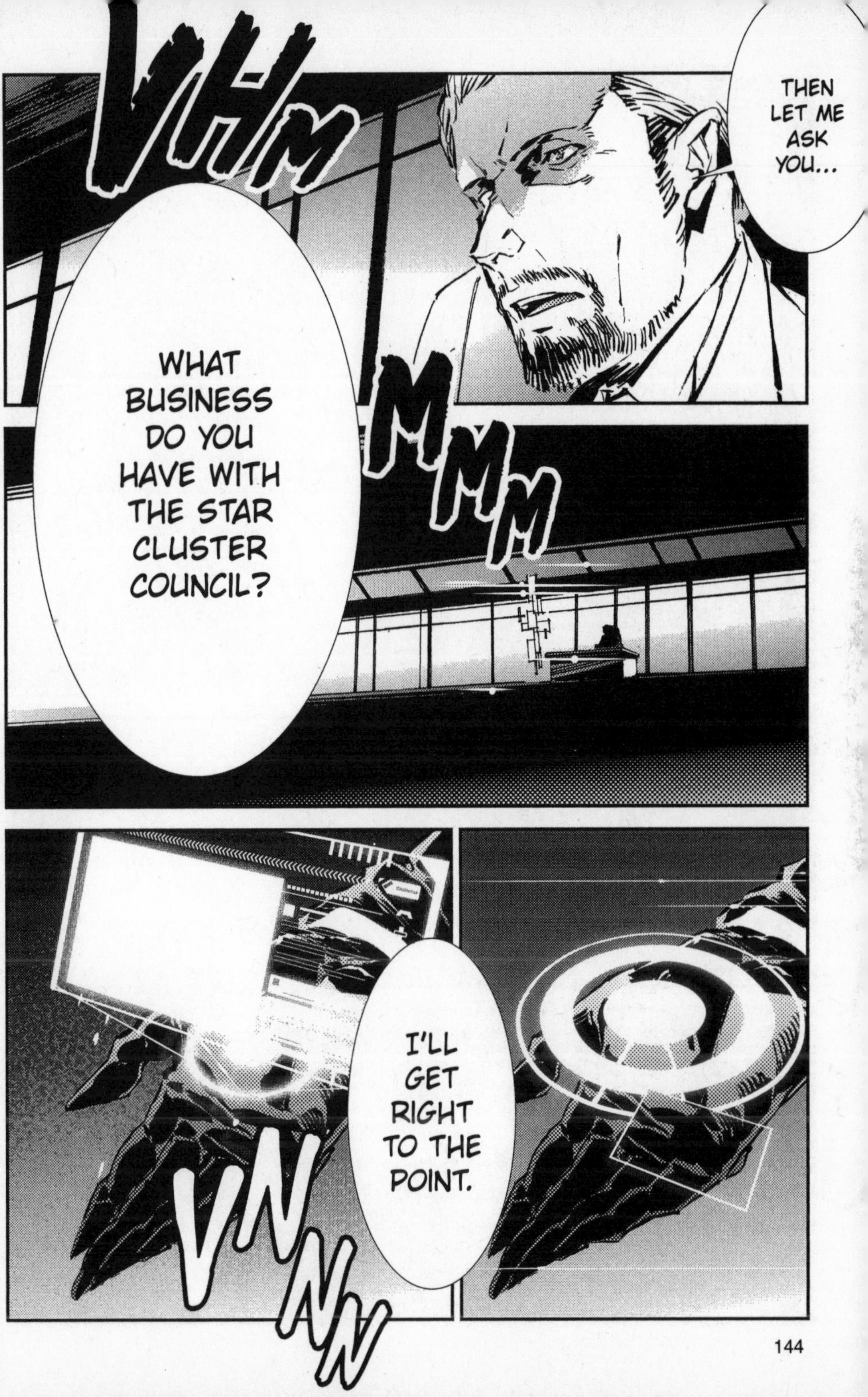
THEN LET ME ASK YOU...
VHMMMMM
WHAT BUSINESS DO YOU HAVE WITH THE STAR CLUSTER COUNCIL?
I'LL GET RIGHT TO THE POINT.
VNNN

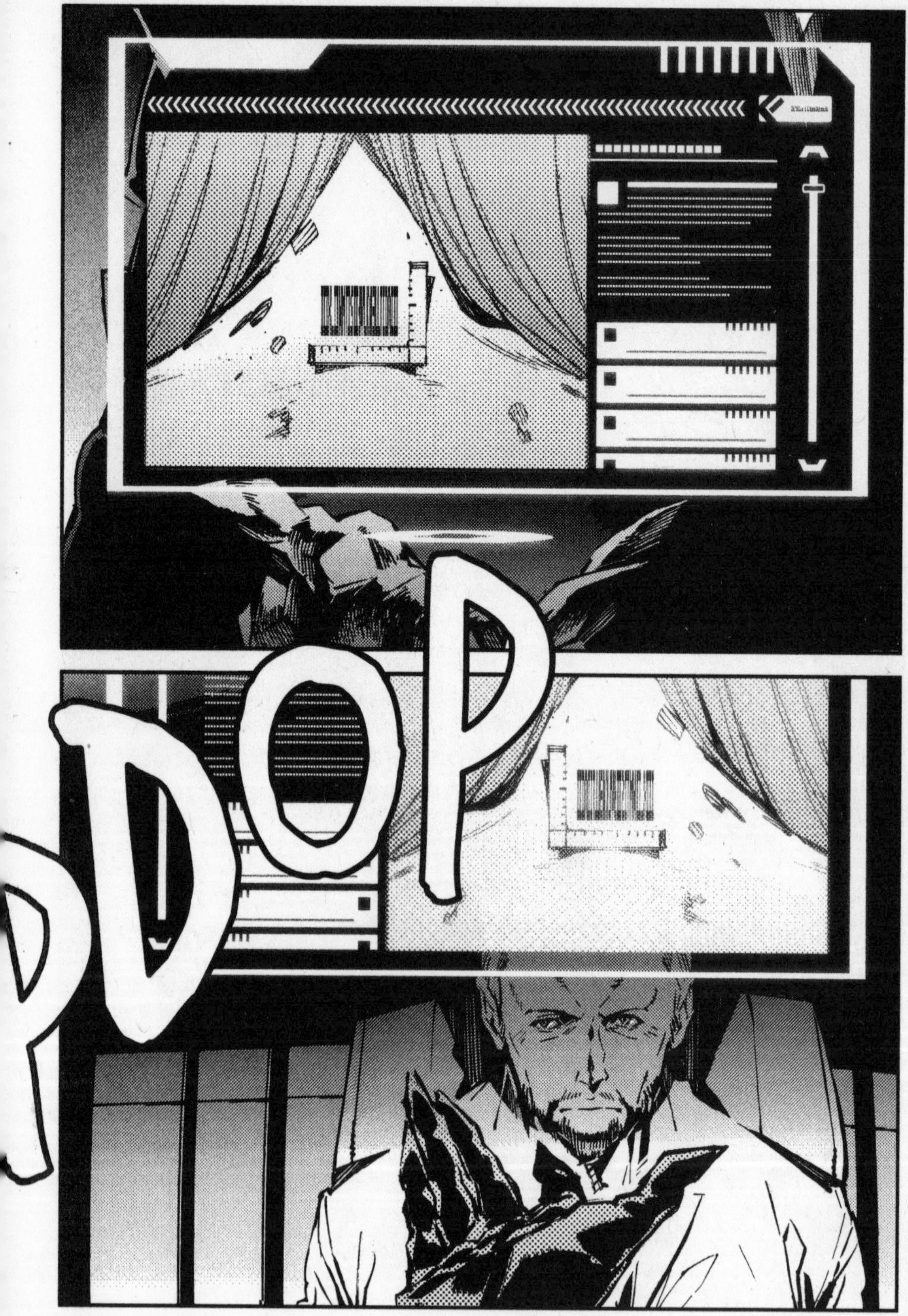
DOP

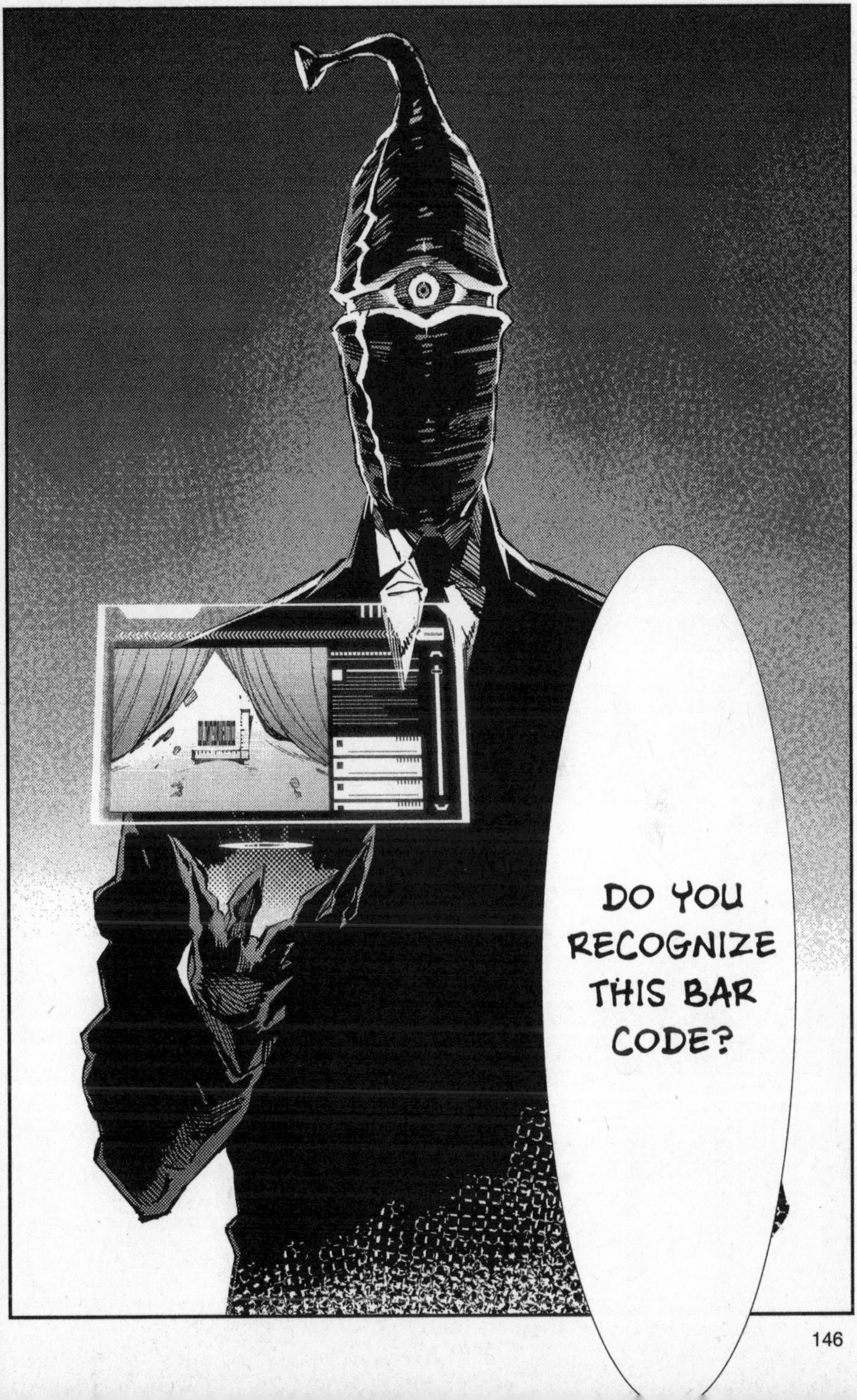
DO YOU RECOGNIZE THIS BAR CODE?

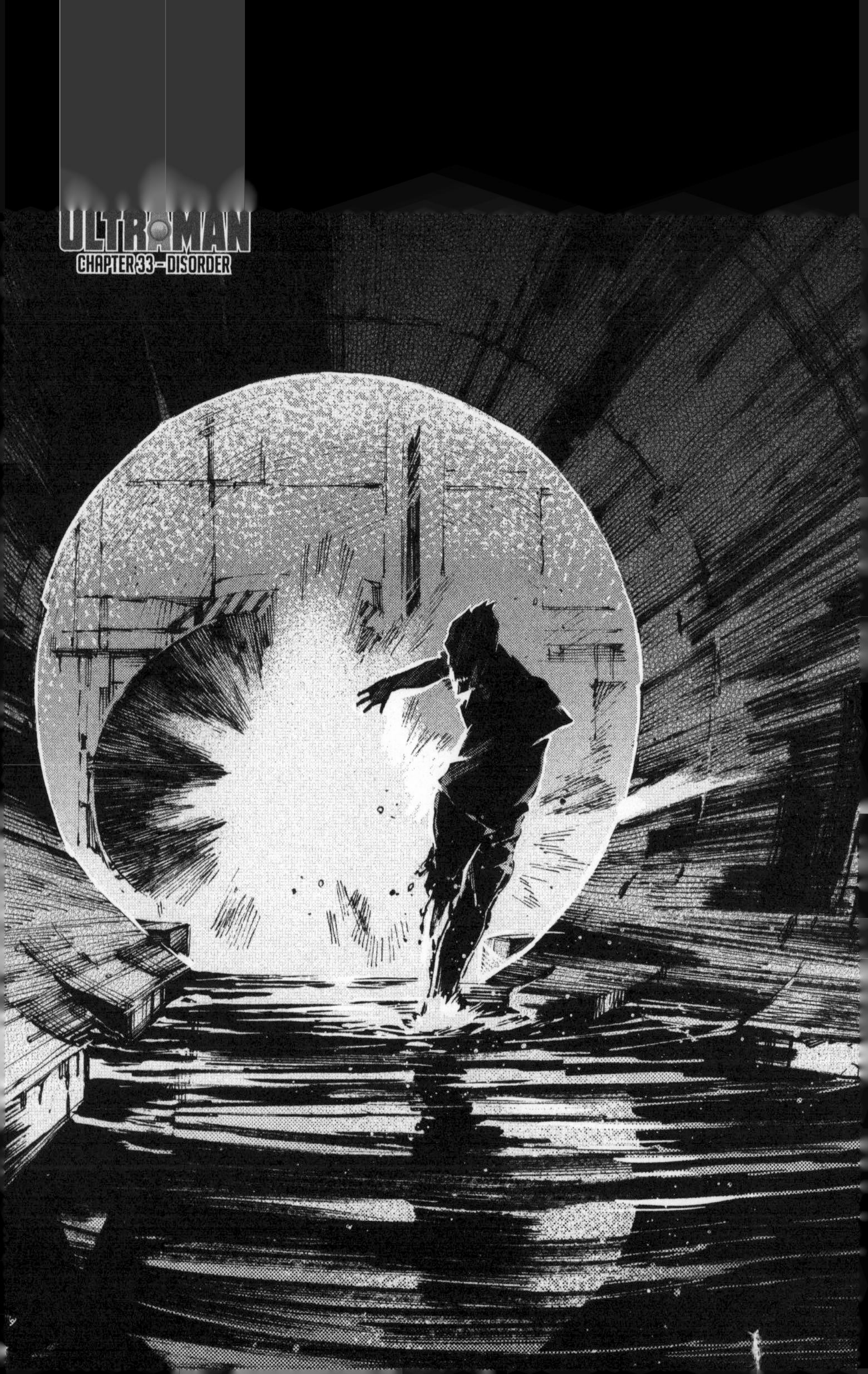
ULTRAMAN
CHAPTER 33 – DISORDER

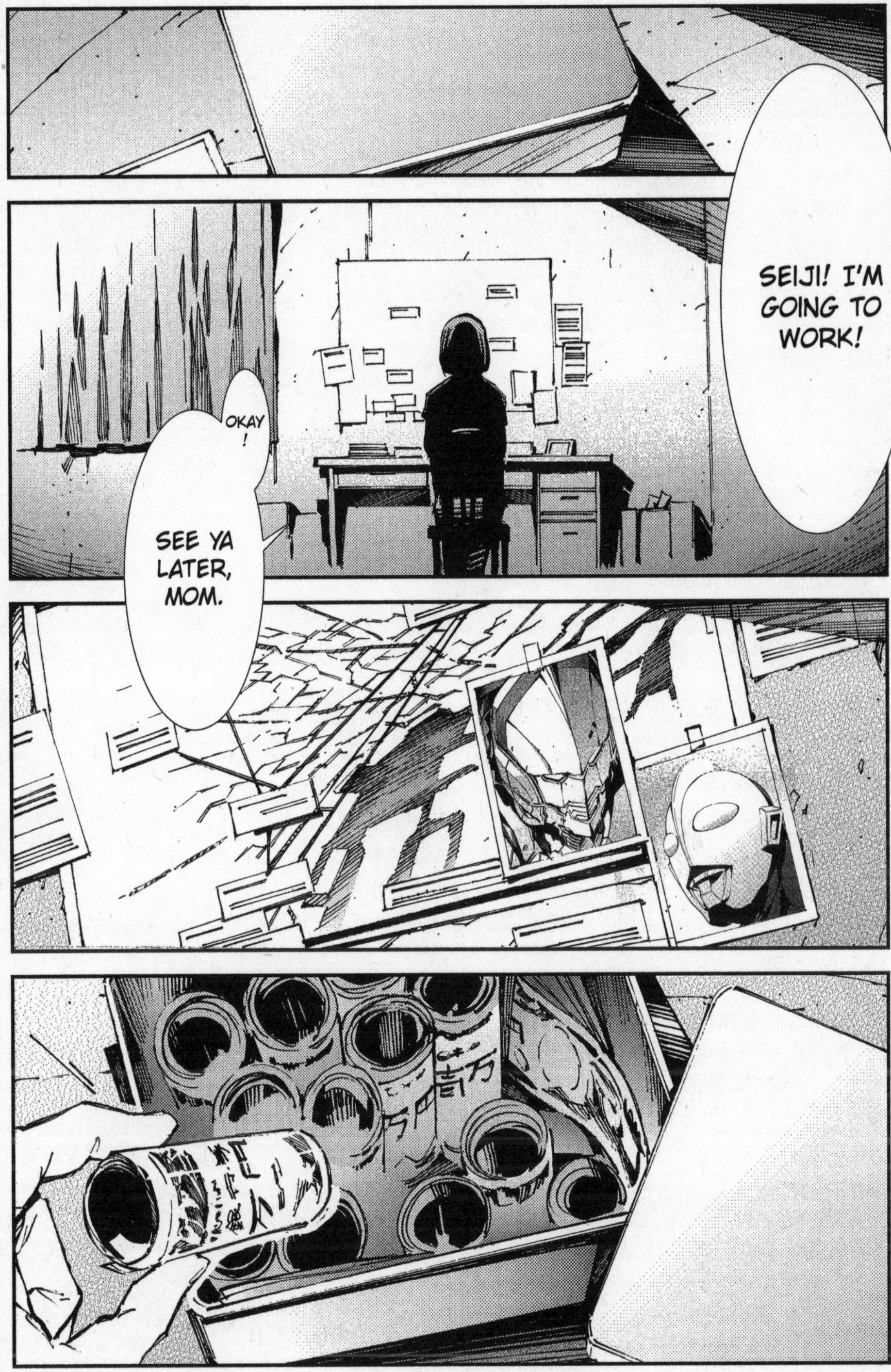
SEIJI! I'M GOING TO WORK!
OKAY! SEE YA LATER, MOM.

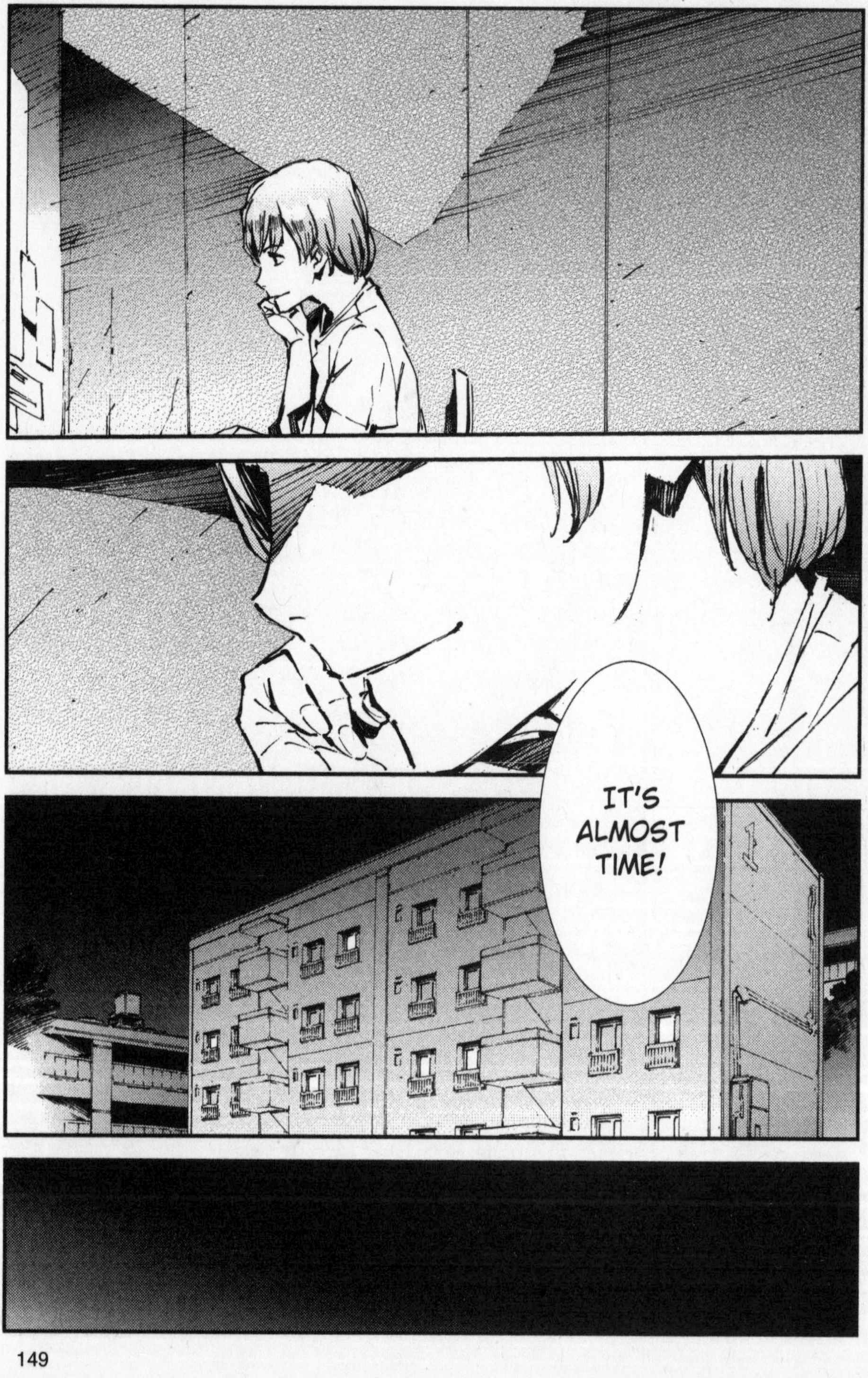
IT'S ALMOST TIME!

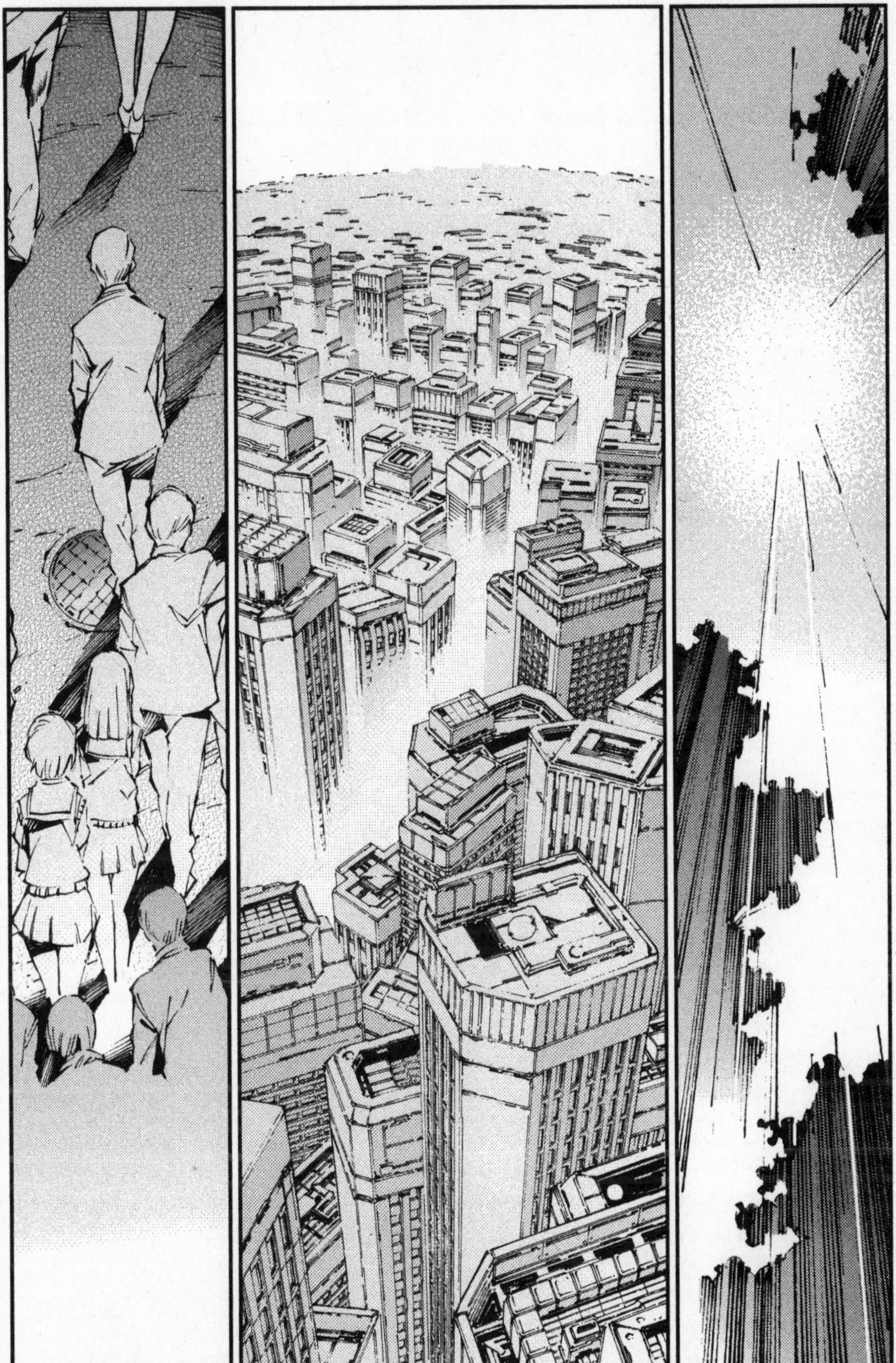

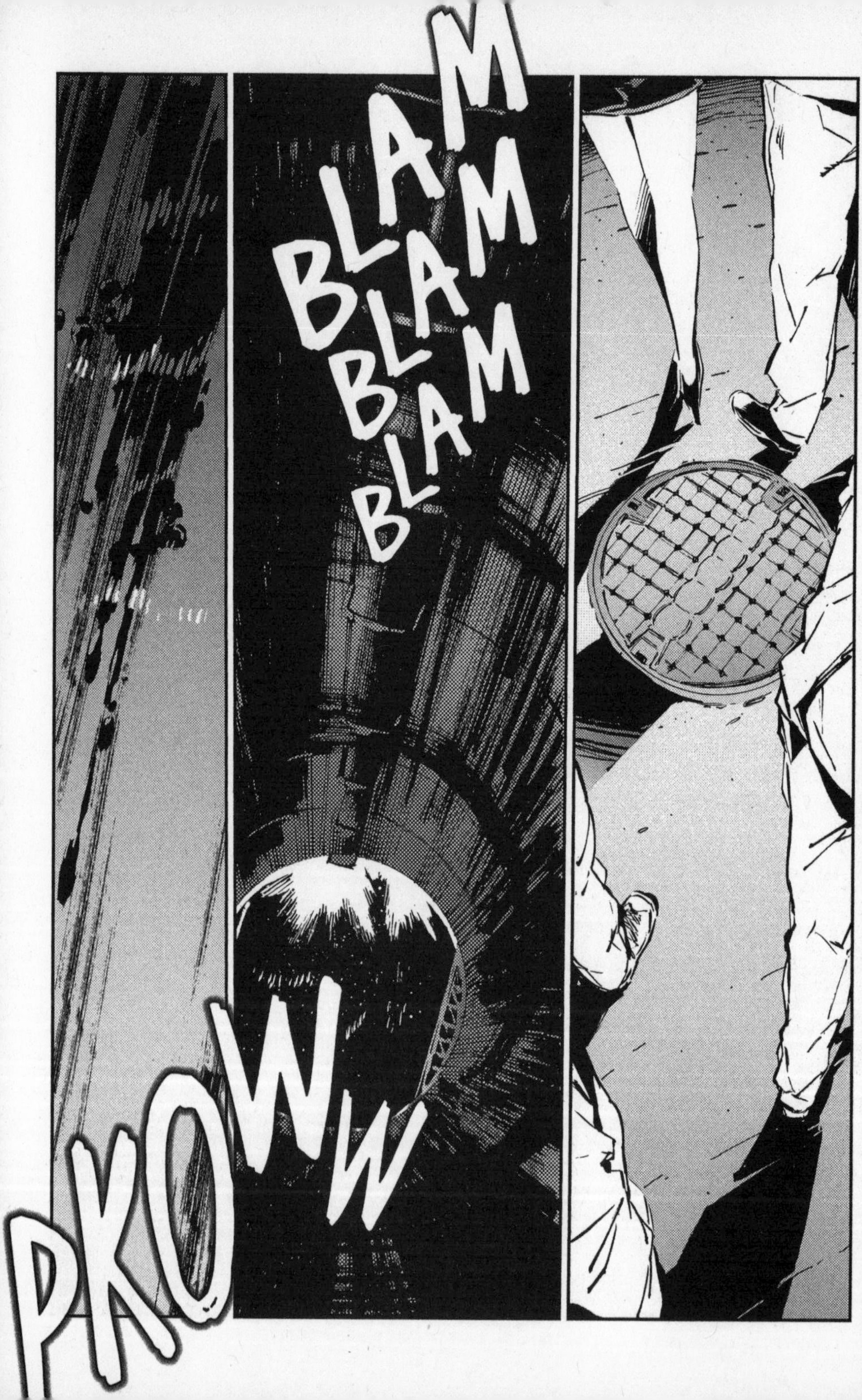
BLAM BLAM BLAM BLAM
PKOWW

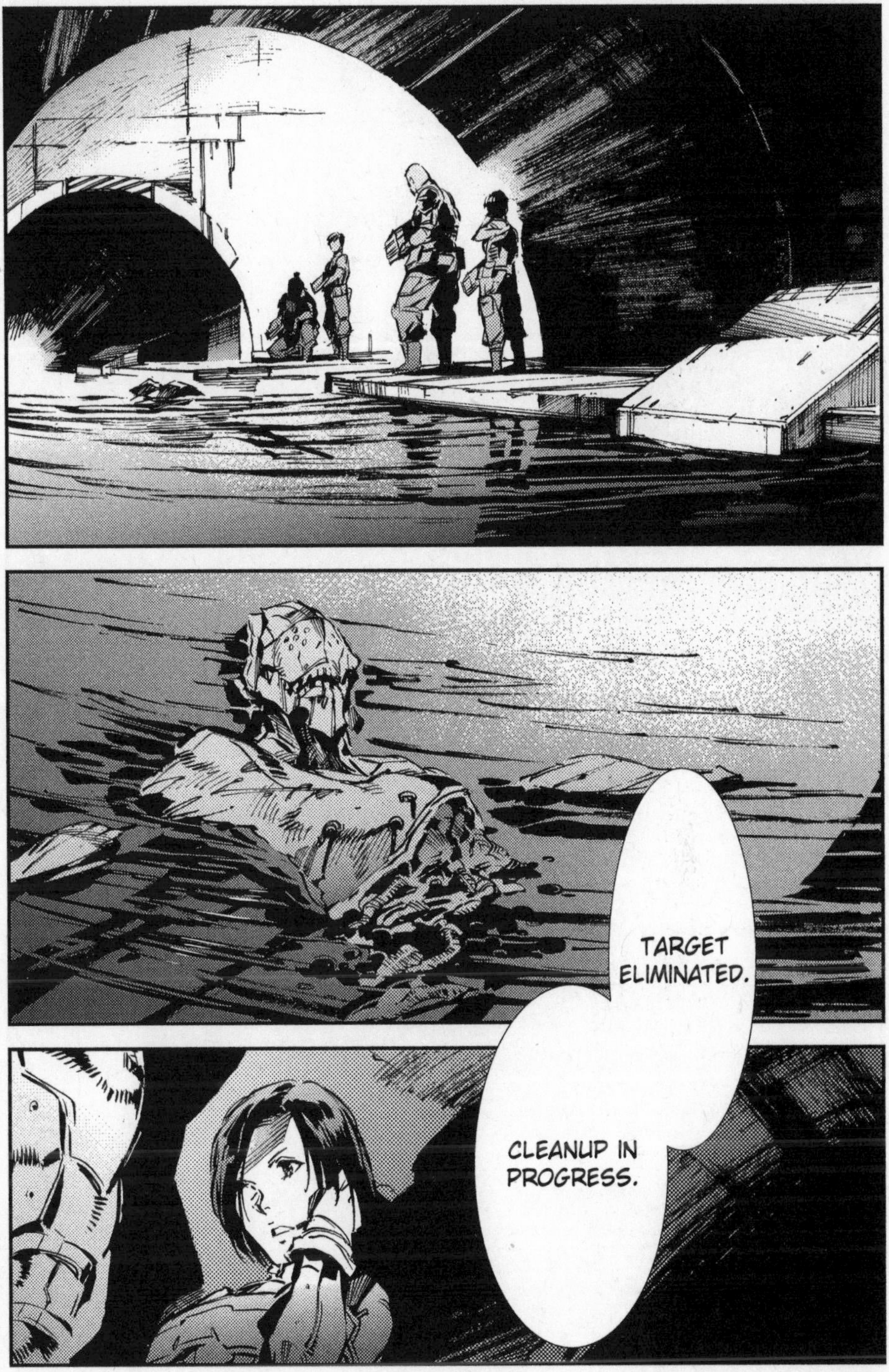
TARGET ELIMINATED.
CLEANUP IN PROGRESS.

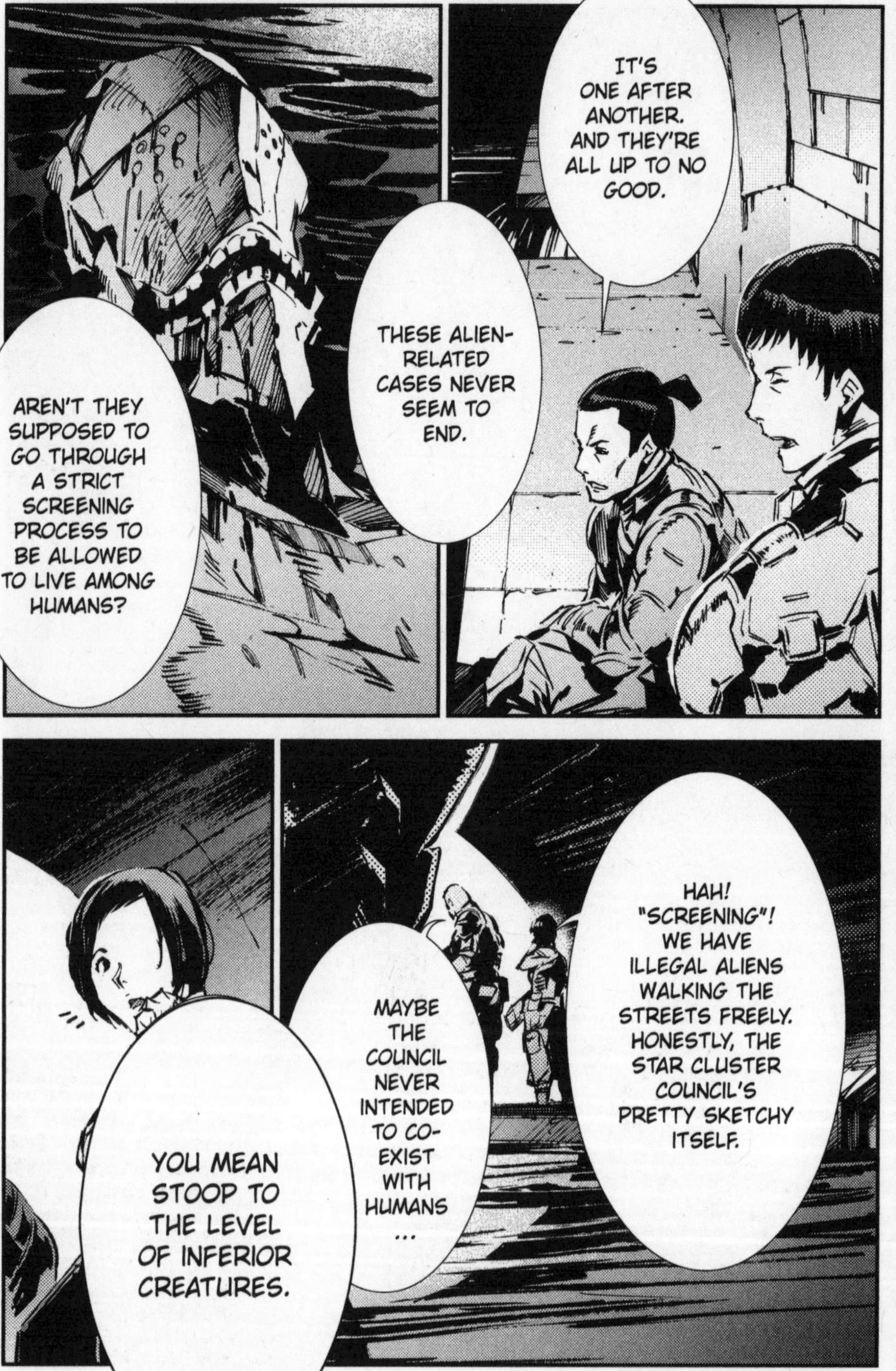
IT'S ONE AFTER ANOTHER. AND THEY'RE ALL UP TO NO GOOD.
THESE ALIEN-RELATED CASES NEVER SEEM TO END.
AREN'T THEY SUPPOSED TO GO THROUGH A STRICT SCREENING PROCESS TO BE ALLOWED TO LIVE AMONG HUMANS?
HAH! "SCREENING"! WE HAVE ILLEGAL ALIENS WALKING THE STREETS FREELY. HONESTLY, THE STAR CLUSTER COUNCIL'S PRETTY SKETCHY ITSELF.
MAYBE THE COUNCIL NEVER INTENDED TO CO-EXIST WITH HUMANS...
YOU MEAN STOOP TO THE LEVEL OF INFERIOR CREATURES.

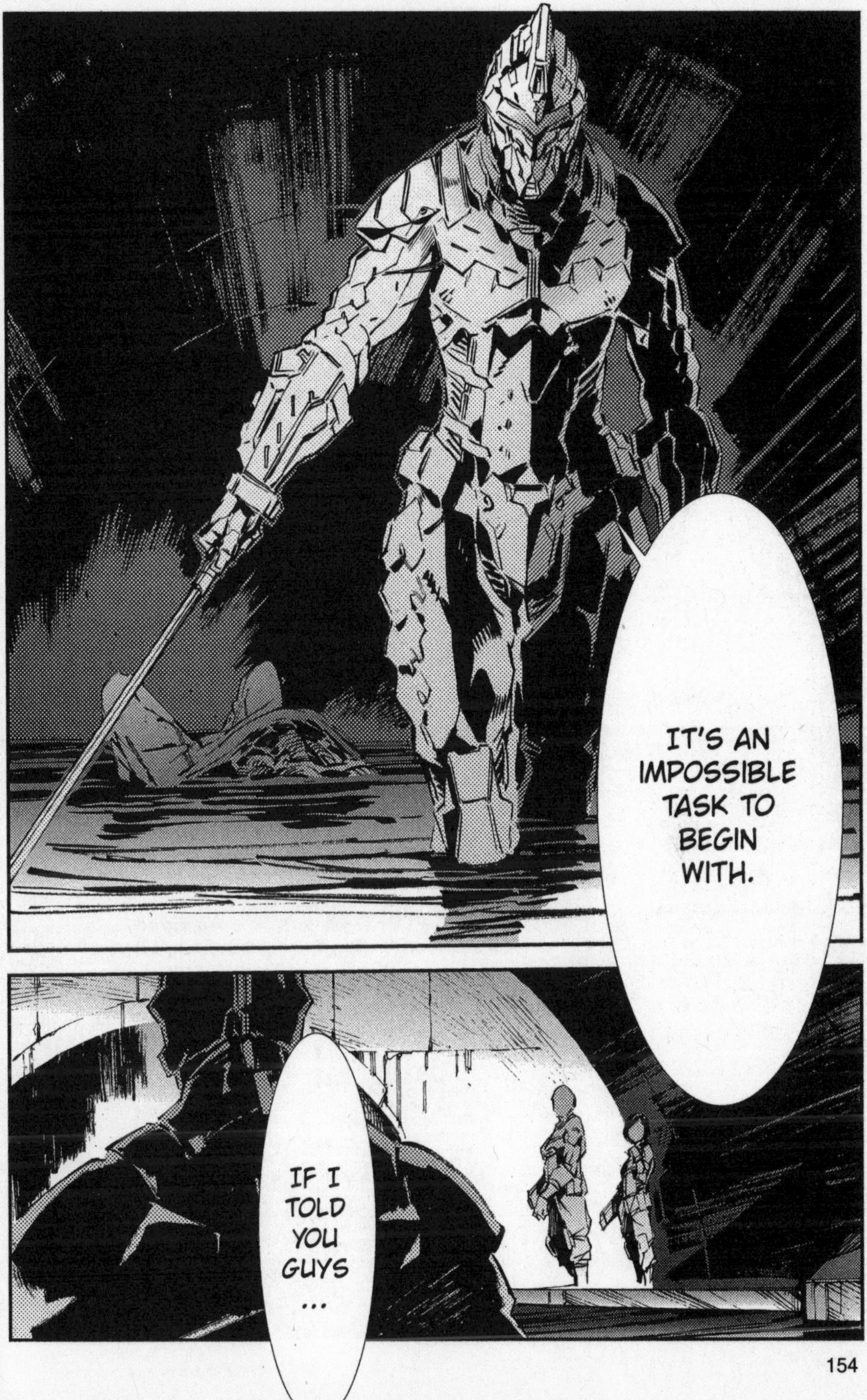
IT'S AN IMPOSSIBLE TASK TO BEGIN WITH.
IF I TOLD YOU GUYS ...

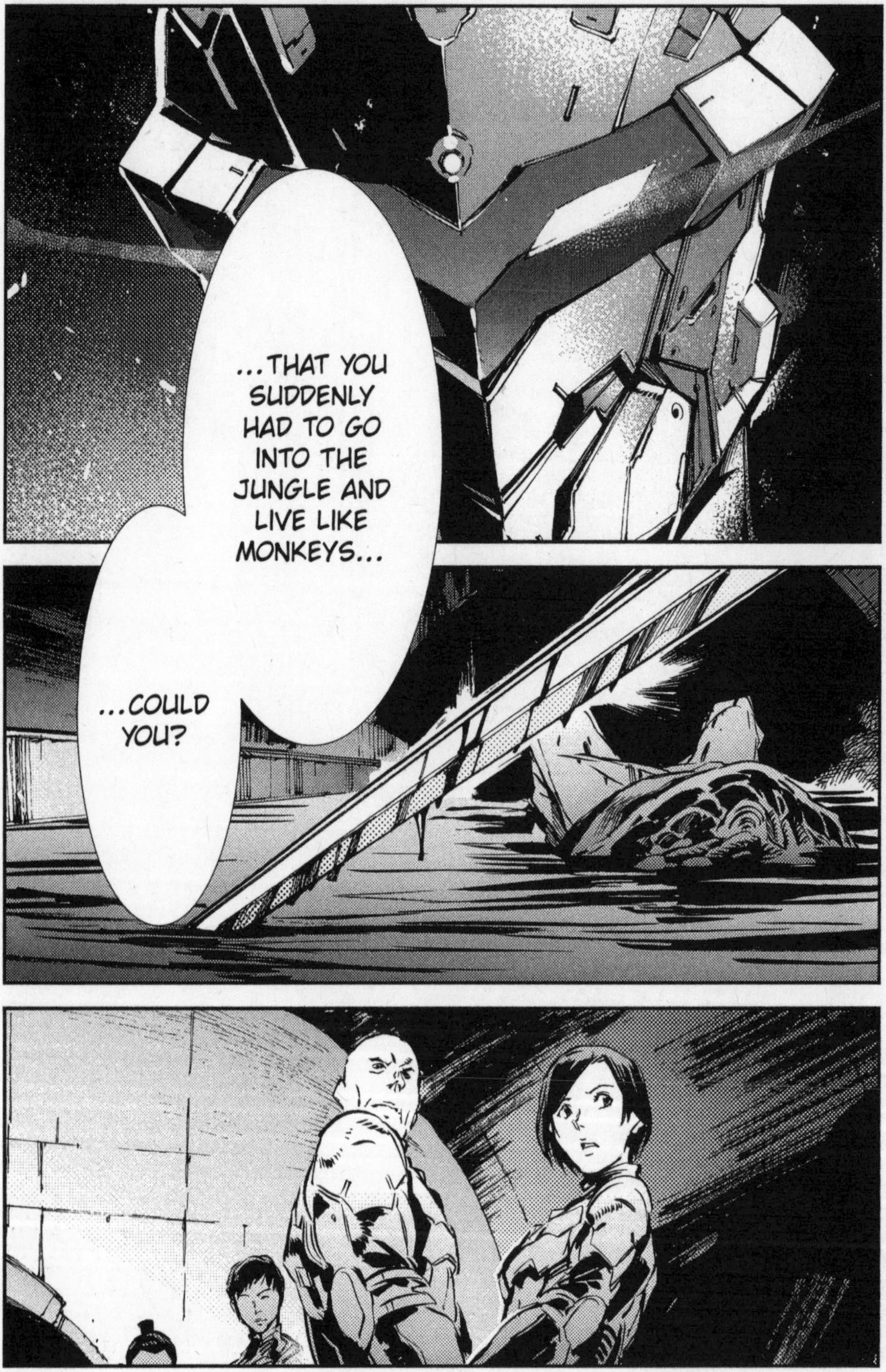
...THAT YOU SUDDENLY HAD TO GO INTO THE JUNGLE AND LIVE LIKE MONKEYS...
...COULD YOU?

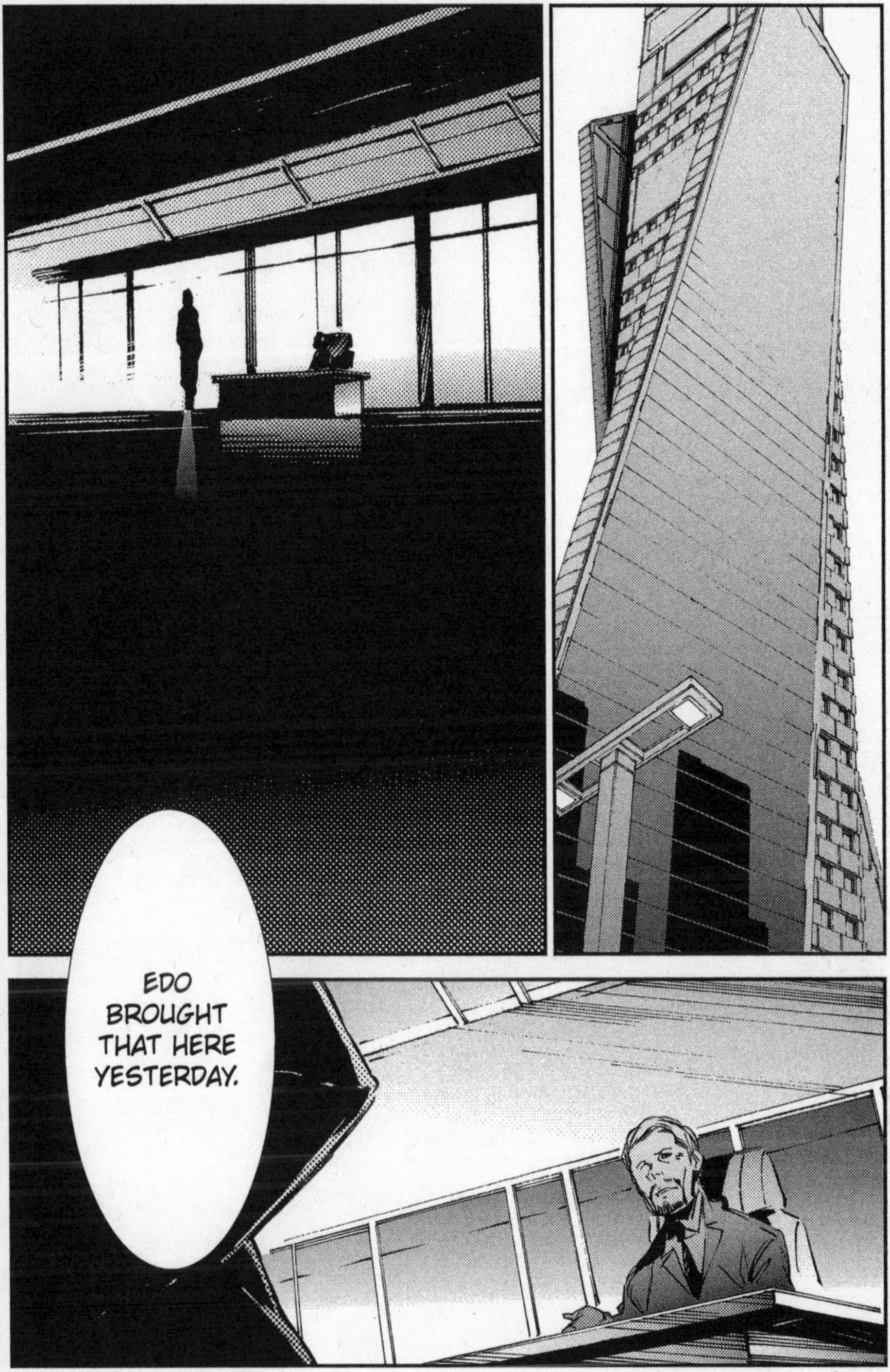
EDO BROUGHT THAT HERE YESTERDAY.

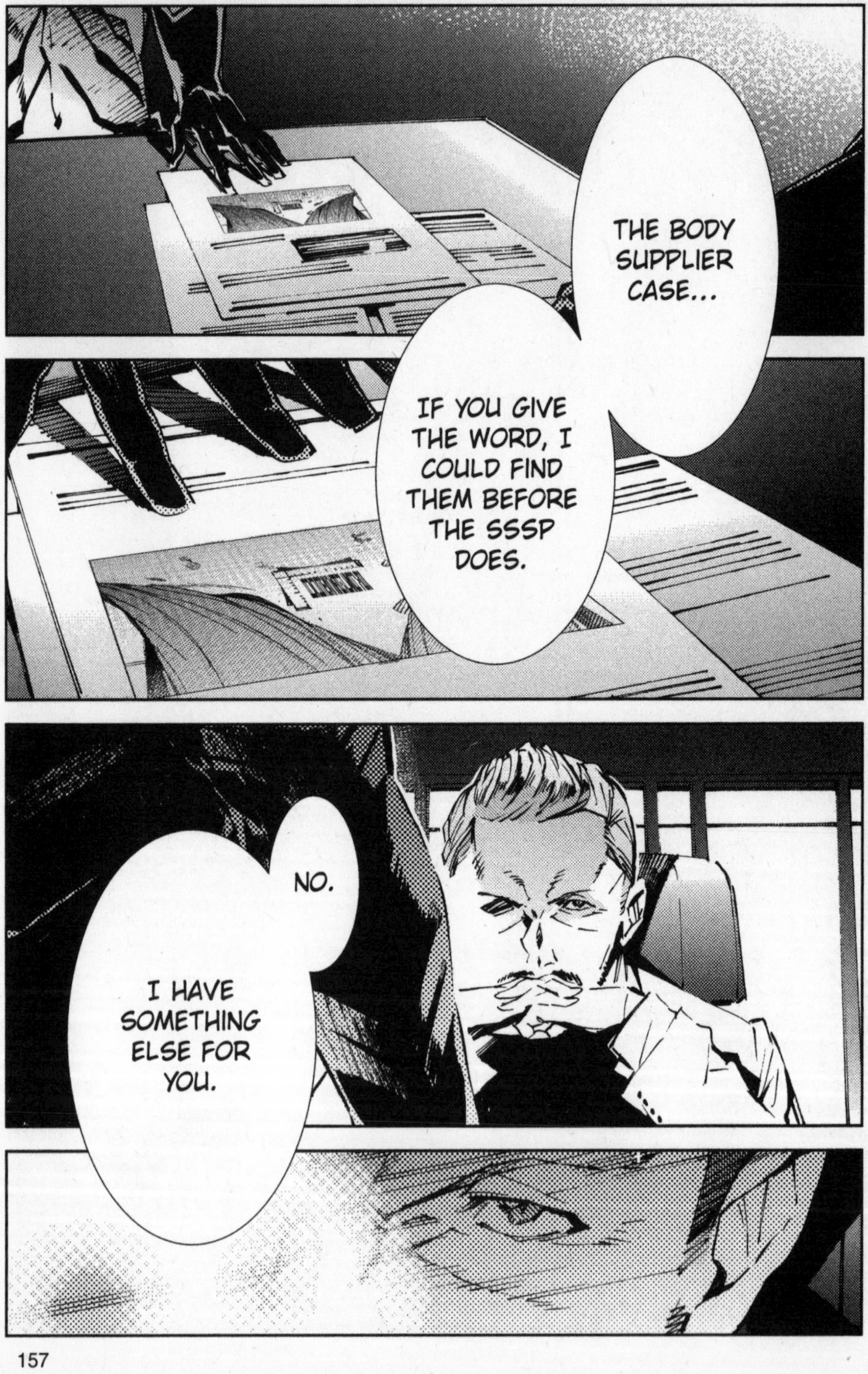
THE BODY SUPPLIER CASE...
IF YOU GIVE THE WORD, I COULD FIND THEM BEFORE THE SSSP DOES.
NO.
I HAVE SOMETHING ELSE FOR YOU.

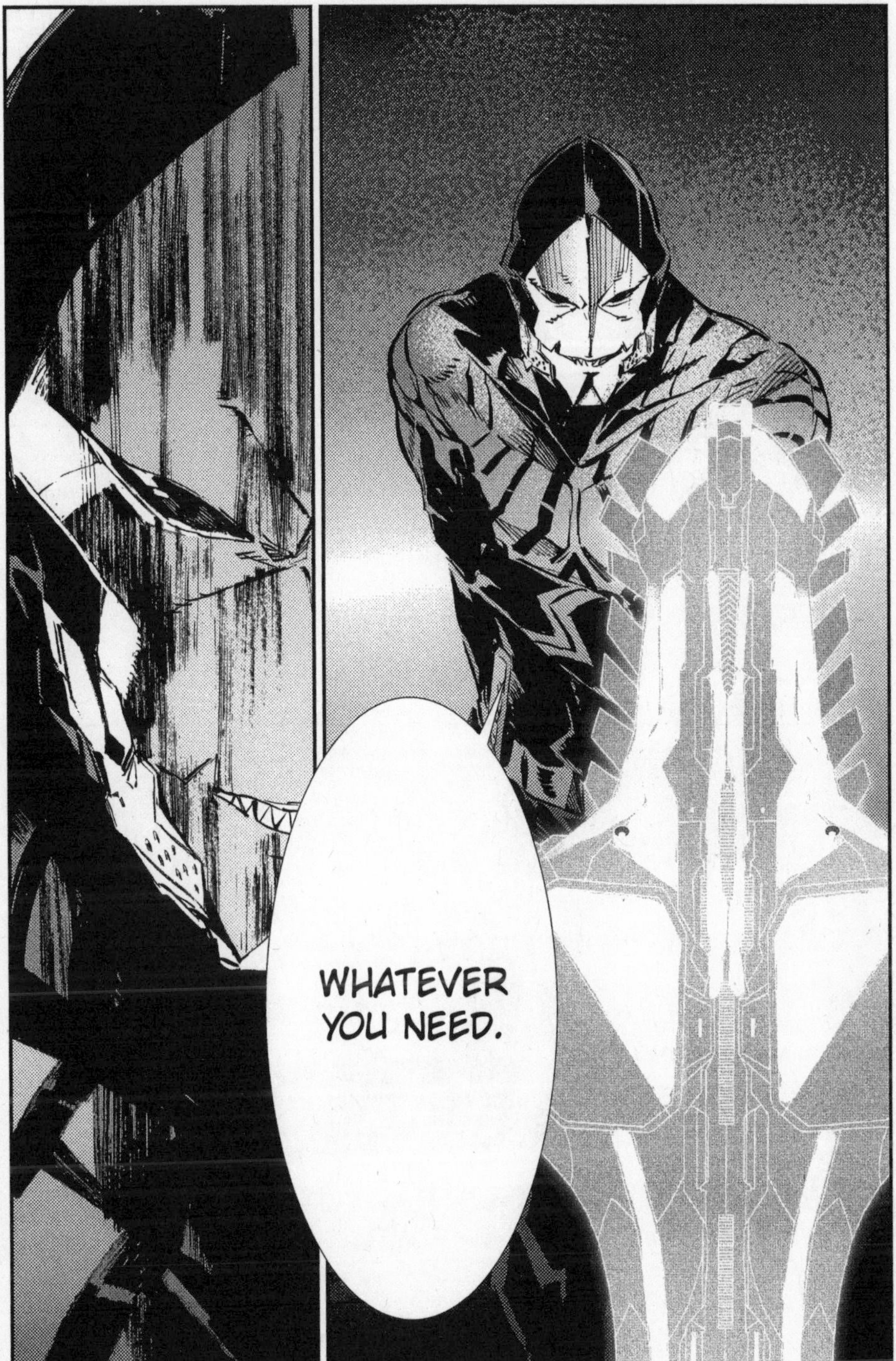
WHATEVER YOU NEED.

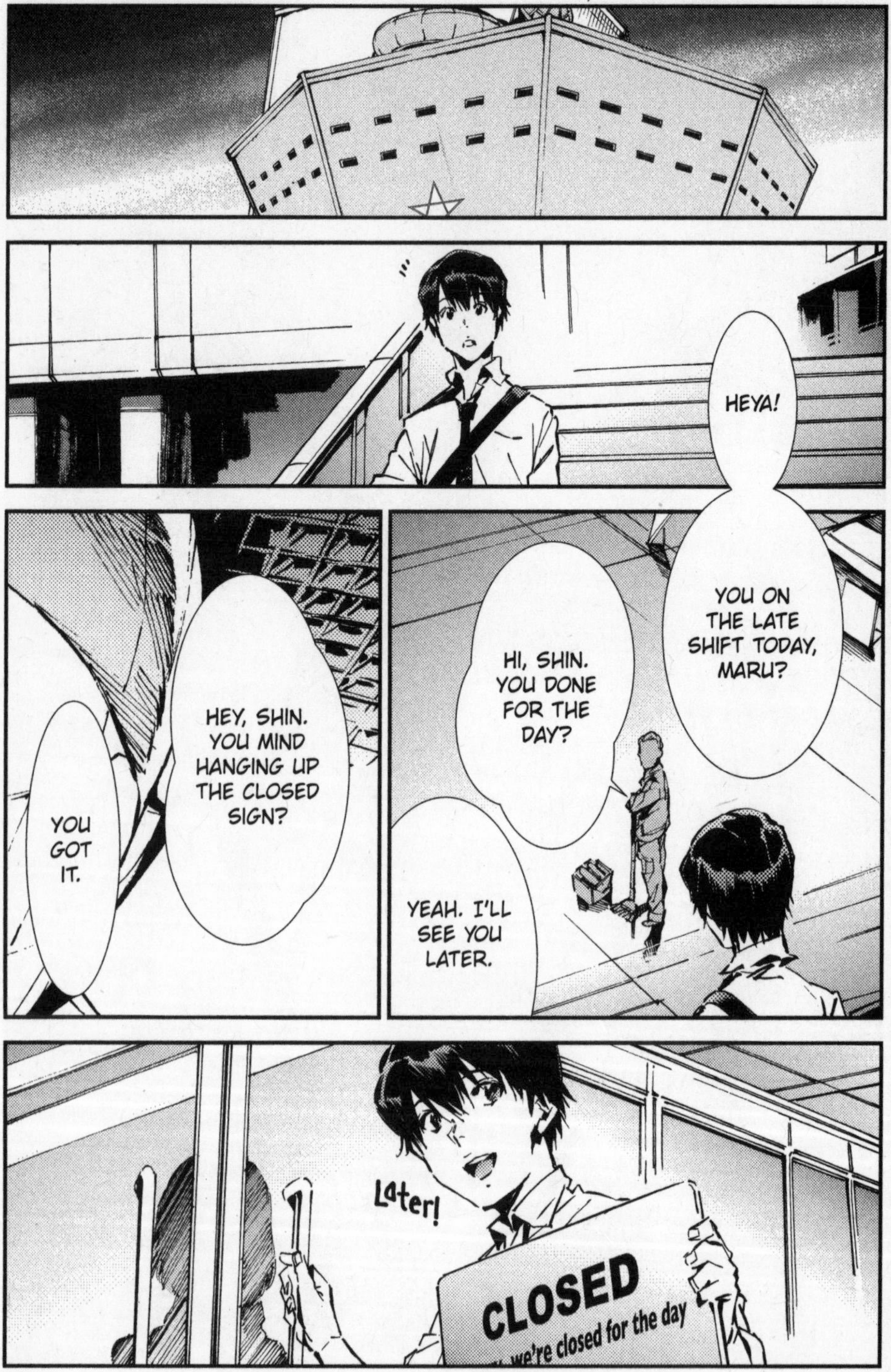
HEYA!
YOU ON THE LATE SHIFT TODAY, MARU?
HI, SHIN. YOU DONE FOR THE DAY?
YEAH. I'LL SEE YOU LATER.
HEY, SHIN. YOU MIND HANGING UP THE CLOSED SIGN?
YOU GOT IT.
Later!
CLOSED
we're closed for the day

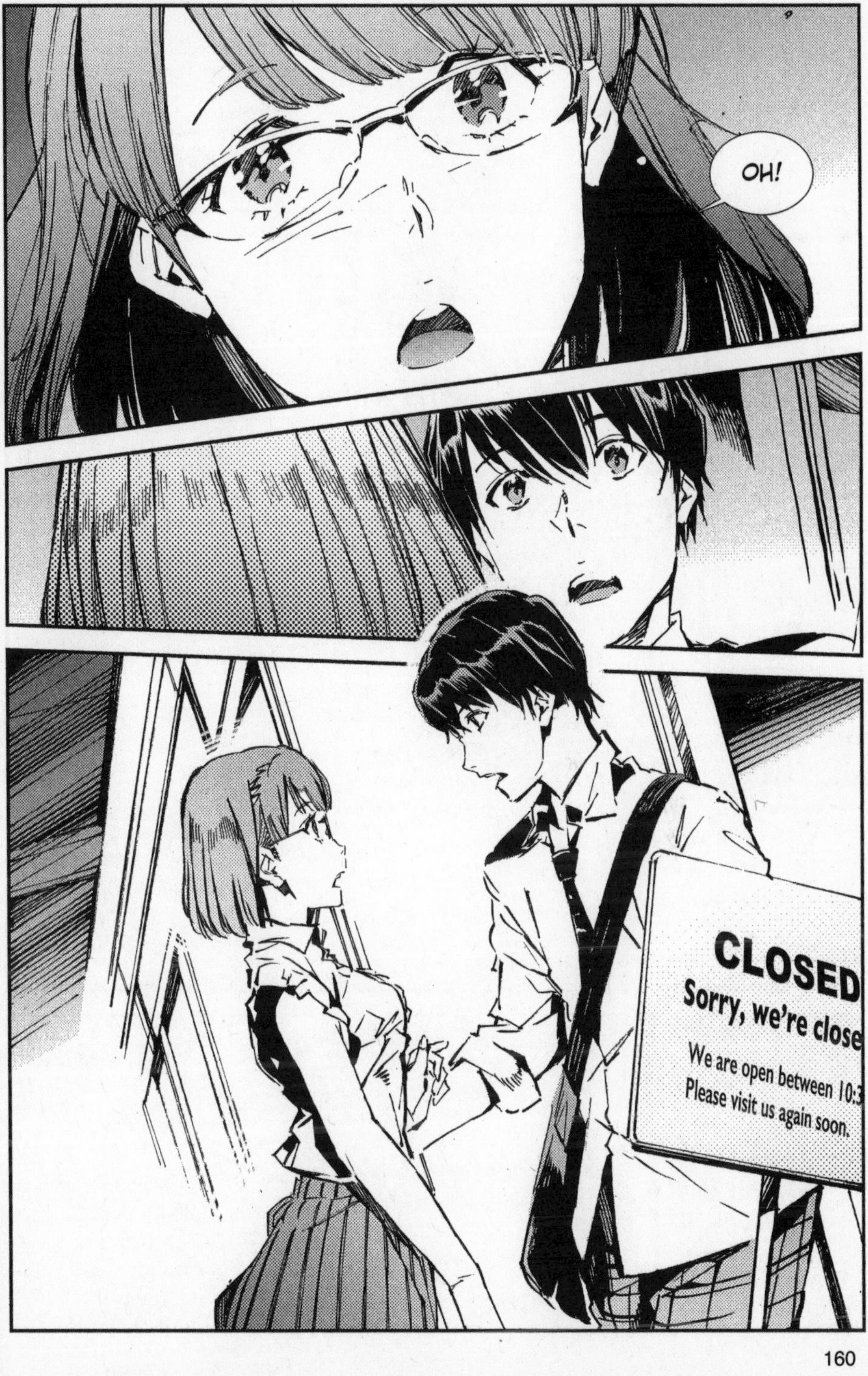
OH!
CLOSED
Sorry, we're close
We are open between 10:3
Please visit us again soon.

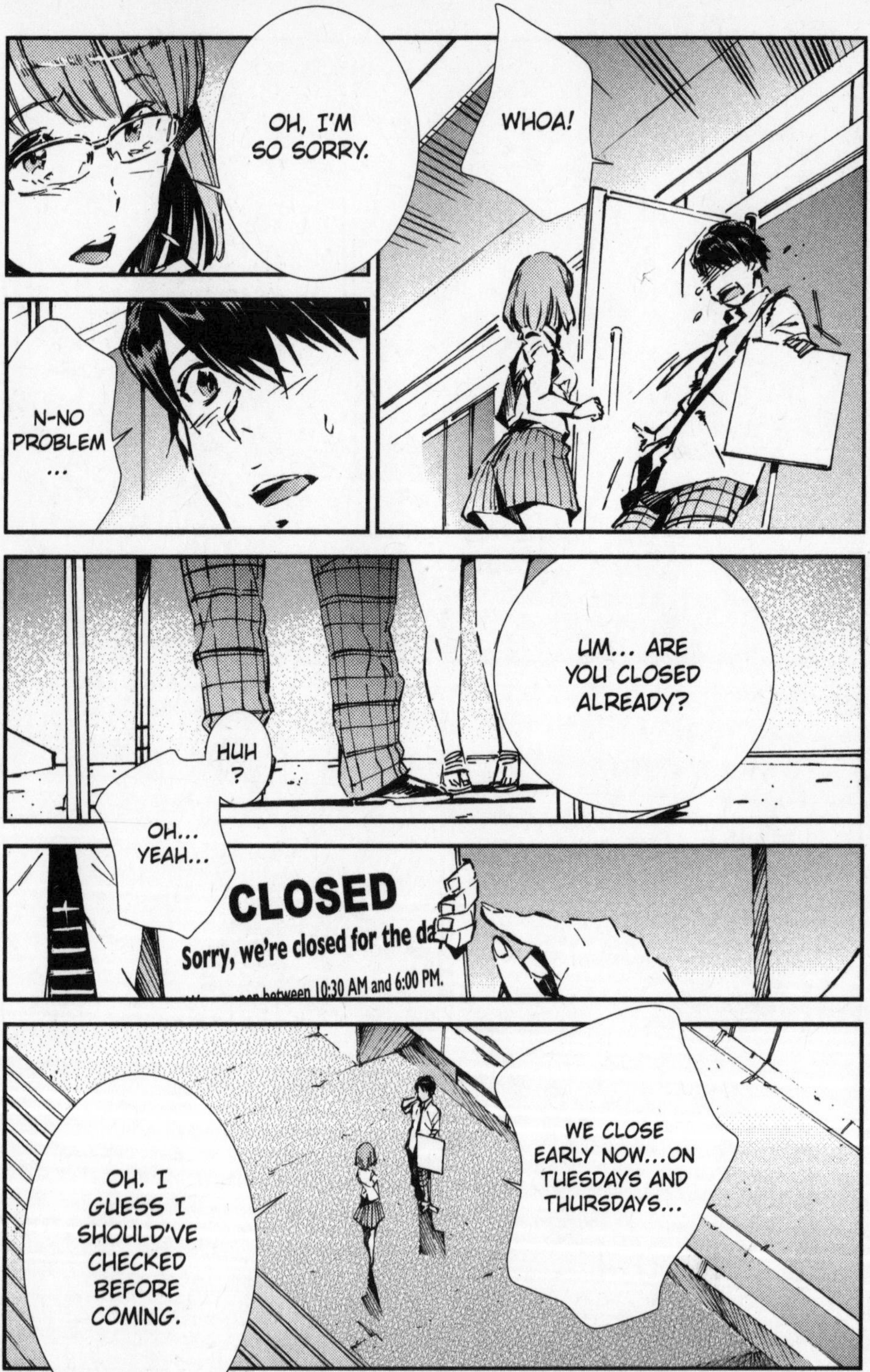
WHOA!
OH, I'M SO SORRY.
N-NO PROBLEM ...
UM... ARE YOU CLOSED ALREADY?
HUH?
OH... YEAH...
CLOSED
Sorry, we're closed for the da
10:30 AM and 6:00 PM.
WE CLOSE EARLY NOW...ON TUESDAYS AND THURSDAYS...
OH. I GUESS I SHOULD'VE CHECKED BEFORE COMING.

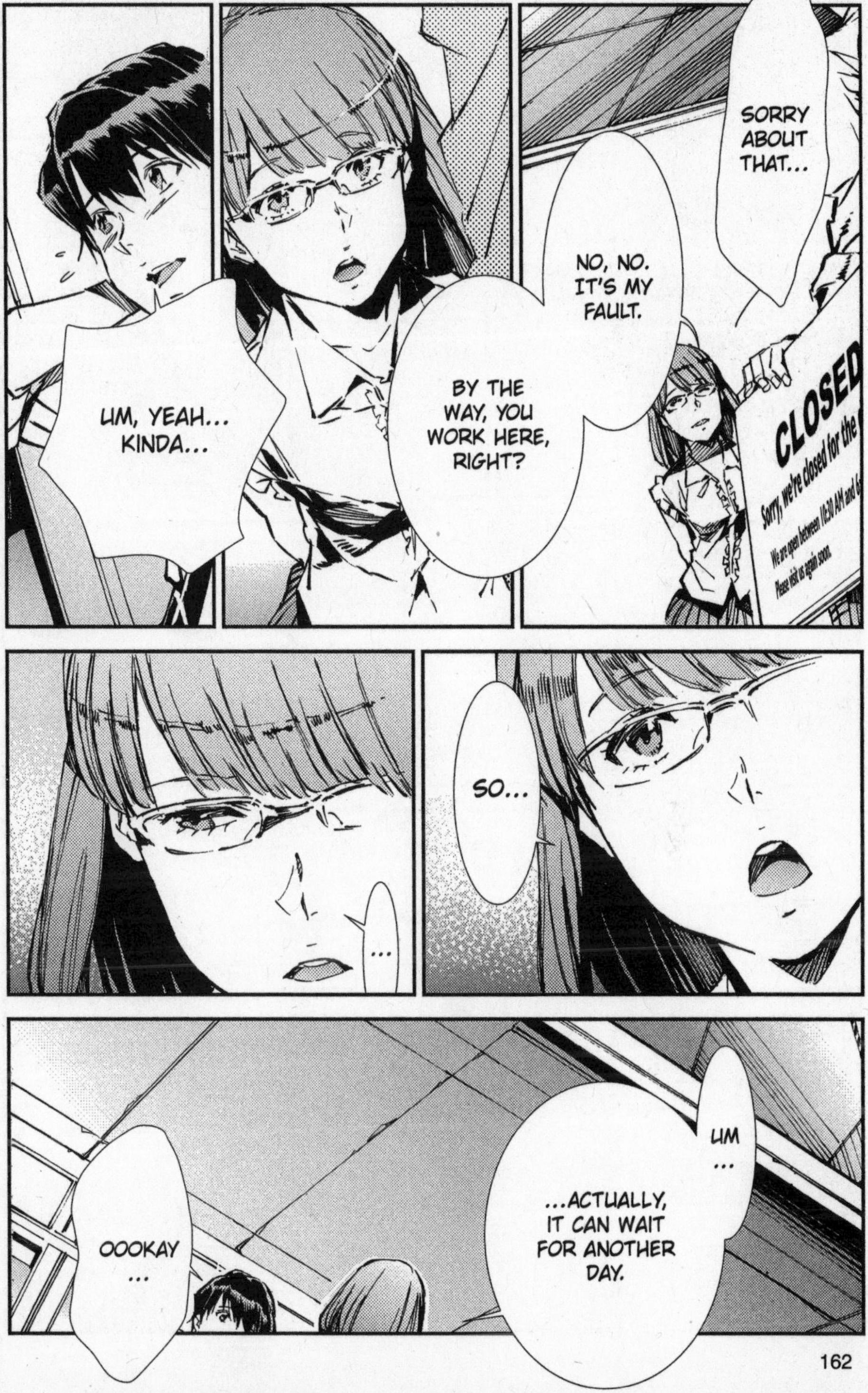
SORRY ABOUT THAT...
NO, NO. IT'S MY FAULT.
CLOSED
Sorry, we're closed for the
We are open between 10:30 AM and 6
Please visit us again soon.
BY THE WAY, YOU WORK HERE, RIGHT?
UM, YEAH... KINDA...
SO...
...
UM ...
...ACTUALLY, IT CAN WAIT FOR ANOTHER DAY.
OOOKAY ...

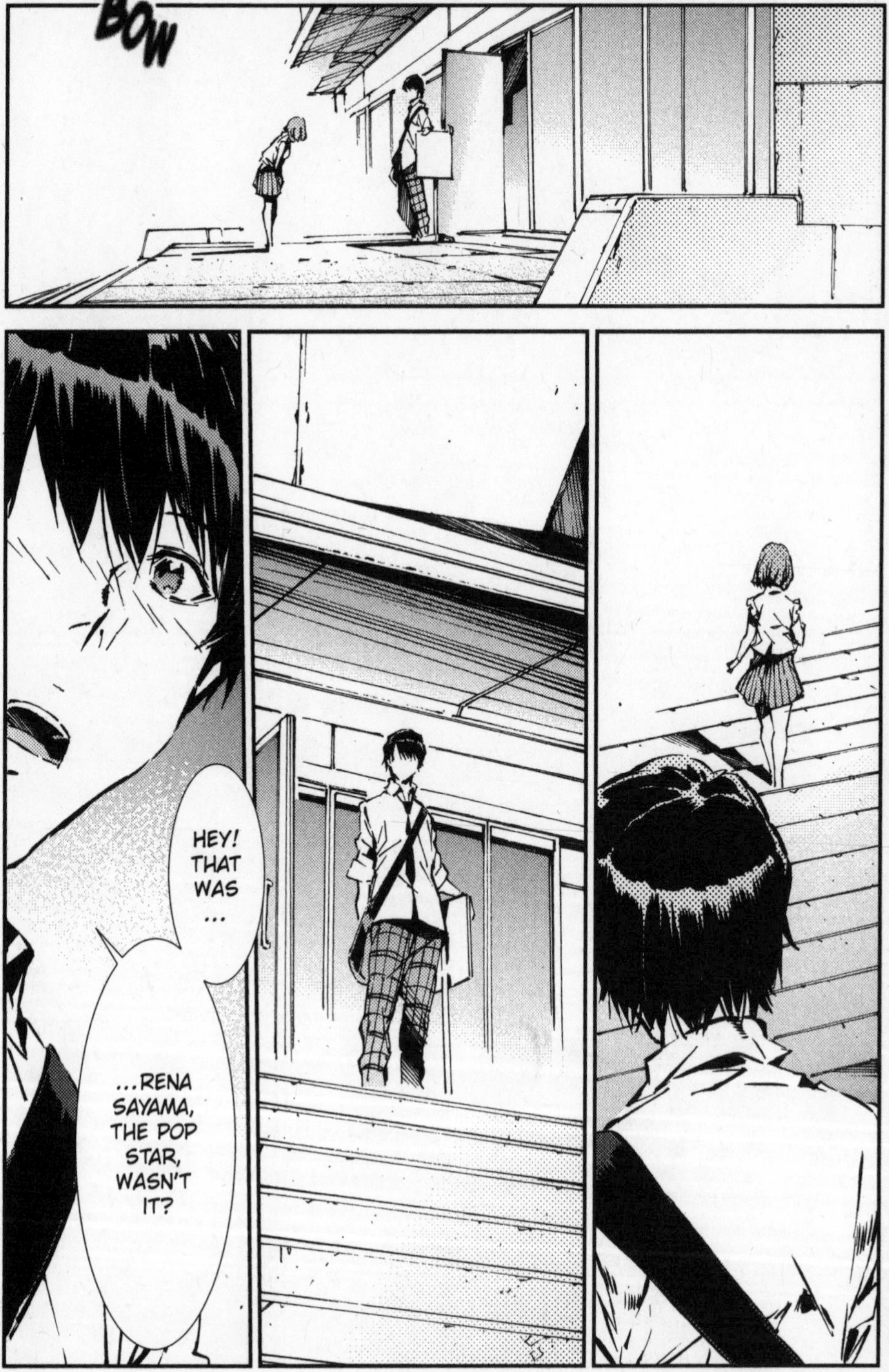
BOW
HEY! THAT WAS ...
...RENA SAYAMA, THE POP STAR, WASN'T IT?

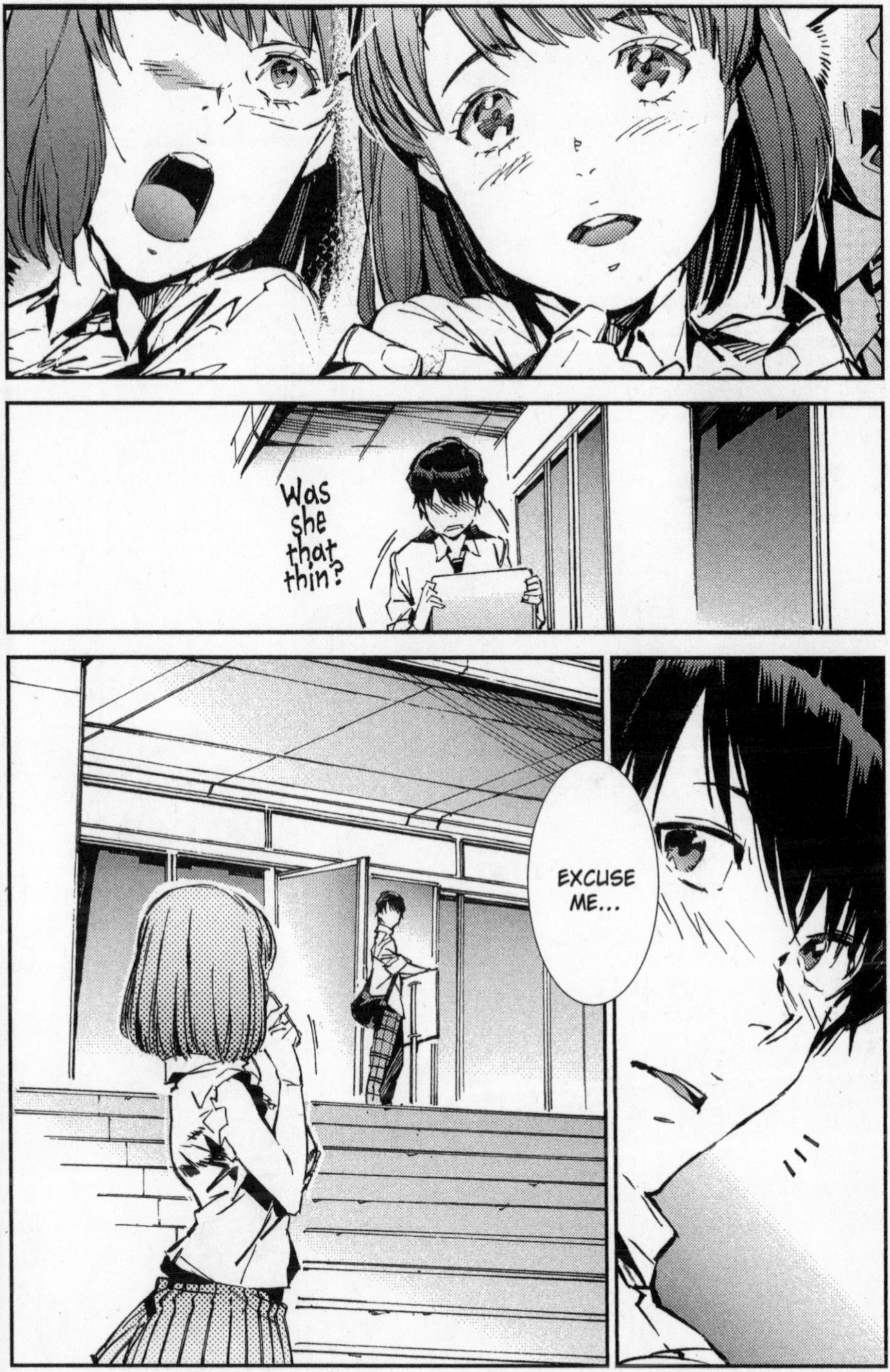
Was she that thin?
EXCUSE ME...

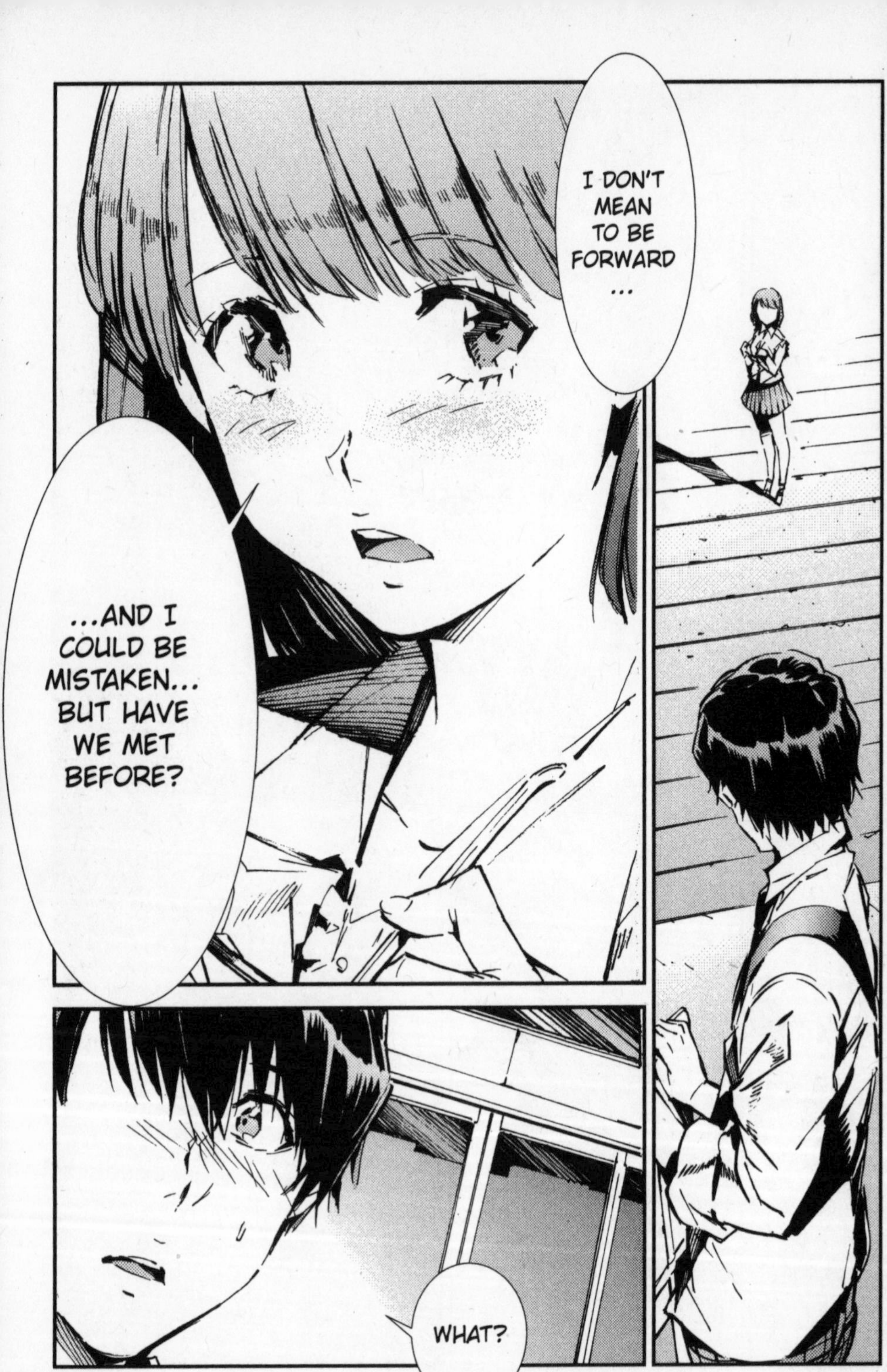
I DON'T MEAN TO BE FORWARD...
...AND I COULD BE MISTAKEN... BUT HAVE WE MET BEFORE?
WHAT?

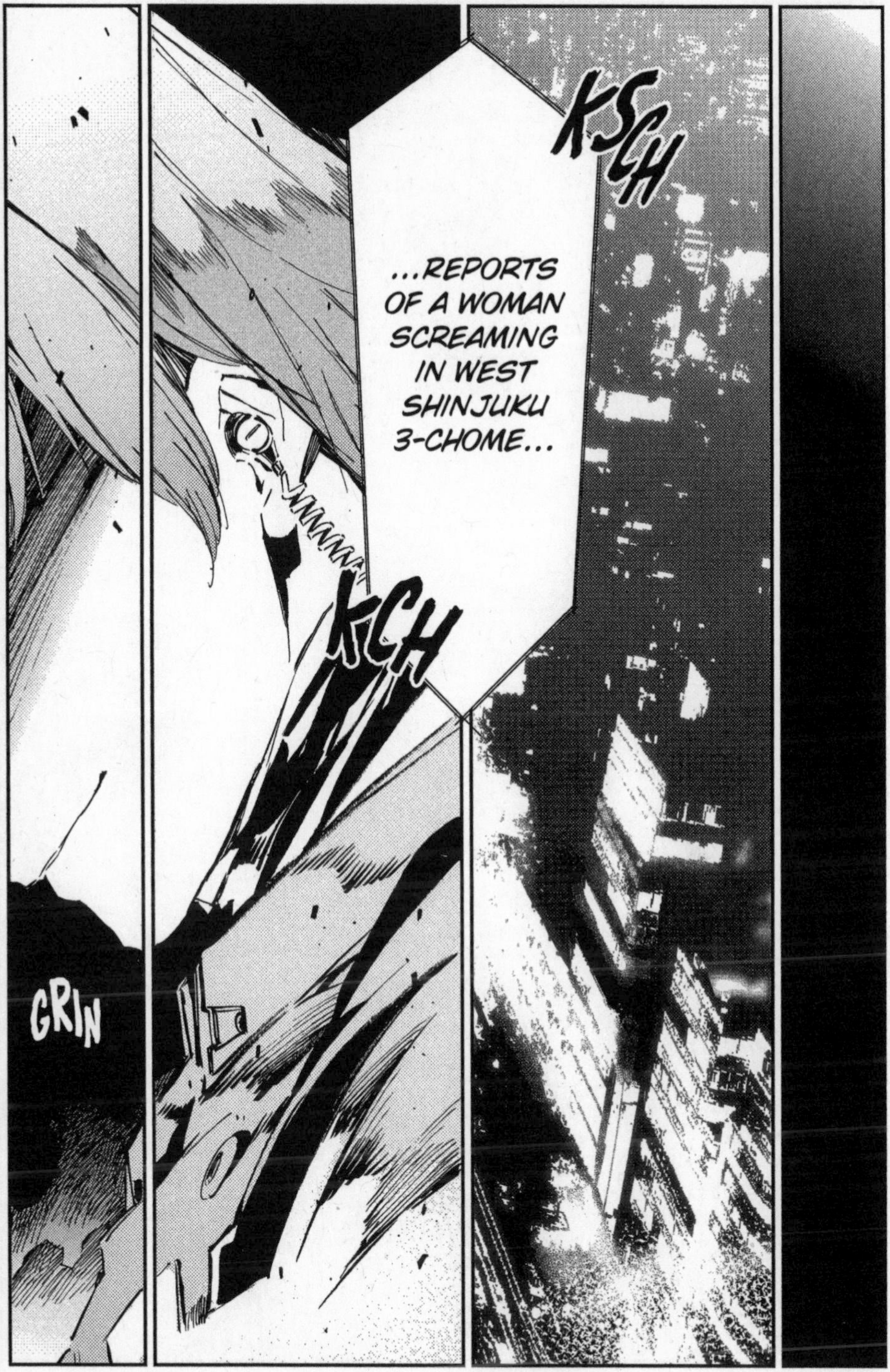
KSCH
...REPORTS OF A WOMAN SCREAMING IN WEST SHINJUKU 3-CHOME...
KCH
GRIN

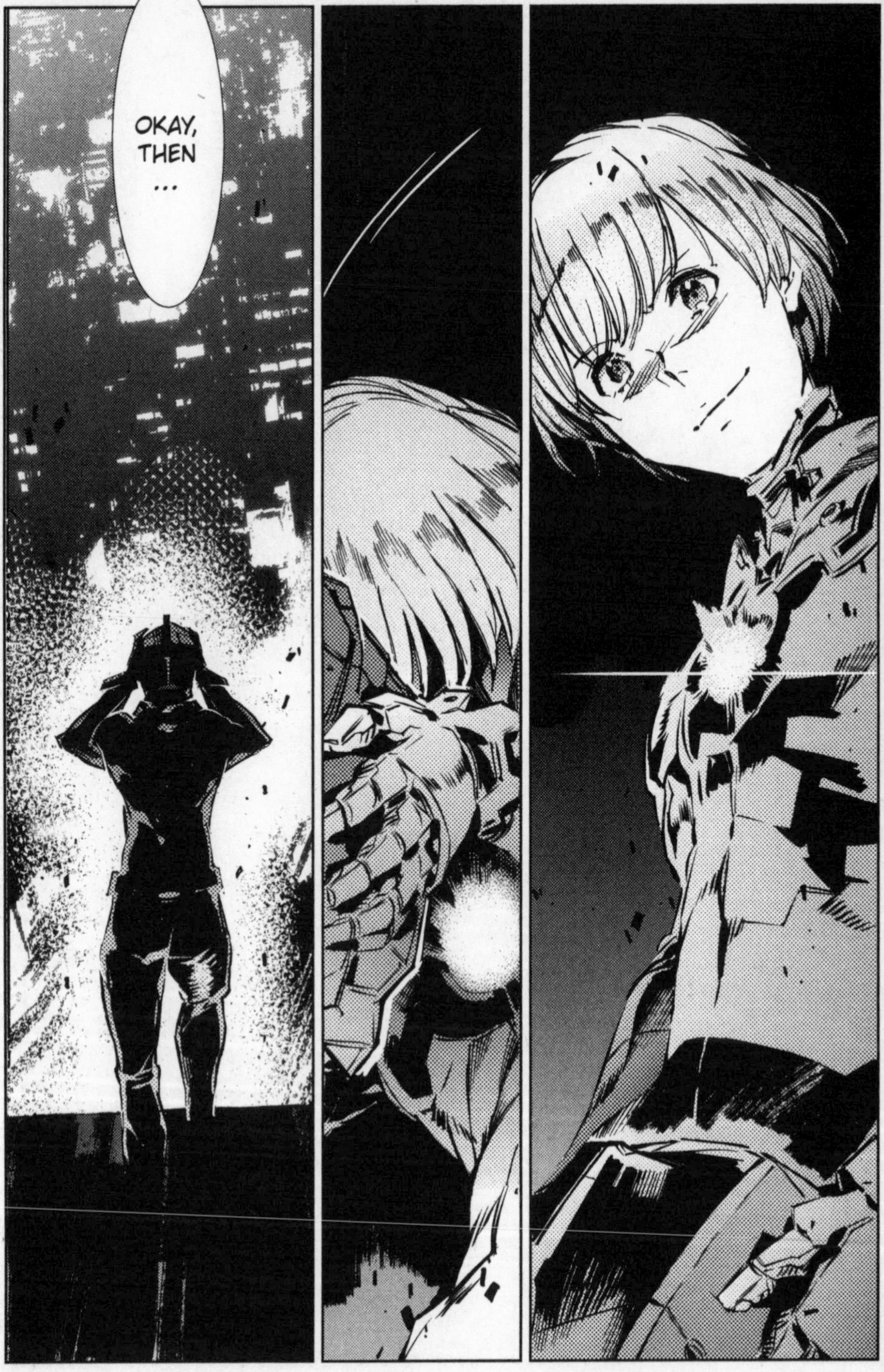
OKAY, THEN ...

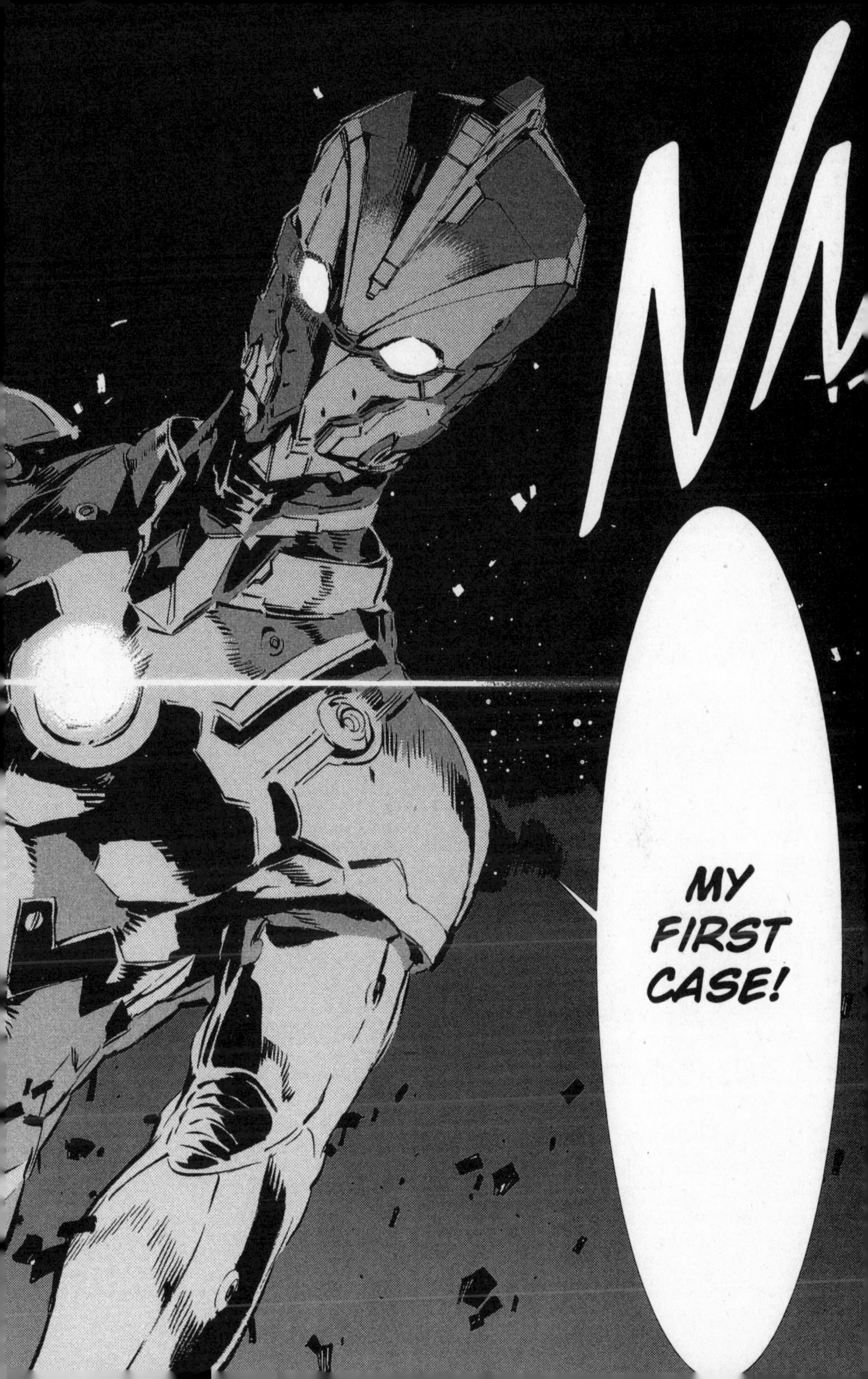
MY FIRST CASE!

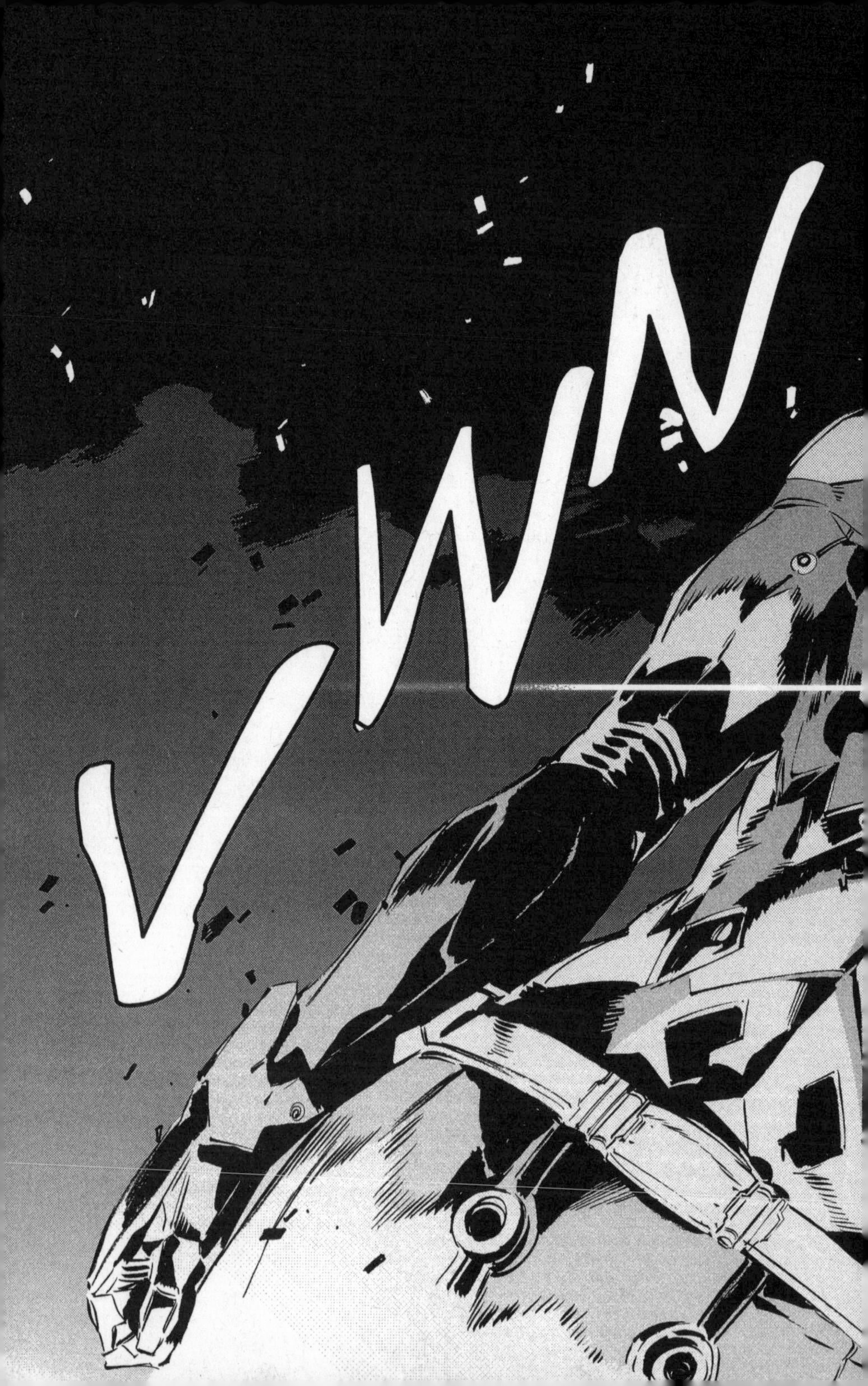
VWN

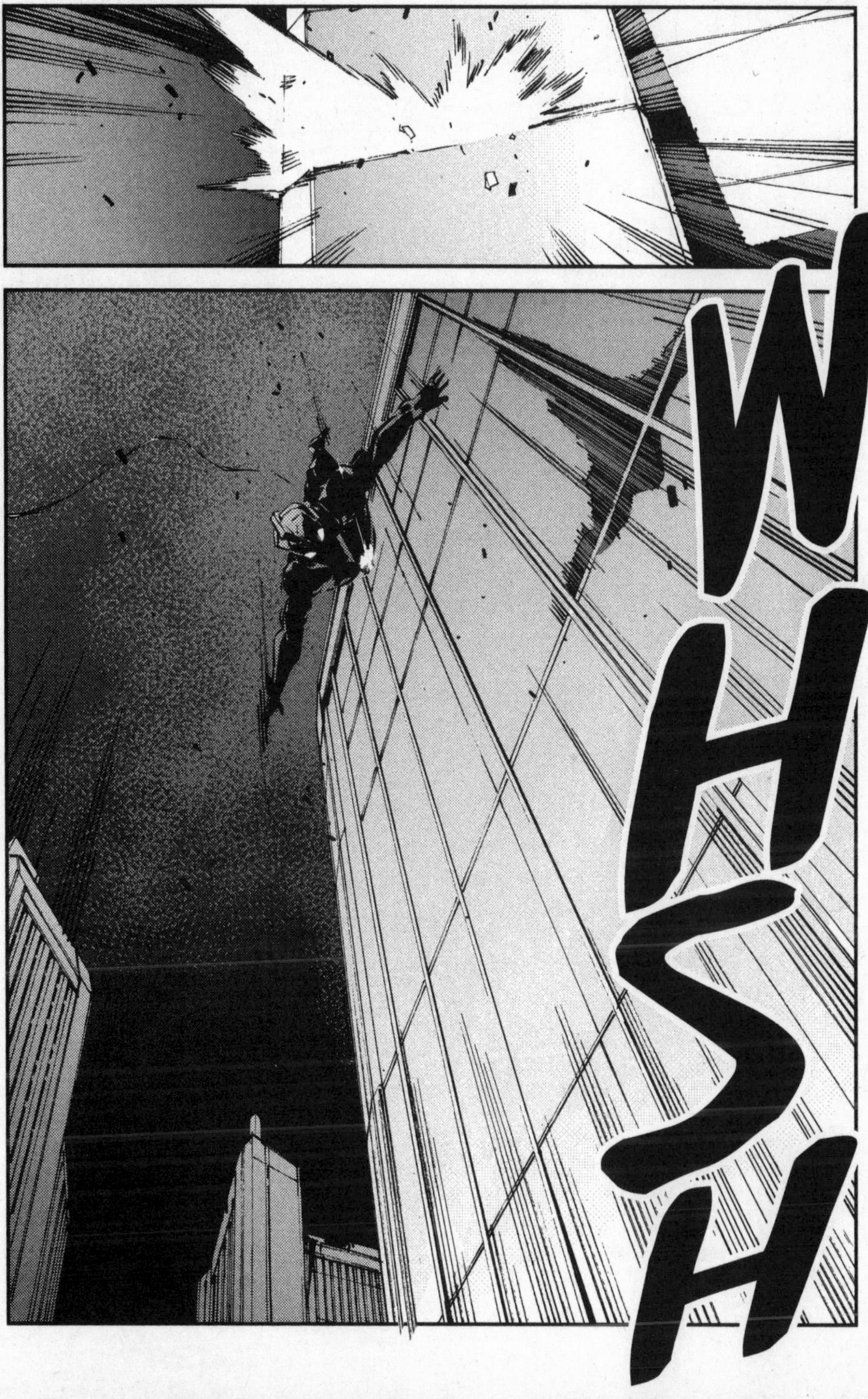
WHSH

ULTRAMAN

CHAPTER 34 – CONTACT

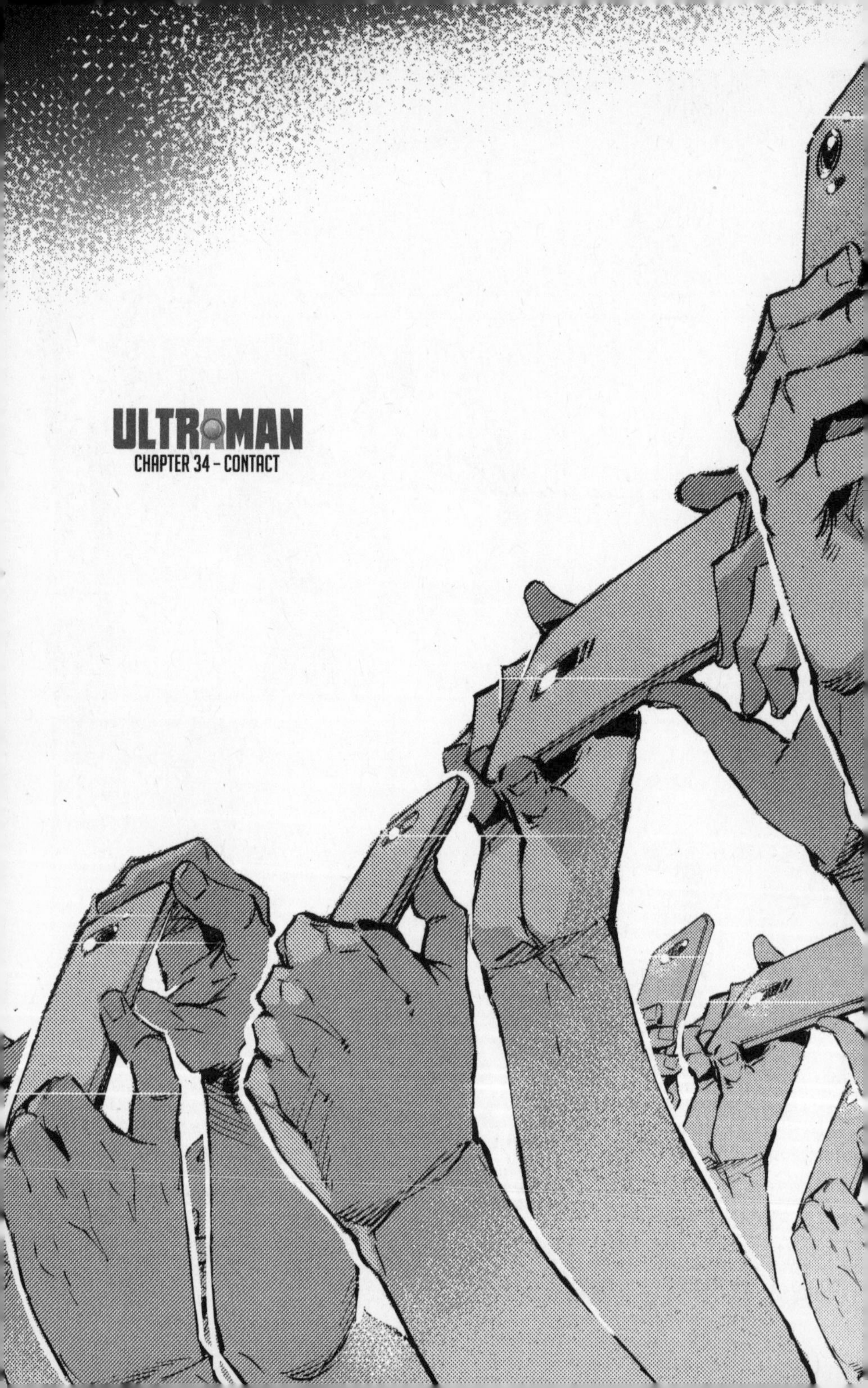

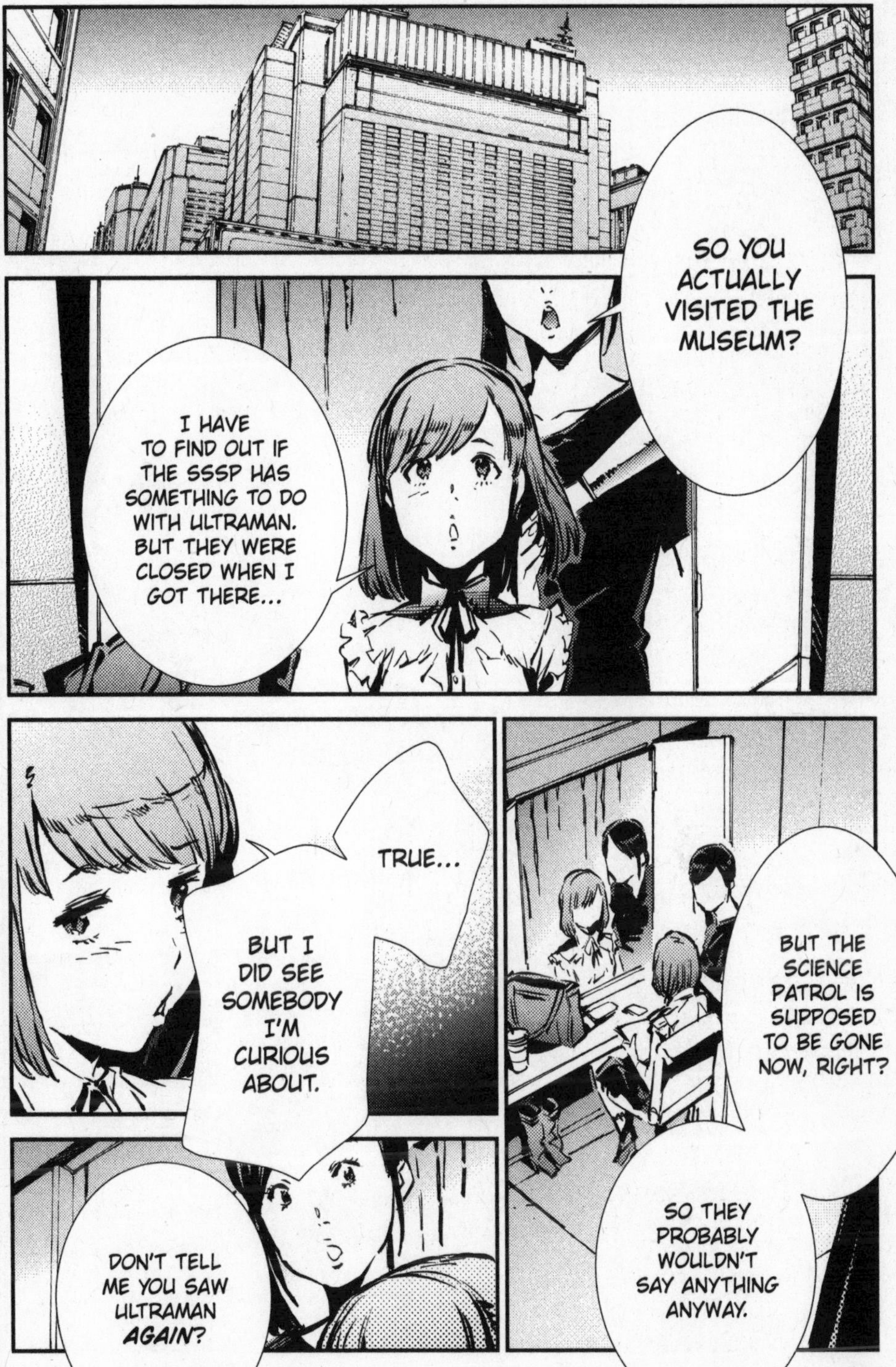
SO YOU ACTUALLY VISITED THE MUSEUM?
I HAVE TO FIND OUT IF THE SSSP HAS SOMETHING TO DO WITH ULTRAMAN. BUT THEY WERE CLOSED WHEN I GOT THERE...
BUT THE SCIENCE PATROL IS SUPPOSED TO BE GONE NOW, RIGHT?
SO THEY PROBABLY WOULDN'T SAY ANYTHING ANYWAY.
TRUE...
BUT I DID SEE SOMEBODY I'M CURIOUS ABOUT.
DON'T TELL ME YOU SAW ULTRAMAN *AGAIN*?

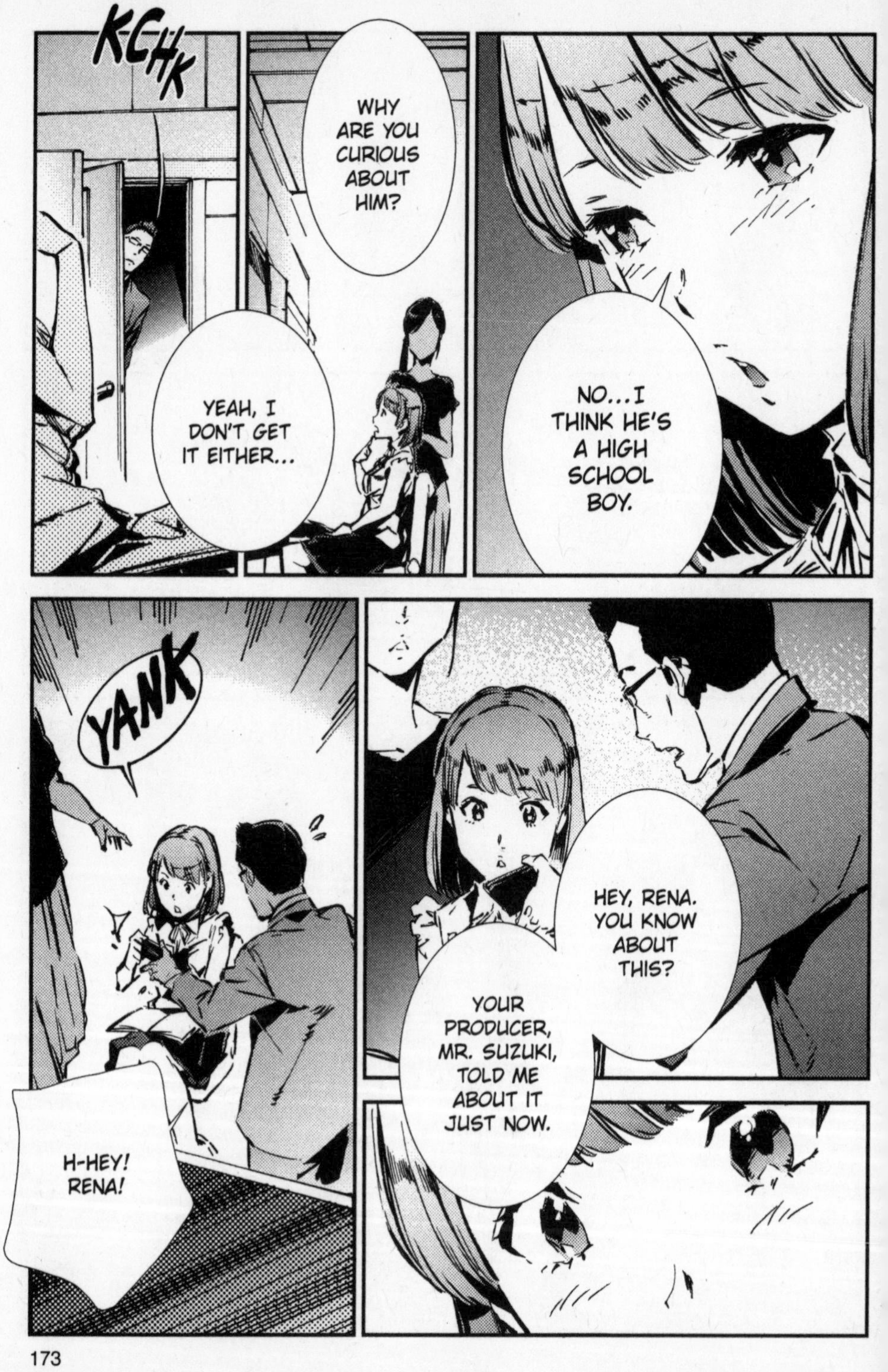
NO...I THINK HE'S A HIGH SCHOOL BOY.
WHY ARE YOU CURIOUS ABOUT HIM?
YEAH, I DON'T GET IT EITHER...
K-CHK
HEY, RENA. YOU KNOW ABOUT THIS?
YOUR PRODUCER, MR. SUZUKI, TOLD ME ABOUT IT JUST NOW.
YANK
H-HEY! RENA!

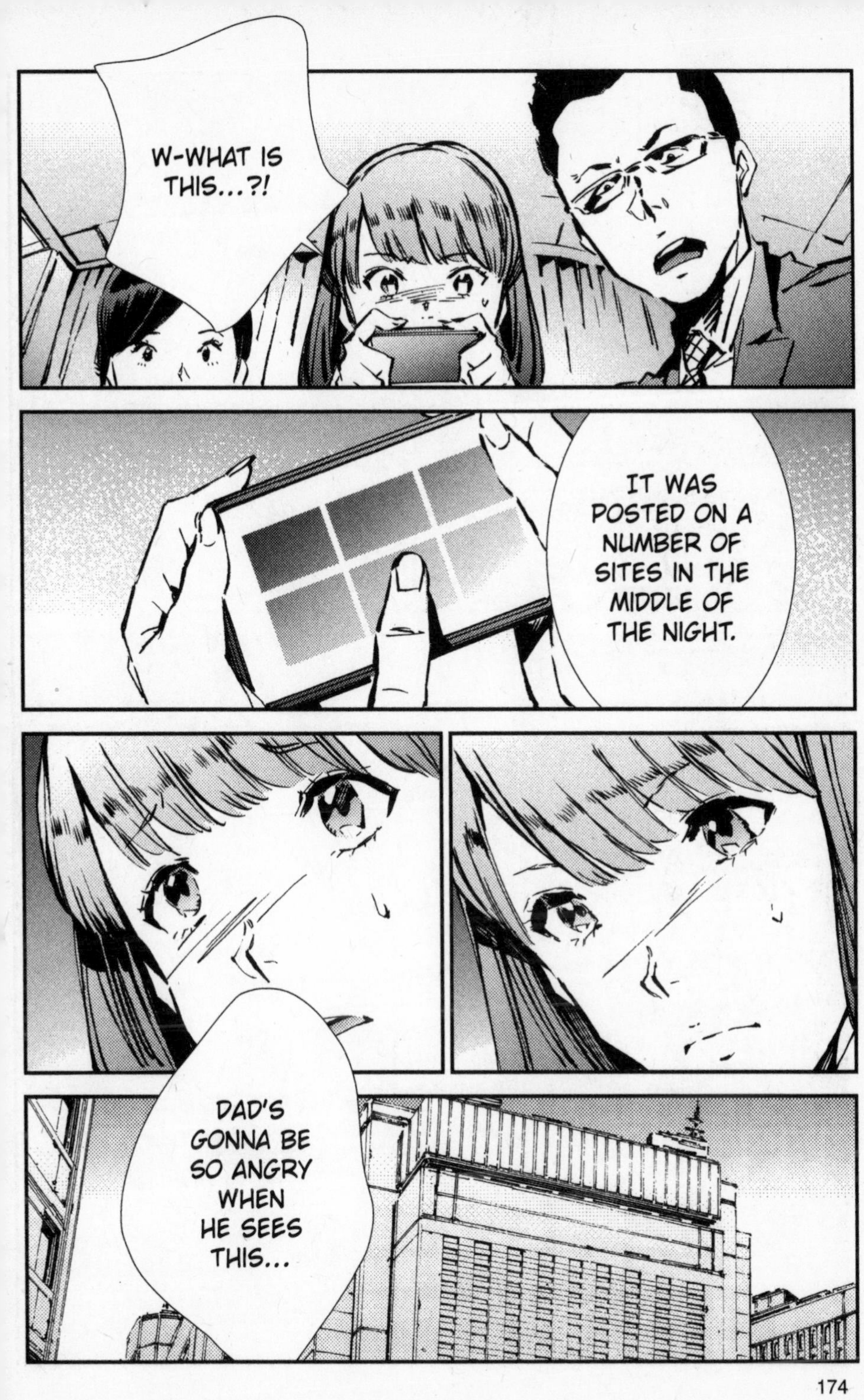
W-WHAT IS THIS...?!
IT WAS POSTED ON A NUMBER OF SITES IN THE MIDDLE OF THE NIGHT.
DAD'S GONNA BE SO ANGRY WHEN HE SEES THIS...

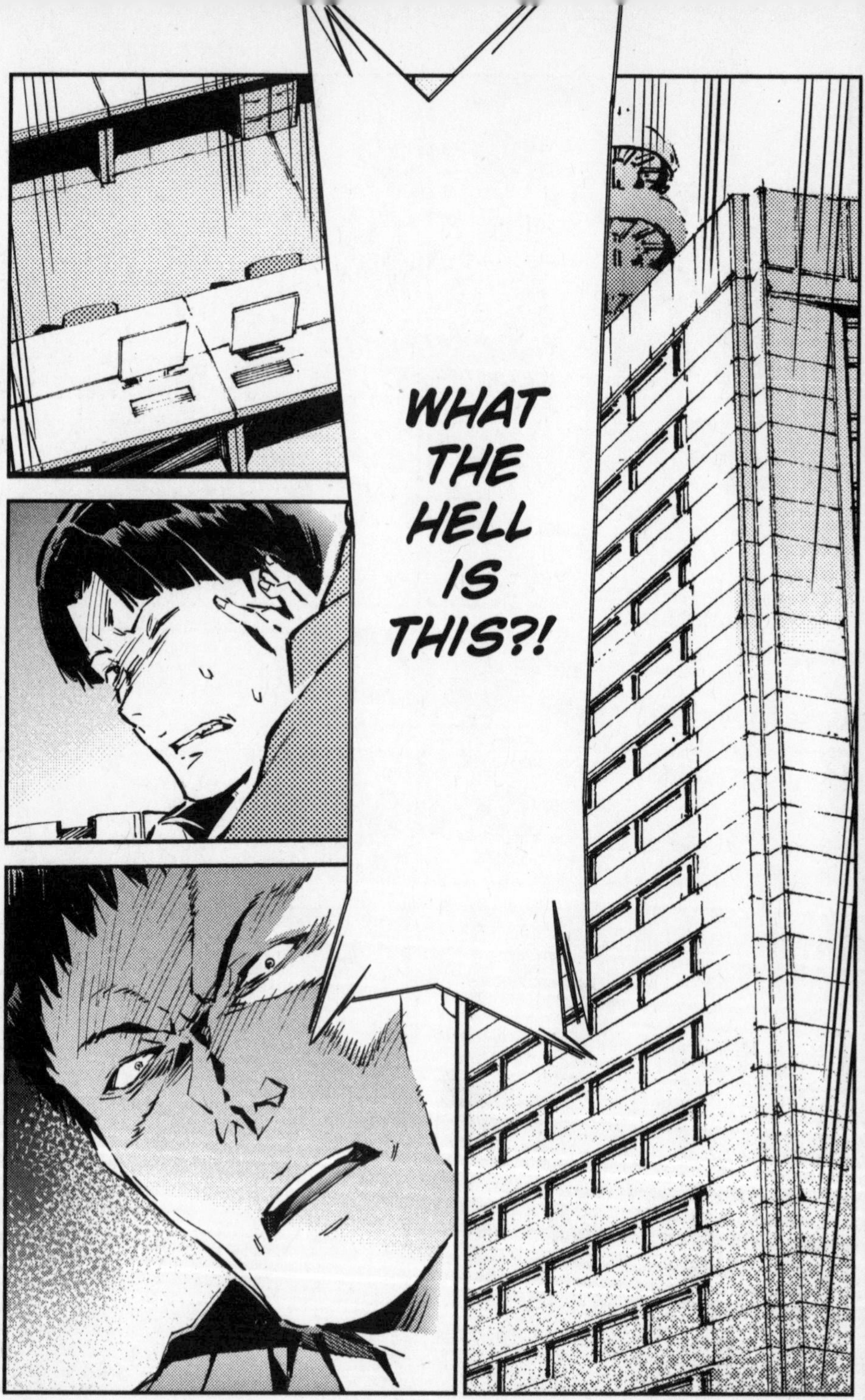
WHAT THE HELL IS THIS?!

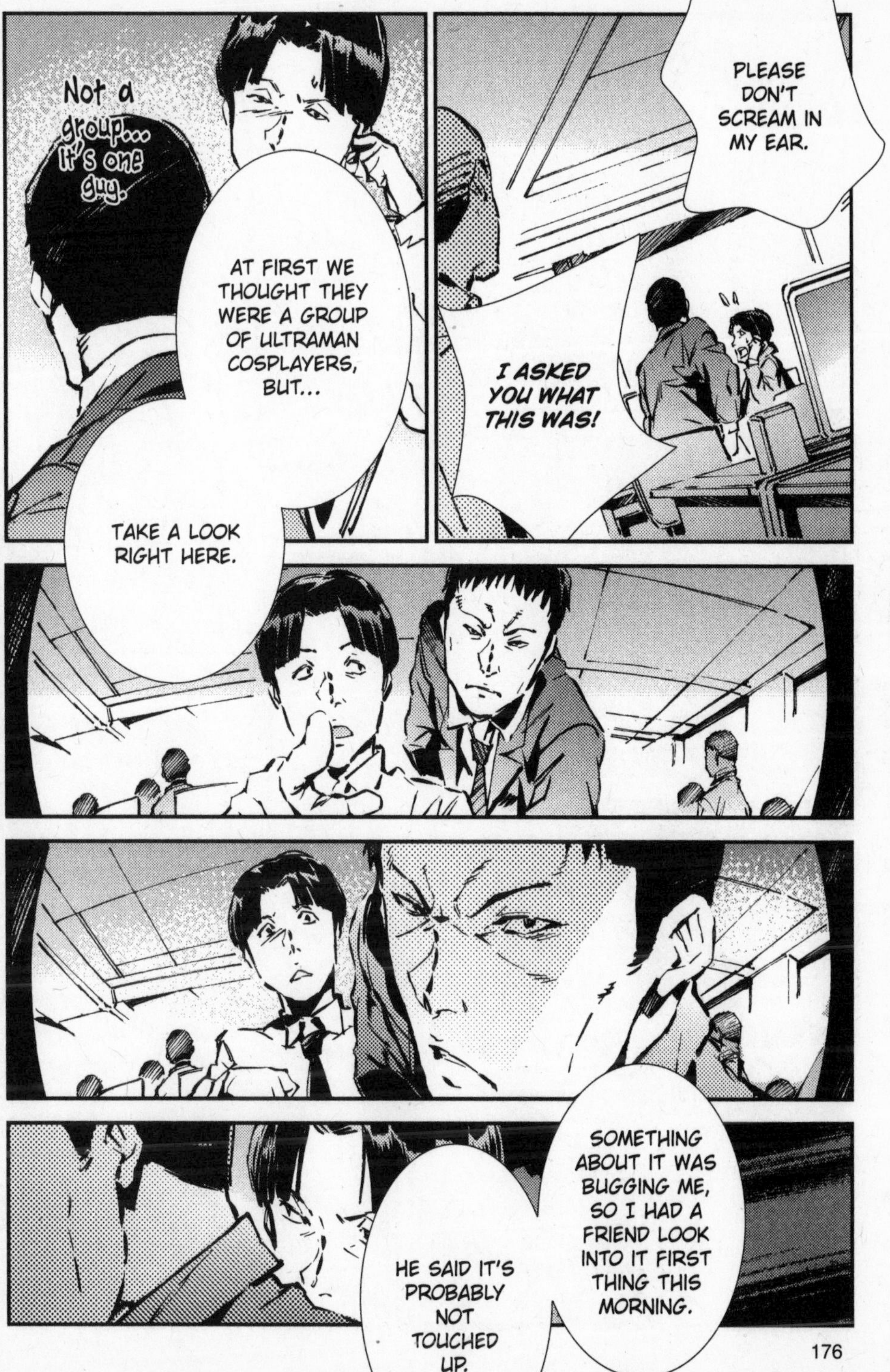
PLEASE DON'T SCREAM IN MY EAR.
I ASKED YOU WHAT THIS WAS!
AT FIRST WE THOUGHT THEY WERE A GROUP OF ULTRAMAN COSPLAYERS, BUT...
Not a group... it's one guy.
TAKE A LOOK RIGHT HERE.
SOMETHING ABOUT IT WAS BUGGING ME, SO I HAD A FRIEND LOOK INTO IT FIRST THING THIS MORNING.
HE SAID IT'S PROBABLY NOT TOUCHED UP.

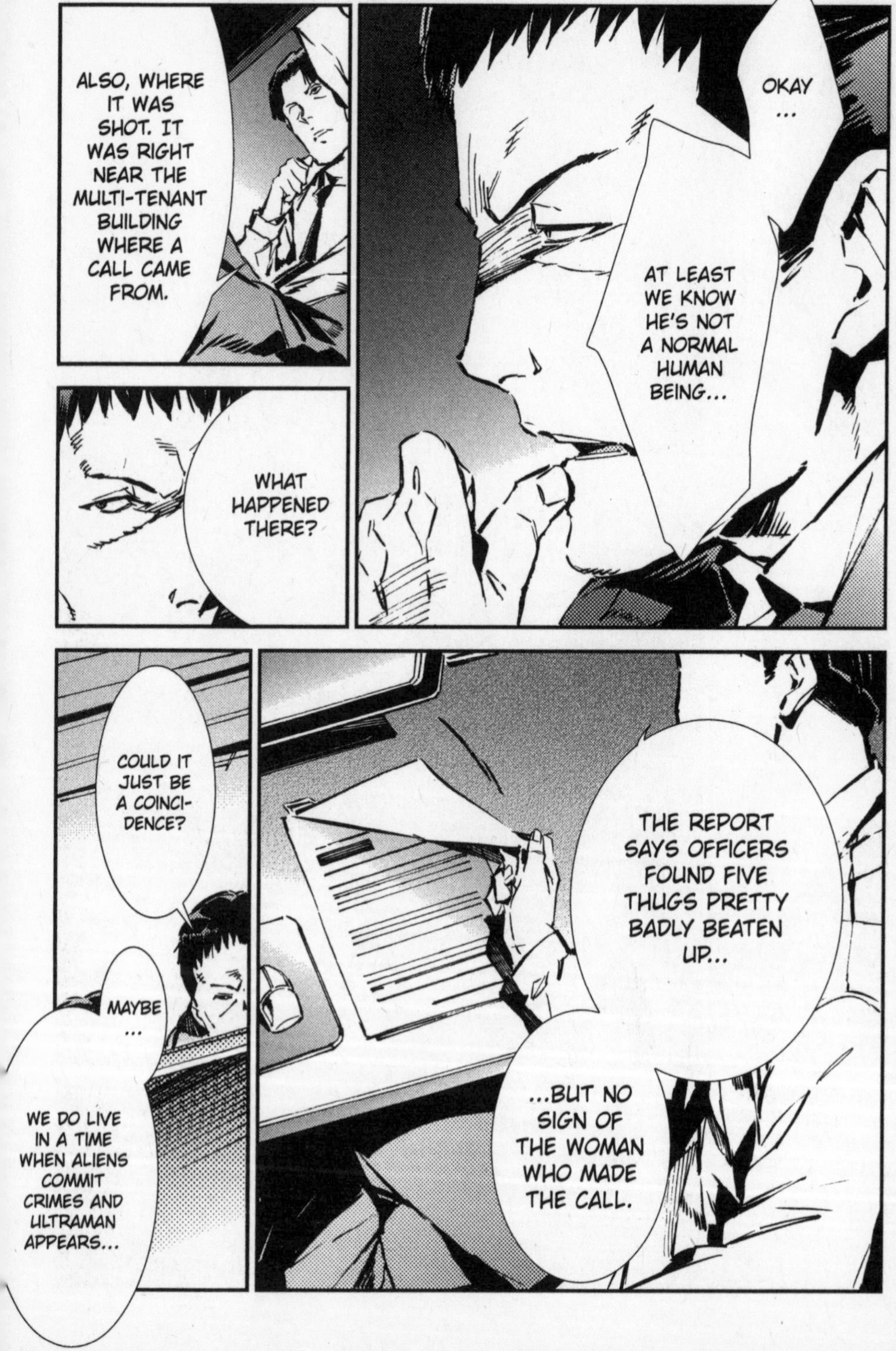
OKAY ...
AT LEAST WE KNOW HE'S NOT A NORMAL HUMAN BEING...
ALSO, WHERE IT WAS SHOT. IT WAS RIGHT NEAR THE MULTI-TENANT BUILDING WHERE A CALL CAME FROM.
WHAT HAPPENED THERE?
THE REPORT SAYS OFFICERS FOUND FIVE THUGS PRETTY BADLY BEATEN UP...
...BUT NO SIGN OF THE WOMAN WHO MADE THE CALL.
COULD IT JUST BE A COINCI-DENCE?
MAYBE ...
WE DO LIVE IN A TIME WHEN ALIENS COMMIT CRIMES AND ULTRAMAN APPEARS...

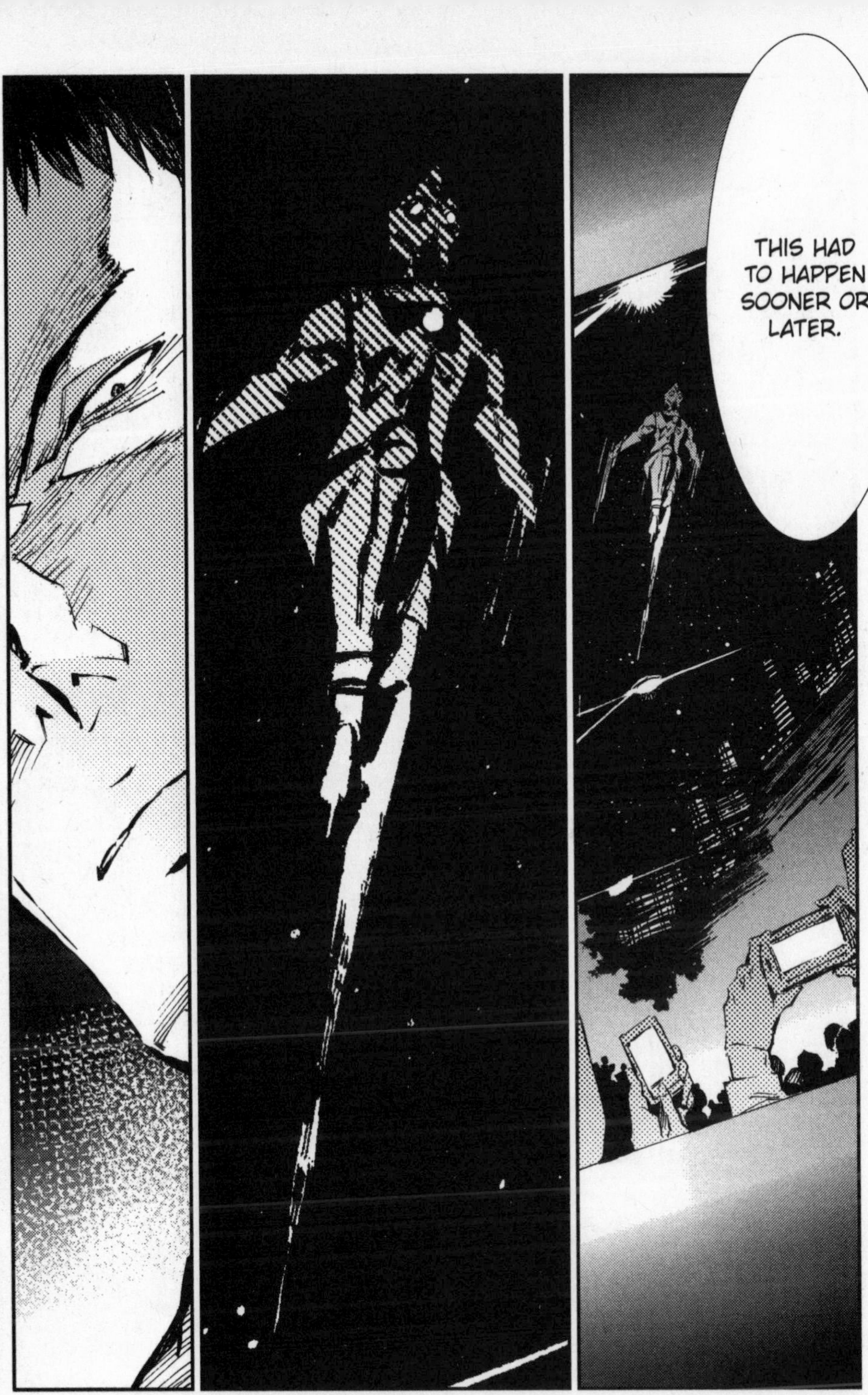
THIS HAD TO HAPPEN SOONER OR LATER.

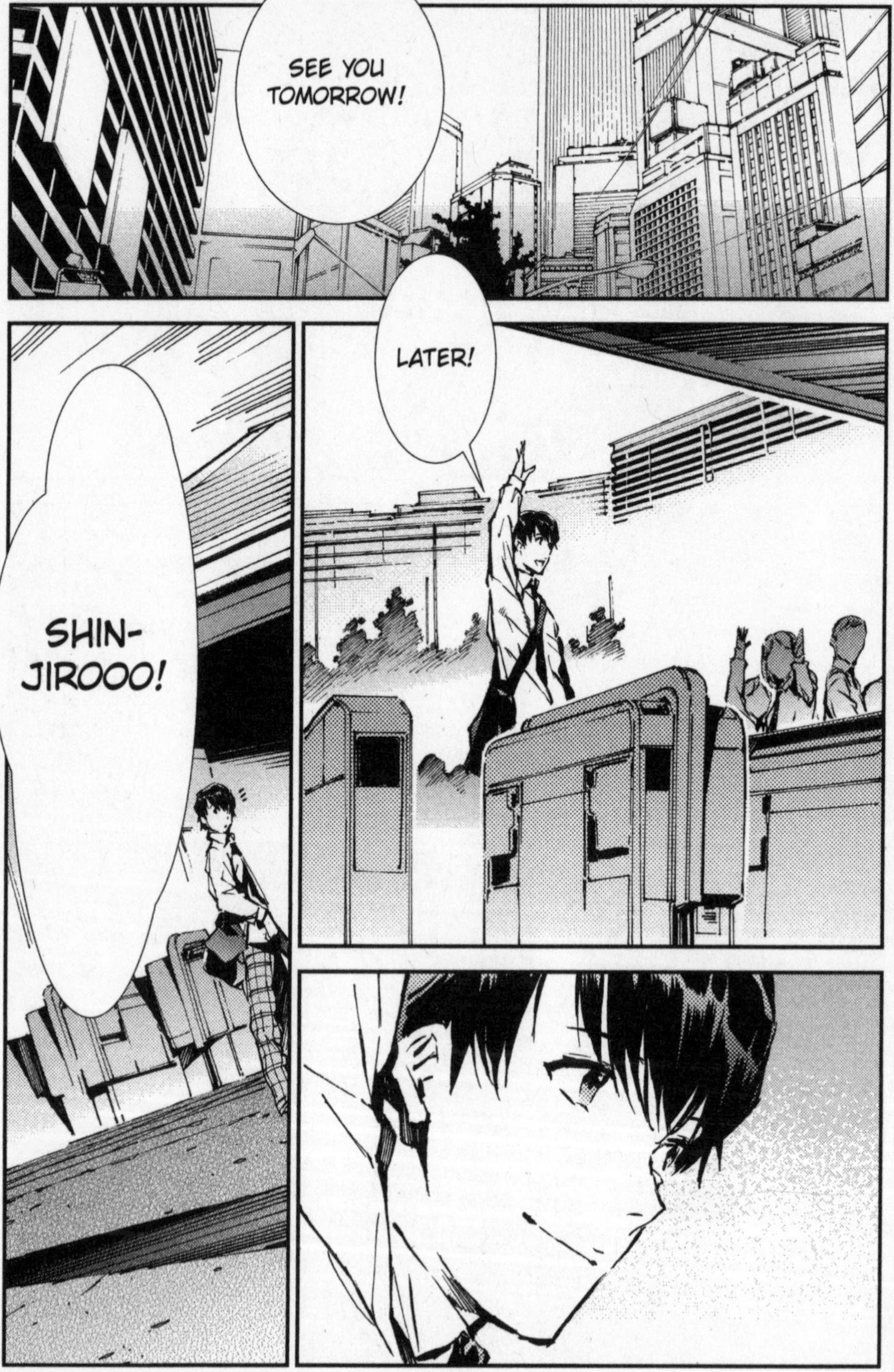
SEE YOU TOMORROW!
LATER!
SHIN-JIROOO!

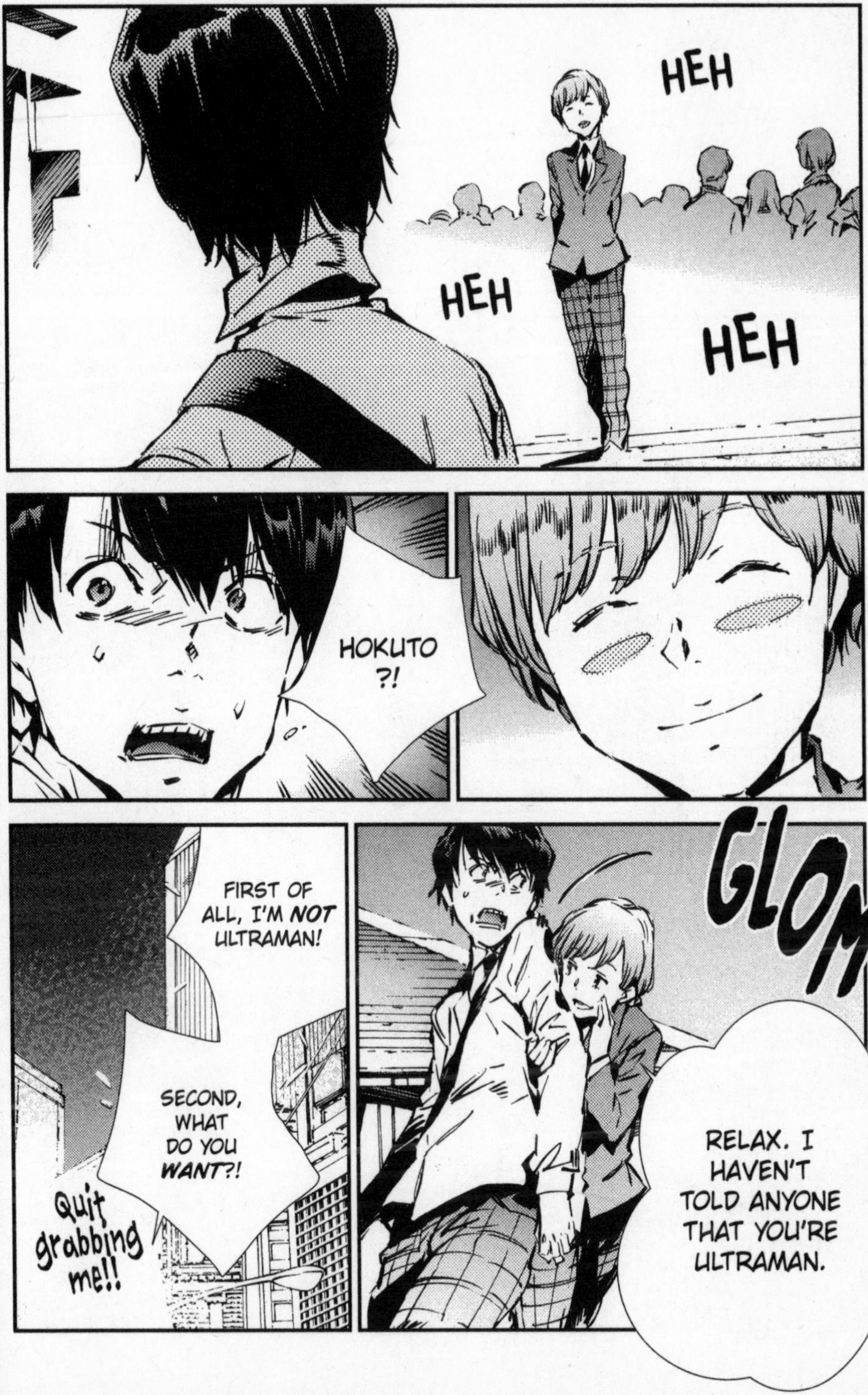
HEH
HEH
HEH
HOKUTO ?!
GLOM
RELAX. I HAVEN'T TOLD ANYONE THAT YOU'RE ULTRAMAN.
FIRST OF ALL, I'M ***NOT*** ULTRAMAN!
SECOND, WHAT DO YOU ***WANT***?!
Quit grabbing me!!

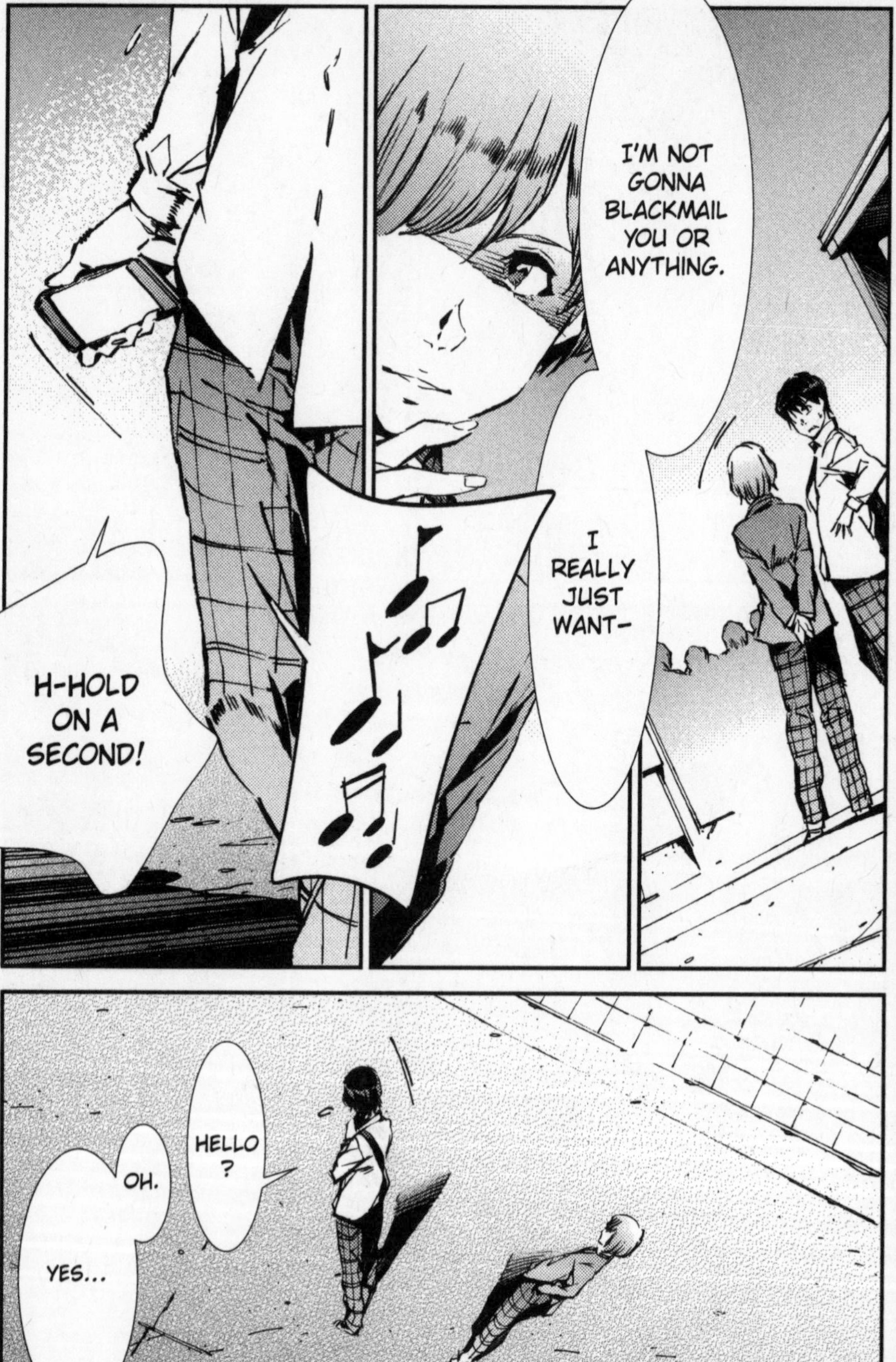
I'M NOT GONNA BLACKMAIL YOU OR ANYTHING.
I REALLY JUST WANT-
H-HOLD ON A SECOND!
HELLO?
OH.
YES...

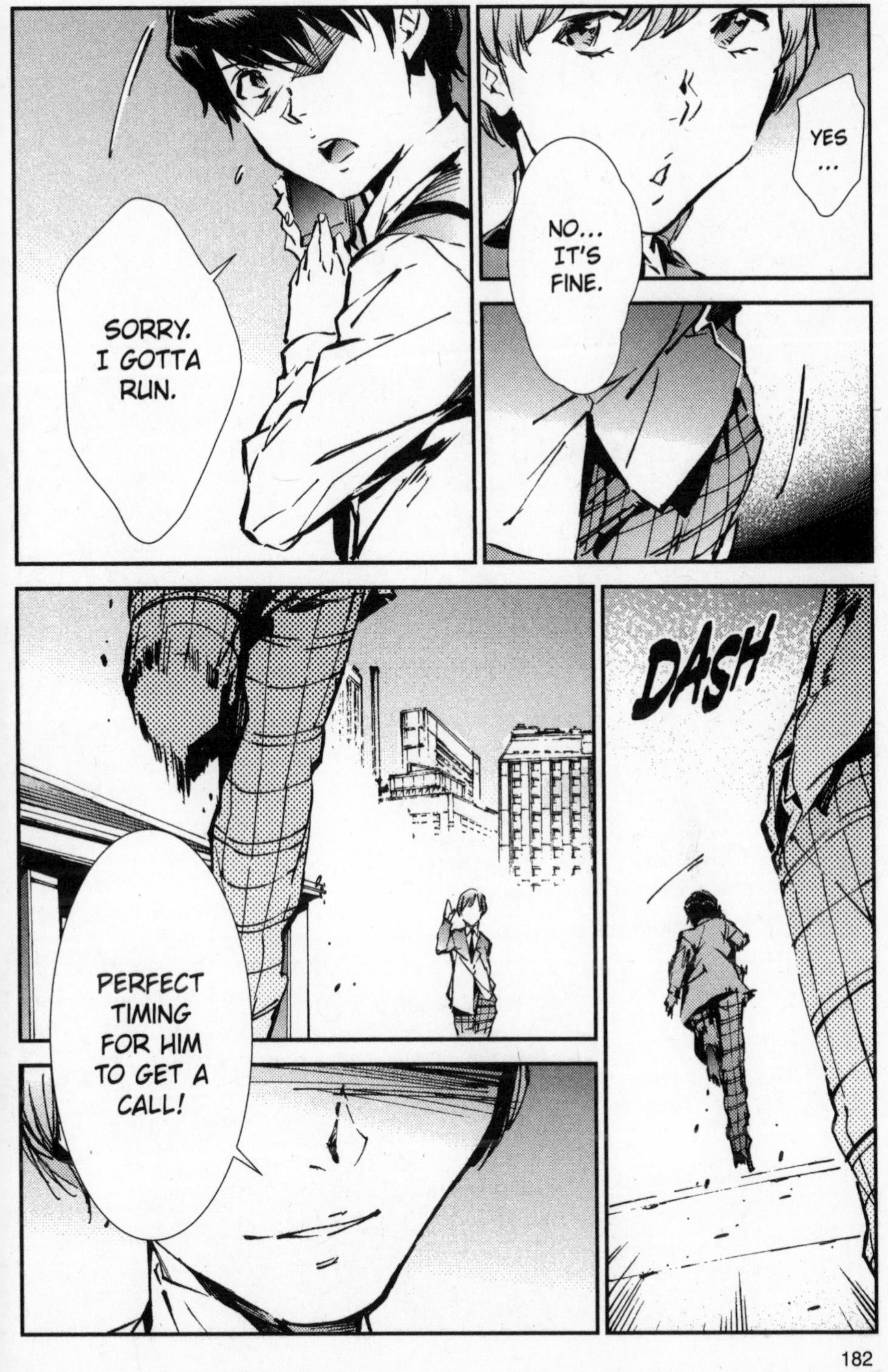
YES ...
NO... IT'S FINE.
SORRY. I GOTTA RUN.
DASH
PERFECT TIMING FOR HIM TO GET A CALL!

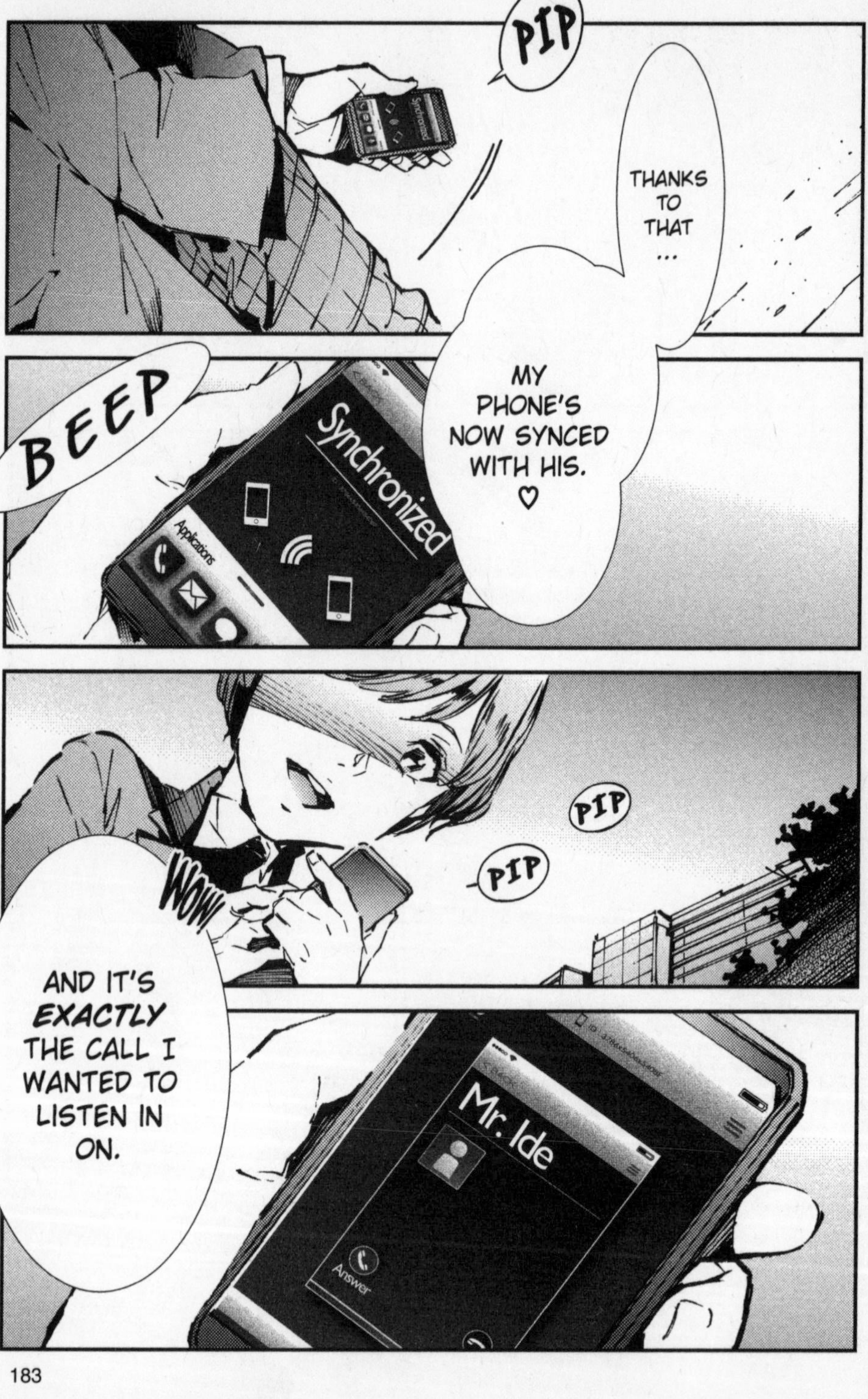
PIP
THANKS TO THAT ...
Synchronized
MY PHONE'S NOW SYNCED WITH HIS. ♡
BEEP
Synchronized
Applications
PIP
PIP
WOW
AND IT'S *EXACTLY* THE CALL I WANTED TO LISTEN IN ON.
Mr. Ide
Answer

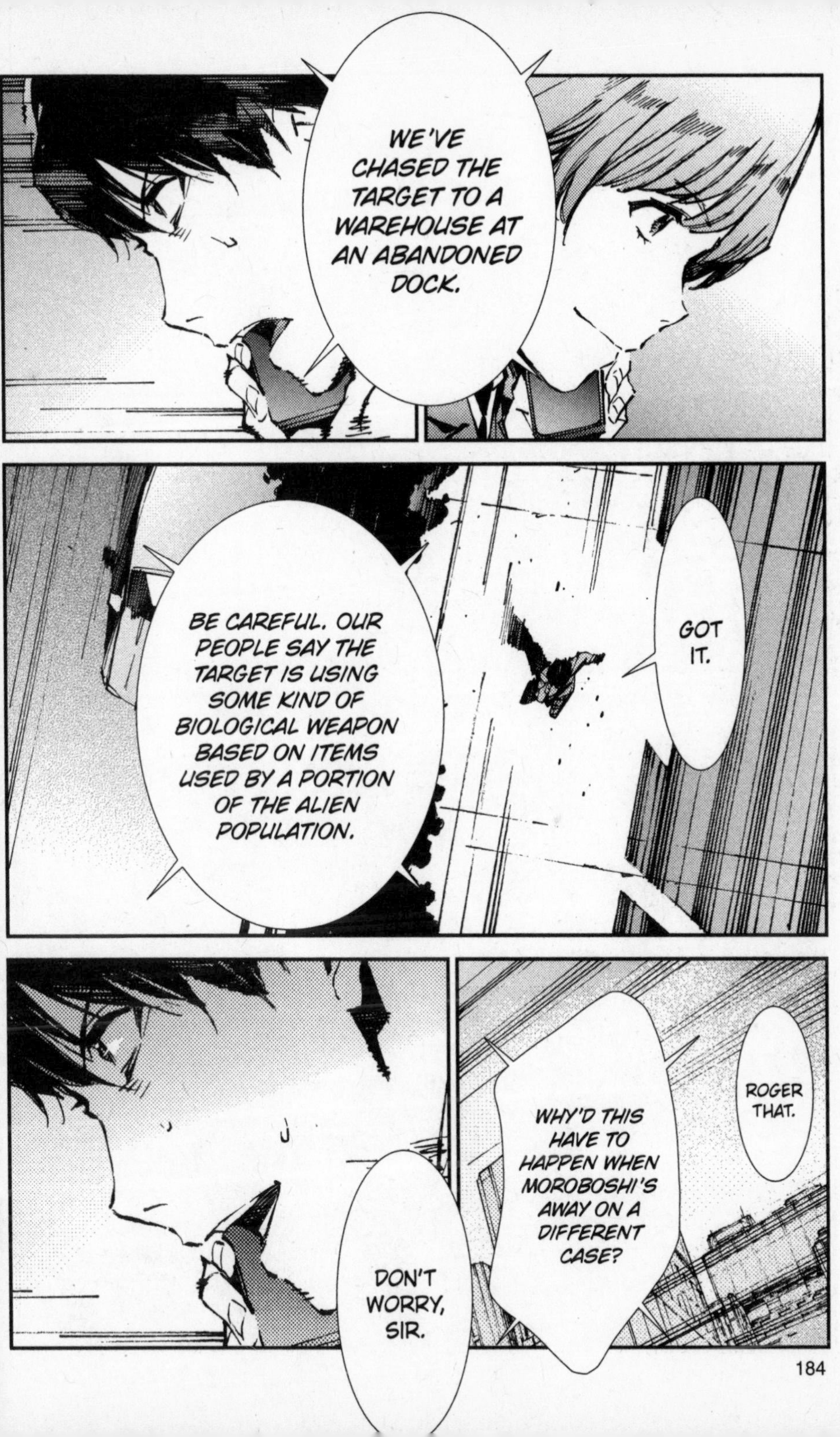
WE'VE CHASED THE TARGET TO A WAREHOUSE AT AN ABANDONED DOCK.
BE CAREFUL. OUR PEOPLE SAY THE TARGET IS USING SOME KIND OF BIOLOGICAL WEAPON BASED ON ITEMS USED BY A PORTION OF THE ALIEN POPULATION.
GOT IT.
ROGER THAT.
WHY'D THIS HAVE TO HAPPEN WHEN MOROBOSHI'S AWAY ON A DIFFERENT CASE?
DON'T WORRY, SIR.

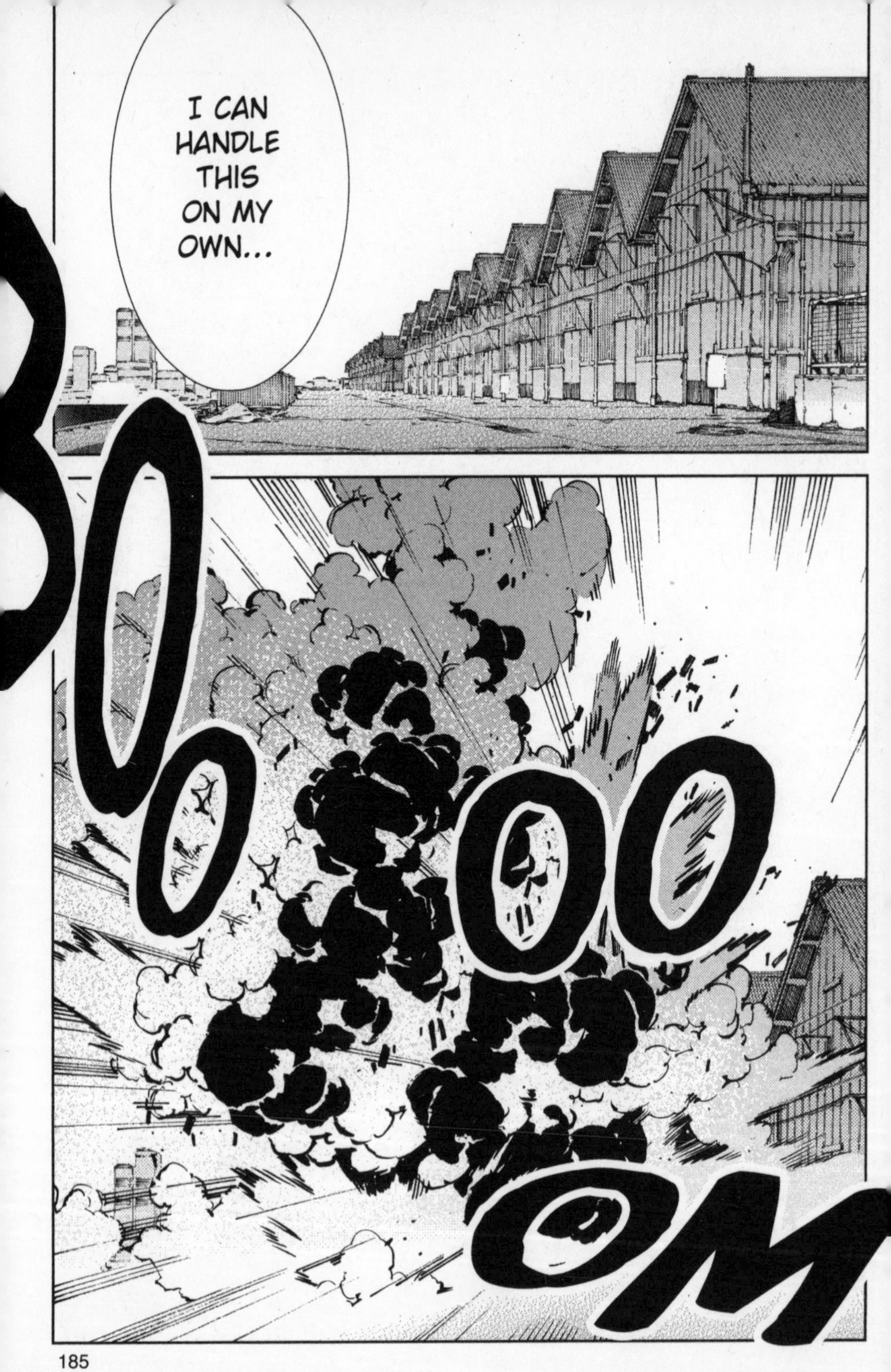
I CAN HANDLE THIS ON MY OWN...
BOOOOOM

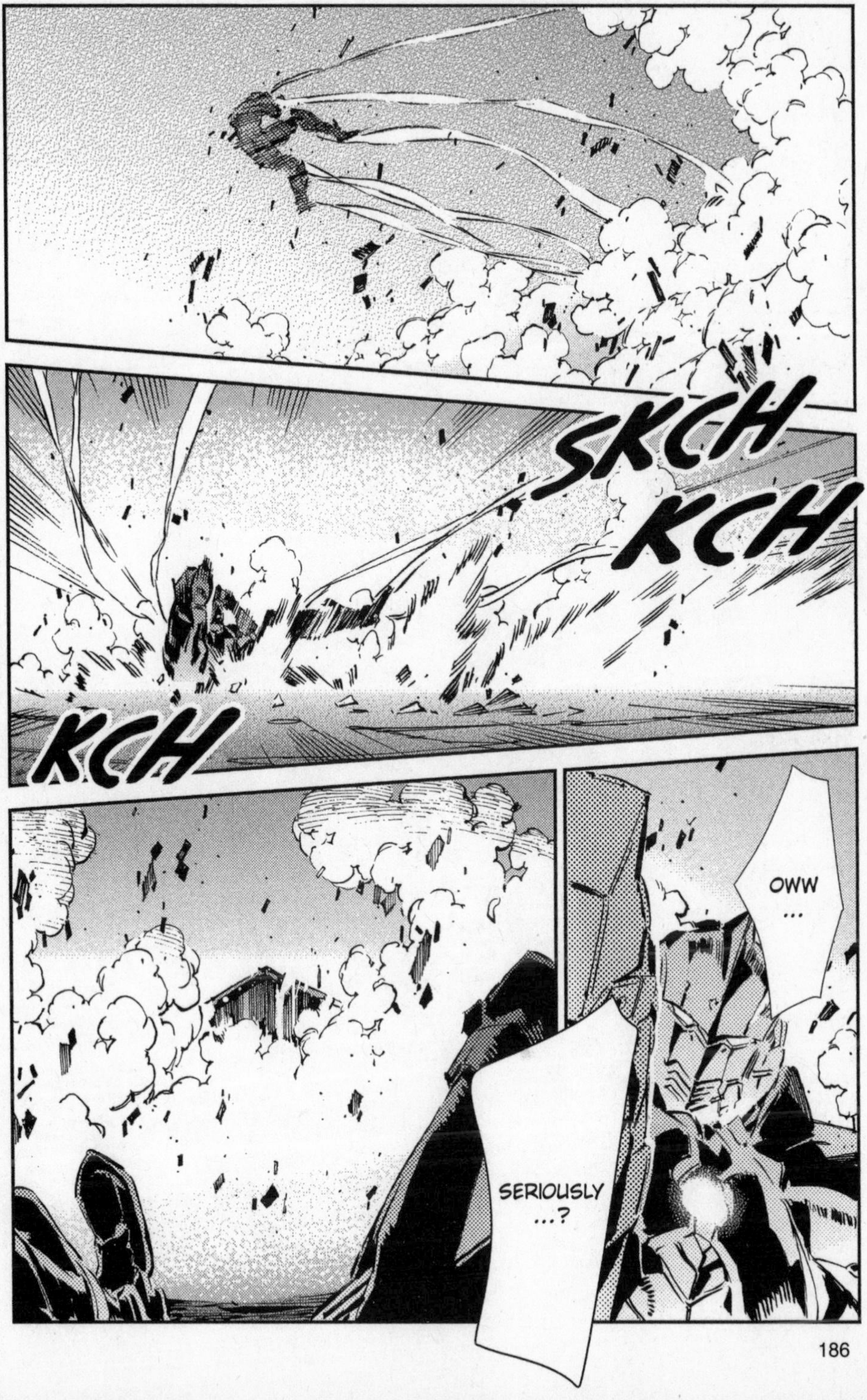
SKCH
KCH
KCH
OWW ...
SERIOUSLY ...?

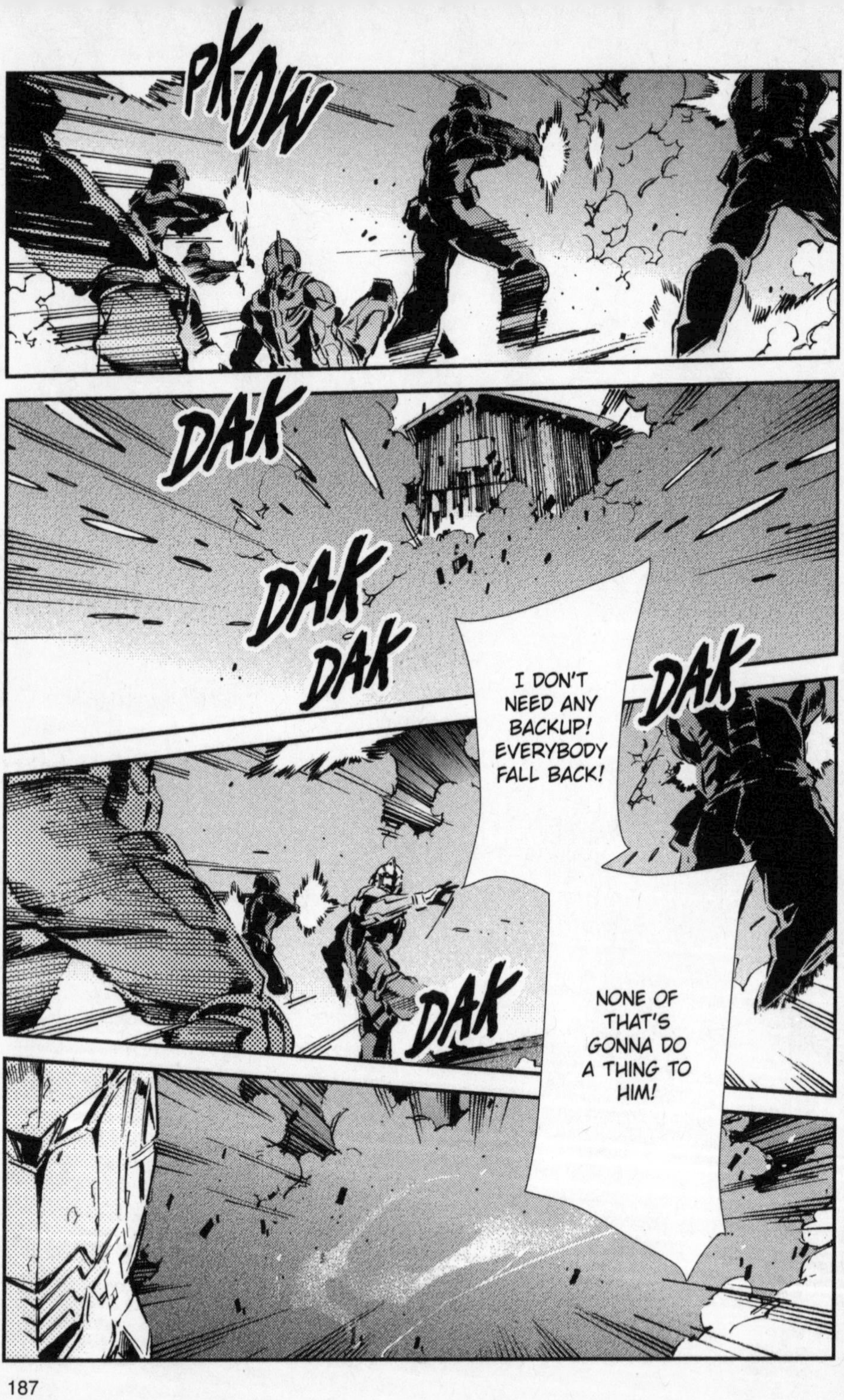
PKOW
DAK
DAK
DAK
DAK
I DON'T NEED ANY BACKUP! EVERYBODY FALL BACK!
DAK
NONE OF THAT'S GONNA DO A THING TO HIM!

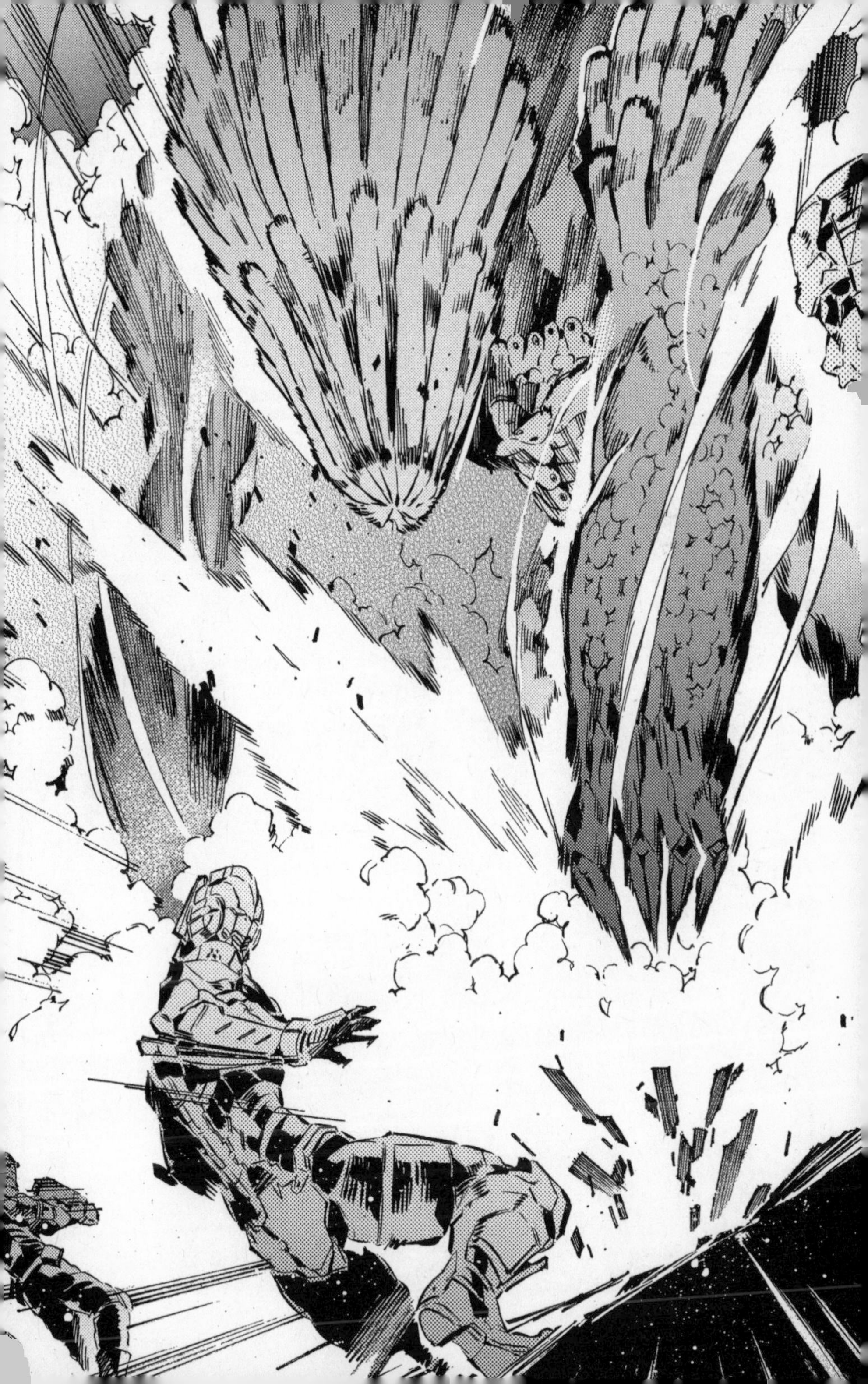

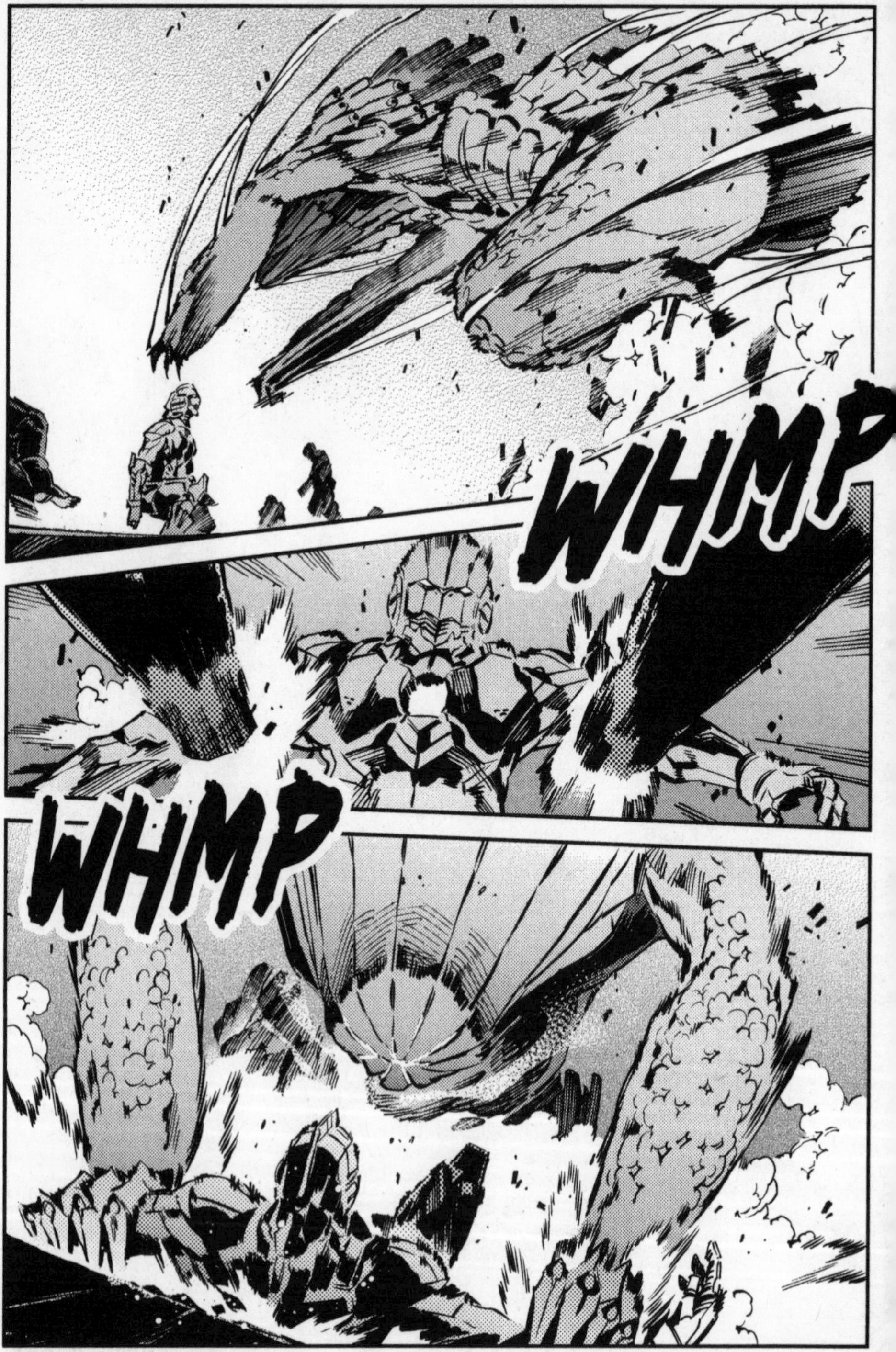
WHMP
WHMP

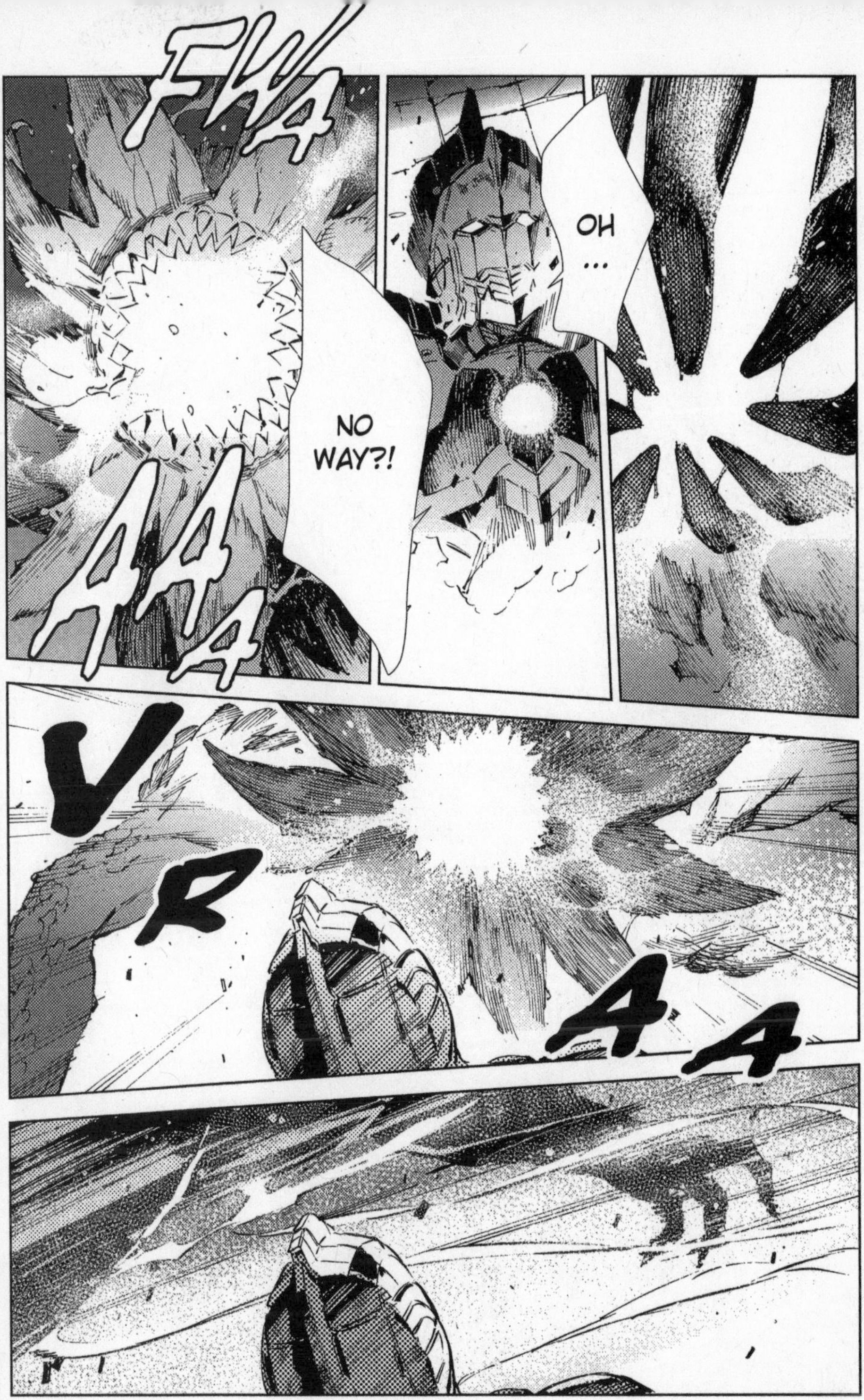
OH ...
NO WAY?!
FWAAAAA
VRAAA

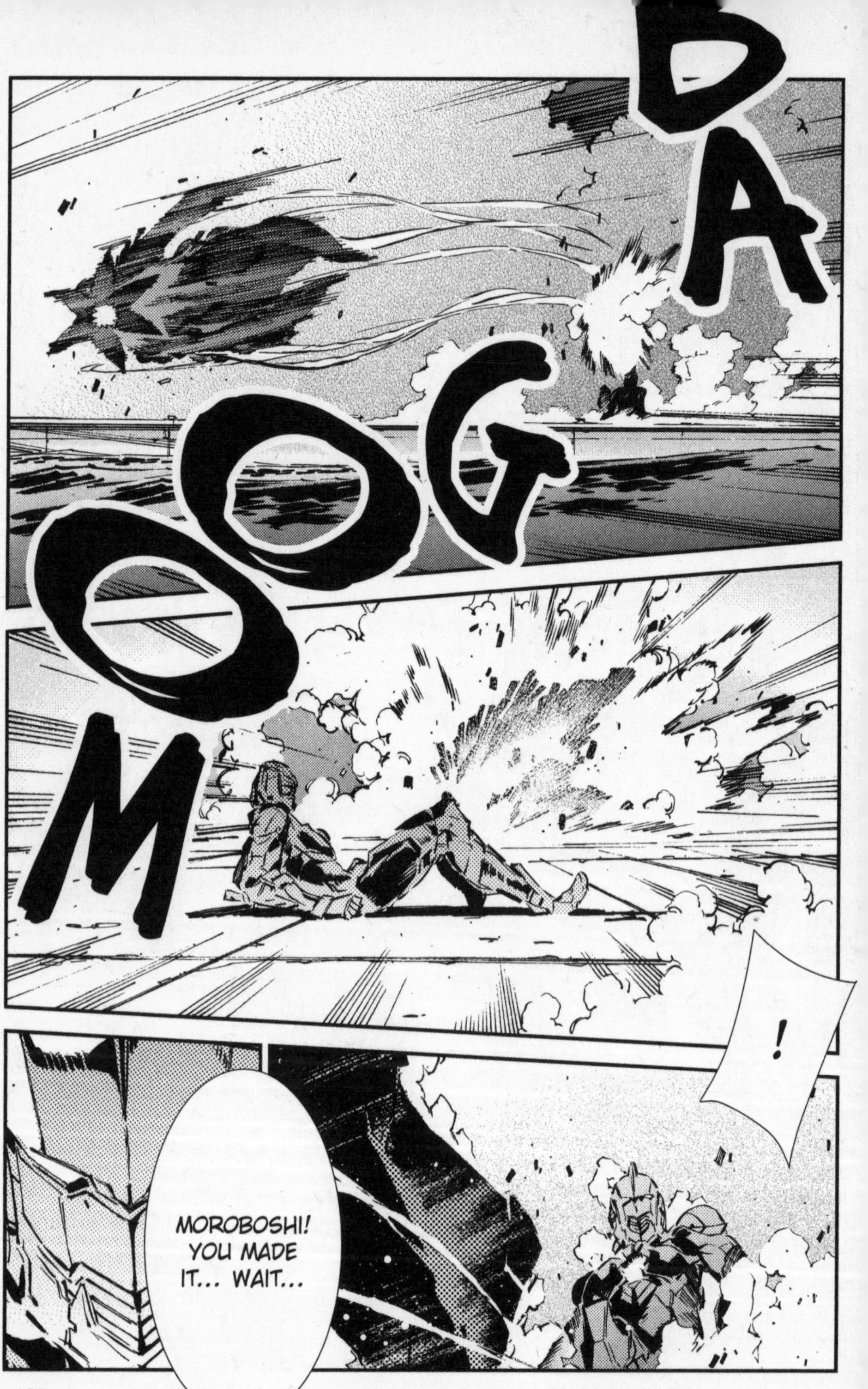
DAGOOM
!
MOROBOSHI! YOU MADE IT... WAIT...

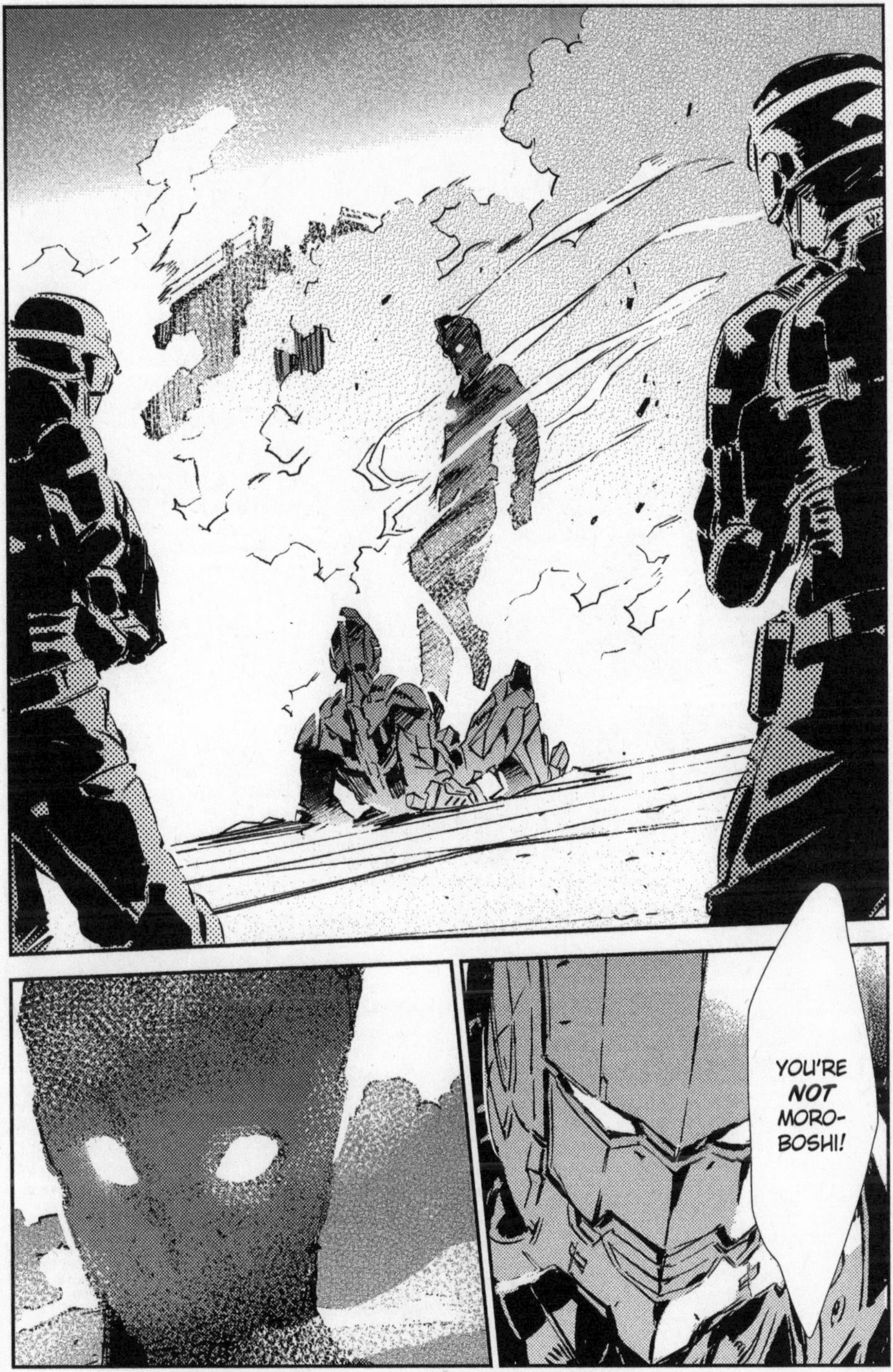
YOU'RE *NOT* MORO-BOSHI!

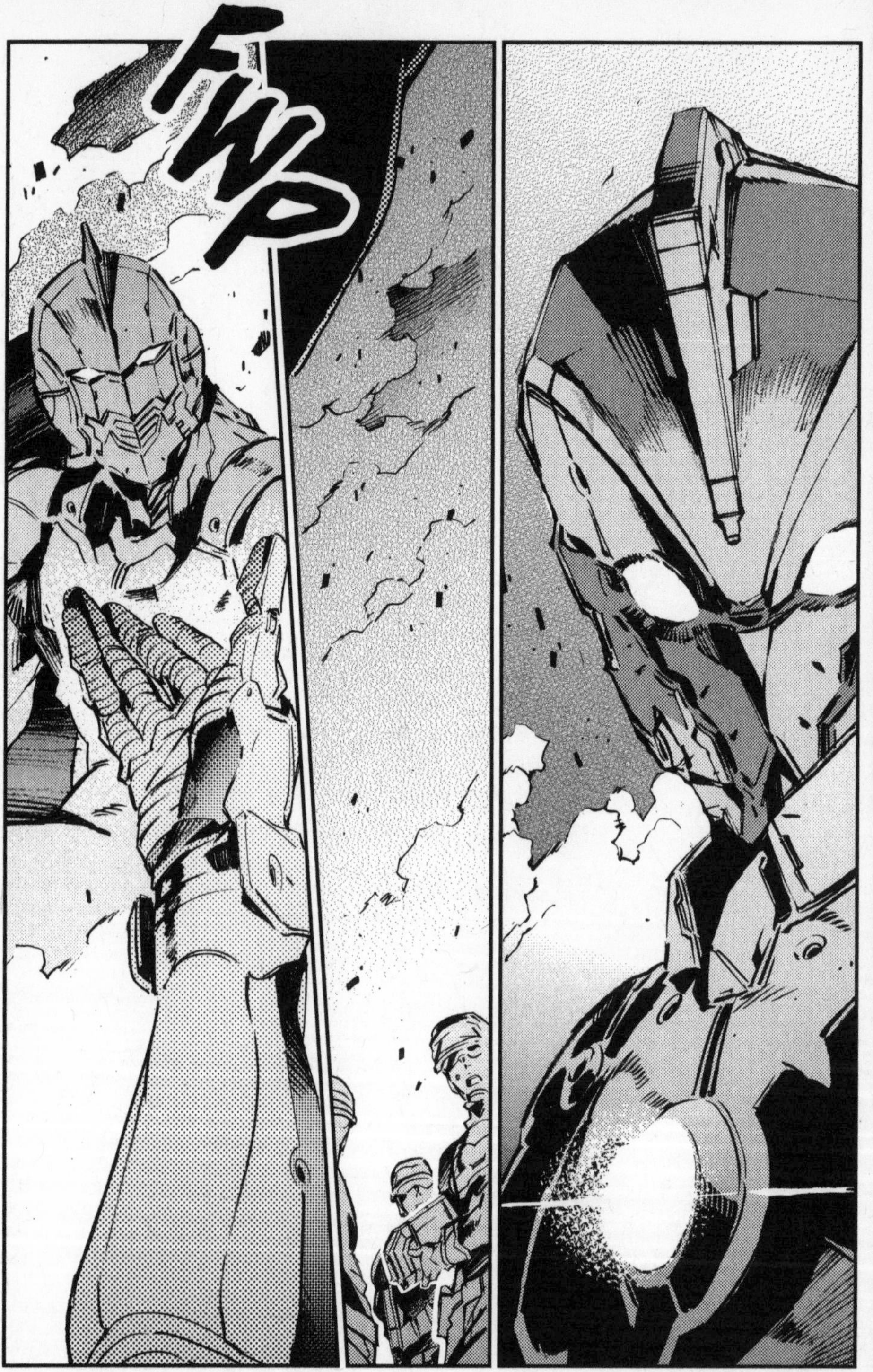
FWP

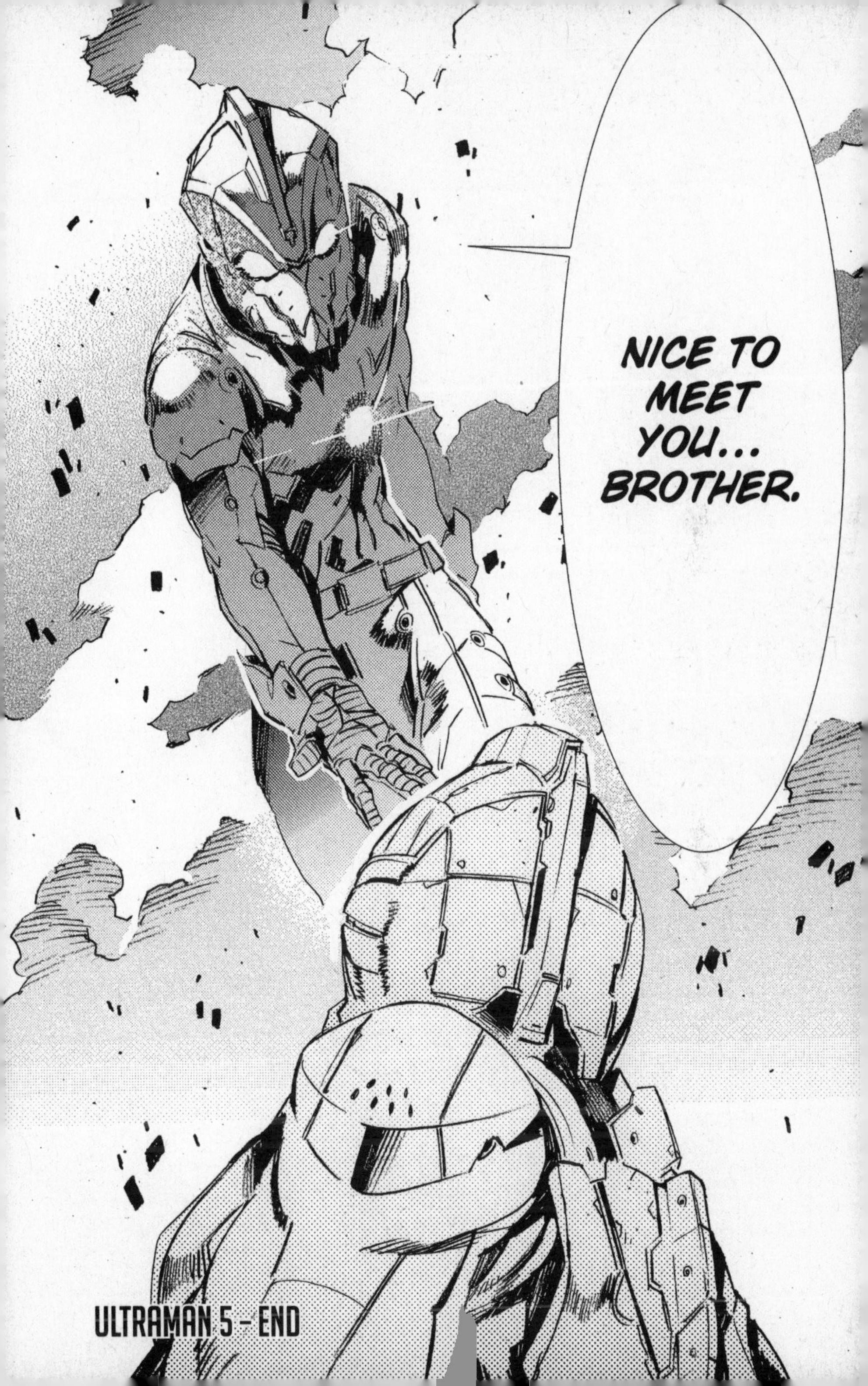
NICE TO MEET YOU... BROTHER.
ULTRAMAN 5 - END

THIS IS THE BEGINNING OF A NEW AGE

An agent of the Immigration Administration Bureau who reports directly to the Star Cluster Council.

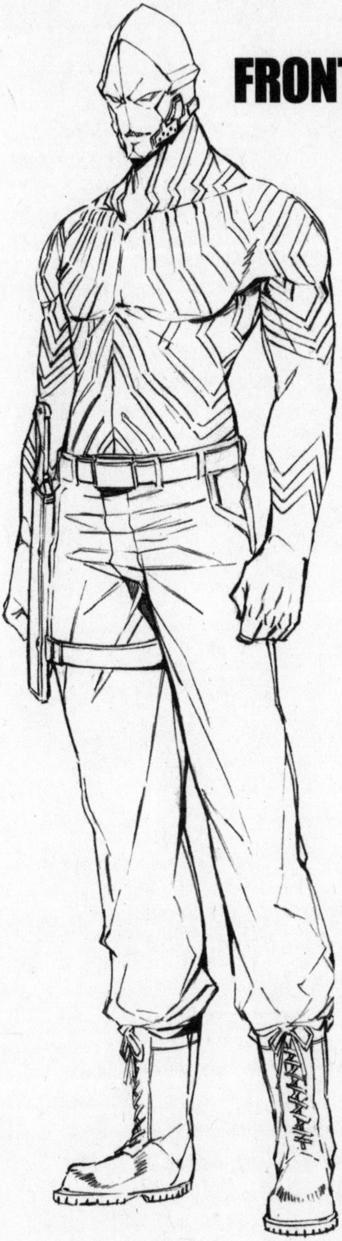

FRONT

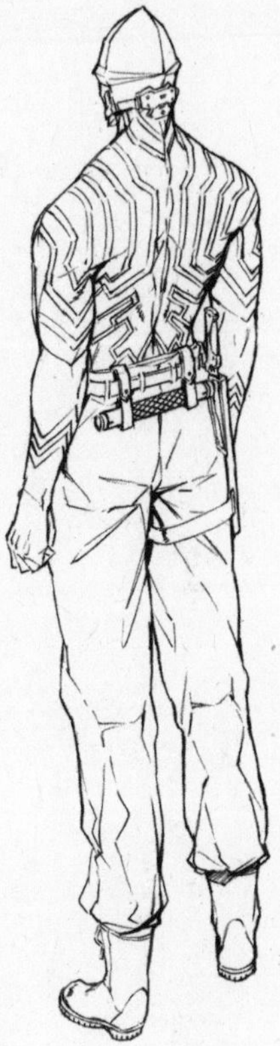

REAR

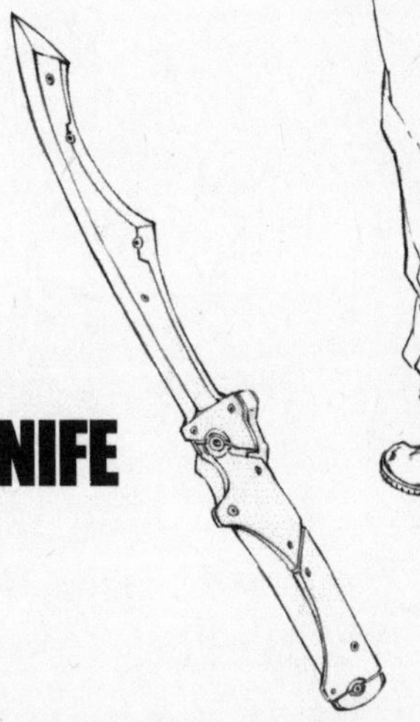

KNIFE

Although his is a warlike race, those of his kind are considerably weaker physically than many other races. Gene manipulation experiments were used in hopes of transforming their bodies into a more powerful state. Adad is the very first test subject. After some twists and turns, he was recruited by the Star Cluster Council.

Skilled at both stick and knife fighting.

The prince of planet Igaru. (Given name: Pigmon.)
Because the Igaru were a peaceful race, they were exploited politically and eventually wiped out. Pigmon was representing his planet at the Star Cluster Council during the genocide and so became the lone survivor. Later, the Council approved his emigration to Earth.

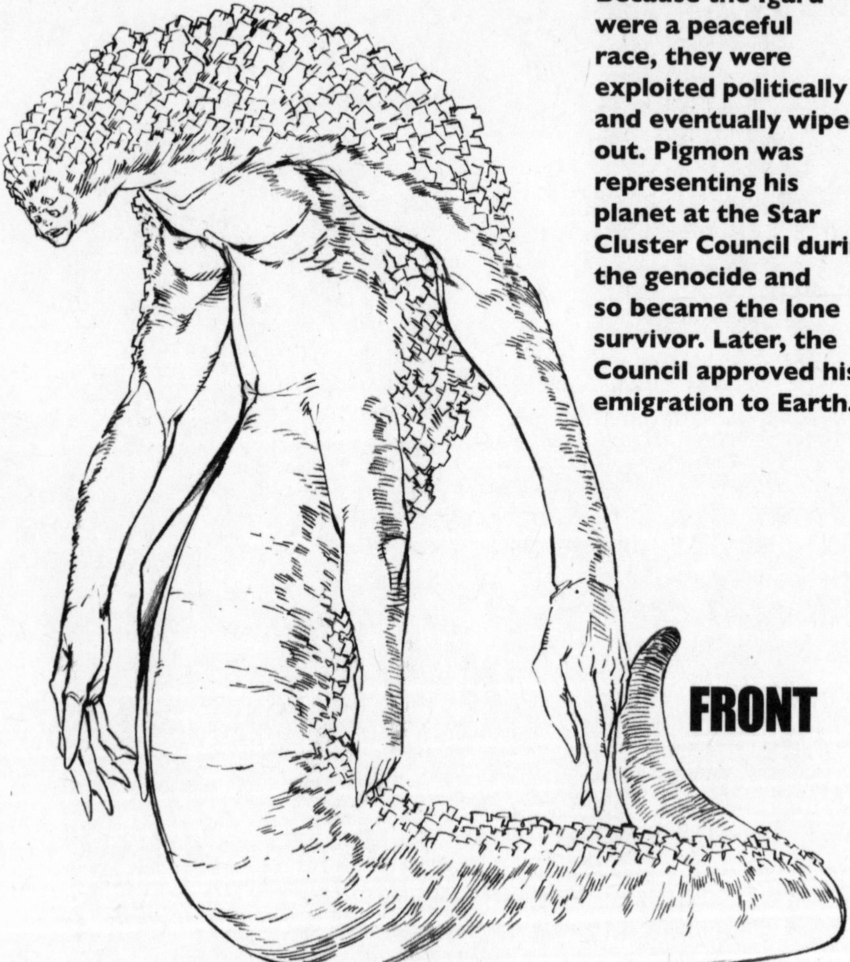
FRONT

Like Red, upon relocating to Earth, he was given medication to alter his shape for life on his new planet. This was done because the area on Earth where aliens live—known as "the City"—has limited space. All those who take up more than a certain cubic volume are required to alter themselves to a more appropriate size.

EIICHI SHIMIZU ✕ TOMOHIRO SHIMOGUCHI

As I wrote in volume 4, Shimoguchi is almost
annoyingly into special effects stuff these days.
So I hit him up with a few questions.

ME: What's your favorite alien?
SHIMOGUCHI: Alien Poll.
ME: What's your favorite monster?
SHIMOGUCHI: Antlar.
ME: Oh, not Gandar? And didn't you say that
     you liked King Joe?
SHIMOGUCHI: KJ is a robot—that's
     a different category.
(I guessed that "KJ" was short for King Joe.)
ME: Then which heroine is your favorite?
SHIMOGUCHI: Mother of Ultra...
(He sounded kind of embarrassed to admit it.)

ULTRAMAN
VOLUME 5
VIZ SIGNATURE EDITION

STORY/ART BY **EIICHI SHIMIZU** AND **TOMOHIRO SHIMOGUCHI**

©2014 Eiichi Shimizu and Tomohiro Shimoguchi / TSUBURAYA PROD.
Originally published by HERO'S INC.

TRANSLATION **JOE YAMAZAKI**
ENGLISH ADAPTATION **STAN!**
TOUCH-UP ART & LETTERING **EVAN WALDINGER**
DESIGN **ALYSA TRINIDAD**
EDITOR **MIKE MONTESA**

Printed in the U.S.A.

Published by VIZ Media, LLC
P.O. Box 77010
San Francisco, CA 94107

10 9 8 7 6 5 4 3 2 1
First printing, August 2016

VIZ SIGNATURE

www.viz.com

HEY! YOU'RE READING IN THE WRONG DIRECTION!

This is the END of the graphic novel

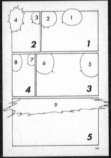

Follow the action this way.

To properly enjoy this VIZ graphic novel, please turn it around and begin reading from RIGHT TO LEFT. Unlike English, Japanese is read right to left, so Japanese comics are read in reverse order from the way English comics are typically read.

This book has been printed in the original Japanese format in order to preserve the orientation of the original artwork.

HAVE FUN WITH IT!